Remote Control

Remote Control
Television, Audiences,
and Cultural Power

Edited by

Ellen Seiter, Hans Borchers, Gabriele Kreutzner,
and Eva-Maria Warth

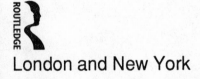

London and New York

First published in 1989

First published in paperback in 1991
by Routledge
11 New Fetter Lane, London EC4P 4EE

Simultaneously published in the USA and Canada
by Routledge, a division of Routledge, Chapman and Hall, Inc.
29 West 35th Street, New York, NY 10001

© 1989, 1991 Ellen Seiter, Hans Borchers, Gabriele Kreutzner, Eva-Maria Warth

Typeset in 10/12 Times by Laserscript Ltd, Mitcham, Surrey
Printed in Great Britain by T.J. Press (Padstow) Ltd, Padstow, Cornwall

British Library Cataloguing in Publication Data

Remote control: television, audiences and cultural power
  1. Television programmes. Audiences
  I. Seiter, Ellen
  302.2'345

Library of Congress Cataloging in Publication Data

Remote control: television, audiences, and cultural power / edited by
  Ellen Seiter ... [et al.].
     p.   cm.
  Papers presented at a symposium held at the University of Tübingen's Heinrich-
  Fabri-Institute, Blaubeuren, Feb. 17-20, 1987, organized by the University's
  Dept. of American Studies.
    1. Television broadcasting – Social aspects – Congresses.
    2. Television audiences – Congresses. I. Seiter, Ellen
  II. Universität Tübingen. Abteilung für Amerikanistik.
  PN1992.6.R46   1991
  302.23'45—dc20   91-34

ISBN 0-415-06505-4

Contents

Contents

List of contributors

Robert C. Allen is Associate Professor of Radio, Television and Motion Pictures at the University of North Carolina at Chapel Hill, USA. He is author of *Speaking of Soap Operas* and *Vaudeville and Film: 1896-1915*, co-author of *Film History: Theory and Practice*, and editor of *Channels of Discourse: Television and Contemporary Criticism*.

Ien Ang teaches at the Institute of Mass Communications, University of Amsterdam, Netherlands. She is author of *Watching "Dallas"* and a member of the editorial collective of *Cultural Studies* and *New Formations*.

Hans Borchers is Professor of American Studies and Media Studies at the University of Tübingen, Germany. He is author of the monograph *Freud und die amerikanische Literatur (1920–1940): Studien zur Rezeption der Psychoanalyse* (1987), and co-author of *Never-Ending Stories: American Soap Operas and the Cultural Production of Meaning* (1991).

Charlotte Brunsdon teaches film and television at the University of Warwick, England. She has worked on popular genres for women and is co-author of *Everyday Television: "Nationwide"* and editor of *Films for Women*.

John Fiske is Professor in the Department of Communication Arts, University of Wisconsin-Madison, USA. He is author of *Television Culture*, co-author of *Reading Television*, and general editor of *Cultural Studies*.

Larry Gross is Professor at the Annenberg School of Communication, University of Philadelphia, USA. He is co-editor of *Image Ethics* and has published widely on television.

Dorothy Hobson is a freelance writer currently working on a biography of Channel 4 Television, 1982-87. She is author of *"Crossroads": The Drama of Soap Opera* and co-editor of *Culture, Media, Language*. She has written, lectured, and broadcast widely on soap opera and television audiences.

Elihu Katz is Professor at Hebrew University in Jerusalem, Israel and at the Annenberg School of Communication, University of Southern California, USA.

He also serves as Scientific Director of the Israel Institute of Applied Social Research. He is co-author of *Mass Media and Social Change* and co-editor of *The Uses of Mass Communications: Current Perspectives on Gratification Research.*

Gabriele Kreutzner is a television scholar working in Stuttgart, Germany. She is author of *Die Fernsehserie "Dynasty": Untersuchung eines populären Texts im amerikanischen Fernsehen der 80er Jahre* (forthcoming) and co-author of *Never-Ending Stories* (1991).

Tamar Liebes is lecturer in the Department of Education at the Ben-Gurion University and the Communications Institute of the Hebrew University in Jerusalem, Israel. Her study, with Elihu Katz, on cross-cultural readings of *Dallas* will soon be published by Oxford University Press.

David Morley teaches Communications in the Department of Human Sciences and is a member of the Centre for Research in Innovation, Culture and Technology, Brunel University, England. He is author of *The "Nationwide" Audience* and *Family Television*, co-author (with Charlotte Brunsdon) of *Everyday Television: "Nationwide"*, and is the editor of the Comedia (Routledge) book series. He is currently working (with Roger Silverstone) on a research project on "The Household Uses of Information and Communication Technologies."

Claus-Dieter Rath is a psychotherapist and a lecturer in the Department of Semiotics, Free University of Berlin (West). He is co-editor of *Rituale der Massenkommunikation* and has published on television.

Jan-Uwe Rogge presently works in the area of media education and family therapy. Together with Hermann Bausinger and Klaus Jensen, he conducted several research projects on media, the family, and everyday life. He is author of *Heidi, Pac-Man und die Video Zombies* and has published widely on television and the family.

Ellen Seiter is Associate Professor of Telecommunications and Film Studies at the University of Oregon in Eugene. Her articles on film and television have appeared in *Feminist Review*, *Journal of Communication*, *Jump Cut*, *Journal of Film and Video*, and *Cultural Studies*. She is currently writing a book about children's consumer culture.

John Tulloch is Associate Professor and Head of Mass Communication at Macquarie University, Australia. He is author of *Television Drama* and co-author of *"Dr Who": The Unfolding Text* and *"A Country Practice": 'Quality Soap'*.

Eva-Maria Warth is Assistant Professor in the American Studies Department, University of Tübingen, Germany. She is author of *The Haunted Palace – Edgar Allan Poe und der amerikanische Horrorfilm (1909-1969)* and co-author of *Never-Ending Stories* (1991).

Preface

It is perhaps symbolic of the pervasiveness of television in our world today that the symposium "Rethinking the Audience: New Tendencies in Television Research," which gave rise to the present volume and the essays it contains, should have taken place at the University of Tübingen's Heinrich-Fabri-Institute in Blaubeuren. Blaubeuren is a small German town hidden away among the hills of the Swabian Alp; Heinrich Fabri belongs to the town's medieval history. One of the founding fathers of the nearby university, he served as abbot to Blaubeuren's Benedictine monastery back in the fifteenth century. Where in Fabri's day scholar-monks had pored over their palimpsests, a group of some forty twentieth-century scholars from all over the world met from February 17 to 20, 1987, to consider what is arguably the most influential palimpsest of our present-day cultural situation – television; their specific goal on this occasion was to discuss television audiences.

The impulse for this gathering originated within a research project on the soap opera as a prominent phenomenon in twentieth-century American culture. The project was planned and undertaken by the University of Tübingen's Department of American Studies in 1985 and funded by the West German Volkswagen Foundation. Although soap operas have for some time been a privileged object of Anglo-American television research, scholarly interest has begun to grow in other countries in direct proportion to the genre's growing global appeal. As the four principal researchers of the project, we soon felt the necessity of involving the project and ourselves in the very lively scholarly debate on television audiences. It was in connection with an ethnographic study we did with American soap opera viewers in the summer of 1986 (see our essay in this volume, pp.223–47) that we decided to organize the symposium.

Motivation to provide a platform for an exchange of opinions about today's trends in television audience research did not come from the project alone, but also from our perception of similar trends in the field of American Studies. To put it in very general terms, the discipline has moved over the past fifteen years from a preoccupation with the artist as the shaper of cultural identity to a growing concern for the social structures undergirding artistic and intellectual creation as well as for the varieties of subcultural expression. At the heart of this new

American Studies paradigm are two important elements. One is the central question of how groups of people generate and reproduce cultural meaning. The other is the ongoing debate over the various methodologies that help us address this question. Janice Radway's 1984 investigation of American women who are habitual readers of romances comes to mind as representative of the new tendencies in American Studies and of their affinity to the current concerns with the readers of television texts.[1]

More than other publications, a collection of essays deriving from a symposium is the product of a collaborative effort. As organizers of the symposium and editors of the ensuing anthology we are very grateful to all who helped us achieve our goals. First and foremost, our acknowledgments are due to the participants of the symposium. Their contributions, both as readers of papers and as speakers during the discussion periods, have made this volume possible. Lack of space unfortunately does not permit us to cite their individual names.

If we make an exception, it is because of a feeling of special indebtedness. Herta Herzog has taken an active interest in the above-mentioned soap opera project since its inception, sharing with us her extensive scholarly experience and her keen insights. While we are very appreciative of her participation in the project, we would also like to express our gratitude for her pioneering research in the field of audience studies – research that goes back as far as the 1930s and that has inspired a whole subsequent generation of scholars.

Special thanks go to those symposium participants whose contributions appear in the present volume. We appreciate their willingness to thoroughly revise their papers and their patience with our sometimes demanding editorial requests.

We would also like to acknowledge our indebtedness to the institutions which made the symposium and, by extension, this volume possible. We are grateful to the Volkswagen Foundation for awarding us a second grant, thereby enabling us to bring together in Blaubeuren a unique group of television scholars, several of whom came from as far away as Australia, Israel, and the United States. Our sincere thanks also go to the University of Tübingen and to the Department of American Studies for providing the logistics indispensable for the organization of an international conference, and to Ute Bechdolf and Margarete Endress for their efficient assistance with all the nitty-gritty details of organizing a symposium and preparing a manuscript.

Finally, we would like to express our gratitude to Jane Armstrong of Routledge for her unfailing support and to Rosamund Howe for her editorial guidance.

Hans Borchers
Tübingen, March 1989

Note

1 Janice Radway, *Reading the Romance: Women, Patriarchy and Popular Culture* (Chapel Hill: University of North Carolina Press, 1984).

Introduction

Ellen Seiter, Hans Borchers, Gabriele Kreutzner, and Eva-Maria Warth

In a recent issue of *Ladies Home Journal*, a psychologist offers advice to readers on "how to recharge your love life and revitalize your marriage." A quiz questions the reader about the amount of time she spends talking to and touching her partner in the course of a typical week. But when the reader turns the page to compute her score on the quiz and assess the health of her interpersonal life, she encounters a nasty surprise. Though the quiz itself included no questions about television viewing, the obedient respondent must now compute substantial penalties for every minute she spends alone or with her spouse watching television. The author, Paul Pearsall, Ph.D., explains:

> Before you analyze your score, you must reduce your MIMs (marital investment minutes) by a penalty deduction. Subtract the time you spend each week, either alone or with your husband, watching TV. TV addiction is one of the most detrimental influences on the American marriage. As a shared addiction it is among the worst, because it robs the relationship of time for intimacy while each person contributes in the theft.[1]

This article exemplifies many of the ways television watching is usually talked about: as an addiction, as a passive, individual activity which precludes direct communication with others, as an impediment to fulfilling family relationships. All these deleterious effects are thought to increase in direct proportion to the amount of time the television is turned on in the home.

There is something suspect about this cluster of beliefs about the effects of television viewing, for, as David Morley puts it in Chapter one of this book, "'television zombies' are always other people. . . . It is a theory about what television does to other, more vulnerable people." These "other" people helpless before the television set are implicitly feminine. Women are the ones responsible for maintaining psychic and social well-being through the institution of the family – the very things television is so often thought to destroy. Beliefs about television viewing have much to tell us about our assumptions about gender, the family, and society, for, as Hermann Bausinger argues, "often people speak of television when they mean society in general."[2] Before introducing the individual papers collected here, we wish to situate this book in relation to the dominant paradigms in media studies today; critique the concept of audience pleasure as it is used in this book; describe the status of "critical" media studies; and finally, discuss the relevance of this work to postmodern theories of television.

Our title *Remote Control* has a double meaning. The institution of television controls us at a distance. It emanates from some place far away, yet it makes its presence constantly felt in our everyday lives. As the gadget we use to change channels, the remote control symbolizes the viewers' selection, control, and manipulation of television broadcasts. Our frustrated "zapping" of commercials has become the American television industry's worst nightmare. The work gathered in this volume does not share a common theoretical or methodological base, but it does share an interest in changing the way we think about television viewing. The authors conceive of television viewing as a complicated social experience, where different meanings are made of television programs by different viewers. The field of mass communications has given us the stimulus-response, or "hypodermic needle," theory of the mass media, with its simplistic notion of direct effects, and the "uses and gratifications" approach with its emphasis on individual, psychological meanings rather than social and ideological ones. Though an enormous number of quantitative studies grounded in these perspectives and insistent on proving the researcher's neutrality and objectivity continue to be conducted every year, they have proven quite inadequate to the task of understanding television viewing. Most of the authors in this volume are academics trained in cultural and critical studies, who bring to bear on the question of audience research an interest in psychoanalysis, semiotics, and Marxism, rather than a background in positivist social science. They are primarily interested in the social contexts of viewing and the way that audiences' interpretations of television programs are influenced by race, nationality, class, age, and gender.

If the uses and gratifications researchers have attempted to upgrade the viewer by stressing an "active" audience, the articles presented here are based on the assumption that television spectatorship is much more complicated than the poles of activity and passivity can accommodate. The authors recognize that much is at stake in talking about television and its assumed effects: political and economic agendas are always served by conceiving of the audience as controlling or controlled, as duped or resistant, as making meanings or receiving them. This book attempts to move cautiously toward a reconsideration of specific audiences, an understanding of the various kinds of pleasure which television can offer, and new perspectives – ones initiated by people outside the academy – on the relationship between ideology and television. No unified theoretical position emerges from these papers. Indeed, many contradictions arise among them, between the critique of television ideology and the analysis of audience pleasures, between the significance of the text and the determinations of the viewing context.

As Charlotte Brunsdon points out in Chapter six television audience studies have proliferated after a period of preoccupation with textual analyses of television, as an attempt, in part, to verify empirically the kinds of ideological readings constructed by (white and middle-class) critics. While the new critical interest in television audiences can be traced to the end of the 1970s and, more specifically, to the publication of David Morley's study of *Nationwide*,[3] it was in 1986 that the debate on television audiences emerged as the focus of scholarly attention at gatherings such as the International Television Studies Conference in London. It was also in 1986 that we planned the symposium at which the papers collected here were eventually presented. While more work on audiences has appeared in the meantime, the essential problematics and challenges posed by audience studies remain the same. This book offers a variety of positions and approaches to research in order to promote debate and scrutiny of this turbulent area of study and debate.

All of the work collected here exists in an uneasy relationship to the mainstream mass communications and sociological research paradigms in the United States. The case studies presented in Chapters seven to twelve deal with extremely small samples, which can make no claims to representativeness. Instead of adopting the neutral objective stance of the mainstream empiricist, the authors are calling for an active and politically engaged production and interpretation of interview material. Rather than offering white middle-class college students (in their role as experimental subjects) as the universe of media audiences, as mainstream mass communications research has often done, the subjectivities of the audiences, including that of the researcher, are not only investigated but tied to specific historical moments and cultural contexts.

A variety of research methods adapted from qualititative sociology have been used in the studies of television viewing collected in this volume. Central to most of these studies is the question how (specific) audiences make meanings and pleasures in their engagement with television programs in the context of everyday life. But to look at television in this context presents many problems. How can we study what goes on when people watch television, when so much viewing takes place in private, in the domestic sphere, in the context of intimate relationships? How can we study talk about television? While there is agreement here on the usefulness of qualitative interviewing techniques, considerable variation exists in terms of contact time, how the interviews were conducted, the appropriate settings for the interviews, the uses of group interviews, and the problem of contacting television viewers willing to be studied and willing to talk about their experience with the media.

At best, we should constantly undergo a process of self-examination about whom this knowledge is for and how it is being presented. The challenge is to describe a variety of experiences with television – women working together in an office (Hobson, Chapter eight), Israel's different ethnic groups (Liebes and Katz, Chapter eleven), German families (Rogge, Chapter nine), the elderly in one housing project (Tulloch, Chapter ten), soap opera fans in the Pacific northwest (Seiter *et al.*, Chapter twelve) – without reducing the participants to essentialist categories: age, race, class, gender. We must look at how the models of audience research proposed here – relying on a particular kind of willing participation and expenditure of time – adapt themselves to the study of social groups who are different from the researcher. In a profession overwhelmingly dominated by middle-class whites, this problem must be openly and regularly discussed. The methodologies of audience research provoke deeply political questions about the role of the academic researcher, which feminist sociologists have been careful to point out.[4] How does the researcher deal with issues involving her own authority, withholding or providing information, and the pretext of neutrality? What is the responsibility of the researcher to her "subjects" or "informants"? Finally, what is the relationship between the scholar's own analysis of the television text and the viewer's? As Ien Ang reminds us (Chapter five), what is at stake in audience studies, no less than in textual studies, is a politics of interpretation.

The goal is for this kind of empirical work to incorporate the perspectives of people of color, of the elderly, gays and lesbians, women, and the poor – those whose voices have not been heard in media research so far, and who do not constitute the desirable demographic groups targeted by advertisers – into the study of the media in society and the development of alternative media.[5]

The politics of pleasure

The idea that television offers its audiences experiences that are genuinely pleasurable, if constrained in ways that are economically and ideologically determined, has been central to the work done by scholars in television criticism since the 1970s. The enormous body of work on television soap operas – a genre once regarded as especially pernicious and objectionable – has had as its impetus the explanation, if not the valorization of the particular kinds of enjoyments it offers its audience, in particular its audience of women. The issue of pleasure has motivated many contemporary studies of popular culture and the popularity of certain television programs often serves as the implicit justification to address such texts as adequate objects of criticism.

In the context in which audience pleasure has recently been used, heady political claims have been made about the experience of television. For John Fiske (Chapter three), oppressed groups use the media for pleasure, and this pleasure involves the production of gender identities, subcultural indentities, class identification, and racial solidarity. Such a position provokes many questions about the definition of pleasure in audience studies. One way to approach the problematic of "pleasure" in audience studies is to ask why this concept is being used at this point to valorize an activity – television viewing – that has usually been represented as particularly harmful? John Fiske argues that the pleasure of television viewing is often oppositional: it is a pleasure that comes from resisting dominant ideology, from defining one's self or one's group or one's subculture as different. In this sense, television reinforces "the power to be different" and therefore, the possibility for change. For this reason, Fiske believes it is necessary for the critic to refuse to judge other people's media pleasures, as criticism and research on culture have historically done. However, we are still far from having developed an adequate, contextualized understanding of the question of pleasure(s) and the media. The issues that scholarship needs to investigate further have been summed up by Simon Frith: when popular culture critics place themselves on the side of the consumer, "the resulting politics of pleasure cannot easily be separated, historically, from the politics of leisure, from struggles over education, time and space, cultural capital or from the question of signifying power – who can make meanings stick?"[6]

Academic enthusiasm over the (re-)discovery of pleasure must be tempered with a number of cautionary points. First, no matter how popular certain media experiences become in terms of sheer numbers, there is nothing inherently progressive about pleasure. But stating the question of pleasure in these terms implies the danger of theorizing the pressing issues in much too abstract terms. Therefore, we have to remind ourselves that the relationship between pleasure and politics has to be historicized, contextualized, and specified. For example, the way that the domestic context of television viewing determines the unequal distribution of pleasures between men and women is a very significant area for study, as David Morley's and Ann Gray's work has demonstrated. Second, as Ien Ang argued in our discussions at Blaubeuren, "you win something when you find something pleasurable, but you can lose something at the same time." In its provision of certain kinds of pleasures, television precludes others. For example, soap operas allow women viewers to take pleasure in the character of the villainess, but they do not provide characters who radically challenge the ideology of femininity. Furthermore, the popularity of US television programs on export around the world should not make us forget that other forms of television might also please (and, possibly, please better). In our concern for audiences' pleasures in such programs, we run the risk of continually validating Hollywood's domination of the worldwide television market. Finally, we must remember to think about other emotional states besides pleasure that may be produced by watching television. For example, television also evokes feelings of rage. As Larry Gross points out in Chapter seven on gay and lesbian audiences, viewers may be enraged at stereotyping and denigrating representations. In our interviews in Oregon (Chapter twelve), we were often reminded that continual commercial interruptions and summer reruns also enrage rather than please viewers. While this may be a more difficult topic for investigation than media pleasures, it may also lead to work with audiences which would have clearer implications for media activism.[7]

Uses of the "critical"

For readers unfamiliar with the range of current debate in the study of television, the ways in which the term "critical" is used in this book may be confusing. Several different meanings of the term come together in the kinds of work included in this volume, and exemplify some of the debates engaging media researchers. Each of these meanings is also associated with a line of argument against audience studies that have been put forward by other scholars in the field.

The term "critical" may simply mean pertaining to the practice of criticism. It is this sense of the term which informs the work of Liebes and Katz, when they use "critical ability" to refer to the kinds of skills that are generally considered the province of the professional critic (Chapter eleven). While "critical" is only sometimes used in this sense in the papers collected here, a background in criticism and a concern with television words, images, and stories as *text* informs much of the work here. Indeed, we are engaged throughout this book not just with audiences, but with the history and practice of television criticism. While questions of textual interpretation have played a crucial role in the British tradition of cultural studies, it has been almost entirely ignored in US mass communications research. Since the 1970s, scholars from literature and film departments have taken on the question of the meaning of television, and dubbed their intellectual terrain "television studies" rather than mass communications. This tradition has tended to produce textual analyses of the media from a vantage point of high culture, especially literary theory.

A second important association of the term "critical" (one which many literature and *Germanistik* scholars would reserve exclusively) is with the so-called critical theory of the Frankfurt School, exemplified by the work of scholars such as Theodor Adorno, Max Horkheimer, Walter Benjamin, and Herbert Marcuse. In this, the narrowest sense of the term, "critical" refers to work which follows in the Frankfurt School tradition by combining psychoanalytic and Marxist theories into a broad social critique.

Today, the term "critical theory" is often used by scholars in a wide range of disciplines to embrace both the work of the Frankfurt School and that of post-structuralists, such as Michel Foucault, Jacques Derrida, and Julia Kristeva. In this usage, critical theory refers broadly to those philosophical traditions which mistrust empiricism and positivism and insist on the relationship between knowledge and power. While many of the scholars represented in this volume share the Frankfurt School's insistence on a "critical" theory of society, they are struggling to overcome deterministic notions of the media's all-pervasive power without going to the other extreme of celebrating the freedom and autonomy of the viewer. In the present debate about the meanings of being "critical," it is increasingly important to understand the political situation which produced the discourse of the Frankfurt School and compare it to the one which produces ours today. In this direction, papers in this volume by Robert Allen, Ien Ang, Charlotte Brunsdon, and David Morley trace the intellectual history of the past twenty years and what produced the interest in television audiences.

Recently, attacks on audience studies have been mounted by some who see this kind of work as implicitly and necessarily collusion – simply doing the industry's market research for it. The alternative offered is doing textual analyses, which are presumably untied to any economic interests. In Tania Modleski's discussion of audience studies – peculiar in that none of her examples involve actual empirical work – the danger is seen in "writing apologias for mass culture and embracing its ideology" and "reproducing in their methodologies the very strategies by which consumer society measures and constructs its audiences."[8] For Modleski being "truly critical" means maintaining a critical distance from mass culture. But this position reflects an anxiety over the contaminating effects of mass culture which is one of the least helpful remnants of the Frankfurt School position. Furthermore, we must recognize how academic and critical discourse on the right and the left also serves a system of class distinctions. As Pierre Bourdieu reminds us:

> The denial of lower, coarse, vulgar, venal, servile – in a word, natural – enjoyment, which constitutes the sacred sphere of culture, implies an affirmation of the superiority of those who can be satisfied with the sublimated, refined, disinterested, gratuitous, distinguished pleasures forever closed to the profane. That is why art and cultural consumption are predisposed, consciously and deliberately or not, to fulfill a social function of legitimating social differences.[9]

Both textual analysis and the study of audiences are bound up with the historical and economic context in which academics work. Neither approach can be seen as free from ideology or the service of political and economic interests: all intellectual labor is implicated in this context. The tendency to represent the conflict as one of *either* audience study *or* textual analysis allows the discussion to degenerate into a squabble over disciplinary turf. Instead, the methodological and theoretical differences of the two approaches should be used to improve understanding of the ambiguities of the academic discourse on television and its cultural significance. To cast the argument in terms of mutually exclusive approaches prevents interdisciplinary work and masks what are presumably the shared interests of television scholars – working toward a more politically engaged research, a better understanding of audiences, and better media.

The "critical studies" perspective cautions against an exuberance over the discovery of "real audiences," the danger of lapsing into a happy positivism in our methodologies, and an overreading of points of resistance. And indeed, political dangers are involved in audience research. Modleski is right to remind us that it is in the media industries' interests to adapt to the pleasures and tastes of economically attractive audience groups. Thus, audience studies *and* textual studies have to be informed by a high degree of theoretical awareness and political responsibility.

Many of these meanings of "critical" are also implicit in the way that the term identifies an area within mass communications research, especially in the US, where it carries a polemical charge by opposing itself to mainstream or institutional research. "Critical communications research" identifies a range of research topics, but often focuses on the political economics of the media. Mike Budd and Clay Steinman have stated the critique of cultural studies by political economists this way:

As cultural studies gains influence in North America, Australia and elsewhere, its work will be increasingly vitiated if it cannot break down the detailed intellectual division of labor which so uncannily resembles that of the capitalist society it seeks to understand. The political economists and others who study concentration of ownership, economic imperialism and other institutional questions may have the mistaken notion that texts, and culture generally, don't matter very much, but that doesn't mean we can ignore economic determination.[10]

The most serious lack in the audience studies presented here is the integration of a political economics perspective. There is a great deal of work which urgently needs to be done in this area. But the political economics perspective should not be used to diminish the importance of audience studies. David Morley (Chapter one) has reminded us of the tendency within Marxist analysis to neglect consumption in order to "prioritize the study of 'production' to the exclusion of the study of all other levels of the social formation." This relentless employment of an economist model adapted from classical Marxism to the media studies has as only one of its shortcomings a firmly masculinist orientation. From the Frankfurt School to Jean Baudrillard, consumption is feminine and bad, production is masculine and good.[11] Often in this book, a simple reversal of terms – the television viewer as producer – is used to redeem the audience. In our efforts to understand the workings of culture and ideology, however, we might do better to rethink the usefulness of the production/consumption dichotomy.[12]

Finally, scholars sometimes use the term "critical" to identify any research which has something negative to say about the media: as though all that is called for is taking a moral stand against the media (as journalists and *The Ladies Home Journal* regularly do). Such a meaning is frequently found in the famous *Ferment in the Field* issue of the *Journal of Communication*, where "critical" occasionally identifies any work which does not involve quantitative and survey research methods. It is this plethora of meanings which has made the term of dubious usefulness as a way of identifying intellectual positions. More interesting than unpacking these differences in usage may be examining why the term "critical" has become so overdetermined in meaning, and why left academics want so badly to identify themselves and define their practices this way.[13]

Postmodernism

At the present time, much of television studies is dominated by a discussion of writing in critical theory and aesthetics which seeks to define the postmodern. Though they share some of the same concepts, postmodern approaches to television have remained somewhat indifferent to audience studies. Defining postmodernism continues to be a very confusing business because of the blurring of boundaries between "postmodernism as a set of stylistic phenomena and postmodernism as a socio-economic phase."[14] Television represents a specific form of commodity culture in a particular phase of late capitalism as well as a medium whose aesthetic strategies implicate a very different spectator from that of cinematic realism or literary modernism. One of the most difficult problems in relating television audience studies to postmodernism is, in Andrew Ross' words, "in effect it (postmodernism) has been used as an epithet to describe a staggering range of objects, practices and styles: right or left, hot or cold, dead or alive."[15]

Audience studies are inspired in part by a recognition typical of postmodernism of "the instability of ideological processes," especially where the media are concerned. In its philosophical versions, one of postmodernism's central notions has been the deconstruction of essentialist concepts of identity. The cherished Enlightenment belief in "the existence of a stable, coherent self" has been thrown into "radical doubt."[16] This is an extremely important development for audience studies, in that it presents the possibility of shifting subjectivities on the part of the viewer. To varying extents, television has been seen simultaneously as symbolizing and as producing this kind of identity crisis.

Jean Baudrillard's work has been influential within television studies. While indebted to the Frankfurt School, he makes a radical break with traditional Marxist positions. His is the latest example of a cultural critique inspired by political economics (the postmodern as label for societies marked by late capitalism's intense need to stimulate consumption) that expresses a massive cultural pessimism in such notorious phrases as "the death of the social." The cultural consumer of postmodernism has been repeatedly compared to the schizophrenic; Baudrillard has drawn him or her as one who "sees himself at the controls of a hypothetical machine, isolated in a position of perfect and remote sovereignty at an infinite distance from his universe of origin."[17] It is no accident that Baudrillard's extremely abstract work has not yet offered much help in the study of the specific social and historical locations of viewers and their interpretations of specific television texts and genres. Thus, in Lawrence Grossberg's words, "a theory that celebrates otherness fails to acknowledge the difference between experiences, real historical tendencies and cultural discourses and meanings, as well as the complex relations that exist between them." In order to account for these differences, we need to move back and forth between the abstract theories of postmodernism and local, particular practices.[18]

In textual analysis, broadcast television has been seen as embodying postmodern aesthetics, with its relentless intertextuality, its reworking of popular culture, its effacement of history. As a theory of aesthetics, postmodernism offers the possibility – yet unrealized – of dissolving the rigid distinctions between high and low art so characteristic of modernism. Television has provided the raw material for the avant-garde to produce postmodern art, while itself borrowing freely from experimental film and video. The problem of periodization which postmodernism poses looms even larger in popular culture criticism than it does in literature and the visual arts. Where and when was modernism, if television is now postmodern? Television critics have found music television, commercials, and programs such as *Miami Vice* or *Moonlighting* to be especially good examples, which lend themselves to the tendency within postmodernist television criticism "to privilege the medium over the message, style over substance, and form over content."[19]

But many television genres, including those which address themselves specifically to women as audience members, have so far failed to fit the mold. In television studies as elsewhere, the postmodern debate has tended to exclude questions of gender.[20] This is perhaps the primary reason why theories of post-modernism do not figure prominently in this book, where feminist readings, domestic politics, soap opera, and particular local practices of television viewing are the primary concern. As Elspeth Probyn has warned: "In the midst of all this – in the timeless pass from the modern to the post, from marxism to postmod-ernism – we seem to have lost the impulse to push politics into the everyday."[21]

While postmodern theory has tended to lead scholars back to the television text, the work presented in this book insists on the necessity of meeting people outside academic culture to discuss television – mindful of just how problematic that interaction may be. What we offer are readings "from below," mindful of their mediation by our own discourses. It is the reluctance of television scholars to engage in this kind of research which may explain the fact that while everyone seems to be talking about television audience studies, surprisingly few of us trained in cultural studies are actually doing them. The reasons for this reluctance may involve the *Angst* of leaving the secure academic context to listen and talk to social groups different from ourselves about television. But such an encounter is a necessary starting point if we are to understand our own positions as academics and the barriers to our political effectivity. As Janice Radway has put it:

> In learning how others actively make their own social worlds differently from the way we make our own, perhaps it might also be possible to identify together those points where articulations and alliances could be forged across borders in the service of a future not yet envisioned and therefore neither necessarily lost nor secured.[22]

The first six chapters take up theoretical considerations in audience studies and the following six consist of case studies of various audiences. The book begins with David Morley's overview of research on media audiences and critical work on television texts. Morley traces the various theoretical influences – semiotics, cultural studies, film theory, psychoanalysis – which have led to a departure from the traditional paradigms of mass-communication research and to an interest in studying media audiences. Morley stresses the role of social factors in the production of meaning from television; the impact of genre on patterns of viewing and negotiations of meaning, and the importance of contextualizing television viewing within the framework of everyday life. His chapter plays an essential role here in introducing the reader to the intellectual history which informs most of the book's contributions.

Similarly, Robert Allen's "Bursting bubbles" traces the development of genre criticism in film and literary theory, defining genre as a classificatory discursive strategy which allows patterns of textual structure to be connected to the groups in society for whom these patterns are meaningful. The term "soap opera" serves as a catch-all for different discursive relationships between a variety of textual features and at least three major interpretative communities: television industry workers, critics, and viewers. For Allen, theories of the viewer's engagement with soap operas are marked by disjuncture between the implications of the term in critical discourse and the ways in which generic knowledge is employed by viewers in making sense of and deriving pleasure from soap operas.

John Fiske suggests abandoning altogether the categories of "text" and "audience" as separate analytical entities. Instead, television watching should be conceived of as a process of meaning production in which the "text" is merely a substratum from which the viewer may construct various realizations. Television must be analysed not in terms of political economy, but in terms of cultural economy, in which viewers reject their role as commodity and become a producer of pleasures and meanings. Television provides flexibility due to specific textual and intertextual characteristics which militate against closure and the inscription of the dominant ideology. Because of the openness of the televisual text and the diversity of patterns of engagement on the part of the viewer, the process of watching television precludes theoretical fixation and can only be approached in terms of moments in the semiotic process, where textual and social lines of force intersect. This approach demands a researcher who is not a detached scientific observer but a critic-as-fan, who shares discursive competence, social history, and pleasures with the viewers under study.

In "Live television and its audiences," Claus-Dieter Rath focuses on live television in terms of production and reception. Live programs – which are especially common on European television – allow insights into institutional value systems such as topicality and what determines the selection of suitable broadcast material. The very mode of live presentation renders events meaningful and important. Rath outlines aspects of viewer engagement which are vital in live broadcasts: the identification of the viewer with physical actions, the alignment of the viewer with the field of vision of the camera, and the merging of the public and private spheres. Through live broadcasts, television forms a collectivity based on the experience, "I also will have seen."

Chapters five and six challenge the methods and the assumptions underlying audience study itself. Ien Ang criticizes recent tendencies which point to a "new consensus" between the previously opposed "critical" and "mainstream" camps in mass communications research. She draws attention to the fact that despite shared terminology, both approaches are based on epistemological concepts which are fundamentally opposed and make any methodological synthesis impossible. For Ang, the positivist will to truth cannot be reconciled with the hermeneutic and political orientation of critical cultural investigations.

Charlotte Brunsdon expresses reservations about the apparent displacement of textual criticism by audience studies. The concentration on diverse modes of television reception is misleading, since all cultural texts may be engaged with in a variety of ways. Brunsdon argues that the interest in audiences expresses a search for the authentic in the study of a medium whose aesthetics is strongly marked by a lack of authenticity. Brunsdon describes the shift from text to audience in the institutional history of television studies as a development from the interest in "redemptive readings" of popular culture texts, from the recognition of intertextuality and postmodernism, and from the use of the autobiographical in feminist criticism. But for Brunsdon the choice of what is recognized as constituting a single text is a political as well as a critical matter, and retaining the notion of the text is therefore crucial to the development of television criticism and aesthetics.

These theoretical articles are followed by case studies of the audience, some of which focus on audiences for particular genres and some on specific groups within the audience. We begin with "Out of the mainstream: Sexual minorities and the mass media." One of the most important insights of the approach to media effects developed by Larry Gross in his work with George Gerbner was that habitual television viewing results in mainstreaming: it "tends to cultivate in viewers . . . a relative commonality of outlooks and values"(see Chapter seven). On the other hand television works towards a "symbolic annihilation" of minorities and their norms and values. Gross draws attention to the important role of the mass media in offering images of the Other, which have an impact on straight audiences, as well as in the particularly difficult process of social identification for gays. Using examples from several media, Gross discusses three patterns of response, ranging from an internalization of mainstream norms to active resistance through film and television productions by and for gays and lesbians.

In "Soap operas at work," Dorothy Hobson investigates the ways in which British soap operas enter the realm of work through everyday conversations with colleagues. Hobson stresses that communication about media contents is interspersed with accounts of personal experience and stories which are frequently only touched upon in the programs under discussion. Apart from providing a permissive framework for articulating personal concerns, conversations about soap operas tend to reinforce group solidarity because they draw on experiences shared by all members of the group.

In "The media in everyday family life," Jan-Uwe Rogge discusses the functions of media use as they are interwoven with a family's need for communication. Rogge recognizes the ways that various interests among family members and their different biographies affect the meaning of the media in everyday life. His emphasis in a research project involving interviews with hundreds of families in West Germany is on change in media consumption and changes in the everyday life of the family. Rogge discusses a number of family case studies to illustrate how changes such as unemployment alter the family's use of and feelings toward television. Rogge argues that the historical individual's media reality has many facets, expressing "cultural orientation and day-to-day life-styles" and defining "interpersonal relationships and the emotional and communicative climate in a family."

John Tulloch's chapter centers on the elderly, a group which has been largely neglected in media studies, which have tended to concentrate on studies of children and youth. As with women viewers, the elderly have been especially prone to stigmatization and stereotyped as manipulated and addicted television viewers. Tulloch's interviews reveal that the meaning of television series derives to a large extent from their integration in daily routines of the elderly and their meticulously executed schedules of organization and caring. In the second part of his chapter, Tulloch examines the way that the social category of age is related to class. Throughout, Tulloch takes a self-reflexive approach to his interviews and raises important questions about ethnographic interviewing as a method.

Tamar Liebes and Elihu Katz compare the interpretations of *Dallas* made by Israeli viewers from four different ethnic communities (Arab, Russian, Moroccan, and kibbutzim). After gathering responses in group interviews, Liebes and Katz analyse the viewers' critical abilities, i.e. how much they discussed the program as a constructed, conventional narrative. The authors did find that viewers outside the US had diverse strategies for defense against the perceived message of *Dallas* and frequently voiced their moral or ideological opposition to the show.

Finally, we present a report on our own research in "'Don't treat us like we're so stupid and naïve': toward an ethnography of soap opera viewers." It is based on a series of group interviews with soap opera viewers in Oregon carried out in 1986. The study is part of a larger research project on the history, production, and reception of American daytime soap operas based in the American Studies Department at the University of Tübingen. Starting with a discussion of recent work on the practical and methodological problems presented by an "ethnography of reading," the paper problematizes the ethnographic principles underlying our interview study. Problems of ethnographic authority as well as the special nature of gendered discourse in all-women interviews are raised in this context. The interview material is analysed in terms of the way that soap operas are scheduled around women's work in the home, the way viewers described the soap opera as text and as genre, and a reconsideration of Tania Modleski's influential work on the textual position of the "ideal mother."

It is this research project which introduced us to the problems of studying the television audience and inspired us to bring together an international group of scholars in Blaubeuren to discuss these issues. This book presents a variety of the positions taken and topics debated at that symposium. We hope that it will lead to a refinement of methods, a clarification of theoretical positions, and a thoughtful reconsideration of television and its audiences.

The academic pendulum swings along the fine line between re-seeing and revisionism: valorisation of consumption replaces insistence on production; recognition of escapism replaces the search for engagement; the centrality of contradiction makes way for the importance of identity; work makes way for relaxation and politics makes way for pleasure. Each of these shifts is important and necessary where it occurs under pressure of a specific theoretical and political demand. The difficulty is in slowing the process which turns a radical shift into a new orthodoxy.[23]

Notes

1   Paul Pearsall, "Love Busters," *Ladies Home Journal*, October 1987, p. 98.
2   Hermann Bausinger, "Tolerant Partners: On the Intertwining of Communication and Para-Communication" (paper presented at the symposium, "Rethinking the Audience: New Tendencies in Television Research," Blaubeuren 1987), p. 11.
3   David Morley, *The "Nationwide" Audience: Structure and Decoding* (London: British Film Institute, 1980).
4   For a feminist consideration of qualitative methodologies see Helen Roberts (ed.) *Doing Feminist Research* (London: Routledge & Kegan Paul, 1981); and Gloria Bowles and Renate Duelli Klein (eds) *Theories of Women's Studies* (London: Routledge & Kegan Paul, 1983). Janice Radway critiques her own research methods in "Identifying Ideological Seams," *Communication* 9 (1986): 93-123, and in her introduction to the British version of *Reading the Romance* (London: Verso, 1987), pp. 1-18.
5   For one of the best examples of work which fulfills this kind of promise see Jacqueline Bobo's "*The Color Purple*: Black Women as Cultural Readers," in Deidre Primbrawm (ed.) *Female Spectators Looking at Film and Television* (London: Verso, 1988), pp. 90-109.
6   Simon Frith, "Hearing Secret Harmonies," in Colin MacCabe (ed.) *High Theory, Low Culture* (New York: St Martin's Press, 1986), p. 57.
7   For a discussion of the political usefulness of rage, see Julia Lesage, "Women's Rage," in Cary Nelson and Lawrence Grossberg (eds) *Marxism and Cultural Interpretation* (Urbana: University of Illinois Press, 1988), pp. 419-28. Lawrence Grossberg has suggested that the study of affect may solve the problems inherent in the issue of pleasure. See his "History, Politics and Postmodernism: Stuart Hall and Cultural Studies," *Journal of Communication Inquiry* 10, no. 2 (1986): 73-4; and "Postmodernity and Affect: All Dressed Up With No Place to Go," *Communication* 10, nos 3-4 (1988): 271-93.
8   Tania Modleski, "Introduction," in Tania Modleski (ed.) *Studies in Entertainment* (Bloomington: Indiana University Press, 1986), pp. xi-xii.
9   Pierre Bourdieu, *Distinction: A Social Critique of the Judgement of Taste*, trans. Richard Nice (Cambridge, Mass.: Harvard University Press, 1984), p. 7.
10 Mike Budd and Clay Steinman, "Television, Cultural Studies, and the 'Blindspot' Debate in Critical Communications Research," in Gary Burns and Robert Thompson (eds) *Television Studies* (New York: Praeger, forthcoming).
11 See Andreas Huyssen's "Mass Culture as Woman: Modernism's Other," in *After the Great Divide* (Bloomington: Indiana University Press, 1986), pp. 44-64; also Tania Modleski's excellent critique of Baudrillard, "Femininity as Masquerade: A Feminist Approach to Mass Culture," in MacCabe, *High Theory, Low Culture*, pp. 32-57.

12 John Caughie has made this argument in "Popular Culture: Notes and Revisions," in MacCabe, *High Theory, Low Culture*, pp. 156-71.

13 For examples of the various positions within mass communications see *Ferment in the Field*, a special issue of *Journal of Communication* 33, no. 3 (1983).

14 Philip Hayward and Paul Kerr, "Introduction" to the *Screen* issue *Postmodern Screen* 28, no. 2 (spring 1987): 5.

15 "Postmodernism and Universal Abandon," *Communications* 10, nos 3-4 (1988): 252.

16 Jane Flax, "Postmodernism and Gender Relations in Feminist Theory," *Signs* 12, no. 4 (1987): 624.

17 Jean Baudrillard, "The Ecstasy of Communication," in Hal Foster (ed.) *The Anti-Aesthetic* (Port Townsend, Wash.: Bay Press, 1983), p. 128. See also Jean Baudrillard, *Simulations*, trans. Paul Foss (New York: Semiotext(e), 1983); Jean Baudrillard, *In the Shadow of the Silent Majorities*, trans. Paul Foss (New York: Semiotexte(e), 1983).

18 Grossberg, "History, Politics and Postmodernism," p. 74.

19 Steven Best and Douglas Kellner, "(Re)Watching Television: Notes Toward a Political Criticism," *Diacritics* (summer 1987): 100.

20 This point has been made by a variety of feminist writers: Jane Flax, "Postmodernism and Gender Relations," pp. 621-41; Terry Lovell, *Consuming Fictions* (London: Verso, 1987), pp. 153-62.

21 Elspeth Probyn, "Memories and Past Politics of Postmodernism," *Communication* 10, nos 3-4 (1988): 309.

22 Janice Radway, "Reception Study: Ethnography and the Problems of Dispersed Audiences and Nomadic Subjects," *Cultural Studies* 2, no. 3 (1988).

23 John Caughie, "Popular Culture: Notes and Revisions," in MacCabe, *High Theory, Low Culture*, p. 163.

hanging paradigms in audience studies

David Morley

Effects, uses, and decodings

The history of audience studies during the post-war period can be seen as a series of oscillations between perspectives which have stressed the power of the text (or message) over its audiences and perspectives which have stressed the barriers "protecting" the audience from the potential effects of the message. The first position is most obviously represented by the whole tradition of effects studies, mobilizing a hypodermic model of media influence, in which the media are seen as having the power to "inject" their audiences with particular messages which will cause them to behave in a particular way. This has involved, from the right, perspectives which would see the media causing the breakdown of "traditional values" and, from the left, perspectives which see the media causing their audience to remain quiescent in political terms, or causing them to inhabit some form of false consciousness.

One finds curious contradictions here. On the one hand, television is accused of reducing its audience to the status of "zombies" or "glassy-eyed dupes" who consume a constant diet of predigested junk food, churned out by the media "sausage factory" and who suffer the anaesthetic effects of this addictive and narcotic substance. However, at the same time as television has been held responsible for causing this kind of somnambulant state of mind (as a result of the viewers' consumption of this "chewing gum for the eyes") television has also been accused of making us do all manner of things, most notably in the debates around television and violence – where it has been argued that the viewing of violent television content will cause viewers to go out and commit violent acts.[1] One point of interest here is that these "television zombies" are always other people. Few people think of their own use of television in this way. It is a theory about what television does to other, more vulnerable people.

The second key perspective has been the work that has developed principally from the uses and gratifications school. Within that perspective, the viewer is credited with an active role, and it is then a question, as Halloran puts it, of looking at what people do with the media rather than what media do to them.[2] This argument was obviously of great significance in moving the debate forward

– to begin to look at the active engagement of the audience with the medium and with the particular television programs that they might be watching. One key advance which was developed by the uses and gratifications perspective was that of the variability of response and interpretation. From this perspective one can no longer talk about the "effects" of a message on a homogeneous mass audience who are expected to be affected in the same way. However, the limitation is that the "uses and gratifications" perspective remains individualistic, in so far as differences of response or interpretation are ultimately attributed to individual differences of personality or psychology. Clearly, uses and gratifications does represent a significant advance on effects theory, in so far as it opens up the question of differential interpretation. However, it remains severely limited by its insufficiently sociological or cultural perspective, in so far as everything is reduced to the level of variations of individual psychology. It was against this background that Stuart Hall's encoding/decoding model of communication was developed at the Centre for Contemporary Cultural Studies, as an attempt to take forward insights which had emerged within each of these other perspectives.[3] It took, from the effects theorists, the notion that mass communication is a structured activity, in which the institutions which produce the messages do have a power to set agendas, and to define issues. This is to move away from the idea of the power of the medium to make a person behave in a certain way (as a direct effect which is caused by stimulus provided by the medium) but it is to hold on to a notion of the role of the media in setting agendas and providing cultural categories and frameworks within which members of the culture will tend to operate. The model also attempted to incorporate, from the uses and gratifications perspective, the model of the active viewer making meaning from the signs and symbols which the media provide. However, it was also designed to take on board, from the work developed within the interpretative and normative paradigms, the concern with the ways in which responses and interpretations are structured and patterned at a level beyond that of individual psychologies. The model was also, critically, informed by semiological perspectives focusing on the question of how communication "works." The key focus was on the realization that we are, of course, dealing with signs and symbols which only have meaning within the terms of reference supplied by codes (of one sort or another) which the audience shares, to some greater or lesser extent, with the producers of messages.

In short, the encoding/decoding model was designed to provide a synthesis of insights that had come out of a series of different perspectives – communication theory, semiology, sociology, and psychology – and to provide an overall model of the communication circuit as it operated in its social context. It was concerned with matters of ideological and cultural power and it was concerned with shifting the ground of debate so that emphasis moved to the consideration of how it was possible for meaning to be produced. It attempted to develop the argument that we should look not for the meaning of a text, but for the conditions of a practice – i.e. to examine the foundations of communication, but crucially, to examine those foundations as social and cultural phenomena. This was the point of interest

17

in socio-linguistics and in the connections with debates in the sociology of education (most notably around the work of Basil Bernstein) which was evident in the early development of the encoding/decoding model.[4] It was also connected to the field of political sociology and notably with the work of Frank Parkin, in so far as his theory of meaning systems which might exist within a given society (dominant, negotiated and oppositional) provided the basis of the three decoding "potentials" identified in the encoding/decoding model.[5] However, it remains a limited model, in so far as it simply provides for the three logical possibilities of the receiver either sharing, partly sharing, or not sharing the code in which the message is sent and therefore, to that extent, being likely to make a dominant, negotiated, or oppositional decoding of the encoded message. Further, following the encounter with the work of Hymes, Bourdieu, and Bernstein the encoding/decoding model also represented an attempt to develop an analysis of the role of social structure in distributing different forms of cultural competence throughout the different sections of the media audience.[6]

In the more recent period, a whole number of shortcomings with the encoding/decoding model of communication have been identified.[7] These criticisms concern, for instance, the extent to which the model tends to conceive of language merely as a conveyor belt for preconstituted meanings or messages; the way in which it tends to confuse textual meaning with the conscious intentions of broadcasters; and the tendency to blur together under the heading of "decoding" what are probably best thought of as separate processes along the axes of comprehension/incomprehension, as opposed to agreement/disagreement with the propositional content of messages. Furthermore, the concept of the preferred reading, which is of course central to the encoding/decoding model, has been subjected to a number of criticisms. At one level one can ask how specific the concept of preferred reading is to the field of news and current affairs television (within which the encoding/decoding model was first applied). How one might effectively transfer that model to the analysis of fictional television remains a problem. There are also further problems about the exact status of the "preferred reading." Is it something which is in the text (a property of the text) or is it something which can be generated from the text by certain methods of semiological analysis, or is it a statement, or prediction by the analyst, as to how most members of the audience will empirically read a given program or message?

There are then a number of problems with the model and in particular with the concept of preferred reading as specified in that model. However, I would still want to defend the model's usefulness, in so far as it avoids sliding straight from the notion of a text as having a determinate meaning (which would necessarily impose itself in the same way on all members of the audience) to an equally absurd, and opposite position, in which it is assumed that the text is completely "open" to the reader and is merely the site upon which the reader constructs meaning. This latter "reader as writer" position seems to unite theories as apparently distanced as those of "uses and gratifications" and many forms of "postmodern" theory. In either case, any notion of particular forms of textual organization as constraints on the production of meaning disappear entirely and the text is seen as infinitely (and equally) open to all interpretations. The point of the preferred reading model was to insist that readers are, of course, engaged in productive work, but under determinate conditions. Those determinate conditions are of course supplied both by the text, the producing institution and by the social history of the audience.

Psychoanalytic theories of the subject

The other key perspective on the audience which has been developed in recent years is the body of work, principally within film theory, based on a psycho-analytic perspective, which is concerned with the positioning of the subject by the text.

Despite the theoretical sophistication of much of this work, in offering a more developed model of text/subject relations it has, until now, contributed little to the empirical study of the audience. This is for the simple reason that those working in this tradition have, on the whole, been content to "deduce" audience responses from the structure of the text. To this extent, and despite the theoretical advances achieved by this work in other respects, I would argue that the psycho-analytically based work has ultimately mobilized what can be seen as another version of the hypodermic theory of effects – in so far as it is, at least in its initial and fundamental formulations, a universalist theory which attempts to account for the way in which the subject is necessarily positioned by the text. The diff-iculty, in terms of audience studies, is that this body of work, premised as it is on universalist criteria, finds it difficult to provide the theoretical space within which one can allow for, and then investigate, differential readings, interpretations, or responses on the part of the audience. This is so quite simply because the theory, in effect, tries to explain any specific instance of the text/reader relationship in terms of a universalist theory of the formation of subjects in general.

From within this perspective emphasis falls on the universal, primary, psychoanalytic processes through which the subject is constituted. The text is then understood as reproducing or replaying this primary positioning, which is then the foundation of any particular reading. My argument would be that, in fact, we need to question the assumption that all specific discursive effects can be reduced to, and explained by, the functioning of a single, universal set of psychic mechanisms – which is rather like a theory of Platonic forms, which find their expression in any particular instance. The key issue is that this form of psychoanalytic theory poses the problem of the politics of the signifier (the struggle over ideology in language) exclusively at the level of the subject, rather than at the intersection between constituted subjects and specific discursive positions – i.e. at the site of interpellation, where the discursive subject is recognized to be operating in interdiscursive space.

In making this argument, I follow Stuart Hall's critique of the Lacanian perspective. Hall argues that "without further work, further specification, the mechanisms of the Oedipus complex in the discourse of Freud and Lacan are universalist, trans-historical and therefore 'essentialist.'"[8] To that extent, Hall argues, these concepts, in their universalist forms, cannot usefully be applied, without further specification and elaboration, to the analysis of historically specific social formations.

This is to attempt to hold on to the distinction between the constitution of the subject as a general (or mythical) moment and the moment when the subject in general is interpellated by the discursive formation of specific societies. That is to insist on the distinction between the formation of subjects for language, and the recruitment of specific subjects to the subject positions of discursive formations through the process of interpellation. It is also to move away from the assumption that every specific reading is already determined by the primary structure of subject positions and to insist that these interpellations are not given and absolute, but rather, are conditional and provisional, in so far as the struggle in ideology takes place precisely through the articulation/disarticulation of interpellations. This is to lay stress on the possibility of contradictory interpellations and to emphasize the unstable, provisional, and dynamic properties of subject positioning. It is also to recognize that subjects have histories and that past interpellations affect present ones, rather than to "deduce" subjects from the subject positions offered by the text and to argue that readers are not merely bearers or puppets of their unconscious positions. It is to insist, with Volosinov, on the "multiaccentuality of the sign" which makes it possible for discourse to become an arena of struggle.[9]

However, it must also be recognized that, within this psychoanalytic perspective itself, the gap between real, empirical readers and the "inscribed" ones constructed and marked in and by the text has increasingly been recognized. To that extent real readers can then be seen to be subjects in history, living in social formations, rather than mere subjects of a single text (cf. the distinction between the inscribed reader of the text and the social subject who is invited to take up this position). This is further to recognize that address is not synonymous with textual address, and that particular positions are a product of textual address in conjunction with the immediate discourses and apparatuses that surround and support it, and that the social subject always exceeds the subject implied by the text. We can point here to the work of Paul Willemen and Steve Neale who developed this break with the ahistorical and unspecified use of the category of the subject.[10] It follows from this break that the meaning produced by the encounter of text and subject cannot be read straight off from textual characteristics or discursive strategies. We have to take into account what Neale so aptly described as "the use to which a particular text is put, its function within a particular conjuncture, in particular institutional spaces, in relation to particular audiences."[11] This is, further, to recognize that the meaning of the text will also be constructed differently depending on the discourses, knowledges, prejudices, or resistances brought to bear on the text by the reader. One crucial factor delimiting this will, of course, be the repertoire of discourses at the disposal of different audiences, and the individual's position in the social formation will tend to determine which sets of discourses a given subject is likely to have access to, and thus to bring to their encounter with the text.

These then are, in my view, the main difficulties with much recent psychoanalytic work, in so far as it is a theoretical perspective which presumes a unilateral fixing of a position for the reader, imprisoning him or her in its structure, so as to produce a singular and guaranteed effect. The text, of course, may offer the subject specific positions of intelligibility, it may operate to prefer certain readings above others; what it cannot do is to guarantee them – that must always be an empirical question. This is, in part, because the subject that the text encounters is, as Pecheux has argued, never a "raw" or "unacculturated" subject. Readers are always already formed, shaped as subjects, by the ideological discourses which have operated on them prior to their encounter with the text in question.[12]

If we are to theorize the subject of television, it has to be theorized in its cultural and historical specificity, an area where psychoanalytic theory is obviously weak. It is only thus that we can move beyond a theory of the subject which has reference only to universal, primary psychoanalytic processes, and only thus that we can allow a space in which one can recognize that the struggle over ideology also takes place at the moment of the encounter of text and subject and is not "always already" predetermined at the psychoanalytic level.

Valerie Walkerdine has recently produced an analysis which addresses the question of how a psychoanalytic mode of analysis might be developed while avoiding the problems of "universalism". Walkerdine sets out to offer an understanding of a particular working-class family's viewing habits and pleasures (and, in particular, the pleasure which the husband derives from watching the *Rocky* films) within the terms of what she describes as an "ethnography of the unconscious." Her concern is with "the production of subjectivity in the actual regulative practices of daily life" and with the "effectivity of filmic representations within the lived relations of domestic practices." In particular, Walkerdine aims to avoid the common problem associated with psychoanalytic accounts which tend to "impose universalistic meanings on particularistic viewing situations."[13] Walkerdine offers an illuminating analysis of a class-specific mode of masculinity. Thus, in seeking to understand this working-class man's obsession with the *Rocky* films, rather than simply understanding the fighting in the films as "macho violence" (and thus the appropriate object of pathologization in a liberal anti-sexist discourse), Walkerdine examines it in relation to this man's own understanding of himself as a "fighter," struggling to defend his (and his family's) rights in an oppressive system. Thus, for this working-class man, for whom advancement through mental labor is not an option, there remains only the body – and the struggle for advancement is then expressed either through manual labor, or ultimately, through fighting. From this perspective then fighting is a key term in a discourse of powerlessness, of a constant struggle not to sink, to get rights, not to be pushed out. In that lived historicity fighting is quite specific in its meaning, and therefore not coterminous with what fighting would mean in a professional middle class household. This is an argument against a universalism of meaning, reading and interpretation.[14]

From my own point of view, Walkerdine's analysis is of interest not simply on account of the important "break" which it makes by developing a mode of analysis derived from psychoanalytic theory which is, for once, historically and contextually specific, but also because it opens up the whole question of how we understand the specific conditions of formation of "pleasures" for particular groups at any one historical moment.

Moreover, the idea of the determining effectivity of the single text which has been the cornerstone of much film theory is not simply deficient when we consider the role of promotional material within the cinema. It is certainly deficient when we consider the consumption of television, given the higher level of interpenetration of different materials across the flow of television scheduling. In this context, Nick Browne has usefully suggested a notion of the televisual text which is quite different from the traditional notion of the discrete and separate text. He proposes the concept of the "supertext" which consists of "the particular program and all the introductory and interstitial materials – chiefly announcements and ads – considered in its specific position in the schedule." He thus argues that the

> relevant context for the analysis of form and meaning of the television text consists of its relation to the schedule, that is, to the world of television and secondly, of the relation of the schedule to the structure and economics of the work week of the general population.[15]

As Larry Grossberg has put it, "not only is every media event mediated by other texts, but it's almost impossible to know what constitutes the bounded text which might be interpreted or which is actually consumed."[16] This is because the text does not occupy a fixed position but is always mobilized, placed, and articulated with other texts in different ways.

However, it can be objected that this new emphasis upon intertextuality runs several risks, notably that contextual issues will overwhelm and overdetermine texts and their specificity. The question is whether, in following this route, we run the danger of arriving at a point in which the text is simply dissolved into its readings.

Texts and readings

The primary issue which contemporary work has opened up in this connection concerns the definition of the text itself. To what extent can we still usefully speak of the separate text, as opposed to what has variously been described as the "paratext" or the "supertext"? I want to begin here by referring to Tony Bennett's work on the problems for textual analysis highlighted in his case study of the "James Bond" phenomenon.[17] In that study, Bennett quotes Pierre Macherey as asking what studying a specific text should entail. Macherey argues that studying a text involves studying not just the text, but also everything which has been written about it, everything which has collected on it or become attached to it, like shells on a rock by the seashore, forming a whole encrustation. At that point the very idea of a separable text becomes problematic. Macherey moves us toward a perspective on the text which, rather than looking at it as a given and separable entity, is concerned with the history of its use and its inscription into a variety of different material, social, and institutional contexts.[18]

John Fiske has called for a re-theorization of the televisual text, which would allow us to investigate its openness by mobilizing Barthes' distinction between "work" and "text." Barthes argued that the work is the physical construct of signifiers, that becomes a "text" only when read.[19] The text, in this formulation, is never a fixed or stable thing but is continually being recreated out of the work. Fiske has extended this argument toward the idea of a "readers' liberation movement," involving a theory of audience reading which

> asserts the reader's right to make, out of the program, the text that connects the discourses of the program with the discourses through which he/she lives his/her social experience, and thus for program, society and reading subject to come together in an active, creative living of culture in the moment of reading.[20]

While I sympathize with this concern with "readers' rights," I would argue that the concept of rights in this context is problematic, in so far as it is perhaps less a question of the readers' rights to make out of a program whatever meaning they wish (which presumably involves a moral or philosophical discourse concerning "rights" in general) than a question of power – i.e. the presence or absence of the power or cultural resources necessary to make certain types of meaning (which is, ultimately, an empirical question).

Jane Feuer has usefully identified a number of the problems which lurk around here. As she notes, from the standpoint of the reception theories on which Bennett draws, the question of what constitutes the text is extremely complex. As she notes, from this perspective it becomes increasingly hard to separate the text from its contemporary encrustations – fan magazines, the ads, the product tie-ins, the books, the publicity articles and so on, and indeed, the very sense of attempting this separation is called into question. Feuer's argument is that this approach endlessly defers the attribution of meaning. Whereas Bennett argues that "the text is never available for analysis except in the context of its activations," as Feuer puts it,

> the reception theorist is asking us to read those activations, to read the text of the reading formation. Thus, audience response criticism becomes another

form of interpretation, the text for which is now relocated. If we take the concept of the "openness" . . . of a text to its logical extreme, we have merely displaced the whole problem of interpretation, for the audience responses also constitute a representation, in this case a linguistic discourse. In displacing the text onto the audience, the reception theorist constantly risks falling back into an empiricism of the subject, by granting a privileged status to the interpretations of the audience over those of the critic.[21]

In Feuer's formulation, the problem is that when one attempts to combine this perspective with empirical audience work,

the authors begin by reacting against theories which assume that the text has a total determinity over the audience. They then attempt to read their own audience data. In each case, the critic reads another text, that is to say, the text of the audience discourse. For the empirical researcher, granting a privileged status to the audience response does not create a problem. But it does for those reception theorists who acknowledge the textual status of the audience response. They then have to read the unconscious of the audience without benefit of the therapeutic situation, or they can relinquish the psychoanalytic conception of the subject – in which case there is a tendency to privilege the conscious or easily articulated response.

Feuer concludes that studies of this type are not necessarily "gaining any greater access to the spectator's unconscious responses to texts than do the more speculative attempts by film theorists to imagine the possible implications of spectator positioning by the text."[22]

Certainly, much of the audience work discussed here (including my own) is inevitably subject to the problems of reflexivity that Feuer raises. In my own research[23] I have offered the reader a "reading" of the texts supplied by my respondents – those texts themselves being the respondents' accounts of their own viewing behavior. However, in relation to the problems of the status of any knowledge that might be produced as a result of this process of "readings of readings" I would still argue that the interview (not to mention other techniques such as participant observation) remains a fundamentally more appropriate way to attempt to understand what audiences do when they watch television than for the analyst to simply stay home and imagine the possible implications of how other people might watch television, in the manner which Feuer suggests.

In the case of my own research, I would accept that in the absence of any significant element of participant observation of actual behavior beyond the interview situation, I am left only with the stories that respondents chose to tell me. These stories are, however, themselves both limited by, and indexical of, the cultural and linguistic frames of reference which respondents have available to them, through which to articulate their responses, though, as Feuer rightly notes, these are limited to the level of conscious responses.

However, a number of other points also need to be made. The first concerns the supposedly lesser validity of respondents' accounts of behavior, as opposed to observations of actual behavior. The problem here is that observing behavior always leaves open the question of interpretation. I may be observed to be sitting, staring at the TV screen, but this behavior would be equally compatible with total fascination or total boredom on my part – and the distinction will not necessarily be readily accessible from observed behavioral clues. Moreover, should you wish to understand what I am doing, it would probably be as well to ask me. I may well, of course, lie to you or otherwise misrepresent my thoughts or feelings, for any number of purposes, but at least, through my verbal responses, you will begin to get some access to the kind of language, the criteria of distinction and the types of categorizations, through which I construct my (conscious) world. Without these clues my TV viewing (or other behavior) will necessarily remain opaque.

The interview method then is to be defended, in my view, not simply for the access it gives the researcher to the respondents' conscious opinions and statements but also for the access that it gives to the linguistic terms and categories (the "logical scaffolding" in Wittgenstein's terms[24]) through which respondents construct their worlds and their own understanding of their activities.

The dangers of the "speculative" approach advocated by Feuer in which the theorist simply attempts to imagine the possible implications of spectator positioning by the text are well illustrated in Ellen Seiter et al.'s critique of Tania Modleski's work (see Chapter twelve of this volume). Seiter et al. argue that Modleski's analysis of how women soap opera viewers are positioned by the text – in the manner of the "ideal mother" who understands all the various motives and desires of the characters in a soap opera[25] – is in fact premised on an unexamined assumption of a particular white, middle-class social position. Thus, the subject positioning which Modleski "imagines" that all women will occupy in relation to soap opera texts turns out, empirically, to be refused by many of the working-class women interviewed by Seiter et al. In short, we see here how the "speculative" approach can, at times, lead to inappropriate "universalizations" of analysis which turn out to be premised on particular assumptions regarding the social positioning of the viewer. This is precisely the point of empirical work – as Ien Ang puts it, to "keep our interpretations sensitive to concrete specificities, to the unexpected, to history" – to the possibility of, in Paul Willis' words, "being surprised, of reaching knowledge not prefigured in one's starting paradigm."[26]

Contexts, media, and modes of viewing

The question here is how we might develop a mode of analysis which combines a focus on the understanding of viewing practices with an understanding of the readings of specific program material in specific contexts. There are three main issues that I wish to address. One concerns the adequacy of the traditional model within film theory, which relates the spectator to the cinema text, or film. The second concerns the problem of the non-transferability of the modes of viewing associated with the cinema to the dominant mode of viewing associated with television. The third is concerned with the need to specify variations within the different modes of viewing of television.

First, I want to consider the theorization of the film audience, within the context of the cinema. Predominantly, within film theory, the subject which is addressed is the subject of the text, i.e. the film. At its simplest, I want to argue that there is more to the matter than the question of the film text, and that it is necessary to consider the context of viewing as much as the object of viewing. Simply put, films traditionally had to be seen in certain places, and the understanding of such places has to be central to any analysis of what "going to the pictures" has meant. I want to suggest that the whole notion of "the picture palace" is as significant as the question of "film." This is to introduce the question of the phenomenology of "going to the pictures," which involves the "social architecture" – in terms of décor and ambience – of the context in which films have predominantly been seen.

Quite simply, this is to argue that there is more to cinema-going than seeing films. There is going out at night, the sense of relaxation combined with the sense of fun and excitement. The very name "picture palace" by which cinemas were known for a long time captures an important part of that experience. Rather than selling individual films, cinema is best understood as having sold a habit, or a certain type of socialized experience. This experience involves a whole flavor of romance and glamor, warmth and color. This is to point to the phenomenology of the whole "moment" of going to the pictures – "the queue, the entrance stalls, the foyer, cash desk, stairs, corridor, entering the cinema, the gangway, the seats, the music, the lights fading, darkness, the screen which begins to glow as the silk curtains are opening."[27] Any analysis of the film subject which does not take on board these questions – of the context in which the film is consumed – is, to my mind, inadequate. Unfortunately most recent work in film theory has, in fact, operated without reference to these issues, and has largely followed the protocols of the literary tradition, in prioritizing the status of the text itself, abstracted from the context of consumption.

Second, I want to raise a query about the possibility of transferring any insights gained from the understanding of the film audience to the different context of the understanding of a television audience. As Larry Grossberg has put it, "film theory rests on the assumed privileging . . . of a particular form of engaged subjectivity . . . [in which] the viewer [is] engaged in a concentrative act in which they are absorbed into the world of the film."[28] Now, not only must this cease to apply in relation to film when we consider its consumption either on broadcast television or on video in the home, since these provide a quite different context of reception, and therefore a quite different set of subject positions for the viewer. The problem is all the more marked if we try to transpose theories developed in relation to the activity of the cinema audience to the activity of the television audience.

26

John Ellis has usefully pointed to the distinctions between cinema and television, in terms of their different regimes of representation, of vision, and of reception. Ellis attempts to sketch out cinema and television as particular social forms of organization of meaning, for particular forms of spectator attention. He argues that broadcast TV has developed distinctive aesthetic forms to suit the circumstances within which it is used. The viewer is cast as someone who has the TV switched on, but is giving it very little attention – a casual viewer relaxing at home in the midst of a family group. Attention has to be solicited and grasped segment by segment. Hence, Ellis argues, the amount of self-promotion that each broadcast TV channel does for itself, the amount of direct address that occurs, and the centrality given to sound in television broadcasting. As Ellis puts it "sound draws the attention of the look when it has wandered away."[29]

Ien Ang has noted that what is particularly interesting here is the way in which Ellis treats the aesthetic modes developed by television, not as neutral or arbitrary forms, but as rhetorical strategies to attract viewers. In short, he offers the beginnings of a rhetoric of television. However, in relation to the third issue noted in the introduction to this section, the need to specify variations in the different modes of viewing television, Ien Ang points out that while Ellis' work is of considerable interest in this respect, he

> continually speaks about broadcast TV in general and tends to give a generalised account of televisual discourse which is consciously abstracted from the specificities of different programme categories, modes of representation and types of (direct) address. (. . . [thus Ellis'] preoccupation seems to be with what *unifies* televisual discourse into one "specific signifying practice"). As a result, it becomes difficult to theorise the possibility that television constructs more than one position for the viewer.[30]

Ien Ang goes on to argue that the point is that

> different types of involvement, based upon different ideological positions can be constructed by televisual discourse. It does not make sense, therefore, to see televisual discourse as a basically unified text without . . . internal contra-dictions . . . [rather] . . . we should analyse the different positions offered to viewers in relation to different parts of the televisual discourse.[31]

In summary, the key issues identified here are the status of the text; the relation of text and context; the usefulness of an expanded notion of the "supertext"; the problem of "medium specific" modes of viewing; and the further problem of variations of modes of viewing within any one medium. It is this set of concerns, I want to argue, which provide the framework within which one must, in fact, consider the particular readings which specific audiences make of individual programs.

Genres, pleasures and the politics of consumption

One of the most important developments in recent work in this field has been the shift from the concern with interpretations of specific films or television programs to the study of patterns of engagement with different types or genres of material. What is at issue here is how we can begin to understand the particular pleasures which particular types (or genres) of material seem to offer to particular audiences in specific social situations. In this respect, Janice Radway offers what I would regard as an exemplary proposal for the appropriate mode of analysis. As she puts it

> a good cultural analysis of the romance ought to specify not only how the wo-
> men understand the novels themselves but also how they comprehend the very
> act of picking up a book in the first place. The analytic focus must shift from
> the text itself, taken in isolation, to the complex social event of reading.[32]

I will return later to this theme, in discussing the need to combine analysis of viewing contexts and modes of viewing with the analysis of specific readings, but first I want to focus on the issue of how popular taste and popular pleasures can be understood. From my own perspective, the most interesting question is that of why particular types of material are particularly attractive to specific segments of the audience. The key reference, most obviously, is to the work of Pierre Bourdieu on patterns of taste, and the distribution of these patterns within different segments of a society.[33] The issue is how best to understand the "fit" between particular cultural forms and particular patterns of taste.

In an earlier period, Barthes suggested that what was needed was an aesthetic based on the pleasures of the consumer. My own argument is that the critical issue is, in fact, the analysis of the particular pleasures of specific audience groups rather than any abstract concern with the nature of "Pleasure" as such. To pursue the latter route would be to risk replicating all the difficulties encountered by the attempt to develop a theory of "the subject in general" in so far as all specific instances of pleasure in all their various forms would be unhelpfully subsumed within the general theory, as mere "replays" of a universalized psychic mechanism.

Here, in fact, it seems quite possible that we have much to learn from the commercial world. In the context of the proliferation of channels and the much heralded advent of "narrow casting," the commercial world has been fast to identify the issue of audience segmentation as one of the keys to the successful pursuit of profit. It is of some considerable interest that, within the realm of British television it was, as Ian Connell has argued, undoubtedly the commercial channel, ITV, which "led the way in making connection with and expressing popular structures of feeling."[34] As Connell argues, by its very logic a commercial station is bound to attempt to meet the tastes and needs of its audience more directly than any station (of a left- or right-wing political persuasion) which takes a more paternalist attitude toward its audience.

There are, evidently, a number of political difficulties running through these debates, as has been well evidenced in Britain certainly by the debates between Ian Connell and Nicholas Garnham concerning the question of commercial television, popular taste, and public broadcasting.[35] These same political difficulties have also been brought into focus in another context, in the debates between writers such as Jane Root and Kathy Myers,[36] who have attempted to analyse the specific forms of pleasure which are offered to consumers (and particularly to women) – as against those such as Judith Williamson[37] who argue that the project of attempting to understand popular pleasures continually runs the risk of ending up as an uncritical perspective which simply endorses popular tastes because they are popular.

In a similar vein to Williamson, Tania Modleski has also recently argued that we face a danger of "collusion" between "mass culture critics" and "consumer society." Modleski's argument is that

the insight that audiences are not completely manipulated, but may appropriate mass cultural artefacts for their own purposes, has been carried so far that it would seem that mass culture is no longer a problem for some "marxist" critics . . . . If the problem with some of the work of the Frankfurt School was that its members were too far outside the culture they examined, critics today seem to have the opposite problem: immersed in their culture, half in love with their subject, they sometimes seem unable to achieve the proper critical distance from it. As a result, they may unwittingly wind up writing apologies for mass culture and embracing its ideology.[38]

Modleski claims that the stress on the "active" role of the audience/consumer has been carried too far. However, she is also concerned that the very activity of studying audiences may somehow turn out to be a form of "collaborating with the (mass culture) industry." More fundamentally, she quotes, with approval, Terry Eagleton's comments to the effect that a socialist criticism "is not primarily concerned with the consumers' revolution. Its task is to take over the means of production."[39]

It seems that, from Modleski's point of view, empirical methods for the study of audiences are assumed to be "tainted" simply because many of them have been and are used within the realms of commercial market research. Moreover, in her use of Eagleton's quote, she finally has recourse to a traditional mode of classical Marxist analysis, the weakness of which is precisely its "blindspot" in relation to issues of consumption – and, indeed, its tendency to prioritize the study of "production" to the exclusion of the study of all other levels of the social formation. The problem is that production is only brought to fruition in the spheres of circulation and exchange – to that extent, the study of consumption is, I would argue, essential to a full understanding of production.

I want to argue that the critical (or "political") judgment which we might wish to make on the popularity of *Dallas* or any other commercial product is a quite different matter from the need to understand its popularity. The functioning of taste, and indeed of ideology, has to be understood as a process in which the commercial world succeeds in producing objects, programs (and consumer goods), which do connect with the lived desires of popular audiences. To fail to understand exactly how this works is, in my own view, not only academically retrograde but also politically suicidal. As Terry Lovell has argued, goods which are produced for profit can only, in fact, acquire an exchange value if they also have a use value to those who consume them. As Lovell puts it:

> the commodities in question – films, books, television programs, etc. – have different use values for the individuals who purchase them than they have for the capitalists who produce and sell them, and in turn, for capitalism as a whole. We may assume that people do not purchase these cultural artefacts in order to expose themselves to bourgeois ideology . . . but to satisfy a variety of different wants, which can only be guessed at in the absence of analysis and investigation. There is no guarantee that the use value of the cultural object for its purchaser will even be compatible with its utility to capitalism as bourgeois ideology, and therefore no guarantee that it will in fact secure "the ideological effect."[40]

Popular forms: soap opera and American culture

I want now to move on, within this general framework, to look in a little more detail at two particular areas of work on the question of the "fit" between particular types (or genres) of programming and particular types of audiences. These two areas are, first, the study of soap opera in relation to a feminine audience and, second, the study of "American culture," American fictional programming (and *Dallas* as a particular instance), in relation to non-American audiences.

In relation to the study of soap opera, the body of work developed by writers such as Tania Modleski, Dorothy Hobson, Ien Ang, Charlotte Brunsdon, Janice Radway, Ellen Seiter *et al.*, and Ann Gray is now extensive and I shall not comment here in detail on it.[41] However, I would argue that what is most interesting about it is precisely the concern to understand how and why it is that this specific variety of programming is found to be particularly pleasurable by women. Whether one locates that pleasure in the homology between the narrative style of the programming and the constantly interrupted and cyclical nature of many women's domestic work-time, or whether one locates the issue centrally around the "fit" between particular feminine forms of social and cultural competence and the particular focus of these texts on the complexities of human relations, the mode of inquiry is, to my mind, exemplary in so far as it takes seriously, and is concerned to investigate in detail, the specific types of pleasures which this particular type of programming offers to a distinct category of viewers.

Ien Ang draws on Pierre Bourdieu's notion that popular pleasures are characterized by an immediate emotional or sensual involvement in the object of pleasure (i.e. the possibility of identification) so that popular pleasure is first and foremost a pleasure of recognition.[42] As Ang says, the question is what do *Dallas* lovers recognize in *Dallas*, and how and why does that pleasure work? Clearly, one part of that identification, for a feminine audience, must be the way in which soap operas do give expression to the contradictions of patriarchy. Thus, even if the women within these narratives cannot resolve their problems, given the structure in which they operate, minimally these are programs in which those problems are recognized and validated. However, these forms of identification themselves are clearly variable. Some soap operas clearly work on a level of empirical realism, in so far as the characters within them are presented as living in situations comparable to those of significant numbers of their audiences (*Brookside* in the UK). In other cases, like *Dallas*, as Ang argues, the realism need not be of an empirical kind. The stories can be recognized as realistic at an emotional level, rather than at a literal or denotative level. As Ang puts it "what is recognized as real is not knowledge of the world, but is subjective experience of the world: a 'structure of feeling.'"[43] As she suggests, it would seem to be this "tragic structure of feeling" in soap opera which, for many women, is what is recognized and is that with which they can identify.

However, *Dallas* can also provide us with a useful bridge to the second theme noted above. This is to focus on *Dallas* not so much as a soap opera but as "yet more evidence of the threat posed by American style commercial culture against 'authentic' national cultures and identities ... i.e. *Dallas* as the symbol of American cultural imperialism."[44] Here the issue becomes not so much one of gender but one of how *Dallas* "works" for non-American audiences, i.e. how and why it can be pleasurable for a whole range of audiences outside of America and indeed, outside of the First World. In this context the most important work is that which has been conducted by Elihu Katz and Tamar Liebes on international readings of *Dallas*.[45] Their project was designed to investigate how it is that US commercial culture can be so popular throughout the world – how it is that such a variety of international audiences can attend to it and indeed seem enthusiastic about it. In short, the issue is, what is it about *Dallas* that is compatible with the lives of its variously cultured viewers? How is this compatibility expressed? Or, negatively, when and where does the program not work? One of the key issues which Katz and Liebes have been concerned to investigate is the way in which certain levels of the program might be expected to be universally understood (for instance the universality of family conflict) whereas decodings of other levels of the program might be expected to vary by social category of viewer, either in terms of nationality, ethnicity, class, or sex. The broad framework within which this project was initially conceived has allowed questions to be asked such as whether the "meaning" of the program is to be found in the genre, in the interactions of the characters, in the moral issues as embodied in these characters, or in the narrative form. As Tamar Liebes herself has written, this research project has not been aimed at "attempting to demonstrate effect, but rather . . . to investigate those processes that are prerequisite to any possible effect, namely, understanding, interpretation and evaluation . . . i.e. to address the question of how American films and television programs can cross cultural and linguistic frontiers."[46]

Their research has thrown up a number of examples of how community members from a variety of ethnic origins negotiate the meanings of the program by confronting the text with their own traditions and their own experience. Moreover, this research has illustrated the important function which programs of this type can serve for viewers in providing them with an "occasion" or forum in which to debate issues of concern to them. As Katz and Liebes have shown, this is not a process which simply goes on in a reflective manner, after the event of program transmission – rather the viewing process itself is likely to include ongoing comment, and indeed debate along these lines. Of further, substantial, interest is the material which the research has produced, not simply in terms of differential interpretations or evaluations of this or that program item, but in relation to the different "angles of vision" (for instance, the distinction between poetic and referential readings) which different groups bring to the program.[47]

In the British context, where the very phrase "wall to wall *Dallas*" has come to represent the notion of television at its very (and quintessentially American) worst, this kind of precise investigation of the specific meaning of the program in different contexts is to be particularly welcomed. What I want to briefly explore now is a further set of issues, within this debate, about the way in which "glossy" American series are held to have "invaded" European culture.

I want to try to relate the argument about cultural imperialism back to the issues raised earlier concerning popular taste, but now from a different perspective. The idea that English or European "high culture" is in danger of being swamped by a relentless deluge of "Americana" is not new. In the British context Dick Hebdige traces these fears back to at least the 1930s, when writers as different as the conservative Evelyn Waugh and the socialist George Orwell were united by a fascinated loathing for modern architecture, holiday camps, advertising, fast food, plastics, and, of course, chewing gum.[48] To both Waugh and Orwell, these were the images of the "soft," enervating, "easy life" which threatened to smother British cultural identity. By the 1950s, the battle lines in this debate were drawn – real working-class culture, quality, and taste on one side; the ersatz blandishment of soft disposable commodities, streamlined cars, rock and roll, crime and promiscuity on the other. As Hebdige says, when anything American was sighted, it tended to be interpreted – at least by those working in the context of education or professional cultural criticism – as the "beginning of the end." Hebdige describes how the images of crime, disaffected youth, urban crisis, and spiritual drift became "anchored together around popular American commodities, fixing a chain of associations which has become thoroughly sedimented in British common-sense."[49] Thus, in particular, American food became a standard metaphor for declining standards. The very notion of the Americanization of television came to stand for a series of associations: commercialization, banality, and the destruction of traditional values.

The debate which Hebdige opens up here goes back centrally to Richard Hoggart's work on *The Uses of Literacy*.[50] Hoggart's book is a detailed appreciation of traditional working-class community life, coupled with a critique of the "homogenizing" impact of American culture on these communities. According to Hoggart, authentic working-class life was being destroyed by the "hollow brightness," the "shiny barbarism," and "spiritual decay" of imported American culture. This lamentation on the deleterious effects of Americanization was, and continues to be, advanced from the left just as much as from the right of the political spectrum. However, Hebdige's central point is that these American products – streamlined, plastic, and glamorous – were precisely those which appealed to substantial sections of a British working-class audience (and, in television terms, were related to the same dynamics of popular taste which lay behind the mass desertion of the working-class audience toward commercial television when it began to be broadcast in the UK in the 1950s). While, from the paternalistic point of view of the upholders of "traditional British values," these American imported products constituted "a chromium hoard bearing down on us," for a popular audience, Hebdige argues, they constituted a space in which oppositional meanings (in relation to dominant traditions of British culture) could be negotiated and expressed.

I would note a number of connections in this respect. First, the point which Hebdige develops about the appeal of American culture to disadvantaged groups within another society is paralleled by Ien Ang's findings concerning the nature of the pleasures offered by American-style commercial programming to working-class audiences in Holland.[51] Second, the work which Tim Blanchard has done in Britain, analysing the differential preferences of various categories of teenagers for different types of television programs, adds some further support to the argument.[52] He identified a pattern among the young people he interviewed in which black English teenagers had a particularly high regard for American programming; this is by no means simply to do with the fact that there are more black characters in American shows, but is closely related to Hebdige's argument about the subversive appeals of certain types of "vulgar" commercial products for subordinated groups.

In concluding this section, I would also like to add one more twist to the story. The images which Orwell and Hoggart use to characterize the damaging effects of American popular culture have a recurring theme: the "feminization" of the authentic muscle and masculinity of the British industrial working class, which they saw as under attack from an excess of Americana – characterized essentially by passivity, leisure, and domesticity, warm water baths, sun bathing, and the "easy life." When the discussion of American programming is combined with the discussion of programming in the form of soap opera, principally understood as a feminine form in itself, we are clearly, from Hoggart's or Orwell's position, dealing with the lowest of the low, or as Charlotte Brunsdon has characterized it "the trashiest trash."[53] Audience research which can help us begin to unpick the threads which lie tangled behind this particular conundrum would seem to be of particular value.

Television and everyday life: the context of viewing

One of the most important advances in recent audience work has been the growing recognition of the importance of the context of viewing. In the case of television this is a recognition of the domestic context. Of necessity, once one recognizes the domestic, one moves rapidly toward questions of gender, given the significance of gender in contemporary modes of domestic organization. I will return to this point, but for the moment, let us begin by noting, with Ien Ang that

> an audience does not merely consist of the aggregate of viewers of a specific program, it should also be conceived of as engaging in the practice of watching television as such . . . so decodings must be seen as embedded in a general practice of television viewing.[54]

In this connection, Thomas Lindlof and Paul Traudt have argued that

> much TV audience research has concentrated on questions of why to the exclusion of what and how. Scholars have attempted to describe the causes and consequences of television viewing without an adequate understanding of what it is and how it gets done.

As they argue, "in order for many of the central theoretical and policy questions to be satisfactorily framed, let alone answered, a number of prerequisite questions concerning what the act of television viewing entails . . . need to be posed and investigated."[55] This is not, by any means, to return to any abstracted notion of the specificity of the medium of television, or even the specificity of television viewing as such, as if that itself were an invariable and homogeneous category. However, it is, first of all, necessary to distinguish television viewing as a practice from, for instance, cinema viewing, or indeed, from the viewing of video.

As Larry Grossberg argues,

> the very force and impact of any medium changes significantly as it is moved from one context to another (a bar, a theatre, the living room, the bedroom, the beach, a rock concert . . .). Each medium is then a mobile term taking shape as it situates itself . . . within the rest of our lives . . . the text is located, not only intertextually, but in a range of apparatuses as well . . . thus, one rarely just listens to the radio, watches TV, or even, goes to the movies – one is studying, dating, driving somewhere else, etc.[56]

In Grossberg's version of the argument,

the indifference of the media displaces the problematic of cultural theory from that of coding ... to that of the apparatus itself ... television makes this displacement particularly obvious and disconcerting – in so far as television viewing constitutes a large temporal part of our lives ... we must note its integration into the mundanities of everyday life, and simultaneously, its constant interruption by, and continuity with our other daily routines.[57]

As Grossberg points out,

one rarely intently gazes at television, allowing oneself to be absorbed into the work, but rather distractedly glances at it or absorbs it into our momentary mood or position ... television is indifferent to us (it doesn't demand our presence, yet it is always waiting for us).

Thus, as he argues, we need to face up to the consequences of the fact that

viewers rarely pay attention in the way that sponsors (or advertisers) want, and there is little relation between the television's being on, and either the presence of bodies in front of it, or even a limited concentration or interpretative activity being invested in it.[58]

Hermann Bausinger approaches the problem of the domestic context of viewing from a similar angle,[59] and quotes the following remark made by an interviewee: "Early in the evening we watch very little TV. Only when my husband is in a real rage. He comes home, hardly says anything and switches on the TV."[60] Bausinger notes that many media analysts would interpret this man's action as signifying a desire to watch TV. However, as Bausinger goes on, in this case "pushing the button doesn't signify 'I would like to watch this,' but rather 'I would like to see and hear nothing.'"[61] Conversely, he notes, later, the opposite case where "the father goes to his room, while the mother sits down next to her eldest son and watches the sports review with him. It does not interest her, but it is an attempt at making contact."[62]

By way of a protocol, Bausinger also helpfully provides us with a number of points to bear in mind in relation to domestic media consumption:

1 To make a meaningful study of the use of the media, it is necessary to take different media into consideration, the media ensemble which everyone deals with today – the recipient integrates the content of different media.
2 As a rule the media are not used completely, nor with full concentration – the degree of attention depends on the time of the day, or moods, the media message competes with other messages.
3 The media are an integral part of the way the everyday is conducted (for example, the newspaper as a necessary constituent part of "breakfast") and (media) decisions are constantly crossed through and influenced by non-media conditions and decisions.
4 It is not a question of an isolated, individual process, but of a collective

process. Even when reading a newspaper one is not truly alone, it takes place in the context of the family, friends.

5 Media communication cannot be separated from direct personal communication. Media contacts are materials for conversation.[63]

In a similar way, Paddy Scannell has usefully analysed what he calls the "unobtrusive ways in which broadcasting sustains the lives, and routines, from one day to the next, year in, year out, of whole populations."[64] This is, in effect, to pay attention to the role of the media in the very structuring of time. Another oblique connection is worth noting here. The perspective which Scannell advances is closely related to Bourdieu's insistence on the materiality of the subject, as a biological organism existing chronologically. This is to emphasize the study of the organization of time as a necessary focus for any sociology of culture. At another level, Scannell's focus is on the role of national broadcasting media as central agents of national culture, in the organizing of the "involvement" of the population in the calendar of national life. Similarly, he analyses the way in which broadcast media constitute a cultural resource "shared by millions" and the way in which, for instance, long-running popular serials provide a "past in common" to whole populations. Here we move beyond both the study of the isolated text, and at the same time beyond any abstract notion of the study of television as an undifferentiated "flow." Rather than having recourse to either of these opposite, but equally inadequate positions, we must attend to the issue of television scheduling and the manner in which, for instance, as Richard Paterson has argued,[65] the broadcasting institutions construct their schedules in ways which are designed to complement the basic modes of domestic organization, but also, inevitably, then come to play an active and constitutive role in the organization of domestic time.

This, then, is to advance a perspective which attempts to combine questions of interpretation with questions of the "uses" of television (and other media), an approach more commonly associated with a broadly based sociology of leisure. This perspective relocates television viewing within the overall context of domestic leisure. Given that television is a domestic medium it follows that the appropriate mode of analysis must take the unit of consumption of television as the family or household rather than the individual viewer. This is to situate individual viewing within the household relations in which it operates, and to insist that individual viewing activity only makes sense inside of this frame. Here we begin to open up a whole set of questions about the differences hidden behind the indiscriminate label of "watching television." It is to begin to consider the differential modes of viewing engaged in by different types of viewers, in relation to different types of programs, shown in different slots in the overall schedule, in relation to different spaces within the organization of domestic life.

Clearly, if we are considering television viewing in the context of the family, things are pretty complicated. First of all one is not able to treat the individual viewer as if he or she were a free or rational consumer in a cultural supermarket.

For many people (and especially for the less powerful members of any household) the programs they watch are not necessarily programs which they will have chosen to watch. In the context of the domestic household, viewing choices must often be negotiated. Moreover, this perspective introduces, as one of its premises, what Sean Cubitt has called "the politics of the living room," where, as he puts it, "if the camera pulls you in to involvement with the screen, the family is likely to pull you out."[66] This is also to try to get beyond the way in which television is often understood – simply as disruptive of family life. It is to look at the way in which television is also used by people to construct "occasions" around viewing, in which various types of interaction can be pursued. This is also to get away from the idea that people either live in social relations or watch television. Rather one must analyse how viewing is done within the social relations of the household.

However, a number of points follow from this. As soon as one thinks about television in the context of social relations then one is inevitably thinking about television in the context of power relations. If one is considering the domestic context, then it will inevitably be gender relations, in particular, that will come into focus, within the household. This is to introduce a whole set of possible connections and disjunctions between gender relations and the organization of private and public life – not least, the differential positioning of women and men within the domestic space of the household. In short, if, for men, their concept of time and space is organized around a notion of "worktime" and the "public" – from which the domestic is a respite, for most women (even those who do work outside the household) the fundamental principles of organization operate in a different way. For them, the domestic is not understood as a sphere of leisure, but rather as a sphere in which a further set of (domestic) obligations take precedence, which complicate and interrupt any desires they may have to watch television. Dorothy Hobson's work on the complicated modalities of women's viewing has explored some of these issues,[67] though again it is worth noting the way in which it is women's viewing which becomes the "marked" category, and the "problem" for analysis – as opposed to the "unmarked" (i.e. masculine) mode of viewing, which constitutes the taken for granted norm of the activity.

In this connection, it is also important to take note of James Lull's work on TV viewing in the domestic context. One of the issues which Lull investigates is the question of "who is responsible for the selection of television programs at home, how program selection processes occur, and how the roles of family position and family communication patterns influence these activities."[68] Lull's point is that program selection decisions are often complicated interpersonal communications activities involving inter-family status relations, temporal context, the number of sets available, and role-based communications conventions. Here we approach the central question of power. And within any patriarchal society the power at issue will necessarily be that of the father. This perspective involves us in considering the ways in which familial relations, like any other social relations, are also and inevitably power relations. Lull's central finding in his survey of control of the television set was that fathers were named (not surprisingly) most often as the person who controlled the selection of television programs.

In essence, as Lull puts it, "the locus of control in the program selection process can be explained primarily by family position."[69] Thus, to consider the ways in which viewing is performed within the social relations of the family is also, inevitably, to consider the ways in which viewing is performed within the context of power relations and the differential power afforded to members of the family primarily in terms of gender and age.

In making these points about the structure of the domestic viewing context, there is a certain sense of simply restating things which we "already know," from our own experience of domestic life. This very insistence on the importance of these banal considerations is made difficult by their "taken-for-grantedness" – as the invisible routines and structures inside of which our lives are organized. In Britain, the results of a study conducted during 1985 by Peter Collett, in which a video camera was placed inside the television sets of a number of different households, thus providing film of families watching television, had notable effects in getting these considerations on to the agenda of public discussion.[70] No one who saw the tapes could really have claimed to have been surprised by what they saw – pictures of people sitting in a room with their back to the television, pictures of empty sofas in front of the screen, pictures of people dressing their children, eating meals, and arguing with each other while seemingly oblivious to the set, etc. However, it seemed that it was only at the point at which this kind of videotape "evidence" of these everyday situations was made available, in the context of respectable scientific research within a framework of behavioral psychology, that it was possible, certainly for the broadcasters, to begin to take these questions at all seriously.

In making these points about the complex nature of the domestic setting in which television is viewed by its audience, I am not arguing for any kind of "new optimism" which would allow us to rest content in the secure understanding that because so many other things are going on at the same time, nobody pays any attention to television and therefore we shouldn't worry about it. Rather, I am trying to move the baseline, against which we precisely should then be concerned to examine the modes and varieties of attention which are paid to different types of programs, at different points in the day by different types of viewers. It is precisely in the context of all these domestic complications that the activity of television viewing must be seriously examined.

Old perspectives for new

Centrally, I have been trying to argue that the most useful work which has been conducted within audience studies in the last few years is that which has taken on board the questions raised about the flow of television, the positioning of the subject, the contextual determinations operating on different types of viewing of different media, alongside a close attention to the varieties of patterns of taste, response, and interpretation on the part of specific members of the audience. Here I would specifically like to support the arguments made by Elihu Katz and Tamar Liebes when they note that they are

> in disagreement with others who believe that the unit of television viewing is better conceptualized as background, or as "a strip" that cuts through an evening's viewing, or as a pervasive barrage of messages about society that is embedded in all of prime time. Our argument is simply ... that certain programs – some more than others – are identified by viewers as discrete stories and, as such, viewing entails attention, interpretation, evaluation and perhaps social and psychological consequences.[71]

It is this kind of close attention to, for instance, the varieties of subject positioning which, I would argue, we need to pursue. Without this kind of detailed empirical attention to what actually happens in particular situations, we run the danger of lapsing into the kind of structuralist perspective which in Peter Dahlgren's words,

> incorporates a view of meaning and consciousness ... and the unconscious ... where the subject is essentially dominated by the object ... [and] the cultural text is reduced to an abstract grammar, with meaning residing wholly in its confines. The negotiation of meaning and the historicity of consciousness is denied."[72]

As Dahlgren continues,

> in the heady wake of the structural reading of Freud it seems that the only alternative to the infamous transcendental subject has been a view which understands the subject not only as decentred by, but also created by, the grammatical structures of the unconscious. The unconscious becomes an abstract drive shaft of history, while the individual subject is emptied of any conscious intentionality.[73]

Similarly, I would want to argue that the varieties of postmodern relativism in which the text is seen as infinitely "iterable" or writable, according to the whim of the subject, are equally unhelpful, if for the opposite reason. The demonstration that theoretically "anything goes," in terms of the potential polysemy of any text, is very different from the demonstration that empirically "just anything" happens when it comes to the actual reading of television texts. Such an approach not only abandons any notion (however attenuated) of the effectivity of the text. It also flies in the face of the empirical evidence we have of the way in which attention, modes of viewing, response, and interpretation are patterned in observable empirical clusters as between different sectors of the audience.

Peter Dahlgren has advanced what, in my view, is a very useful definition of a perspective which he describes as a concern with the "social ecology" of viewing. He attempts to combine this perspective with a concern for what he also describes as the different "epistemic bias" of different media (in so far as each medium fosters a somewhat different dispositional relationship between itself and its audiences) and indeed, a concern with the differential "epistemic biases" of particular types of television material. In a similar vein, Robert Deming has advanced an analysis of the ways in which specific channels offer particular positionalities to their viewers,[74] and Ellsworth remarks on the way in which MTV (the American all-music cable channel)

> offers student-age viewers a place to stand in relation to other individual groups in the culture ... a social identity ... that positions the inscribed viewer as a middle-class consumer of rock music with enough money to purchase record albums, concert tikets, fan magazines and rock influenced fashion, while excluding and evaluating those who are female, ethnic, working-class.[75]

Thus, as Deming argues,

> the position "I" assume, when called by *Dynasty* is different from but related to the position I assume when called by *Dallas* ... I am called to assume a position vis-a-vis those two texts, but not all that I am is so called, only that which is appropriate ... I bring with me, as a Real Social Subject, all my genre-, program-, and culture-specific competence but, again, *only* [what] is appropriate to the subject-text position.[76]

It is this level of differentiation of subject positions in relation to different types of material which, it seems to me, is important for us to explore.

In short, this is to examine the material varieties of the positioning of the subject, not in some transhistorical or universalistic mode, but from a perspective which would also properly involve very material questions about the physical organization and inhabitation of the domestic space within which television is ordinarily viewed.[77]

The object of study, from this perspective, then focuses on systems of cultural behavior and is necessarily concerned with the organization of diversity.[78] Here one can most usefully look for guidance to that body of work in socio-linguistics which has been concerned with the study of communicative acts, in particular socio-cultural contexts. My own argument is that the study of viewing will most effectively be pursued along these same lines.

To make these points is to argue, ultimately, for the return of the somewhat discredited discipline of sociology to a central place in the understanding of communication. In this connection, I shall close by quoting from Richard Nice who, some years ago, in a commentary on the significance of Pierre Bourdieu's work, argued that

> those who seek to expel sociology ... in favor of a strictly internal analysis of what happens on the screen, or how the viewing subject is articulated, can only do so on the basis of an implicit sociology which, in so far as it ignores the social realities of the differential distribution of cultural competences and values, is an erroneous sociology, the more insidious for being unrecognized.[79]

Notes

1   Jane Root, *Open the Box* (London: Comedia, 1986).
2   James Halloran (ed.) *The Effects of Television* (London: Panther Books, 1970).
3   Stuart Hall, "Encoding/Decoding," in Stuart Hall, Dorothy Hobson, Andrew Lowe, and Paul Willis (eds) *Culture, Media, Language* (London: Hutchinson, 1980), pp. 128-38.
4   Basil Bernstein, *Class, Codes and Control*, 3 vols (London: Routledge & Kegan Paul, 1973).
5   Frank Parkin, *Class Inequality and Political Order* (London: Paladin Books, 1973).
6   See, for example, Dell Hymes, "On Communicative Competence," in J.B. Pride and J. Holmes (eds) *Sociolinguistics* (Harmondsworth: Penguin, 1972), pp. 269-93; Pierre Bourdieu, *Distinction* (London: Routledge & Kegan Paul, 1984); Bernstein, *Class*.
7   See, for example, Justin Wren-Lewis, "The Encoding-Decoding Model: Criticisms and Redevelopments for Research on Decoding," *Media, Culture, and Society* 5 (1983): 179-97.
8   Stuart Hall, "Some Problems with the Ideology/Subject Couplet," *Ideology and Consciousness* 3 (1978): 118.
9   Stuart Hall, "Recent Developments in Theories of Language and Ideology," in Hall *et al., Culture, Media, Language*, pp. 157-62.
10 Paul Willemen, "Notes on Subjectivity," *Screen* 19, no. 1 (1978): 41-69; Steve Neale, "Propaganda," *Screen* 18, no. 3 (1977): 9-40.
11 Neale, "Propaganda," p. 39.
12 Michel Pecheux, *Language, Semantics and Ideology* (London: Macmillan, 1982).
13 Valerie Walkerdine, "Projecting Fantasies: Families Watching Films" (unpublished paper, University of London, 1986).
14 ibid.
15 Nick Browne, "The Political Economy of the TV (Super) Text" (paper presented at the International Television Studies Conference (ITSC), London, 1986).
16 Larry Grossberg, "The In-Difference of Television," *Screen* 28, no. 2 (1987): 33.
17 Tony Bennett, "Text and Social Process: The Case of James Bond," *Screen Education* 41 (1982): 3-14. See also Tony Bennett and Janet Woollacott, *Bond and Beyond: The Political Career of a Popular Hero* (London: Macmillan, 1987).
18 Pierre Macherey, *A Theory of Literary Production* (London: Routledge & Kegan Paul, 1978). See also "An Interview with Pierre Macherey," *Red Letters* 5 (1977): 3-9.
19 Roland Barthes, *Image-Music-Text* (London: Fontana, 1977).
20 John Fiske, "TV and Popular Culture" (paper presented at Iowa Symposium on Television Criticism, 1985).
21 Jane Feuer, "*Dynasty*" (paper presented at ITSC, London, 1986).
22 ibid.
23 See David Morley, *The "Nationwide" Audience: Structure and Decoding* (London: British Film Institute, 1980), and David Morley, *Family Television: Cultural Power and Domestic Leisure* (London: Comedia, 1986).
24 Ludwig Wittgenstein, *Tractatus Logico-Philosophicus* (London: Routledge & Kegan Paul, 1961, p. 40).
25 Tania Modleski, "The Search for Tomorrow in Today's Soap Operas," in her *Loving with a Vengeance: Mass-Produced Fantasies for Women* (Hamden, Conn.: Archon, 1982), pp. 85-109.
26 Ien Ang, "Wanted: Audiences: On the Politics of Empirical Audience Studies," Chapter five of this volume; Paul Willis is quoted in Ang's essay.

27 Andrew Buchanan, quoted in Philip Corrigan, "Film Entertainment as Ideology and Pleasure" (unpublished paper, University of London, 1984).

28 Grossberg, "The In-Difference," p. 32.

29 John Ellis, *Visible Fictions: Cinema, Television, Video* (London: Routledge & Kegan Paul, 1982), p. 162.

30 Ien Ang, "The Battle Between Television and Its Audiences," in Phillip Drummond and Richard Paterson (eds) *Television in Transition* (London: British Film Institute, 1986), p. 256.

31 ibid., p. 257.

32 Janice Radway, quoted in Robert C. Allen, *Speaking of Soap Operas* (Chapel Hill: University of North Carolina Press, 1985), p. 185.

33 Bourdieu, *Distinction.*

34 Ian Connell, "In Defence of the Tyranny of Popular Taste" (paper presented at the ITSC, London, 1984).

35 Nicholas Garnham, "Public Service Versus the Market," *Screen* 24, no. 1 (1983): 6-27.

36 Root, *Open the Box*; Kathy Myers, *Understains: The Sense and Seduction of Advertising* (London: Comedia, 1985).

37 Judith Williamson, "The Problems of Being Popular," *New Socialist* (September 1986): 14-15.

38 Tania Modleski, "Introduction," Tania Modleski (ed.) *Studies in Entertainment* (Bloomington: Indiana University Press, 1986), p. xi.

39 Eagleton, quoted in Modleski, "Introduction," p. xii.

40 Terry Lovell, *Pictures of Reality: Aesthetics, Politics and Pleasure* (London: British Film Institute, 1981), p. 60.

41 Modleski, *Studies*; Dorothy Hobson, *"Crossroads"* (London: Methuen, 1982); Charlotte Brunsdon, "Notes on Soap Opera," in E. Ann Kaplan, (ed.) *Regarding Television – Critical Approaches: An Anthology,* American Film Institute Monograph Series, vol. 2 (Frederick, Md.: University Publications of America, 1983), pp. 76-83; Janice Radway, *Reading the Romance* (Chapel Hill: The University of North Carolina Press, 1984); Ellen Seiter, "The Role of the Woman Reader" (paper presented at the Cinema Studies Conference, 1981); Ann Gray, "Women and Video" (paper presented at the ITSC, London, 1986).

42 Ien Ang, *Watching "Dallas"* (London: Methuen, 1985).

43 ibid., p. 45.

44 ibid., p. 46.

45 See, for example, Elihu Katz and Tamar Liebes, "Mutual Aid in the Decoding of *Dallas*: Preliminary Notes from a Cross-Cultural Study," in Drummond and Paterson (eds) *Television in Transition*, pp. 187-98.

46 Tamar Liebes, "Ethnocriticism: Israelis of Moroccan Ethnicity Negotiate the Meaning of *Dallas*," *Studies in Visual Communication* 10, no. 3 (1984): 46.

47 In this connection, see also John Corner and Kay Richardson, "Reading Reception" (paper presented at the ITSC, London, 1986).

48 Dick Hebdige, "Towards a Cartography of Taste 1935-1962," in his *Hiding in the Light* (London: Comedia, 1987).

49 ibid.

50 Richard Hoggart, *The Uses of Literacy* (London: Penguin, 1957).

51 Ien Ang, "The Vicissitudes of Progressive Television," *New Formations* 2 (summer 1987): 91-106.

52 Tim Blanchard, unpublished thesis, Institute of Education, London, 1986.

53 Charlotte Brunsdon, "Women Watching TV" (paper presented at the Women and the Electronic Mass Media Conference, Copenhagen, 1986).

54   Ien Ang, "The Battle Between Television and Its Audiences," in Drummond and
      Paterson (eds) *Television in Transition*, p. 252.
55   Thomas Lindlof and Paul Traudt, "Mediated Communication in Families," in
      Mary S. Mander (ed.) *Communications in Transition: Issues and Debates in
      Current Research* (New York: Praeger, 1983), pp. 261-62.
56   Grossberg, "The In-Difference," pp. 34-5.
57   ibid.
58   ibid.
59   Hermann Bausinger, "Media, Technology and Daily Life," *Media, Culture,
      Society* 6 (1984): 343-51.
60   ibid., p. 344.
61   ibid.
62   ibid., p. 349.
63   ibid., pp. 349-50.
64   Paddy Scannell, "Radio Times" (paper presented at the ITSC, London, 1986).
65   Richard Paterson, "Planning the Family: The Art of the Television Schedule,"
      Screen Education 35 (1980): 79-85.
66   Sean Cubitt, "Top of the Pops," in Len Masterman (ed.) *Television Mythologies.
      Stars, Shows, and Signs* (London: Comedia, 1984), p. 48.
67   Hobson, *"Crossroads."*
68   James Lull, "How Families Select Television Programs," *Journal of Broadcasting*
      26, no. 4 (1982): 801.
69   ibid., p. 809; see also James Lull, "The Social Uses of Television," *Human
      Communication Research* 6, no. 3 (1980): 197-209.
70   Peter Collett and Roger Lamb, "Watching Families Watching TV" (report to
      Independent Broadcasting Authority, 1986).
71   Katz and Liebes, "Mutual Aid," p. 198, note 1.
72   Peter Dahlgren, "The Modes of Reception: For a Hermeneutics of TV News," in
      Drummond and Paterson (eds) *Television in Transition,* p. 240.
73   ibid., p. 247.
74   Robert H. Deming, "The Television Spectator-Subject," *Journal of Film and
      Video* 38 (summer 1985): 48-63.
75   Elizabeth Ellsworth, "Critical Media Analysis, Radical Pedagogy and MTV"
      (unpublished paper, quoted in R. H. Deming, "Television's Inscribed Spectator"
      (Fredonia College, unpublished paper)).
76   Deming, "The Television Spectator-Subject," pp. 54-6.
77   See, for example, Patricia Palmer's comments on the physical distance from the
      screen taken up by children in relation to favorite or less favorite programs, in her
      paper "The Social Nature of Children's TV Viewing" (presented at the ITSC,
      London, 1986). See also David Morley and Roger Silverstone, "Domestic
      Communications: Technologies and Meanings" (paper presented at the ITSC,
      London, 1988).
78   See Dell Hymes, "On Communicative Competence," in Pride and Holmes (eds)
      Sociolinguistics, pp. 269-94.
79   Richard Nice, "Bourdieu: A 'Vulgar Materialist' in the Sociology of Culture,"
      Screen Education 28 (1978): 24.

Chapter two

Bursting bubbles:

"Soap Opera," audiences, and the limits of genre

Robert C. Allen

The shop seemed to be full of all manner of curious things – but the oddest part of it all was that, whenever she looked hard at any shelf, to make out exactly what it had on it, that particular shelf was always quite empty, though the others round it were crowded as full as they could hold.

"Things flow about so here!" she said at last in a plaintive tone, after she had spent a minute or so in vainly pursuing a large bright thing, that looked sometimes like a doll and sometimes like a work-box, and was always on the shelf next above the one she was looking at. "And this one is the most provoking of all – but I'll tell you what – " she added, as a sudden thought struck her. "I'll follow it up to the very top shelf of all. It'll puzzle it to go through the ceiling, I expect!"

But even this plan failed: the "thing" went through the ceiling as quietly as possible, as if it were quite used to it.

Lewis Carroll
Through the Looking-Glass[1]

Genre is so basic to our notions of what literature is that, as Terence Hawkes has put it, "a world without a theory of genre is unthinkable, and untrue to experience."[2] For most of its 2,000 years, genre study has been primarily nominological and typological in function. That is to say, it has taken as its principal task the division of the world of literature into types and the naming of those types – much as the botanist divides the realm of flora into varieties of plants.

When eighteenth- and nineteenth-century European biologists went out to arrange all living things into types and sub-types, they did so secure in the belief that their perception of similarity and difference corresponded to the way the world really was. They were merely the recorders – certainly not the creators – of ontological distinctions in the living world. Similarly, genre theorists have until fairly recently presumed that their classification of the world of literature was also based on features objectively and indisputably existing in the text itself.

Today, although the empiricism of much of modern science protects the biologist from self-doubt, the literary theorist finds it increasingly difficult to hold to the notion that a literary genre is a "thing" or that genre study is merely the disinterested mapping of the literary world. Genre describes not so much a group of texts or textual features as it does a dynamic relationship between texts and interpretative communities. To assign a name to a group of texts – fantasy, romance, western – is to appropriate a linguistic signifier for use within a particular discursive system. The appropriation of the same signifier by groups occupying vastly different positions within society implies that individuals within a culture share a common language, but not necessarily that they share the same discourses and hence the same meanings. Reframing genre as a classificatory discursive strategy allows us to reconnect perceived patterns of textual structure and reader expectation with the groups in society for whom those patterns are meaningful. It also helps to reconnect the uses of language by particular groups with their goals and aspirations.

My purpose in this chapter is to suggest that far from naming a static group of texts and thereby defining their nature and meaning, the term "soap opera" much more problematically describes several different sets of discursive relationships between a variety of perceived textual features and at least three different types of interpretative communities: what I will call the industrial, critical, and viewer communities. In other words, "soap opera" is appropriated within at least three different discursive systems. Further complicating matters is that fact that whatever it is to whom, the soap opera is a transnational and transcultural phenomenon, so that for each of these three types of interpretative communities and corresponding discursive systems there are distinctive instances for each national culture. Finally, each country's experience with the range of texts to which the term "soap opera" has been applied is different. It is a bit like ornithologists, taxidermists, and bird watchers from a dozen different countries all talking about birds, but in one country there are only eagles; in another pigeons and chickens but no eagles; in another macaws and pigeons but no eagles or chickens; and so on.

I want to concentrate on the use of the term "soap opera" within contemporary critical discourse,[3] since as scholars we are the interpretative community with the greatest responsibility to be self-conscious and self-critical about our use of language. Also because media criticism seems to be moving away from a text-oriented notion of critical practice and toward an audience- or viewer-oriented one, the relationship between genre and audience emerges as all the more important in contemporary media studies. The appropriation of the term "soap opera" within contemporary critical discourse occurred at a particular historical moment, and within the context of larger and somewhat differing critical and political projects. By examining this history and recontextualizing the use of the term "soap opera," I hope to suggest some of the reasons why "soap opera" has been constructed as it has as a figure in the discourse of contemporary media criticism. At the very least I wish to make a case for the obvious: that we cannot afford to assume an unproblematic relationship between the term "soap opera" and either its signified or its referent.

The practice of discussing contemporary television programming in terms of genre – at least that practice as I am familiar with it in British, Australian, and American media studies – developed as much out of cinema studies as literary studies. Genre analysis was a logical adjunct to the *auteur* theory of cinema, which so influenced Anglo-American cinema studies in the 1960s and early 1970s. Auteurism, in addition to providing the embryonic field of cinema studies with a mantle of "theory," quite literally helped to define the object of cinema studies by perceiving and naming difference where earlier critics had seen only sameness, and, conversely, by "uncovering" unity and coherence (within the corpus bearing the name of an *auteur*) that had been unseen by those not predisposed to look for it. As Andrew Sarris put it, *auteur* critics were able to see individual trees within the forest of Hollywood cinema.

Given the nature of the Hollywood mode of production, it is not surprising that early *auteur* critics found the key works of Howard Hawks, John Ford, Alfred Hitchcock, and other *auteurs* to be – in Hollywood argot – formula pictures, or genre films: combat films, westerns, screwball comedies, suspense films, etc. Industry, audience, and critical recognition of generic patterns of characterization, setting, and narrative organization both presented a challenge to the *auteur* theory and demonstrated its ultimate validity – at least in the eyes of Peter Wollen and others. The challenge came from the possibility that the "world view" of a director such as John Ford might actually emanate more from the conventions of the western genre than from Ford's manipulation of those conventions. The "proof" of the validity of the *auteur* approach came when the director's world view could be discerned across genres.

For our purposes, cinema auteurism and genre study are important not only for providing organizational schema for the study of screen narratives, but also for foregrounding popular narrative forms (and in some cases critically despised forms) and making them the object of "serious" scholarly discourse. Although there would continue to be a critical community for whom the science fiction or musical film would be critically illegible, by the early 1970s graduate courses at major universities were being taught on the later westerns of John Ford, the melodramas of Douglas Sirk, and the horror films of Val Lewton. Furthermore, the inherent link between commercial Hollywood genres and their mass popularity over time gave genre criticism a cultural, if not yet sociological, as well as aesthetic cast.

Genre study in the United States and Great Britain really came into its own as auteurism waned and the structuralist star rose in the early 1970s. Although some critics attempted to accommodate auteurism within the framework of structuralism and semiotics, auteurism's inherent emphasis on the vision (conscious or unconscious) of the individual artist made this at best an uncomfortable accommodation. The film genre, on the other hand, could be read as a sort of unauthored but culturally accepted narrative *langue* and each genre film a particular utterance. In Thomas Schatz' *Hollywood Genres*, for example, each genre was seen as embodying a different cultural opposition, the irreconcilability of which necessitated obsessive reworking within each film and accounted for the genre's popular appeal.[4]

From its inception, cinematic genre study has been caught in what Andrew Tudor has called an empiricist dilemma: a genre is defined in terms of features drawn from a set of texts already identified by the analyst as containing the defining features of the genre. This circularity afflicts genre study in literature as well, of course, but not so severely. Cinematic genre scholars were intrigued by the continuing mass popularity of certain types of Hollywood films and were interested in linking textual markers to audience desire and, presumably, to audience interpretation. Tudor's own solution to the empiricist dilemma, articulated in 1970, was to define genre as an interplay between film maker, film, and audience: genre becomes, in Tudor's words, "what we collectively believe it to be," and, in turn, what film makers believe we collectively believe it to be.[5] Tudor even hints that in order to establish what audiences expect a western to be like we might have to ask them. However, the textuality of the dominant semiotic model of film operation, in its ascendance in 1970, combined with a general anti-positivist suspicion of anything approaching empirical research, militated against genre analysts taking Tudor's sociological advice to heart. Genre study survived in film study without having to tackle its central conceptual contradiction in large measure, I think, because it contributed to a larger project of discovering useful analytical differences among popular texts and, within these patterns of difference, complex, coherent systems of signification and pleasure production.

With the hegemony of Lacanian/Althusserian film theory in the mid-1970s (sometimes referred to as *Screen* theory), the project of genre study was temporarily side-tracked as Hollywood cinema once again was analysed in terms of similarity rather than difference. The classic realist cinematic text came to be seen as an awesomely effective machine for subject production and interpellation, whose mechanisms functioned before and across any generic distinctions. But just when the trees of popular commercial cinema were in danger of blending imperceptibly into yet another critical forest, genre study – this time aligned with feminist challenges to the more rigid versions of 1970s film theory – once again pointed out the danger of assuming that all popular narratives operated on all spectators in the same way.

Feminist film scholars looked to genres in which the construction of masculine/feminine difference allowed for the possibility of more than one reading and/or in which the film's address seemed to be to a female rather than a male spectator: the *film noir*, melodrama, and the musical.[6] The remapping of cinema studies that resulted from the strong feminist intervention in film theoretical debates not only pushed previously ignored genres into the center of film study, it implicitly highlighted the relationships of different groups of viewers to different types of popular narrative.

It is at this historical moment – that is, the late 1970s and early 1980s – and as a result, at least in part, of the conjuncture of these and other intellectual forces that the soap opera emerges on the critical agendas of scholars on both sides of the Atlantic. In the United States especially interest in the soap opera also signals the increasing fascination of film scholars with television as an object of study. It is no coincidence that much of the important recent critical work done on American serial drama is by scholars trained primarily in cinema studies: Sandy Flitterman-Lewis, Jeremy Butler, Ellen Seiter, Jane Feuer, Patricia Zimmerman, and Louise Spence, among others. Some of this interest was no doubt stimulated by the somewhat belated practical recognition that television had long usurped film's position as the predominant form of popular entertainment in America. But film scholars were also fascinated by the challenges that the most mundane forms of television represented to film theoretical orthodoxy. For example, in his monograph on cinema genres, Stephen Neale maintains that

> the coherence of mainstream narrative [a category that would include Hollywood film genres] derives largely from the way in which disphasure is contained as a series of oscillations that never exceed the limits of "dramatic conflict" (that never, therefore, exceed the limits of the possibility of resolution), and from the way in which such conflict is always, ultimately, articulated from a single, privileged point of view.[7]

The soap opera, by this definition at least, would not be a mainstream narrative at all, since it is predicated upon the infinite delay of closure. Furthermore, as Sandy Flitterman-Lewis argues with particular reference to the American daytime serial drama, "where in the cinema the reverse-shot structure works together with the point-of-view system to bind the spectator into a position of coherence and fictive participation, in television, the effect is just the opposite."[8]

Interest in the soap opera can also be seen as part of a larger project among feminist scholars to work out the nature of the relationships obtaining between female viewers and readers and types of popular narrative primarily designed for and largely consumed by them. It is here, of course, that Tania Modleski's work on "feminine" popular narratives, produced first as her doctoral dissertation and then published in book form in 1982 as *Loving with a Vengeance*, proved to be crucial in framing much of the critical discourse on soap operas to follow. For Modleski, the daytime serial drama represents a narrative form diametrically opposed to more male-oriented novels and films: a feminine form of narrative structure, which inscribes its reader as ideal mother, values dialogue over action, disperses the viewer's attention over huge extended families of characters, and forever retards ultimate resolution.

In Great Britain, two other trends helped to open up a space for "soap opera" in critical discourse. The first was a concern over representations of class in popular media and a reconsideration of scholarship on class and "the popular," as it had been promulgated by Hoggart, Leavis, Williams, Thompson, Gramsci, and others. As Richard Dyer makes clear in his introduction to the 1981 BFI monograph on *Coronation Street*, this particular "soap opera" allows three distinct but related lines of inquiry to be brought together: interrogations of "the popular," representations of working-class life, and representations of gender:

> The series lays claim to being "about" working-class culture and is also marked by the presence of strong and positive female characters. It thus supplies social images that are conspicuous for their rarity on British television, and that are necessarily of particular interest to anyone working within broadly Marxist and/or feminist perspectives, as is the case in this book.[9]

The second trend was one toward the inclusion of the audience – and not just their subject positions or textual inscriptions – on the agenda of media studies. In his 1980 monograph on *Nationwide*, David Morley is concerned "with the ways in which decoding is determined by the socially governed distribution of cultural codes between and across different sections of the audience." The text, he goes on to say, "cannot be considered in isolation from its historical conditions of production and consumption."[10]

Dorothy Hobson's doctoral dissertation-turned-book, *"Crossroads": The Drama of a Soap Opera*, considers the production and consumption of what was in 1982 *Coronation Street*'s chief ratings rival. For Hobson *Crossroads* represents an opportunity to explore media popularity as a cultural phenomenon and the curious relationship between that popular appeal and near unanimous disdain visited upon the program by critics in the popular press. Although she does not put it in these terms, Hobson recognizes that the term "soap opera" has been constructed within an "other" critical discourse – a discourse that conditions the relationships between programs bearing that appellation and both their producers and viewers. Hobson finds that the contradictory position of whatever is called a "soap opera" is bound up with its address to and popularity among women viewers. Thus, despite its status as an advertising vehicle within the commercial television sector, Hobson finds soap operas to be "progressive" texts by virtue of their "raising of problems which are seen as relevant to their [women's] lives."[11]

Finally, critical interest in serial drama in the late 1970s and early 1980s was prompted by the enormous success of *Dallas* in the United States in the mid-1970s and its even more startling popularity elsewhere – first in Britain in 1978 and then in countries around the world. *Dallas* was framed within critical discourse as a "soap opera," I suspect, in part because it had already been framed that way by the popular and industry press in the United States, but also because its perceived narrative seriality, prominent female characters, and dramatic concern with heterosexual romance, kinship, and family sufficiently related it, on the one hand, to American daytime serials, and, on the other, to British serials such as *Crossroads*, for it to be brought under the same generic designation. Furthermore, as Jane Feuer makes clear in her 1984 essay on *Dallas* and *Dynasty*, these texts provided an opportunity to apply psychoanalytic, feminist, and ideological analyses of Hollywood melodrama to television. Thus, although she acknowledges important differences between daytime and prime time serials, she chooses to set them aside ("For the purposes of this article") in order to examine the relationship between melodrama and the serial form. She coins the term "television melodrama" to describe a genre that includes daytime serials, *Dallas* and *Dynasty*, and serial cop and medical shows (*Hill Street Blues* and *St. Elsewhere*).[12]

The transnational popularity of *Dallas* raised a collateral but distinct set of critical and cultural issues that had not arisen with respect to "other" "soap operas": the "Americanness" of *Dallas* and its representation of entrepreneurial capitalism, wealth, and region; the show's interpenetration of the realms of business, politics, sexuality, and family; the continuing cultural invasion of other countries by American popular media; and simply accounting for the mass popularity of *Dallas* among viewers around the world.

The five years since the publication of Hobson's book – the first British book that I am aware of that uses soap opera in its title – have seen the publication of many more books and articles about something called but seldom explicitly defined as "soap operas," with still more research, books, and articles in progress. Some of the works have examined particular programs (Ien Ang's *Watching "Dallas"* and John Tulloch and Albert Moran's *"A Country Practice" : 'Quality Soap,'* to name the two most notable examples); others have considered a range of texts. All have invoked the term "soap opera" to frame their enterprises.

To this point in the history of the appropriation of the term "soap opera" in contemporary critical discourse, I would argue, it has not been particularly important to specify with great precision and in each case the relationships marked out by that term between programs and analysts, programs and institutions, programs and other modes of critical discourse, and programs and audience groups – any more than it was seen as necessary by feminist theorists a few years ago to specify the limits of the *film noir* or the melodrama. What was for them important and has been for the analysts of soap opera is the function of a particular generic designation to mark analytically productive difference. However vaguely defined and however related to particular programs, the term "soap opera" has provided a convenient and useful framework within which to examine programs whose narrative structure would seem to be fundamentally at odds with that of the classic realist text, whose "ideological problematics" (to use Charlotte Brunsdon's term[13]), modes of address, and methods of pleasure production would seem to be quite different from other forms of television, whose audiences would appear to be constituted differently from those for "mainstream" television, and whose place in the lives of many of those audience members renders soap time a special time of day.

However, as one reads back through these critical analyses, one can detect traces of a largely unspoken unease regarding what a soap opera is for whom. In the opening essay of the *Coronation Street* monograph, "The Continuous Serial – a Definition," Christine Geraghty studiously avoids using the term "soap opera" at all and warns in a footnote that the definition she gives of the continuous serial applies only to British television and radio serials and not

American ones. In the Introduction that precedes her essay, however, Richard Dyer conflates the continuous serial and the soap opera and by the beginning of the second paragraph has added a new term: the continuous soap opera. *Coronation Street*, he informs us, is a typical instance of one of broadcasting's most typical forms.[14] To further confuse matters, Marion Jordan's essay refers to the style of *Coronation Street* as "soap opera realism," placing the program in the same genre as *The Liver Birds*, although she admits that the latter is "a series rather than a serial, and not classified by the programmers as drama." Having constructed a genre consisting of *Coronation Street* and perhaps one other program (she mentions no others), Jordon then tells us that "in terms of narrative management, [*Coronation Street*] fits the genre pattern of Soap Opera Realism perfectly," as well it might.[15]

As already mentioned, Jane Feuer's 1984 essay collapses US daytime and prime-time serials into a single category, the television melodrama. However, Annette Kuhn's essay on "Women's Genres," which follows Feuer's in the same issue of *Screen*, explicitly excludes "prime-time serials like *Dallas* and *Dynasty*" from her formulation of soap opera, even though it includes US daytime along with early evening UK serials. No explanation is given for this constitution of the genre.[16]

In her book on *Crossroads* Dorothy Hobson gives as "a very basic definition of soap opera" a program "that is a continuous drama serial which should be transmitted daily." Thus, as she points out, "in this sense there are no soap operas on British television." Although she relies upon Modleski's discussion of American daytime serials as the basis for her conception of the "soap opera's" narrative and thematic concerns, Hobson distinguishes between British and American soaps primarily on the basis of production values: "One major difference between the genre as it has developed in America and Britain is the vast budgets which are allocated to soap operas in the USA." Many of the serials shown on the BBC are, she says, "imports of expensively produced, high gloss American television soap operas." Since, so far as I know, American daytime serials rarely have been shown in Great Britain, these lavishly produced soap operas must be American prime-time serials such as *Dallas, Dynasty*, and *Falcon Crest*. Thus, the American soap opera is defined in relation to daytime serials and then stretched to include prime time serials as well.

Yet Hobson makes clear that the viewers with whom she spoke regard *Crossroads* and *Dallas* as two quite different types of viewing experience. Summarizing the comments of one viewer with regard to *Crossroads'* representation of Birmingham life, Hobson concludes:

> What she is saying is that it does not present a glamorized image of life either in its contents or in its production style. ... She also reveals how viewers watch a programme like *Crossroads* for one kind of appeal and expect an entirely different type of production and content when they watch a programme like *Dallas*[17].

Here Hobson opens up the possibility – one she does not pursue or even comment upon – of disjunctures between discourses circulating around what she has called "soap opera" and of the parsing of viewing experience by viewers themselves in ways the analyst has not taken fully into account. Charlotte Brunsdon's quite useful essay on the "gendered audience" for *Crossroads* argues that "just as a Godard film requires the possession of certain forms of cultural capital on the part of its audience to 'make sense' . . . so too does *Crossroads*/soap opera." Among the three categories of such competencies, Brunsdon includes generic knowledge: "familiarity with the conventions of soap opera as a genre."[18] This is a point few would take issue with; however, it begs the questions: "How is that generic knowledge structured?" And "Of what terms is it constituted?"

But these two questions beg a third: "By whom is this generic knowledge used in making sense and deriving pleasure?" Again because of the legitimate desire of scholars to interrogate gender differences in film/television texts and viewing experiences, the "femaleness" of "soap opera" has been foregrounded in recent research.[19] I certainly recognize the distinction between a feminine subject position – constructed through textual address, and through program publicity, scheduling, advertisements and other forms of situating discourse – and the social constitution of audiences for various forms of programming. The fact that the audience for various "soap operas" might not be 100 per cent female in and of itself no more vitiates an argument for the form's femininely inscribed spectator than does the sexual heterogeneity of the film-viewing audience vitiate the argument for the masculinely inscribed viewer for most forms of Hollywood cinema. However, as Annette Kuhn has asked with specific reference to soap operas,

> what precisely does it mean to say that certain representations are aimed at a female audience? However well theorized they may be, existing conceptualizations of gendered spectatorship are unable to deal with this question. This is because spectator and audience are distinct concepts which cannot – as they frequently are – be reduced to one another.[20]

By conflating audience and gender address we might be obscuring important differences among audiences for types of programs as well as differences in the relationships between audience groups and the spectator positions inscribed within texts. Just as feminist interrogations of spectator inscription in the Hollywood cinema opened up a theoretical space for a consideration of the relationship between social subjects and subject positions, might not opening up a similar space with regard to the soap opera illuminate the viewing experiences of different socially constituted groups?

I can only mention the fact that very little work has been done – at least by scholars not in the employ of the television industry – to pin down the social and demographic constitution of audiences for various types of serial drama in the United States, Great Britain, and Europe. On the basis of data provided me by the Office of Social Research at the National Broadcasting Corporation (NBC), it appears that a majority of the adult audience for most forms of prime-time programming – not just serials – is female. Even the programs currently scheduled against *Dallas* and *Dynasty* (*Miami Vice* and *Magnum PI*) have adult audiences that are more than 50 per cent female. By the same token, the audience for *Dallas* is nearly one-third male. Daytime serial audiences, on the other hand, are on average nearly 80 per cent female. The above figures for male viewership of "gender-specific" forms may well under-represent actual male viewing, since some males are reluctant to admit they watch "soap operas" at all. David Buckingham's research on *EastEnders* viewers suggests that this is the case in Britain as well.[21] Furthermore, the image of the male viewer of serial dramas staying in the living room only because he is outnumbered or overpowered by female members of the household is challenged by at least one Broadcast Audience Research Bureau study, which in November 1985 found that 69 per cent of a sample of male viewers of *EastEnders* specially chose to watch it, while only 15 per cent watched as a result of someone else's choice and only 7 per cent because they felt there was nothing else worth watching.[22]

We must also be aware that viewing patterns vary within program types, by region, by class, and over time. In many instances, historical changes in viewer demographics do not occur by accident but are encouraged by campaigns to attract new categories of viewers or to shift the demographic center of viewership from one group to another. In the mid-1970s, for example, American daytime serial producers attempted to counter the "graying" of their audiences by introducing younger characters and plotlines thought more likely to appeal to teenagers and women in their twenties. By 1982, over 40 per cent of American college students were watching soap operas, and today one out of every seven viewers of *General Hospital* is under the age of 18.[23] In Britain, *Coronation Street* has added younger characters; *Crossroads* (before its demise) attempted to "upscale" its audience; and both *EastEnders* and *Brookside* appear to have been successful in attracting large teenage followings.

I hope my critique of the appropriation of "soap opera" in contemporary critical discourse does not obscure my admiration for and debt of gratitude to the work of these scholars who have done much to reinvigorate the study of television in the United States. I think that one reason for my concern over the minimizing or eliding of the discursive nature and functions of genre designations stems from a recognition that, in the United States at least, "soap opera" has been a term activated within the supervisory discourses of traditional mass communication research and traditional criticism (as well as in their more popularized variants) in order to hierarchize media experiences and texts by gender, and having done so to create a large, undifferentiated "other world" to which they (those gendered texts and viewing experiences) could be conveniently consigned.[24] I am not in the least suggesting that the scholars whose work I have discussed are unaware of the discursive "encrustation" of "soap opera" (indeed, for several it is precisely the marginalization by sex of certain television texts that has given impetus to their study of soap operas) or that they in any way share the assumptions or goals of these groups. It is just that I believe that for practical and political reasons it is important that we do not – however inadvertently – contribute to the reification of the term "soap opera" and, more positively, that we build on the work already done within contemporary criticism on "soap operas" (however defined) by refining our conceptualizations of audience, textual engagement, textual inscription, and the discourses in which they and their analyses are embedded.

Notes

1   Lewis Carroll, *Through the Looking-Glass* (London: Octopus Books, 1978).
2   Terence Hawkes, *Structuralism and Semiotics* (London: Methuen, 1977), p. 101.
3   By the term "contemporary critical discourse" I mean to mark out those approaches to the study of cultural production that have followed from or developed in reaction to the "structuralist revolution." I also mean to differentiate this cluster of critical approaches from what might be called "traditional" or pre-structuralist critical practice. The figuring of "soap operas" within the latter is examined in my *Speaking of Soap Operas* (Chapel Hill: University of North Carolina Press, 1985), pp. 11-18. Differences between contemporary and traditional criticism as they relate to television analysis are discussed in Robert C. Allen (ed.) *Channels of Discourse: Television and Contemporary Criticism* (Chapel Hill and London: University of North Carolina Press/Methuen, 1987), pp. 1-16.
4   Thomas Schatz, *Hollywood Genres* (New York: Random House, 1981).
5   Andrew Tudor, "Genre and Critical Methodology," in Bill Nichols (ed.) *Movies and Methods* (Berkeley: University of California Press, 1976), pp. 118-26.
6   See, for example, E. Ann Kaplan (ed.) *Women in Film Noir* (London: British Film Institute, 1978); and Rick Altman (ed.) *Genre, the Musical* (London: British Film Institute, 1981).
7   Stephen Neale, "Genre and Cinema," in Tony Bennet, Susan Boyd-Bowman, Colin Mercer, and Janet Woolacott (eds) *Popular Television and Film* (London: Open University/British Film Institute, 1981), pp. 12-13. Extracted from Stephen Neale, *Genre* (London: British Film Institute, 1980).
8   Sandy Flitterman-Lewis, "Psychoanalysis, Film, and Television," in Robert C. Allen (ed.) *Channels of Discourse*, p. 195.
9   Richard Dyer, "Introduction," in Richard Dyer, Christine Geraghty, Marion Jordan, Terry Lovell, Richard Paterson, and John Stewart (eds) *"Coronation Street"* (London: British Film Institute, 1981), p. 2.
10 David Morley, *The "Nationwide" Audience: Structure and Decoding* (London: British Film Institute, 1980).
11 Dorothy Hobson, *"Crossroads": The Drama of a Soap Opera* (London: Methuen, 1982), p. 35.
12 Jane Feuer, "Melodrama, Serial Form, and Television Today," *Screen* 25 (1984): 4-16.
13 Charlotte Brunsdon, *"Crossroads*: Notes on Soap Opera," *Screen* 22, no. 4 (1981): 34.
14 Christine Geraghty, "The Continuous Serial – a Definition," and Richard Dyer, "Introduction," in Dyer *et al.*, *"Coronation Street"*.
15 Marion Jordan, "Realism and Convention," in Dyer *et al.*, *"Coronation Street"*, pp. 27-39.

16   Annette Kuhn, "Women's Genres," *Screen* 25 (1984): 18-28.
17   Hobson, *"Crossroads,"* pp. 26, 27, 120.
18   Brunsdon, *"Crossroads".*
19   In Dyer *et al.*'s *Coronation Street* monograph, a female audience is for the most part assumed, as is a corresponding dislike of the program by men. Terry Lovell (p. 50), for example, says the program provides a validation of a set of concerns women see as "theirs." To which she adds: "No wonder men dislike it." However, in his article on the production context of *Coronation Street* which follows Lovell's essay in the volume, Richard Paterson notes that between 1975 and 1980 the audience for the program in the Granada-controlled market included a "static but quite high male viewership" (p. 56).
        Brunsdon, at the beginning of her article *"Crossroads,"* cites demographic research on American radio serial audiences conducted before and during World War II to support her statement that "the audience for soap operas is usually assumed to be female" (p. 32). Furthermore, she argues, the scheduling of *Crossroads* in the early evening hours (5.30-7.30 p.m.) implies a predominantly female audience sought by broadcasters, as opposed to prime time, "which is expected to maximise on a male audience" (p. 33). However, so far as I am aware, *Dallas, Dynasty,* and other American prime time serials have always been scheduled during prime time in Britain.
        Hobson (*"Crossroads,"* p. 119) interviewed only female viewers of *Crossroads.* There are male viewers as well, she admits, "but the proportion is much smaller." However, she does not state how "small" that proportion is. Ang generated the body of audience discourse she analysed in *Watching "Dallas" : Soap Opera and the Melodramatic Imagination* (London: Methuen, 1985) by placing an advertisement in a "women's" magazine. Not surprisingly, only three of the responses to this ad. were from men.
20   Kuhn, "Women's Genres," p. 21.
21   David Buckingham, *Public Secrets: "EastEnders" and Its Audience* (London: British Film Institute, 1987).
22   Broadcast Audience Research Bureau Audience Reaction Service, "Report on *EastEnders,*" November 26, 1985, Booklet Part B, p. 4. Eighty per cent of female viewers reported that they specially chose to watch, and only 7 per cent because someone else chose. Unfortunately for media scholars in the United States and Great Britain (and perhaps in Europe as well), studies conducted by BARB, Nielsen, and other companies are regarded as proprietary information and made available only to clients. Those clients are specifically enjoined from publishing or sharing these data with others – although in some cases sympathetic "clients" are willing to help scholars. The data on US viewing were prepared by Hans Stipp, Director of Social Research, NBC. I am grateful to him for his assistance.
23   "They're Watching," Brochure, ABC-Television Social Research Unit, 1982.
24   In Allen, *Speaking of Soap Operas,* I discuss the encrustation of the term "soap opera" in social science discourse in the United States. Despite the recent fashionability of daytime serial viewing among American college students and the popularity of prime-time serials, soap opera viewing continues to carry with it a social stigma for many viewers. The nature of that stigma and viewers' strategies for dealing with it are discussed in a recent and as yet unpublished study by Alison Alexander and Virginia Fry: "Interpreting Viewing: Creating an Acceptable Context" (paper presented at the Conference on Culture and Communication, Temple University, Philadelphia, Pa., 1986).

Chapter three

Moments of television:

Neither the text nor the audience

John Fiske

A group of people in front of the television set, spines curved weakly on the couch, drinks or snacks in hand, eyes glued to the screen is, I suppose, the commonsense model of television and its audience. What is on the screen is the text, the people watching, multiplied a millionfold, are the audience. In the not too distant past there have been theories of both the text and the audience that, unfortunately for them and us, have taken this model for the uninspected base of their assumptions, for the scene the model paints is both typical and realistic. Its problem lies in its easy categorization of the viewers into "the audience" and the screen into "the text".

I wish to dissolve both categories. First, there is no such thing as "the television audience," defined as an empirically accessible object, for there can be no meaningful categories beyond its boundaries – what on earth is "not the television audience"? The "television audience" is not a social category like class, or race, or gender – everyone slips in or out of it in a way that makes nonsense of any categorical boundaries: similarly when in "it" people constitute themselves quite differently as audience members at different times – I am a different television "audience" when watching my football team from when watching *The A-Team* with my son or *Days of our Lives* with my wife. Categories focus our thinking on similarities: people watching television are best modeled according to a multitude of differences.

Similarly, the television text, or program, is no unified whole delivering the same message in the same way to all its "audience." The old literary idea of the organic, self-contained text has been exploded so comprehensively that there is no need for me here to contribute further to its demolition. But we still need the term, or something like it to refer to television's meaning-making potential, though we might do better to make it less concrete, less comfortable to handle, and to use the word "textuality" whose abstraction signals its potentiality rather than its concrete existence. What the set in the living-room delivers is "television," visual and aural signifiers that are potential provokers of meaning and pleasure. This potential is its textuality which is mobilized differently in the variety of its moments of viewing.

Textuality is realized in the making of sense and the production of pleasure, and central to this process is the inescapable intertextuality of our culture, a point I shall return to later. For the moment I wish only to point out that we have now collapsed the distinction between "text" and "audience." The textuality of television, the intertextuality of the process of making sense and pleasure from it, can only occur when people bring their different histories and subjectivities to the viewing process. There is no text, there is no audience, there are only the processes of viewing, – that variety of cultural activities that take place in front of the screen which constitute the object of study that I am proposing.

The viewer

This model, or models, will involve people and television, despite our resolution not to separate them into categories of audience and text. This paper is primarily concerned with textuality: but in order to discuss that I must briefly set out my assumptions of viewers without whom textuality could not be constituted out of television.

Watching television is a process of making meanings and pleasures, and this process is determined by two parallel and interlocking sets of forces. I use the word "determine" in its literal sense of setting the boundaries, not in its more common mis-sense of authoritarian social imperatives – thou shalt be, do, feel, react as society determines. Determination, then, refers to a bounded terrain within which people have the space to exercise some power over their meanings, pleasures, subjectivities. People can and do make their own culture, albeit within conditions that are not of their own choosing. How much power is available within this terrain, and how fixedly its boundaries are determined are matters of considerable debate, in which I align myself with those who propose that ideological and hegemonic theories of popular culture have overestimated the power of the determinations and underestimated that of the viewer.

The two intertwined sets of determination are the social and the textual, the one working upon the subjectivity of the viewer, the other upon the textuality of television, and I wish to argue that the correspondence between subjectivity and textuality is so close that the two leak into each other at every point of contact.

Viewers within this determined terrain are subjects constituted by late-capitalist societies. Such societies are characterized by heterogeneity – a vast shifting range of subcultures and groups which are finally structured by their relationship to the system by which power is unequally distributed in them. Any one person, or television viewer, forms a number of shifting alliances within this heterogeneity, she or he enters the social system via differently constituted and shifting social formations: the metaphor of a nomadic subjectivity is a productive one here.[1] Any one viewer, then, may at different times be a different viewing subject, as constituted by his or her social determinants, as different social alliances may be mobilized for different moments of viewing: to return to our spatial metaphor, the socially constituted viewing subject may occupy different spaces within the determined terrain according to the social alliances appropriate to this specific moment of making sense of and finding pleasure in the television experience. Hall refers to a similar process as "articulation."[2] Here he uses both senses of the word, first as speech, that is a symbolic system used to make sense of both self and experience, and second as flexible linkage. Hodge and Tripp's school students who made sense of *Prisoner* by aligning themselves with the prisoners, the wardens with school teachers, and the prison with the school were articulating, in both senses of the word.[3] They were using the television program to "speak," or make sense of their experience of institutionalized subordination and thus to make sense of themselves as subordinated subjects, and they did this by articulating (linking) their viewing of a soap opera set in a women's prison with their social experience of school.

But many of the same students also enjoyed *Sale of the Century – Prisoner* and *Sale of the Century* were the most popular programs amongst Australian junior high school students in 1983. Here, the program was articulated with school in a way that produced quite different meanings and pleasures.[4] Making sense of popular television, then, is the process of activating meanings from it, and this process is controlled within more or less determined boundaries by the socially situated viewer. The text will be a source of popular pleasure when these meanings become part of that larger cultural process by which the subject makes sense of his or her material existence. For social experience is like a text: it can only be made meaningful when a social subject brings his or her discursive competencies to bear upon it. The shifting alliance of formations that constitute social experience for the subject allows for a potentially unlimited range of social differences so that each person may be constituted differently, yet these differences are to be explained not by the individual differences of psychology but by the variety of intersections of social alliances and social relations.

Social experience is like intertextuality. It is a vast interlocking potential of elements that can be mobilized in an unpredictable number of ways. Any social system needs a system of meanings to underpin it, and the meanings that are made of it are determined only to an extent by the system itself. This determination allows adequate space for different people to make different meanings though they may use a shared discursive repertoire in the process. The subject is not fully subjected – the sense we make of our social relations is partly under our control – and making sense of social experience necessarily involves making sense of ourselves within that experience.

This potential of meanings that constitutes our social experience must not be seen as amoeba-like and structureless. Just as post-structuralism and discourse theory must not be allowed to evacuate a notion of material social relations, so too, my argument in favor of difference and a relatively empowered, relatively loosely subjected, subject must not blind us to the determining framework of power relations within which all of this takes place. In a similar vein, the emphasis on the power of the viewer to achieve certain meanings from the potential offered by the text can only be understood in terms of a textual power and a textual struggle that are remarkably similar to social power and social struggle. Making sense of social experience is an almost identical process to making sense of a text.

What television delivers is not programs but a semiotic experience. This experience is characterized by its openness and polysemy. Television is not quite a do-it-yourself meaning kit but neither is it a box of ready-made meanings for sale. Although it works within cultural determinations, it also offers freedoms and the power to evade, modify, or challenge these limitations and controls. All texts are polysemic, but polysemy is absolutely central to television's textuality.

Television as cultural commodity

Television is a cultural commodity. It works within an economically determined capitalist economy, but when we have said that about it we have said both much and remarkably little. There is a financial economy within which wealth circulates, and a cultural economy within which meanings and pleasures circulate, and the relationship between them is not as deterministic as some theorists have proposed. In the financial economy television is programs and advertisements, not textuality. A program is a commodity produced and then sold to distributors. In distribution its role changes and it becomes not a commodity, but a producer, and what it produces is a new commodity, the audience which is then, in its turn, sold as a commodity to advertisers. The ramifications of this financial economy are fascinating, but they are not the topic of this paper. I wish to concentrate more on the cultural economy.

Here the role shift undergone by the program in the financial economy – that from commodity to producer – is now undergone by the audience, whom I left as a commodity sold to the advertiser. But in the cultural economy the audience rejects its role as commodity and becomes a producer, a producer of meanings and pleasures, and at this moment stops being "an audience" and becomes different materializations of the process that we call "viewing television."

While the metaphor of a cultural economy is a productive one, we must not let it blind us to differences between it and the financial. Meanings and pleasures do not circulate in the cultural economy in the same way that wealth does in the financial. In the first place there is no exchange of money at the point of sale or consumption. Television *appears* to be free, however it may actually be paid for. Payment has no direct relationship to consumption – people can consume as much as they wish and what they wish with no thought of what they are able to afford. Watching an opera or a concert by Dire Straits costs no more than a quiz show or a rerun sitcom.

This liberation from economic constraints frees the viewer from the subordinate role in the market economy, that of "consumer" who, by definition, gives more than he or she receives. This crucial difference between the television commodity and other more material goods in the market-place foregrounds the considerable freedom won by the viewer in the shift from consumer in the financial economy to producer in the cultural. Meanings and pleasures cannot be owned or bought and sold in a way that grants proprietorial rights over them to some but denies them to others. Bourdieu's theory of cultural capital needs re-examination: for him cultural capital works for one section of the bourgeoisie (the intelligentsia) similarly to the way that economic capital works for the business section.[5] It works to maintain power in the hands of the powerful, advantaged minority, whether that power be expressed in economic or cultural terms. We need to add to this notion that of a popular cultural capital that puts bourgeois culture under constant pressure. Hobson, for instance, has shown how the women viewers of *Crossroads* had made the program theirs, had constituted it as their cultural capital that they could draw upon to articulate their social relations and social identities – the meanings and pleasures of the program were theirs, not the male producers'.[6] Similarly, Hodge and Tripp have shown how Australian Aboriginal children have made American westerns into their cultural capital.[7] They constructed a cultural category, a tool to think with, that included them, American Indians, and American blacks in a way that enabled them to find in the western some articulation of their subordination to white imperialism and, presumably, to identify with instances of resistance to it. Such a reading position will, we may predict, affect the sense they make of the inevitability of the final narrative defeat of the Indians or non-whites. It was their ability to make a non-white sense from, and find non-white pleasures in, a genre of white imperialism and colonialism that made it popular with them. Without this ability to be the producers of their own culture, the makers of their own meanings and pleasures, it would be difficult to account for Aboriginals' choosing to watch westerns.

This freedom of the viewer to make socially pertinent meanings and pleasures out of television is considerable. Tulloch and Moran found that school students in working-class and middle-class areas made completely different sense out of an episode of the Australian soap *A Country Practice* which dealt with youth unemployment.[8] The working-class students articulated it with their social experience and found in it the sense that the economic system was at fault in not providing enough jobs for the people. The middle-class students, on the other hand, found meanings that supported the system and placed the blame upon the failures of the (working-class) individuals: for them the unemployed were the undereducated, and the episode's meanings for them were produced by the socially derived discourses of class, education, and economics that they brought to bear upon it. A group of Arab viewers in Katz and Liebes' study of different ethnic group readings of *Dallas* found it incompatible with their own culture that Sue Ellen, escaping with her baby from her husband, should return to her father; so they "rewrote" it in their conversation about the program, making her return to her former lover, not to her father.[9] Of course, this freedom is inherent in all popular art, not just television: Michaels, for instance, has found that Aboriginal viewers of *Rambo*, who derived great pleasure from the movie, "rewrote" considerable areas of it.[10] They found pleasure in Rambo's conflict with authority (presumably his Hispanic, non-white appearance, his verbal inarticulateness, and his opposition to the white officer class will have helped here), but could find neither sense nor pleasure in his "patriotic," nationalistic motivation. Instead they constructed for him a tribal or family motivation by inserting him into an elaborate kinship network with those he was rescuing, which enabled them to make sense of the movie in a way that paralleled the way they made sense of their social relations both with each other and with white power. The fact that the film was a favorite with both Ronald Reagan and Australian Aboriginals must not lead us to assume any affinity between the two, nor between the meanings and pleasures that each produced from the same cultural commodity.

The (usually) scatological versions of television commercial jingles produced by school children provide an extreme example of this "rewriting" process which is itself typical.[11] Most viewers of course do not need to rewrite television to this extent to find pleasurable meanings in it, but these examples demonstrate that the freedom is there; they are not a distinct form of perverse or aberrant viewing, but an exaggerated and therefore explicit example of the normal process of making meanings and pleasures from television.

This model differs essentially from that underlying political economy in stressing the relative autonomy of the cultural economy from the financial to which political economy traditionally grants considerable, if not total, determinate power. The political economy model is thus unable to progress beyond seeing the audience as a commodity, or in defining it other than in market terms, those of demographic headcounting. Equally it cannot conceive of the text except as the free lunch that catches the audience for the advertisers. Of course the audience is a commodity, of course the text is a free lunch: but neither definition comes within a mile of adequacy. Political economy cannot conceive of television audiences as being socially diverse and therefore capable of producing different socially pertinent meanings from the same commodity, nor of conceiving of this productive activity as pleasurable. It thus cannot conceive of the cultural commodity as a text that requires reading, and thus as capable of serving the contradictory interests of both the producers in the financial economy and of the viewers in the cultural: it cannot conceive of the text as a site of struggle for the power to make meanings; or of the notion that what finally determines the meanings and pleasures provoked by a text is the social situation of the viewer-reader, *not* the interests of the producers and their ideological investment in consumer capitalism. This leads to another crucial factor in the cultural economy which political economy is unable to take into account, and that is popular discrimination. The people choose to make some texts popular, and some not, and this process of choice is essentially a popular one: however hard the industry may try through market research, promotion, advertising, and scheduling to influence popular choice, its failure rate is enormous. It has thus been forced into producing what Garnham calls a "repertoire" of products from which the public is invited to choose.[12] And it does not know which of its products will be chosen: if it did, it could concentrate on producing a narrower and thus more profitable repertoire. As it is, twelve out of thirteen records fail to make a profit, as do the vast majority of films on their cinema release. Television shows are regularly axed in mid-run. Political economy cannot conceive of any audience activity that opposes the interests of the producers, whether this activity be one of semiosis or of discrimination.

My position differs from that of political economy in locating at least equal, if not greater, power in the cultural economy. The interests of the financial economy would be best served by producing and reproducing the smallest number of hit products: the cultural needs of the constantly shifting alliances of its audiences force the industry into its constant search for products that have enough originality to meet these shifts, but yet retain enough familiarity to meet both the audience expectations and developed competencies, and the routinized production practices of the producers. The major drive for innovation and change comes from the audience activity in the cultural economy, and from the relationship of this activity to larger movements in the political and social system. Television's rehabilitation of Vietnam in shows like *Magnum PI*, *Simon and Simon*, or *The A-Team* has participated in the 1980s shift of American values to the Reaganite masculine right, but did not originate it. Similarly, shows like *Designing Women*, *Golden Girls*, and *Cagney and Lacey* are part of the redefinition of gender meanings, but the spur to redefine them came from the changing material conditions of women. In both cases, it was the cultural economy's dialectic relationship with the socio-political system at the level of the meanings of social experience that fed into the financial economy and caused the economic success and therefore the reproduction of these genres. Theorizing the audience as commodity blinds us to the subtleties and complexities of these social forces.

Of course the audiences' freedom and ability to make their socially pertinent meanings out of television's text, even though these meanings may be beyond both the prediction and the control of the producers, is, at one level, exactly what the producers want: they neither know nor care what meanings and pleasures their audiences produce, their concern is solely with the headcount and the demographics. But only a tiny proportion of audience members are converted into purchasers or even potential purchasers. We must be chary of singular definitions of such multifarious (and ultimately untenable) categories as text and audience. Just as television's textuality can simultaneously serve the economic needs of its producers and the cultural pleasures of its audiences, however oppositional these functions may be to each other, so the audience can, at one and the same time, fill the contradictory roles of commodity and cultural producer. Russian Jews, newly arrived in Israel, read *Dallas* as capitalism criticizing itself: such a process can hardly be described as one of commodification.[13] Of course the industry will attempt, often successfully, to produce programs that invite and encourage the audiences' powers as meaning-producers, but their commercial intention can only describe a part and, I would argue, a small part, of the audiences' activities within the cultural economy.

The democracy of the television text

I wish to adapt Barthes' theory of the writerly text by describing television as a "producerly text."[14] A producerly text does not prescribe either a set of meanings or a set of reading relations for the viewer: instead it delegates the production of meaning to the viewer-producer. It differs, however, from the writerly text in that it is not avant-garde and does not shock the reader-writer into learning new discursive competencies in order to read-write it: rather it offers provocative spaces within which the viewer can use her or his already developed competencies.[15]

Television can only offer its viewers the flexibility of its producerliness because of its textual and intertextual characteristics: all of which constitute it as a particularly polysemic medium. I wish to deal with these under four main headings: 1) segmentation and syntagmatic gaps; 2) intertextuality; 3) time and seriality; 4) heteroglossia (many-languagedness). For the purposes of my argument, I will take as read the means by which the dominant ideology is structured into the text as an agent of closure working to oppose polysemy. My attention, then, will be focused on the counterforces of openness and flexibility.

Segmentation and syntagmatic gaps

Williams' famous characterization of television viewing as an experience of "flow" is useful in so far as it stresses television's lack of textual boundaries, but within it he seems to suggest that the consequent contradictions and lack of formal organization are regrettable rather than a positive textual characteristic.[16] Ellis' use of the term "segmentation" is more productive:[17] television's continuous flow is actually fragmented into an often jarring experience of segments in which discontinuity, sequence and contradiction take precedence over continuity, consequence, and unity. Channel switching and zapping merely exaggerate and exploit this characteristic. Segmented texts are marked by abrupt transitions from segment to segment that require active, experienced, televisually literate viewers to negotiate. Abrupt changes from plot to plot in soap operas are, to television illiterates, as confusing as the change from movie to promo. to ad. were for Williams on his first experience of US television. (Television illiterates, of course, are those whose textual experience is of books, movies, or theater where the textual characteristics are quite different from those of television.) The segmentation of television allows for connections between its segments to be made according to the laws of association rather than those of consequence, logic, or cause and effect. They are therefore much looser, much less textually determined, and so offer the viewer more scope to make his or her own connections. They resist textual hierarchization. The differential mode of attention given to television means that the viewer views some segments more intently than others: this is paralleled semiotically by the viewer's ability to give greater significance to some segments than others. Thus Lewis found that viewers of a news story exploited the contradictions between a live insert and the studio narrative framework in a way that accorded semiotic precedence to the insert, even though the textual structure was attempting to subordinate it to the narrative framework and thus to close off many of the meanings that viewers reportedly found in it.[18] The prioritization of some segments over others is performed by the viewers rather than the text.

The segmentation opens up the syntagmatic gaps in television's narrative so that the viewer has to "write" in the connection.[19] The largest, and most obvious of these gaps are those produced by television's seriality. Many authors have shown how, for instance, women viewers of soap opera write their own "scripts" in their heads as they predict the future of the serial, and check these scripts against the ones actually broadcast.[20] This activity and the gossip that it involves generate considerable pleasure, for they involve the viewers in a producerly relationship with the text: the viewers draw upon the same sort of cultural competencies as do the actual scriptwriters – they know the conventions of soap opera, they know the need to appeal to an audience, they know the difference between the soap opera world and the real world, yet know that the connections between the two must be readily available. They adopt a position of equality with the scriptwriters, a position that gives them the right not only to predict future developments, but to attempt to influence them directly by writing to the producers/scriptwriters.[21]

Segmentation not only opens up syntagmatic gaps, it also allows for a wide variety of syntagmatic relations to be made. Williams failed to see that television's apparent unawareness of the contradiction between the syntagmatically related segments of a news story about Indian Civil Rights protests at Wounded Knee and the promos for a cowboys and Indians movie later in the evening were capable of producing a number of possible meanings about Indianness in American society. Similarly, *Dallas* in Malaysia is viewed as pornography by many males. Its syntagmatic relations with the rest of Malaysian television and its intertextual relations with a largely Muslim culture allow its sexuality to provoke a different set of meanings and pleasures from those for many of its American viewers.

Television's syntagmatic gaps and their range of potential syntagmatic relations resist the organizing and controlling forces of its narrative and ideological closure.

Intertextuality

Intertextuality is not a property unique to television but it does work in televisually specific ways. Barthes' notion that culture is a web of intertextuality, that all texts refer only to other texts and never anchor their referral in a final reality, sets up a useful framework from which to start.[22] He alerts us to the idea that represented events and characters can be understood only in terms of their intertextual relations, so that a "killing" on a detective show can only be made sense of in terms of its relations with a murder story on the news or in the newspapers, or other representations in novels, films, theater, fairy stories, and so on. Culture as a web of intertextual meanings recognizes no boundaries of genre or medium. Similarly, the "wronged mother" is an intertextual figure. Intertextuality of this sort is not the fleshing out of the meanings of one text by references to others, but rather a meaning potential that exists in the spaces between texts, a cultural resource bank that texts and readers can draw from and contribute to equally but differently. Barthes' theory is important because it denies both the uniqueness of the text and its authority to impose its meanings. But this general theory needs to be made more specific if we are to operationalize it in the study of television. I suggest there are four dimensions of intertextuality that require study.

Primary relations

These are the ones elaborated in Barthes' theory. All representational texts and their readers have equal access to this intertextual resource bank and the texts relate not to each other directly, as in the old literary sense of allusion, but indirectly via this intertextual potential. At one level this can deny genre and medium boundaries, at another the concepts of genre and medium act to organize, direct, and thus limit intertextual relations.

Secondary relations

The excessiveness and openness of primary texts in our culture have produced a huge industry of secondary texts that advertise, promote, criticize, and respond to the primary texts of television, film, literature, and so on. Relations between these and the primary texts are direct and specific: secondary texts relate to specified primary ones and these intertextual relations are their sole *raison d'être*. They work to activate certain meanings rather than others, to legitimate certain pleasures rather than others.[23] They can be arranged on a scale that stretches from producer interests at one end to viewer interests at the other. At the first are studio publicity and promotions which can indicate some of the meanings and pleasures which the producers believe their viewers will find and which they hope will help to produce the audiences as commodity.

At the other end are viewers' letters to fan magazines sharing their responses amongst other fans. Somewhere in the middle lie the professional critics who purport to speak for viewers but generally fail because the discourse of formal criticism originates at a social point occupied by only a minority of viewers. More useful and more widely used are the articles which give background or insider information about players, conditions of production, studio business, and so on. All these secondary texts work to activate and often extend the meanings of the primary texts. They are intertextual enablers.

Biographical gossip about soap opera players can indicate some of these intertextual operations. It invites fans to explore the intertextual relations between the representation and the real, or rather between texts of higher and lower modality. The biographies are texts of higher modality than the soap operas themselves, and the "real life" details of the biography of the player can be used to validate or interrogate the verisimilitude of the represented character. They can also provide insight into the mode of production: they give details of the player's acting skill, of his/her hard work, and the conditions under which that work is performed. They provide insider information about players' earnings and contracts, and thus extend the fan's pleasures by extending the primary texts.

Fans will predict the future of a character not only according to their knowledge of the soap opera conventions, but also according to knowledge that only secondary texts can provide – whether the player is pregnant in "real life" or whether she or he is asking for too much money for the next contract. There is also a sense in which those secondary texts provide a "ghost text," like the ghost image on a television set with poor reception, so that viewers of *Cagney and Lacey*, for example, can understand and enjoy both the relationship between the two characters and that between the two players in a complex play of intertextual and intermodal relations between primary and secondary texts that involves a simultaneous surrender to, and distancing from, the illusion of realism. These secondary texts increase the viewer's sense of power over the meanings and pleasures offered by the primary texts because they grant them access to, and thus allow them to participate in, the mode of representation. The pleasure of making meanings is greater by far than that of finding them ready-made.

Oral culture

People talk about television: television is a great promoter of gossip. Katz and Liebes, for instance, argue that part of the popularity of *Dallas* derives from the ease with which its soap opera form enables it to intersect with a variety of oral cultures.[24] People's talk about television is not just a response to it, but is read back into it: our friend's gossip about a program influences our reading of it.

Oral culture is a product of its immediate social formation, so the way that television is talked about provides us with two sorts of clues – clues about how television is being assimilated into the social formation and how that social formation is read back into the text, and clues about which meanings offered by the text are being mobilized in this process. This form of intertextual relations is a bridge between the textual and the social, and is a crucial, if methodologically difficult, area of study.

Methodologically more accessible is a secondary form of this talk, and that is its written form, either in the newsletters and publications of fan clubs or in the letter columns of the press and fanzines. Also methodologically accessible are the verbal responses of viewers to researchers. All of these verbal responses are, of course, not cold data, the verbal equivalent of galvanic skin responses, but texts that require the same sort of theoretical investigation as do the primary texts, and that can only be understood in terms of their intertextual relations with them.

The subject and the social formation

Material social experience is made sense of by textualizing it, by bringing a culture's discursive resources to bear upon it. As argued earlier, reading a social experience parallels reading a text. This does not mean that the reading relations of the two are identical; clearly they are not, because they operate in different modalities. Essential to textual pleasure is an awareness, to whatever extent, of its textuality. The pleasure in playing with the boundary between the represent-ation and the real involves a recognition of their differences as well as of their similarities. Textual experience and social experience are different, but not totally unconnected. The discursive repertoires and competencies that are involved in making sense of each overlap, and inform one another. These discursive resources are also the ones that determine the production of subjectivity, so that the subject is an interdiscursive potential: subjectivity is like textuality, capable of actualization in different forms at different moments. The relations between textual experience, social experience, and subjectivity are perhaps the most methodologically inaccessible; but theoretically and politically, they are amongst the most important of all.

Intertextual relations are almost infinitely complex and diverse. They are activated at the moment of viewing, and the process of viewing can only be described in relation to them. They are inherent neither in the text nor in the viewer, but in their interaction in the cultural process. They are an agent of openness in the text and invite or require considerable semiotic activity from the viewer. Activating them in some ways rather than others is one of the ways in which a viewer exercises "cultural authority" over his or her text by exploiting its producerly potential.

Time, seriality, and semiotic democracy

Television's lack of "authority" over its viewers, its democratic delegation of so many of the meaning-making functions, points us to another set of textual characteristics. One of these is television's "liveness" or "nowness."[25] Television's world appears to be occurring in the same time as the world of the viewer. Novels and movies are records of the past – we know that the end of the narrative has already been written as we watch or read the opening scenes, but in television serials, at least, the future appears to be as unwritten as our own. This sets up the empowering reading relations that I have already noted in which viewers feel they have both the right and the ability to influence the future narrative. Television has no author in the sense of authority.

Television's nowness and its lack of textual authority are closely allied. Its attempt to present itself as "live" is a recognition that "liveness" is a normative and defining characteristic which sets up specific reading relations. Suspense in sport or in game shows is quite different if they are seen as "live" rather than recorded, and the hermeneutic engagement of the viewers is changed. They are not engaged in solving enigmas and predicting narrative outcomes that a power-ful author-role has already experienced and resolved, but are rather invited to experience the suspense and its anxious uncertainty as less mediated, more direct, and thus more open to their own inflections of it. Similarly, the hermeneutic engagement of the viewer of soap opera, with its sense of an unwritten future, is different from that of the cinema spectator or novel reader. The "liveness" of quiz shows like *The Dating Game* or *Perfect Match* invites viewers to bring their own social expertise of pairing people off, or of reading into people from inadequate clues, and to measure this expertise against that of the contestants in a much freer way than if the shows had been presented as a record of who chose whom and for which reasons. The apparent coincidence of the time frames of the show and of the viewers resists the closure inherent in an already written text.

At a micro level, this authorial absence works much less obviously. The speed with which television has to be produced makes it less well "crafted" than, for instance, film. But this lack of craftsmanship is also a lack of authorial intervention: for instance, the absence of post-production in soap operas may, in the financial economy, be simply explained in terms of costs and returns, but in the cultural economy its meanings are quite different. The result is that actions on the screen take place in the same time scale as "reality": they cannot, in the editing process, be speeded up by having "dead" bits removed. This helps the impression that the events on the screen are happening "now" and are not an authored account of events in the past.

The "nowness" of news, like that of sport, takes a different form, but has similar effects. The author-figure of news is explicit, there on the screen, telling us what has happened. Because his or her authorial status is explicit, it is therefore challengeable and, often, challenged. The live "inserts," however controlled they may be by the conventional narrative structure of the news story and the bulletins of which it is a part, rarely fit perfectly into the ideological slot prepared for them. There are always rough edges, unresolved contradictions that intransigently resist the explicit authorship of the bulletin. Television news is the result of a constant struggle between authorial control and a sense of an unwritten, unruly set of events that resist this control. The haste with which news has to be produced means that its authorial control is both visible and inefficient. The contradictions between the "voice of authority" and "the imperative of the real" keep news and sport well within television's producerly mode.

In sport this is explicit. Sports commentary is the authored text that exists simultaneously with the "events" it is writing about: the opportunity for viewers to "produce" their own scripts is openly offered and, frequently, eagerly accepted. The constant flow of background and statistical information, of slow motion replays, of replays from different angles and distances, gives the viewers the insider information and therefore the power to make meanings that is normally the cultural property of the author to be released in controlled doses to the reader. The authorial function of the commentators invites, and frequently receives, oppositional challenges from the viewers and television, along with a host of secondary texts, provides the material upon which such challenges depend. This insider information is similar to that given by fan magazines. It works similarly in that it increases the viewer's awareness of the constructedness of the text and, thus, encourages a producerly relation to it. Access to the mode of representation is an important source of pleasure for the literate readers whom producerly texts demand: and today's television viewers are, of course, exceptionally televisually literate. Again the reading relations of television tend toward a democracy rather than an autocracy.

Television's seriality works to underpin these closely allied appearances of nowness and unwrittenness, for, like them, it works with a sense of a future which denies closure. However completely the plot of one episode is closed off, the situation never is. All television series have some characteristics of serials – the relationships between the characters and the possibilities of the basic situation are never completed or resolved, but remain open, reverberating, and ready for reactivation next week. In action and detective series, the sense of an author, of the writtenness of the text, may be much stronger than in many other television genres, and the "nowness" of the action much less in evidence, but television's tension between the forces of closure and of openness, between authorial and viewer authority, still remains central to the textual experience they offer. It is also pushing them to develop contradictory ways of foregrounding their own constructedness, a point I shall return to in the next section.

Heteroglossia

Television's segmentation and its democratic delegation of semiosis make it necessarily heteroglossic, and its heteroglossia is a precondition for its semiotic democracy and its segmentation. Unity, continuity, and consequence are textual signs of an author function whose authority is exerted in the creation of a comparatively stable, comparatively uncontradictory, locus from which to make sense of the text and of the world that we are invited to experience through it. This author function, of course, must not be reduced to an individual author: it is often performed by institutional conventions and practices, and finally is a discursive practice in an Althusserian model of ideology. But however this authorial function is characterized, it is essentially a force toward homogeneity.

The diversity of television's modes of reception, the diversity of social formations within which it may be viewed, and the diversity of cultural systems and subsystems with which its meanings will be connected require us to understand television in terms of diversity and difference rather than of unity and homogeneity. It is a diversity of voices which resist any authorial hierarchization, but which can be listened to differentially by different viewers and hierarchized differently at different moments of viewing. Different segments can and do speak with different voices, often contradictory ones.

One basic textual characteristic that enables television to speak contradictorily is its semiotic excess. Television's main semiotic energy is, according to Hartley, not in producing meanings, but in policing and controlling the excess of meaning it cannot help producing.[26] Fiske argues that the excess allows television first to offer the meanings preferred by the dominant forces, but that the overspill of such meaning allows for resisting or at least evasive meaning to escape this control; and Feuer argues it allows for the viewer to produce a counter-text.[27] By exceeding the norms, television draws attention to them and to their ideological function, and by doing so opens up the possibility for contradictory meanings and pleasures to be made. One of Ang's subjects was a Marxist who found in the excessiveness of *Dallas* a critique of capitalism; another was a feminist who used its excess of sexist display to produce oppositional, and vocally expressed, pleasures.[28] Elsewhere I have argued that devices such as irony, metaphor, and jokes depend upon a collision of discourses that generates more meaning potential than any authorial function can control: they depend upon contradictions within segments rather than between them, a micro-level heteroglossia.[29] Television's recent tendency to self-reflexivity, the explicit acknowledgment of its textuality, is a good example of this collision of discourses and the way it delegates semiotic power to the viewers. When characters in shows like *Moonlighting* refer to the writers or walk off the set, when *Miami Vice* breaks the 180-degree rule and draws attention to its stylistic devices, or when *Magnum PI* is shot partially in black and white in an explicit reference to *film noir*, television is setting up contradictions with its own realistic mode: it is simultaneously inviting and shattering the illusion of realism. It is significant that this tendency is clearest in those television genres that are most "authored," closest to a novel or film, for in these realistic fictional genres television has had to devise different methods from those of sport or news by which to draw attention to its authorial authority, to demystify it, and, thus, to allow the viewer access to it in a producerly way. The "willingness" of realism's "willing suspension of disbelief" is central to the pleasures of viewing, those producerly pleasures of access to the process of representation, and the reading position that this access promotes. This playful toying with the boundary between our sense of the representation and of the real exploits the final contradiction in popular art forms which depend, at least in part, upon realism's request to willingly suspend disbelief, and it is a necessary contradiction for television to exploit. For realism is essentially a unifying, closing strategy of representation, it is necessarily authoritarian. But the pleasures of television are democratic, to be found in its diversity, so the fracture of realism, the inclusion of the viewer into the process of representation is necessary if television is to be popular in a heterogeneous society.

Of course, television viewers realized this long before its producers. Women viewers of soap opera have long been adept at playing with this boundary between the representation and the real.[30] Their oft-chronicled and oft-derided belief in the represented characters as "real" people is not only a knowing self-delusion entered into to increase their pleasure, but is also one they are able to extricate themselves from at will, particularly at the first sign of displeasure.[31]

It is typically accompanied by a critical awareness of the conventions of soap opera, and of its conditions of production. There is a pleasure in playing with television's textuality, in exploiting one's ability to submit oneself to, and to distance oneself from, its illusion of reality that is finally a democratic one, for it allows the viewer both control of reading relations and access to the process of representation.

Pleasure, semiosis, and difference

The relationship between pleasure and meaning needs to be rethought. Universalistic notions of pleasure derived from psychoanalytic theory do not get us very far in understanding something as diverse as television. Similarly, notions of *jouissance* and affective pleasure require an intensity of viewing and a loss of subjectivity that do not accord with television's typical modes of reception. Television is not an orgasmic medium. Any theory of televisual pleasure must be able to account for both the diversity of the televisual experience and the activity of the viewers within it: it must derive from the social heterogeneity of viewers and of moments of viewing, and from a notion of television textuality as delegated semiosis, what we may call its semiotic democracy.

The pleasures of television lie not just in the meanings it provokes, but also in the access it offers viewers to the process of representation itself. This invites them to adopt a producerly reading relation to its textuality that is necessary if they are to produce from it meanings and pleasures that are subculturally pertinent to them. This producerly relation to the text is a non-subjected one that is a precondition for pleasure. It has its parallel, too, in the world of the social, for it is discursively similar to the subject's process of making sense of social experience and of the social system that provides the conditions for that experience; this process, of course, involves also making sense of our own subjectivity. For this process to be pleasurable there must be some sense of control over at least part of it, some sense of participation in it, and certainly no sense of being excluded from it. There is no pleasure in being totally subjected by the social system or in being made a "cultural dope" by a text.[32] Semiotic democracy entails the subject's power to participate in and inflect meanings of text, social experience, and subjectivity.

The power inherent in this process is both pleasurable and political. But of course it is not undetermined or limitless. Power can only exist in the experience of resistance: democracy is only necessary (or pleasurable) in the face of autocratic forces. The power and the pleasure of making one's own subculturally pertinent meanings out of television can only exist in recognition that opposing semiotic forces are at work in the text. The process of making meanings out of television involves the recognition of authorial, centralizing lines of semiotic force against which the viewer-produced, decentered, democratic meanings are opposed. The centripetal-centrifugal metaphor is a useful one here: the pleasures of television are diverse, around the circumference, and can exist only in unstable, shifting moments of balance with the opposing centripetal forces that seek to center, unify, and provide ready-made meanings. But the model works in both ways. Television expects to be disagreed with: its centripetal forces depend upon centrifugal ones.

This viewer-disagreement, this viewer-challenge, goes beyond the challenge to the meanings that television offers and becomes pleasurable when it becomes a challenge to the power to make meanings. This is when it also becomes political. For the power to make meanings, albeit within conditions not of our own making, is the power to be different. This power to be different can only be understood as power if it is seen in relations of resistance to homogenizing forces. In a liberal pluralistic model of society there is neither power nor threat in social difference; consequently social differences are seen as contributing to social harmony and stability rather than as motors for social change. The social model I prefer is one that characterizes the agencies of social power as working hegemonically to minimize the awareness of social differences, to construct a common sense of social relations that emphasizes harmony and commonality. The power to be different, then, is a resistive power and one that keeps alive the possibility of social change.

Any social system requires a system of meanings to underpin it, to stabilize it, or destabilize it. Popular television can never have a direct radical or subversive effect and it is fruitless to propose that it ought to. However many feminist readings and pleasures women may find in soap opera, the viewing experience *of itself* will never bring them out on the streets in anti-patriarchal revolution. The domains of entertainment and of politics are simply not interconnected along such direct, cause-and-effect channels. But neither is each domain completely autonomous from the other.

The domain of entertainment deals in the interior pleasures of the meanings of texts, of self, and of social relations; any resistance within it is semiotic, not social. Semiotic resistance may not pass beyond the world of the interior, but this does not invalidate it. Angela McRobbie argues that fantasy is a private, intimate experience which can be part of a strategy of resistance or opposition for it constitutes an area that cannot be finally colonized and is, paradoxically, as real an experience as "baby sitting or staying in to do the washing."[33]

The power to think differently from the way preferred by the structures of dominance has a political dimension, even if the meanings produced by such thought remain interior and are not circulated subculturally. The political effectiveness of the minority whose resistance takes the form of organized social action depends upon the support of a grass-roots body of the people who are thinking similarly resistant thoughts. Though this semiotic resistance need not translate into direct political resistance, it can, even if the politics is that of the family rather than the state. Seiter *et al.* found a soap opera fan whose pleasure in a woman character's extramarital affair translated into a direct, if playful, challenge to her husband.[34] Radway found similarly that some women readers of romance novels found that their reading gave them the increased self-confidence to stand up to and oppose the patriarchal power in their marriages.[35] The difference between semiotic resistance and socio-political resistance is not at all clearly defined: the interior is, to coin a phrase, the political.

The origins of social change do not lie in cultural representations, but in material social conditions. Cultural representations obviously have an important role to play in the meanings they can provoke people to make of these social conditions, and television can and does participate to an extent in offering progressive, if not radical, meanings. But I would argue that television's political effectivity and its progressive potential lie rather in its ability to devolve the power to make meanings rather than in any alternative meanings it may offer. Its delegated semiosis encourages the production of semiotic differences which in turn enable social differences to be maintained.

Not all social differences are subjected to the forces of homogenization in the same way. Racial differences, for instance may, as in *The Cosby Show*, be "whitened" or homogenized (I suspect, in the absence of direct evidence, that it offers more pleasurable meanings of race to whites than it does to blacks), or they may be largely ignored, or written out of the system. This may result in such groups not watching television (Morley found that unemployed black girls did not watch *Nationwide* because it offered them nothing[36]) or, if they choose to watch they become ingenious almost to the point of deviousness in finding black pleasures and meanings in white texts – witness the Aboriginal readers of *Rambo* and westerns quoted above. Gans discovered different oppositional reading relations amongst Boston's Italian community in the 1960s.[37] Young males would enjoy jeering at white Anglo-Saxon television heroes in a way that gave them pleasure and empowerment in their sense of ethnic difference: these were not the pleasures of accommodation to the dominant, but of the subordinate asserting their pride in their difference. Oppressed and silenced groups will only enjoy television which offers them the opportunity to participate in this semiotic democracy with its ability to empower the subordinate by providing the opportunity of making resisting meanings of text, society, and subjectivity, and thus to provide a sense of self-confidence in the subordinate that enables their maintenance of social difference, their resistance to the hegemonizing, incorporating process of homogenization.

Television's heteroglossia reproduces social heterogeneity. The contradiction between television's status as an authored text and its apparent unwrittenness that allows the viewer access to the authorial role of making meanings reproduces the struggles for power and (semi-)autonomy in a capitalist democracy. Social change can only be motivated by a sense of social difference, and television, far from being the agent of homogenization that pessimists in the past have feared, is more productively understood as an enabler, if not an active agent, of diversity and difference.

Critical intervention

Television's textuality is not bounded by the titles and credits of a program, subjectivity cannot be confined within the skin or history of an individual, and similarly viewing television cannot be confined to the periods when the set is switched on. Television is not only part of the process of viewing, or reading or talking about it, but it is also part of our cultural lives when its presence is less direct, less obvious. We need to investigate ways in which a television fan watches movies in a cinema or attends a live ballgame: we need to probe how a middle-aged fan of *Miami Vice* makes sense of his own shabby dress. Television is part of family relations and family politics, it is part of gender relations and politics, part of consumer relations and politics. Again, a comprehensive map of all the cultural processes, of which television viewing is only one, is both impossible and unnecessary. What is needed is the investigation of instances that are no more and no less typical than other instances. And the emphasis should be not on what people do, not on what their social experience is, but on how they make sense of it. Their recorded words and behaviors are not data giving us their reactions and meanings, but instances of the sense-making process that we call culture, clues of how this process works and can be actualized.

The ability of the critic to intervene in the politics of popular culture, to counter the forces of domination and support those of resistance or evasion, depends upon a far more sympathetic and detailed understanding of the cultural economy than we have so far achieved. The traditional critical emphasis from the left has focused upon the power of the industry and upon the power of ideology and hegemony. This has led us to locate the appropriate sites of intervention in the processes of production and representation. A more effective, if methodologically much more difficult, focus for intervention might be the diversity of sites of reception, but instrumental simplicity should not be the only factor in our choice of appropriate political action.

The main problem facing the critic today is to understand popular pleasures and popular discrimination, and on the basis of this understanding to decide how and if to intervene in both the production and reception of texts. It may be that open heteroglossic texts such as *Dallas* (which Altman characterizes as a "menu" from which viewers choose[38]) are actually socially and politically more progressive than more closed, monoglossic texts, even ones that prefer more apparently progressive meanings. The progressiveness of popular television may lie in heteroglossic programs that not only promote the dominant ideology but that also offer opportunities to resist, oppose, and evade it. As yet, we just do not know.

We can only find out by paying more attention to the moments of reception for only here can we determine which texts and which characteristics of those texts offer their polysemy for semiotic mobilization by the subordinate, and how these semiotic differences are produced and circulated subculturally. We also need to discover why some members of subordinated groups are more productive or more resistant viewers than others. The critic can only intervene effectively on the basis of adequate understanding, and on the basis of a deep respect for the pleasure that the subordinate make from their popular culture. It may seem unfortunate that it is commercially motivated mainstream television that is best able to offer these pleasures, but possibly the commercial imperative has brought its producers to a closer relationship with popular social experience than the more distantly theorized political-moral-aesthetic position of those with both a social conscience and a social power has been able to achieve.

The question facing progressive critics may now need reversing: rather than asking how it is that the culture industry makes people into commodities that serve its interests, we should now be asking how it is that the people can turn the products of the industry into *their* popular culture and can make them serve *their* interests.

Social differences are produced by the social system but the meanings of these differences are produced by culture: the sense of them has to be constantly produced and reproduced as part of the subject's experience of these differences. Viewer-driven meanings made from texts and subculturally driven meanings made of social experience involve the pleasures of producing meanings rather than the subjection of being produced by them, and make it possible to maintain a consciousness of those abrasive, uncomfortable social differences that hegemonic common sense works so hard to smooth over.

And television plays a crucial role in this; though it is produced by the culture industry and bears within it the lines of hegemonic force, it is met by the tactics of the everyday. De Certeau argues that social power and the power to make meanings that serve the interests of the dominant work strategically, that is, they work in the manner of an occupying army, in a massively organized structure of power.[39] But they are met by the tactics of guerrilla warfare, by tactical, fleeting raids upon their weak points which are not organized into any master plan, but which exploit the particularities and possibilities of each tactical moment. According to de Certeau, "people make do with what they have," and in the heavily bureaucratized and industrialized society of late capitalism, what people have is what is provided for them by the institutions and industries of capitalism. It is through these that the social strategy is put into practice, but its effectivity must not be read simply from its intent or from the strength of the forces at its disposal. It is not only the US army in Vietnam and the Soviet army in Afghanistan that have been unable to devise a strategy to beat guerrilla tactics. What we need to investigate, after de Certeau's provocative theorizing, is the everyday tactical, and therefore pleasurable, uses of these cultural resources (albeit industrially produced), the everyday deployment of the tactics of evasion, expropriation, and resistance.

The links between semiotic power/resistance/pleasure and the maintenance of resistive social differences, the role of television in this, and the part that all this can play in social change are theoretically arguable. What I would like to see is the methodologically daunting project of tracing actual instances of these links being made, of these processes being actualized, of the delineation of the multitude of cultural processes at work in the different moments of viewing television.

Notes

1   Lawrence Grossberg, "The In-Difference of Television," *Screen* 28, no. 2 (spring 1987): 28-46.
2   Lawrence Grossberg (ed.) "On Postmodernism and Articulation: An Interview with Stuart Hall," *Journal of Communication Inquiry* 10, no.2 (summer 1986): 45-60.
3   Robert Hodge and David Tripp, *Children and Television* (Cambridge: Polity Press, 1986). *Prisoner*, (screened in the US under the title *Prisoner – Cell Block H*) is an Australian soap opera set in a women's prison. Hodge and Tripp (p.49) found that school students identified many similarities between school students and prisoners:

1   pupils are shut in;
2   pupils are separated from their friends;
3   pupils would not be there if they were not made to be;
4   pupils only work because they are punished if they do not and it is less boring than doing nothing at all;
5   pupils have no rights; they can do nothing about an unfair teacher;
6   some teachers victimize their pupils;
7   there are gangs and leaders amongst the pupils;
8   there are silly rules which everyone tries to break.

These similarities enable *Prisoner* to provide the students with an imaginative "language" with which to think through their experience of powerlessness in the school. The meanings of subordination were those of the subordinate, not of the dominant, and there is evidence that students found these meanings both pleasurable and empowering.
4   *Sale of the Century* and *Prisoner* were both "articulations" of school in that both could be linked with school and could be used differently to "speak," or make sense of, the school experience. See John Fiske, *Television Culture* (London and New York: Methuen, 1987).
5   Pierre Bourdieu, "The Aristocracy of Culture," *Media, Culture, and Society* 2, no. 3 (July 1980): 225-54.
6   Dorothy Hobson, *"Crossroads" : The Drama of a Soap Opera* (London: Methuen, 1982).
7   Hodge and Tripp, *Children and Television*.
8   John Tulloch and Albert Moran, *"A Country Practice" : 'Quality Soap'* (Sydney: Currency Press, 1986).
9   Elihu Katz and Tamar Liebes, "Mutual Aid in the Decoding of *Dallas*: Preliminary Notes from a Cross-Cultural Case Study," in Phillip Drummond and Richard Paterson (eds) *Television in Transition*, (London: British Film Institute, 1985), pp. 187-98.
10   Eric Michaels, "Aboriginal Content: Who's Got it – Who Needs it" (paper presented at the Australian Screen Studies Association Conference, Sydney, December 1986).

11   Fiske, *Television Culture*; e.g. Sydney children in 1982 and 1983 were singing their version of a Tooheys beer commercial: "How do you feel when you're having a fuck, under a truck, and the truck rolls off? I feel like a Tooheys', I feel like a Tooheys', I feel like a Tooheys' or two" (Children's Folklore Archives, Australian Studies Centre, Curtin University).

12   Nicholas Garnham, "Concepts of Culture: Public Policy and the Cultural Industries," *Cultural Studies* 1, no.1 (January 1987): 23–37.

13   See Tamar Liebes and Elihu Katz' chapter in this volume, pp. 204–22.

14   Roland Barthes, *Writing Degree Zero* (New York: Hill & Wang, 1977).

15   Fiske, *Television Culture*.

16   Raymond Williams, *Television: Technology and Cultural Form* (London: Fontana, 1974).

17   John Ellis, *Visible Fictions: Cinema Television Video* (London: Routledge & Kegan Paul, 1982).

18   Justin Wren-Lewis, "Decoding Television News," in Drummond and Paterson, *Television in Transition*, pp. 205–34.

19   Robert C. Allen, *Speaking of Soap Operas* (Chapel Hill: University of North Carolina Press, 1985).

20   See, e.g., Charlotte Brunsdon, "Writing about Soap Opera," in Len Masterman (ed.) *Television Mythologies: Stars, Shows and Signs*, (London: Comedia, 1986), pp. 82-7; Tulloch and Moran, *Country Practice*; and Fiske, *Television Culture*.

21   Tulloch and Moran, *Country Practice*.

22   Roland Barthes, *S/Z* (London: Cape, 1975).

23   Tony Bennett, "The Bond Phenomenon: Theorizing a Popular Hero," *Southern Review* 16, no.2 (1983): 195–225.

24   Katz and Liebes, "Mutual Aid."

25   Stephen Heath and Gillian Skirrow, "Television: A World in Action," *Screen* 18, no. 2 (summer 1977): 7-59; Jane Feuer, "The Concept of Live Television: Ontology versus Ideology," in E. Ann Kaplan (ed.) *Regarding Television*, (Frederick, Md.: University Publications of America, 1983), pp. 12–22.

26   John Hartley, "Encouraging Signs: TV and the Power of Dirt, Speech and Scandalous Categories," in W. Rowland and B. Watkins (eds) *Interpreting Television: Current Research Perspectives* (Beverly Hills, Calif.: Sage, 1984), pp. 119–41.

27   Fiske, *Television Culture*; Jane Feuer, "Melodrama, Serial Form and Television Today," *Screen* 25, no. 1 (January-February 1984): 4–16.

28   Ien Ang, *Watching "Dallas": Soap Opera and the Melodramatic Imagination* (London and New York: Methuen, 1985).

29   John Fiske, "Television: Polysemy and Popularity," *Critical Studies in Mass Communication* 3, no. 4 (December 1986): 200–16.

30   Hobson, *Crossroads*, and Ang, *Watching "Dallas"*.

31   John Davies, "The Television Audience Revisited" (paper presented at the Australian Screen Studies Association Conference, Brisbane, 1984); and Fiske, *Television Culture*.

32   Stuart Hall, "Notes on Deconstructing 'The Popular,'" in Robert Samuel (ed.) *People's History and Social Theory* (London: Routledge & Kegan Paul, 1981), pp. 227–40.

33   Angela McRobbie, "Dance and Social Fantasy," in Angela McRobbie and Mica Nava (eds) *Gender and Generation* (London: Macmillan, 1984), pp. 130–61.

34   See the chapter by Seiter *et al.* in this volume, pp.223–47.

35   Janice Radway, *Reading the Romance: Women, Patriarchy and Popular Literature* (Chapel Hill: University of North Carolina Press, 1984).

36   David Morley, *The "Nationwide" Audience: Structure and Decoding* (London: British Film Institute, 1980).

37   Herbert Gans, *The Urban Villagers: Group and Class in the Life of Italian Americans* (New York: The Free Press, 1962).

38   Rick Altman, "Television/Sound," in Tania Modleski (ed.) *Studies in Entertainment: Critical Approaches to Mass Culture* (Bloomington: Indiana University Press, 1986), pp. 39–54.

39   Michel de Certeau, *The Practice of Everyday Life* (Berkeley, Calif.: University of California Press, 1984).

Chapter four

Live television and its audiences:

Challenges of media reality[1]

Claus-Dieter Rath

At the end of his televised address to the nation on New Year's Eve 1986, West German Chancellor Kohl asked for God's blessings for 1986. For a while it was not quite clear whether this was due to a lapse or a technical problem. Next day, the first day of 1987, the network apologized and broadcast the correct New Year's address. The prerecorded cassette had been mixed up with the one from the year before. One of the commentators on the glitch wrote:

> Shouldn't we – the people – be upset about being fed with canned material on this dignified and festive occasion? I think it is reasonable to give a live address if one wants to be taken seriously. Besides, it would be the best guarantee against mixing up cassettes, be it intentionally or by stupid mistake.[2]

Live broadcast as a risk factor

This was one of the rare occasions when something went wrong with a prerecorded broadcast. But then, generally speaking, live broadcasts are much more risky both from a technical and from a content point of view. We need of course to distinguish between regular, well-prepared routine live broadcasts and special, out-of-schedule live events. Among the former are sports shows like soccer games, car races, ski competitions, most studio discussions and talk shows, news and public affairs programs, religious services, reports from the stock exchange, some concerts and theater plays, certain game shows on Saturday evenings. The second group includes the coverage of catastrophes, national predicaments, festivities, and public anniversaries, important speeches by political leaders or parliamentary debates, etc. As a rule, events of this second type are mostly broadcast in an improvised way, since they are assumed to be of particular or even urgent interest to the public. The regular program schedule is then abandoned in favor of the rhythm of events.[3]

Live broadcast as a choice in programming

From a technical point of view, live television is no real necessity any more. Since the late 1950s, when AMPEX developed electronic video-recording facilities, preproduction techniques have allowed for an effective control of the television program. Nevertheless, live broadcasts continue to exist just as in the early days of television. Over the last decade they have become more and more appreciated – at least by European audiences and television producers. We find a growing number of live interviews and reports as part of the evening news or of certain public affairs programs. Discussions of the meet-the-press variety, rock concerts (often broadcast in several countries simultaneously or even worldwide), talk shows, and live sports programs are increasingly represented on television. This tendency has actually gone so far that live transmission is presently regarded as a special quality of television. Let us examine some of direct broadcasting's essential dynamics.

Live as an "impure" broadcast

Although the viewer knows that he or she is sharing the event via the eye of the camera, direct broadcasting supports the illusion of one's immediate presence on the scene, the impression that one is an eyewitness. This supposedly direct view occurs almost in real time. Broadcasting time lasts as long as the cameras are running.[4] Thus, the program is put together not by integrating several versions of one take at the editing table, but by the spontaneous development of the events in front of the camera and by the moment-to-moment decisions of the television crew, who often become "actors" on the scene.[5] This is why, in a live broadcast, footage which would have been cut out of a recording will actually get aired. Mistakes – or what are considered such – cannot be erased. The live broadcast is an "impure" broadcast.

The choice of topics

First of all, obviously, the mediated event is chosen among an infinite number of events, since television has, of course, its economic and temporal limitations. Among the major constraints producers work under are the need to make money and the banal but important consideration that the viewers' day has only twenty-four hours. Therefore, selection has to take place, selection among items of information, topics, and images to be put on the air. One of the main criteria for this decision is the degree of topicality of a forthcoming or ongoing event. Its definition determines the placing and timing given to an event – and supposedly the extent of the audience's attention. Live broadcasts based on the assumption of an event's topicality have consequently become eagerly sought-after commodities in the world of television – to the point where public and private television stations compete for them. This race for topicality and the live broadcast not only reflects changes in technology, but, more importantly, also in the social fabric in general and consequently in aesthetics.[6]

Topicality

Approaching topicality[7] phenomenologically, we can describe it by distinguishing between the set of opposites shown in Figure 4.1.

Figure 4.1

Topicality	vs.	Non-topicality
something new, news	vs.	something old, known for a long time
here and now	vs.	experience, tradition
emerging, vanishing	vs.	existing
urgent, imminent, hot	vs.	long-term, boring, lukewarm
alarm, horror	vs.	habit, the habitual
moment	vs.	duration
dynamic	vs.	structure
concrete	vs.	abstract[8]

Essentially, then, topicality is an instrument for producing attention. Or, to turn this around: the individual or a group pays attention to an event as soon as it is marked by special, topical signs, a certain number of which are known in all cultures and to all people: love and death, faithfulness and treachery, existence and danger, power and failure, gain and loss.[9]

Topicality as a social condition

Proneness to topicality varies from one society to another, from one area of life to another, from individual to individual, and from one situation to another. While in static or "cold" (Lévi-Strauss) societies topicality is mainly constituted by cyclical events (rites of hunting and cultivating, of sacrifices, of initiation, of war, etc.), the modern, historical, "hot" societies tend to be permanent generators and consumers of topicality.[10] Among the factors conducive to this dynamization are the process of capitalist industrialization with its overall acceleration of public and private areas of life, changing political power constellations, daily stock exchange quotations, transport conditions in the big cities, news program schedules, special announcements interrupting their rhythms, fashions determining who or what is "in" or "out." But even "hot" societies may have their "colder" and their "hotter" phases (economic crisis, civil war).

The impact of media topicalities

Individuals living in modern societies are in a certain sense subjected to a permanent process of initiation through media topicalities. Media events generate a cultural climate or mood which may become decisive for a period of our lives.

There are three aspects of viewer involvement with television broadcasts. First, physical involvement: it functions via identification with the physical actions of television's actors (sportsmen, game competitors, fighters, dancers, lovers, etc.) as well as with the dynamics of sound-track and of camera movements and montage. Second, linguistic involvement: through the presentation of the event by means of sight and sound (the language of cameras, editing, reporters' commentaries, etc.) the illusion of being there and of sharing the view via the eye of the camera is created. Television thus becomes an electronic network. Third, social and cultural involvement: the spectator is brought into time through a linkage of macro- and micro-practices of power, between the public sphere and private daily life, between the idea of collective life and the rituals of the television viewer.

In a broad sense, the live media event presents a timing which is socially compelling. It guarantees our being in time, our being up to date. We may speak of live television, which thereby functions as an apparatus of synchronization, as an audio-visual implantation into the social body's "interdependence-chains." [11]

Event – story – history

If the journalistic or media-bureaucratic routine is interrupted, this happens, as we have discussed, in the name of a topical event. Since the latter connotes something new, extraordinary, unprecedented, right now emerging, it is viewed in relation to history, in terms of the (future) classification of the event in a historical continuum. Our feeling is one of taking part in a historical event.

If a present or past event is declared to be of historical relevance, it must in some way rise above the everyday chaos of factual details. As a special "point in time"[12] it must be specifically linked to the past and the future. It must also have a special quality of content – a quality that attributes continuity to the plurality of facts and fragments of the "discrete images in time."[13] Thus an event, we may say, is being subjected to the "chronological coding"[14] of historiography. Lévi-Strauss calls historiography "never history but the history-for,"[15] that is, history for an imaginary other – an absent subject like a future viewer, listener or reader, people from other societies, etc. The individual occurrence gets short-circuited into a fictitious historical stream, and the event gains socio-cultural sense. Thus live broadcast narration, with its visual, verbal, and sound commentary, integrates the event into the symbolic order provided by historical and cultural continuity. We are dealing with a process which posits a specific relationship between moment and structure.

Seen from the angle of the viewer, the apparently empty time of his or her everyday life is transformed into full time – time filled by public or publicized events. Life becomes full of supposedly significant events. The viewer becomes part of the social fabric through the sudden impact of the "world outside" upon a moment in his or her memory; in a flash these episodes of "public interest" add fragments to his or her own life story. The viewer's life becomes a story, since what emerges is a holographic social space, an electronic 3-D picture, in which the individual suddenly appears as part of a symbolic structure.[16] More precisely, attending the integration of a topical event, which may happen to be a relatively shocking occurrence, into the symbolic forms of story and history, can help the viewer, via identification, to integrate his or her individually perceived traumas and subjective phantasies into the grids of symbolic, cultural order.[17] In this sense, television broadcasts represent cultural authority – even if they are not considered to be, or labeled as, cultural broadcasts.

We are familiar with this type of extension of our everyday imagination and experience, from participating in festivities or mass events – like national anniversaries, parades, and public trials – from witnessing pickets or street demonstrations or, still in some countries today, executions. The "Hands across America" event which took place in 1986 is a recent example of this type. It is a type which signals affirmation or protest against the established order. Generally speaking, the relationship between maintaining and overthrowing public order which we observe in such traditional mass events appears to be a decisive element of live television.[18]

Television as part of social power-relations

It does not take a sociological training to regard television as an institution of power. A viewer's dissatisfaction with a program will trigger responses such as: "That's what they want to make us believe!"[19]

As an announcement medium and one that provides conformity with the spirit of the time, television combines micro- and macro-practices of power. It is a guiding medium both for those who control a station and for the watching and listening subjects who ensure reality by means of television, by taking it as a guide for their lives.[20] Thus, an essential function of television lies in its capacity for semantic and syntactic mediation, which is independent of the individual program, be it news, political propaganda, or an entertainment show. Therefore the power relation between television and the audience is already operative on the level of its network form. This is not to say that the television institution is necessarily a totalitarian instrument, since

> in itself the exercise of power is not violence; nor is it a consent which, implicitly, is renewable. It is a total structure of actions brought to bear upon possible actions; it incites, it induces, it seduces, it makes easier or more difficult; in the extreme it constrains or forbids absolutely; it is nevertheless always a way of acting upon an acting subject or acting subjects by virtue of their acting or being capable of action. A set of actions upon other actions.[21]

There is a conflict between television and political-economic institutions on the one hand and television and the audience on the other which is often grounded in the concept of "inappropriate" representation of facts, i.e. restrained or exaggerated consideration of an event. Within the social institution of television conflicts may arise, when, for instance, a live-broadcast participant acts unsuitably or is ill-mannered and "the audience" (which might be individuals or representatives of parties or pressure groups) protests by telephone, or an editor or TV director intervenes. The consequences may be the broadcast's immediate interruption or sanctions against those who were in charge of the program (commentators or editors will no longer be in charge of the program or will lose their jobs). It might also happen that the mediated event itself initiates a dynamic which leads to the broadcast's cancellation because of ethical, moral, political or aesthetic considerations (if it deals with obscenity, atrocities, suffering or dying people, scandals, etc.). The need for topicality requires suspense and the extraordinary (extremes, sensations, the exotic, the monstrous, etc.). Not infrequently, television is involved in such a dynamic, because an event's representation must maintain its topical quality (something has to happen) and its "telegeneousness" (i.e. it must be technically and dramaturgically accessible). In its search for the extraordinary, television as a power institution runs the risk of becoming overwhelmed by it. Thus a program could itself become involved in the creation of a scandal by provoking a real drama, directly intervening in the action.[22]

On the other hand, we can observe as well that the mere presence of a station's emblems ("Are you filming for TV or for yourself?") will feed back on to the event. The presence of television cameras will cause the characters who participate in the event to stage themselves for television. We shall return to this point.

In the light of these considerations we are led to focus on a triple set of issues which may be distinguished from one another:

1   the television institution's interrelation with a specific event, i.e. estimation of its topicality, reactions to the event (ignoring, minimizing, dramatizing, blowing it up), considerations about the political, financial, and technical risks of a coverage, the internal limitations of its time grids.
2   the spectator's interrelation with the specific event, i.e. what does the event signify to him or her, does it have a subjective topicality for the spectator?
3   the spectator's interrelation with the television institution, i.e. how does he or she judge the station's way of dealing with the event by symbolizing and codifying it, by showing and telling what is "reality"?

Showing and telling the event

It would be wrong to assume that the live/non-live opposition has anything to do with the reality/fiction opposition or with the realism/*mise-en-scène* dichotomy. Without any doubt the event at the scene can be falsified by the broadcast. Live editing has at its disposal not only the whole range of camera techniques and sound engineering but also a large variety of advanced electronic devices (like picture and lettering inserts, acoustical and color effects, etc.) to manipulate image and sound.

Needless to say, what we get to see on a live broadcast has already been prepared and selected by live-editing on the control monitors. It has been scanned and given a rhythm; the camera people and the speakers have already commented on the event.

For Umberto Eco live television is "an improvised report."[23] The director tries to impose an order on an amorphous situation. It is his or her job to tell a story by interweaving diverse elements. Relying on organization, choice of elements, and their composition, tonality, and style, the director has to blend qualitatively and quantitatively different kinds of event sequences. The result may be an exciting drama, but it will always be the director's symbolization or interpretation. "The producer's choice becomes a composition, a narration, a discursive reunion of images, analytically detached from the context of an entire series of simultaneous and overlapping events."[24] What intervenes between the event and its representation is the order of discourse to which television producers are subjected.[25]

Live suspense

What live broadcasts share with other program types, such as television features or fictional series, is their dramatic intensity. "Action" and "drama," of course, are aesthetic concepts deriving in their audio-visual form from the theater and the cinema, and as such they have to be constructed. Therefore, the dramatic quality of fictional programs may be much higher than that of direct broadcasting. But "live" television adds another dimension to these characteristics: like dramatic incidents on the street or in the family, "live" television is endowed with the special notion of an encounter with the "real." Its particular attraction lies in the promise of the unforeseeable. An example is the tragic Brussels 1986 soccer game with its panic scenes and the succeeding slaughter right in front of the cameras.

"Live" is in opposition to "canned," "recorded" – just as fresh food stands in contrast to canned food. But as fresh food is not the same as raw food, a live event is not the same as the "real." It is rather a symbolic approach to the "real." As René Magritte put it:

> The mystery is obviously something unrecognizable, which is to say that it is not representable, either iconographically or symbolically. Thus I am not looking for a representation of the mystery but for pictures of the visible world, which are united in an order that evokes the mystery.[26]

If, then, the unforeseeable breaks into the "live" broadcast, the representation will tend to destroy – at least for an instant – television's firmly established symbolic order. In this instance, something gets out of control, and often the authority is not able to stamp the event with its symbols; for a split second we find ourselves in a non-legal space. Here, at the outer edge of the symbolic, a moment of horror is constituted. The viewers then judge the unfolding discourse or even the speechlessness of the media agent according to what they perceive in sight and sound about that particular instance. They judge whether or not the right words are found, whether an adequate *mise-en-scène* is constructed, thus reintegrating the event into the specific symbolic, cultural order.

Topicalities and (pseudo-)myths

Although eagerness for topical events – as stories – is an effect of the historical invention of the electronic media and, even before, of the press and cinema, its origins lie beyond them, in a socio-cultural shift that took place in the course of the twentieth century.

In 1933, the cultural philosopher Walter Benjamin pointed out the gradual decline of "experience": after the disturbing experiences of the First World War and inflation, the transmission of the human heritage from generation to generation – expertise, maxims, various forms of knowledge as an aid for the single subject acting in and interpreting the world – was no longer decisive.[27] Under the impact of these shocking historical events, traditional wisdom and experience were superseded by the immediate present, the momentarily meaningful, by topical actuality. What emerged was a specific disposition toward the present moment.[28] This shift from experience to actuality represents, on the one hand, an enormous challenge to and – consequently – change in perception and aesthetics; and on the other, paradoxically, it leads to an invasion of imperative pseudo-myths.

> This tremendous development in technology has brought along an entirely new form of poverty for mankind. And the reverse fact of this poverty is the oppressive wealth of ideas, which has come with the revival of astrology and yoga wisdom, Christian Science and palmistry, vegetarianism and gnosis, scholasticism and spiritualism, and has been spread among – or rather, over – the people. For it is not a case of true revival, but one of galvanization.[29]

The extinction of experience is not synonymous with the extinction of mythical structures. Rather, the extinction of certain types of tradition (i.e. the transfer of experience) can increase the value of others, something which is confirmed by the significance of such phenomena as sensational journalism or human interest stories. Here, each occurrence is presented as a recurrence of certain (sentimental or scandalous) patterns and dynamics – but in the form of a shocking event.

As Benjamin pointed out, referring to the cinema audience's perceptive situation,

> the film is the art form that is in keeping with the increased threat to his life which modern man has to face. Man's need to expose himself to shock effects is his adjustment to the dangers threatening him. The film corresponds to

profound changes in the apperceptive apparatus – changes that are experienced on an individual scale by the man in the street in big-city traffic, on a historical scale by every presentday citizen.[30]

Catching the moment

Live broadcasting attempts to capture the significant moments of an event. This is why it sometimes lasts unbearably long. The climax must be waited for. It is not always possible to increase suspense by presenting images or by the speaker's intervention. Often, "nothing" happens: the soccer game has not started yet, the president of the republic has not yet appeared in front of the waiting crowd to make his declaration, the missile launch has been postponed, latest election results are not yet in. But the cameras transmit images. We are there and we stay there, for the long-awaited "unexpected" could happen in just a moment. This type of expectation can be produced – on different levels and with different intensities – by the hesitation of a quiz candidate, the private confessions of a talk-show guest, star appearances, sports records, speeches to the nation in cases of emergency, or by a possible catastrophe or an assassination attempt during an official state occasion.[31]

What fascinates us, while we are still waiting, is the aura of the "inaccessible," that which can be imagined, yet – due to subjective and social censorship – is not actually perceived. The uncanny is the major characteristic of live television. We, as assumed eyewitnesses, can see the unfolding of the event, perceive what "evokes the mystery," in Magritte's words. What is expected to occur (and what causes the suspense) is a moment of truth.

Let us take as an example the – extraordinary – live coverage of situations in which an individual or a group of people are trapped in a cave or mine, i.e. situations which prohibit visual access. What we wait for in these instances is *evidence*, the visualization of facts. In 1949, Kathy Fiskus' tragic entrapment was commented upon as paradigmatic of television:

> Two television stations, KTTV and KTLA, kept their cameras focussed on the scene continuously for twenty-seven hours. The coverage was set down as a milestone for the medium's development comparable to radio's spectacular performance on the occasion of Floyd Collins' entrapment in Kentucky in 1925.[32]

Of course, hundreds of movies are based on the same situation (calamities in Arctic stations, submarines, hotels, aeroplanes, elevators, etc.), but live television works like an *epiphany*: the appearance of a hidden or lost, a desired object. It may appear from one moment to the next. Will the victim live or die? Who is guilty? Will Mother Earth set her prisoners free? Are there any heroes to snatch the victim from the jaws of death? What we are facing here are facts (birth and death) which can be dealt with in terms of stories. Birth and death cannot "tell themselves" since they are hypolinguistic phenomena, but they have an enormous cultural and subjective value, as we can easily perceive if we examine our birth phantasies or our phantasies of danger, threat, and death. As discourse events they appear in the form of myths, pseudo-myths or narrative stereotypes. Thus, the events themselves acquire the status of topicality, because in a particular socio-political situation they trigger phantasms of universal or at least broad cultural range. They become local, regional, national, or even planetary affairs which we face privately in our cosy living-rooms.

This concept is reinforced by public statements such as those which followed the 1949 incident:

> A little girl was dead. That was the news – just one little girl. Three days ago only a few people knew the name of this little girl. Yesterday there was no one in this country and few in other civilized countries who had not heard of three-year-old Kathy Fiskus of San Marino, California. Millions upon millions followed the heartbreaking story as they did no other news of the day . . . . Yet, even Kathy's father and mother must have felt that something like a miracle of human compassion had taken place. Their little daughter had suddenly become a symbol of something precious in all our lives. Two great world wars and many smaller ones have cost the lives of multitudes.[33]

In this case we can observe how a perhaps not too uncommon incident became a topic of nationwide symbolic meaning. Thus sometimes a private event can become an emblematic affair whose solution symbolically stands for the state of things.

Since live broadcasts are produced for a "mass audience," they don't deal with unique objects for individual viewers. Rather, the specific uniqueness implied here is signified by the collective, simultaneous perception of an event charged with symbolic value. In this sense, we can say that something like a "live aura" exists. It inscribes its audiences into the social order of what can be called the "television community."

Acting audiences

The most heterogeneous kinds of "media events" are projected into our living room: partly simulations or deceptions, partly real events whose procedures are oriented toward television broadcasting.[34] Small-scale events which are inaccessible to the "masses" and "insignificant" are blown up into media events, thereby transforming themselves.

There are different ways for viewers to participate from their living-room armchairs: they can express their approval or disapproval of a particular topic in a television discussion by simply dialing a certain telephone number, an action which will immediately register on the screen, or they can express their own opinion directly in some broadcasts by passing on information to them.[35] These real-time interventions, by the way, work also as a kind of guarantee of simultaneity.

Sometimes, the public may even act directly at the scene. It may be present as an applauding audience in the studio or perhaps one individual may participate in an entertainment show or ask critical questions in a political feature. Occasionally, the audience takes matters into its own hands: after a reported accident the audience may become curious and rush to the scene.

This is illustrated by the following example. In the early summer of 1981 in Vermicino, near Rome, a little boy fell into an uncovered well. For two days and two nights Italian television devoted three channels to uninterrupted reporting of the rescue work which failed. The entire nation (including the press) followed the developments. Attracted by the broadcasts, new actors thronged to the site, claiming to be "saviors": alpinists, speleologists, acrobats, and contortionists, all took turns to be roped down into the well to attempt to grasp the child. Each of these actors thus played a role in this macabre live-television show.[36] Significantly it happened at a time of national political-economic crisis. Therefore, as in the 1949 example, "saving the child" also meant saving one's own way of live.

As a new geographic entity, a sovereign "state," with its own guarantors, the "space of the broadcast media" cuts across the geographies of power and social life which together define national or cultural space. New modes of ordering reality emerge at the push of a button: the world of television language, television geography, television community. Television thus can *create* social reality, an ability of a quite different order from merely improving family or community life. What is decisive is not merely the medium's influence on reality, but its power to constitute reality. Television events are able to work as an electronic platform: only a small number of political and social issues have the same power.

The television community

The relationship between viewer and medium cannot be described in terms of a system of representation which would allow viewers to make judgments about whether or not they are adequately represented in the programs they watch. The point is rather that viewers experience themselves as being "socialized," as belonging to a kind of electronically constituted society whenever and as long as they watch television. The experience of watching television may therefore be described not so much by the words "I see," as by the words "I am among those who will have seen." This sense of collectivity established by shared visual perception is reminiscent of the kind of communities which may develop around movie stars (such as fan clubs) or certain literary texts, as for example the community formed by the readers of a particular newspaper, or religious communities which – like the Christian Church – are founded on scriptures. Live programs which are transmitted worldwide – such as the "mondovision" Band Aid concert in July 1985 – may establish a sense of united humanity, thus inviting the spectator to become a part of an imaginary totality. Long before the advent of television, yet acutely aware of the social implications of the visual, Georg Simmel, a German social philosopher, observed in 1908: "The immediate

89

generation of very abstract, unspecific social phenomena is . . . privileged by the proximity of viewing and a lack of closeness in verbal interaction."[37]

Listening to a sermon or to a public speech by a political or cultural personality is based not only on a desire to hear the message, but, as Umberto Eco notes, also on the wish "to experience the event: to hear also the others, to take part in a collective happening."[38] He adds, commenting on new forms of cultural performances:

I presume people who go to the stadiums to hear Beethoven follow the symphony from beginning to the end, but what counts is the collective rituality – as if that which used to be the High Culture can be reaccepted and placed in a new dynamics provided it also permits encounters, experiences in common.[39]

It thus seems that even in the age of mechanical reproduction, we may find a vestige of what Walter Benjamin called "ritual value" (or cult value) in television events: the mass of the audience celebrates its role as observer of the social body, examining whether things are the way they ought to be, an attitude which may often take on the characteristics of an obsession.[40]

Mass reproduction is aided especially by the reproduction of masses. In big parades and monster rallies, in sports events, and in war, all of which nowadays are captured by camera and sound recording, the masses are brought face to face with themselves. This process . . . is intimately connected with the development of the techniques of reproduction and photography. Mass movements are usually discerned more clearly by a camera [in the German original *Apparatur*, which is a more comprehensive term] than by the naked eye.[41]

The representatives of the television community

Due to the millionfold reproduction of their televised images, people on the screen become – at least for a moment – celebrities, celebrities who belong to everybody, who immediately become ours. But at the very moment of its constitution, the aura is dispersed. The people on the screen belong to those who share them, who scrutinize them, as indicated in comments like: "My goodness, how old he has become!" "He is still wearing the same tie!" "Look at this haircut!" or "Look at that one!"

Such self-exposure and visibility claim their price. One is either rejected as a flop, bore, or failure by the audience and the critics, or one is accepted and promoted to the status of a representative or leading figure of the (imaginary) television community – with all its consequences. People who are familiar from the screen – popular show hosts or MCs, anchor persons or people who simply attain television stardom by appearing in studio audiences (let alone athletes or pop stars whose careers are promoted by television appearances) – are usually the objects of merciless curiosity and – just like chiefs of tribal communities – become subjected to permanent attention both on the screen and in their private lives. They become objects of desire, including the desire for physical contact, and, after a while, find themselves, in many cases symbolically, in some instances even psychically, sacrificed.

The attention given to these representatives of television communities indicates that the most important aspect of a (live) broadcast is not only its particular topic, but, essentially, the success or failure of the anchor person, the sports reporter, or the talk show host. In fact, this is precisely what distinguishes the live television star from the movie star: for the latter it is crucial to imbue the assigned role in the film with one's personal "aura" or "character," while it is presence of mind and the style with which a given situation is mastered which count for the former.

In the name of the audience

While it is true that television stars preside over their (media) communities, they also act in front of cameras and microphones, which is the form in which the invisible audience of millions confronts them. In this situation they are under the same pressure to avoid mistakes as athletes, a fact which may lead to terrible accidents as when athletes in dangerous sports such as slalom skiing push themselves beyond their limits under the pressure of the live camera eye.

Both network directors and television critics continue their arguments in the name of "The Audience," even if what is really at stake are ratings and cultural prestige. In the international political scene, the audience becomes a more and more imaginary, yet nevertheless quite effective factor of power. Thus Philippine ex-president Marcos' loss of power may be explained as partially due to live broadcasts by North American television companies, as when ABC News commentator George Will "grilled Marcos via satellite last November [1985]; it was one of those put-up-or-shut-up challenges."[42] After this event, many Americans shared the feeling of Tom Shales who wrote in the *Washington Post*: "Suddenly we are all terribly aware of the Philippines, but we don't fully know why." Shales continues:

> Dictators of the world take note: Clean up your acts, or risk a U.S. media invasion. President Ferdinand Marcos thought he could go on television and defeat it. Instead he became the star of a continuing saga that played a real-life version of "Sins." He played the sinner.[43]

The article depicts a grim perspective on the interrelationship between politics and the audience: "Revolution, it appears, can now take the form of serialized talk show."[44]

Notes

1　This essay is based on my article "Live/Life: Television as a Generator of Events in Everyday Life," in Phillip Drummond and Richard Paterson (eds) *Television and Its Audiences: International Research Perspectives* (London: British Film Institute, 1988), pp. 32-7.

2　From a letter to the editor of *Der Spiegel* 3 (1987): 10; my translation.

3　Of course, a previously recorded live broadcast, a film, or a feature can also be "an answer" to a special socio-cultural event, for example, the death of a famous actor.

4　This is a common feature in live broadcasts and early forms of videotaping, when video-editing facilities were not available, at least not for non-commercial groups. This phenomenon could serve as a starting point for further reflections on the relationship between styles and aesthetics of (early) video and live television.

　　We now also have live playbacks: points of major interest can be watched again immediately, mostly from other perspectives and in slow motion, while the event goes on simultaneously (meanwhile, we may be assured by the reporter: "Don't worry, you won't miss anything important while watching the replay.") Thus a kind of micro-memory becomes part of direct broadcasting, a technical innovation not yet available when Umberto Eco wrote (in 1962/7) that "there is no narrative trick by which a time-lapse could be created within the autonomous time of the broadcast event" (*Das offene Kunstwerk* (Frankfurt: Suhrkamp, 1977), p. 189; my translation. Italian original: *Opera aperta* (Milano: Bompiani, 1967)).

5　For example, by fencing off and illuminating a space, cameramen and reporters moving on to the scene, etc.

6　As Walter Benjamin put it: ". . . unspectacular social changes often promote a change in receptivity which will benefit the new art form." *The Work of Art in the Age of Mechanical Reproduction*, trans. Harry Zahn (New York: Schocken Books, 1969); reprinted in John G. Hanhardt (ed.) *Video Culture* (Rochester, NY: Visual Studies Workshop Press, 1986), p. 52, Note 26).

7　Because of its shared etymological root, the German term *Aktualität* appears to be adequately translatable into French (*actualité*), but poses problems in English. Here the term may occasionally mean "topicality," "actuality," "currency," "significance," etc., depending on the particular context. "Actuality" refers to "what really is." In the sense of "topicality," the concept covers three areas: (1) speed of information transmission, (2) the latest (production, distribution, and reception of latest news), (3) societal, cultural, and personal concern and interest. See Claus-Dieter Rath, "Changes in the Concept of 'Aktualität' ('topicality') in the Age of New Electronic Communication Technologies" (paper presented at the conference "The Press and the New Technologies – the Challenge of a New Knowledge," organized by the Commission of the European Community, Brussels, November 1985).

8　On a theoretical level, however, these opposites are related differently, since highlights, extraordinary events such as festivities etc., can be considered as indispensable for the maintenance of a given established order.

9　Tabloids usually rely on these topics of universal interest, which are projected into the world of stars and crowned heads. The topics are constantly exploited to provide a continuous stream of topical news (see, for example, the "Royal Watchers" in Great Britain). The tabloids offer examples of how topicality can be deliberately constructed; this may be contrasted to the process of "developing topicality." Both types are combined in those cases in which the media create a kind of extra-medial topicality (provocation, falsification, insinuation, alarmist reports, scandals, scoops, etc.).

10   Claude Lévi-Strauss, *The Raw and the Cooked: Introduction to a Science of Mythology*, trans. John and Doreen Weightman (Chicago: Universtiy of Chicago Press, 1979).

11   One cannot imagine . . . that oneself could ever experience events without reference to a tightly knit framework of time measurement, such as hours of the day or the sequence of calendar years. In actual fact, however, this specific time experience is bound up with a stage of social development at which societies could not function without a differentiated and firmly institutionalized framework of time measurements – a society with long interdependence-chains binding the social functions of many thousands of people to each other and thus requiring very close coordination of their activities in terms of time. It is well known that people of less differentiated societies neither possess nor need timing devices of our kind.
         (Norbert Elias, "Scientific Establishments," in Norbert Elias, Herminio
         Martins and Richard D. Whitley (eds) *Scientific Establishments
         and Hierarchies, Sociology of the Sciences: A Yearbook*, vol. 6
         (Doordrecht, Boston, London: Reidel, 1982), p. 17)

12   Georg Simmel, "Das Problem der historischen Zeit" (1916), in *Brücke und Tür* (Stuttgart: Koehler, 1957), p. 49; my translation.

13   ibid., p. 55.

14   Claude Lévi-Strauss, *The Savage Mind* (London: Weidenfeld & Nicolson, 1966).

15   ibid., p. 297.

16   See Claus-Dieter Rath, "The Invisible Network: Television as an Institution in Everyday Life," in Phillip Drummond and Richard Paterson (eds) *Television in Transition* (London: British Film Institute, 1985), pp. 199-204.

17   An object or a process becomes topical on condition that it contains the themes listed above – on the level of a direct physical stimulus (e.g. pain; "primary or hypolinguistic code"), on the level of a linguistic message (e.g. indication of a conspiracy or a symbolic gesture; "secondary, i.e. linguistic or sign code"), or on the level of an entire cultural and social order (e.g. collapse or devaluation of certain forms of social exchange; "tertiary, i.e. hyperlinguistic or text code"). In this process a past, a distant event, or products of the imagination are brought into a relationship of simultaneity, are brought into the present – i.e. into the field of political slogans which suggest dangers or conflict solutions, or into the field of fashion design "for 'with it' people," since, "while reality precedes thought, it takes different forms according to the way the subject deals with it" (Jacques Lacan, "Some Reflections on the Ego," *International Journal of Psychoanalysis* 34, part 1 (1953): 11).

18   See Michel Foucault, *Discipline and Punish: The Birth of the Prison* (New York: Vintage/Random House, 1979).

19   The major source of detachment, however, is the knowledge that the mass media are part of the outside world, and that therefore they cannot be trusted. West Enders enjoy making fun of the media as much as they enjoy the programs. As one of my neighbours put it, "We heckle TV just like we used to heckle the freaks at the circus when we were kids." . . . In effect, the mass media are approached with some of the same ambivalence as other features of the outside world. This in turn allows the West Ender to interpret the media content so as to protect himself from the outside world and to isolate himself from its messages unless he wishes to believe them. Because of his suspicion of the mass media as an institution, the appearance of people and values of which he approves demonstrates that they are there because they are superior and cannot be held back.
         (Herbert J. Gans, *The Urban Villagers: Group and Class in the Life
         of Italian-Americans* (New York: The Free Press, 1962), pp. 194-5)

20   Perhaps the equivocal nature of the term *conduct* is one of the best aids for coming to terms with the specificity of power relations. For to "conduct" is at the same time to "lead" others (according to mechanisms of coercion which are, to varying degrees, strict) and a way of behaving within a more or less open field of possibilities. [Translator's note: Foucault is playing on the double meaning of the French verb *conduire* (= to lead or to drive) and *se conduire* (= to behave or conduct oneself), which corresponds to the noun *la conduite* (= conduct or behavior).] The exercise of power consists in guiding the possibility of conduct and putting in order the possible outcome. Basically, power is less a confrontation than a question of government. . . . To govern, in this sense, is to structure the possible field of actions of others. The relationship proper to power would not therefore be sought on the side of violence or of struggle, nor on that of voluntary linking (all of which can, at best, only be the instruments of power), but rather in the area of the singular mode of action, neither warlike nor juridical, which is government. . . . Power is exercised only over free subjects, and only insofar as they are free. By this we mean individual or collective subjects who are faced with a field of possibilities in which several ways of behaving, several reactions and diverse comportments may be realized.

> (Michel Foucault, "Why Study Power: The Question of the Subject; How is Power Exercised?" in Hubert L. Dreyfus and Paul Rabinow (eds) *Michel Foucault: Beyond Structuralism and Hermeneutics*, 2nd edn, with an afterword by and an interview with Michel Foucault (Chicago: The University of Chicago Press, 1983), pp. 220-1)

21   ibid., p. 220.
22   See the controversies about "responsible," "honest" vs. "irresponsible," "dishonest" journalism.
23   Eco, *Das offene Kunstwerk*, p. 192; my translation. See the chapter "Zufall und Handlung. Fernseherfahrung und Ästhetik (Ästhetische Strukturen der Live-Sendung; Freiheit der Ereignisse und Determinismen der Gewohnheit)," pp. 186-211.
24   ibid., p. 190.
25   Michel Foucault, "The Discourse on Language," in *The Archaeology of Knowledge*, trans. A. M. Sheridan Smith (New York: Harper/Colophon, 1972).
26   Interview with Pierre du Bois, in René Magritte, *Sämtliche Schriften*, ed. André Blavier (München: Hanser, 1981; Paris: Flammarion, 1979), p. 543; my translation.
27   Walter Benjamin, *Illuminations*, trans. Harry Zohn (New York: Schocken Books, 1969).
28   See Georg Simmel, "Das Abenteuer," in *Philosophische Kultur* (Berlin: Wagenbach, 1983), p. 15.
29   Walter Benjamin, "Erfahrung und Armut," in *Gesammelte Schriften*, vol. II, 1 (Frankfurt: Suhrkamp, 1977), pp. 214-15; my translation.
30   Benjamin, *The Work of Art*, p. 52, note 29.
31   Thus, the live broadcast of the tragic Challenger Space Shuttle lift-off in January 1986 was watched by a relatively small audience compared to previous launches. The enterprise had developed into a routine matter and was no longer conceived of as risky. President Reagan, who, up to this point, had apparently always watched such events live on television, had to watch the catastrophe on a video recording.
32   *New York Times*, April 4, 1949, p. 38.
33   *New York Times*, April 11, 1949, p. 24.

34   See the study on the Royal Wedding, 1981, by Daniel Dayan and Elihu Katz,
      "Rituels publics à usage privé: metamorphose télévisée d'un mariage royal,"
      Annales. Économies, Sociétés, Civilisations 1 (1983): 3-20.
35   See Rath, "The Invisible Network."
36   See also Billy Wilder's film *The Ace in the Hole*, originally titled *The Big
      Carnival*, dealing with a case of entrapment in a cave as media sensation, and
      Woody Allen's *Radio Days* with the case of the dramatic but futile rescue action
      of little Polly Phelps who fell into a well. A recent case of worldwide live TV
      focusing on an entrapment in a well was the one of little Jessica McClure (October
      1987, in Midland/Texas):

> Alert and recovering from a two-and-a-half-day ordeal in an abandoned well, an
> 18-month-old girl underwent minor surgery at the hospital at Midland, Texas. The
> girl, Jessica McClure, who was rescued Friday night at the climax of a
> life-and-death drama that brought wild cheers, sobs of joy and world attention to a
> depression-weary city of 90,000 people in West-Texas, was tired but in a stable
> condition. . . . Millions of people across the country and around the world watched
> the drama on television. The three major networks inter rupted their programs.
>   Friday night Jessica, barefoot, dirty and strapped to a board like a papoose, was
> raised up from the well to a thundering chorus of hurrahs and horns from crowds
> that overwhelmed the rescue site. At Midland Memorial, where Jessica was rushed
> to the emergency room, a parade of cars circled late into the night and the
> switchboard was inundated with well-wishers' calls from around the world.
> Thousands of teddy bears began pouring in.
>
> (*New York Times*, October 18, 1987, p. 28)

37   Georg Simmel, *Soziologie. Untersuchungen über die Formen der
      Vergesellschaftung* (Berlin: Duncker & Humblot, 1968), pp. 488-9; my translation.
38   Umberto Eco, "Culture as Show Business" (1980), in *Travels in Hyperreality.
      Essays*, trans. William Weaver (London: Picador, 1987), p. 154.
39   ibid., p. 155.
40   This should be considered in the context of the relation between obsessive
      neuroses and visuality.
41   Benjamin, *The Work of Art*, p. 52, note 32.
42   *Washington Post*, February 24, 1986, pp. D1, D2.
43   ibid.
44   ibid., p. D1.

Chapter five

Wanted: Audiences.

On the politics of empirical audience studies

Ien Ang

In his pioneering book *The "Nationwide" Audience*, David Morley situates his research on which the book reports as follows: "The relation of an audience to the ideological operations of television remains in principle an empirical question: the challenge is the attempt to develop appropriate methods of empirical investigation of that relation."[1]

Although this sentence may initially be interpreted as a call for a technical discussion about empirical research methods, its wider meaning should be sought in the theoretical and political context of Morley's work. To me, the importance of *The "Nationwide" Audience* does not so much reside in the fact that it offers an empirically validated, and thus "scientific" account of "the ideological operations of television," or merely in its demonstration of some of the ways in which the television audience is "active." Other, more wide-ranging issues are at stake.

Since its publication in 1980, *The "Nationwide" Audience* has played an important role in media studies, especially in Britain, western Europe, and Australia, not so much because of its inherent "informational" value, but because of its strategic position in the field of qualitative empirical research on media audiences – a field that has gone through a rapid development in the 1980s. It seems fair to say that Morley's book forms a major moment in the growing popularity of an "ethnographic" approach on media audiences – Morley himself termed his project an "ethnography of reading."[2] This type of qualitative empirical research, usually carried out in the form of in-depth interviews with a small number of people (and at times supplemented with some form of participant observation), is now recognized by many as one of the most adequate ways to learn about the differentiated subtleties of people's engagements with television and other media.

This "ethnographic" approach seems to be gaining popularity in both "critical" media studies and "mainstream" mass communications research.[3] A sort of methodological consensus seems to be emerging, a common ground in which scholars from divergent epistemological backgrounds can thrive. On the one hand, qualitative methods of empirical research seem to be acceptable because they offer the possibility to avoid what C. Wright Mills has termed abstracted empiricism,[4] which is often leveled at quantitative methods by "critical" scholars; on the other hand, some "mainstream" audience researchers at least have acknowledged the limitations on the kind of data that can be produced by large-scale, quantitative survey work, and believe that ethnographically oriented methods can overcome the shortcomings observed. Given this enthusiastic, rather new interest for the qualitative aspects of television viewing, I would like to reflect upon its general implications for our understanding of television audiences. What kind of knowledge does it produce? What can this manner of doing empirical research on audiences mean? In short, what are the politics of audience "ethnography"?

It is my intention in exploring these questions to try to clarify some of the issues that are at stake in developing a *critical* perspective in empirical audience studies. The term "critical" – as I would like to use it here – refers first of all to a certain intellectual-political *orientation* toward academic practice: whatever its subject matter or method of analysis, essential to doing "critical" research would be the adoption of a self-reflexive perspective, one that is, first, conscious of the social and discursive nature of any research practice, and, second, takes seriously the Foucaultian reminder that the production of knowledge is always bound up in a network of power relations. By characterizing "critical" research in this way, that is as an orientation rather than as a fixed "paradigm," I aim to relativize the more rigid ways in which "critical" and "mainstream" research have often been opposed to one another. Formally speaking, positions can only be "critical" or "mainstream" in relation to other positions within a discursive field. The two terms thus do not primarily signify fixed contents of thought, but their status within a whole field of thinking. The relations of force in that field can change over time: what was once "critical" (or marginal) can become part of the "mainstream"; what was once "mainstream" (or dominant) can lose its power and be pushed aside to the marginal. Furthermore, as Larry Grossberg has usefully remarked, the term "critical" can bear uneasy arrogant connotations: after all, is there any scholar whose work is not "critical" in some sense?[5]

This does not mean, of course, that the distinction is totally devoid of any substantive bearings. Historically, those scholars who are committed to doing "critical" work have been led in their research agendas by certain philosophical, theoretical, and political influences and currents, which have shaped their interests and perspectives, and profiled their problematics. For example, in media studies the "critical" tradition, whose beginnings can be located in the work of the Frankfurt School, has generally derived its philosophical inspiration from continental schools of thought such as Marxism and (post)structuralism. In terms of research problematics, it has mainly been concerned with the analysis of the ideological and/or economic role of the media in capitalist and patriarchal society, while its epistemological underpinnings are generally characterized by a strident anti-positivist and anti-empiricist mentality.[6]

This distrust of positivist empiricism on the part of "critical" theorists, however, does not necessarily imply an *inherent* incompatibility between "critical" and empirical research, as is often contended by "mainstream" scholars.[7] Indeed, if doing "critical" research is more a matter of intellectual-political orientation than of academic paradigm-building, then no fixed, universal yardstick, theoretical or methodological, for what constitutes "critical" knowledge is possible. On the contrary, in my view what it means to be critical needs to be assessed and constantly reassessed in every concrete conjuncture, with respect to the concrete issues and directions that are at stake in any concrete research field. In other words, I am proposing an *open* and *contextual* definition of "critical" research, one that does not allow itself to rest easily on pre-existent epistemological foundations but – on the contrary – engages itself in reflecting on the ways in which it contributes to our understanding of the world.

In the following, I hope to clarify some of the implications of this perspective on doing "critical" research for an evaluation of the current developments in audience studies. More concretely, what I will discuss and try to elaborate in this chapter is what I take as the political and theoretical specificity of the cultural studies approach as a "critical" perspective, from which David Morley, coming from the Birmingham Centre for Contemporary Cultural Studies, has developed his work.[8] I will set this perspective on audience studies against the uses and gratifications approach, in which an interest in the "ethnographic" has been growing recently. In doing this it is not my intention to construct an absolute antagonism between the two approaches. Rather, I would like to highlight some of the differences in preoccupation in both approaches, in order to specify how the project of audience ethnographies can take on a "critical" outlook in the sense I have outlined. Before doing this, I will first give a short sketch of the intellectual arena in which Morley intervened.

Against textual determinism

The "Nationwide" Audience appeared at a time when critical discourse about film and television in Britain was heavily preoccupied with what Morley, following Steve Neale, calls an "abstract text/subject relationship," formulated within a generally (post)structuralist theoretical framework.[9] In this discourse, primarily developed in the journal *Screen*, film and television spectatorship is almost exclusively theorized from the perspective of the "productivity of the text." As a consequence, the role of the viewer was conceived in purely formalist terms: as a position inscribed in the text. Here, the subject-in-the-text tends to collapse with "real" social subjects. In this model, there is no space for a dialogical relationship between texts and social subjects. Texts are assumed to be the only source of meaning; they construct subject positions which viewers are bound to take up if they are to make sense of the text. In other words, the reading of texts is conceived here as entirely dictated by textual structures.

It is this model's textual determinism that fueled Morley's dissatisfaction. Theoretically, it implied an ahistorical, asocial, and generalist conception of film and television spectatorship. Methodologically, the analysis of textual structures alone was considered to be sufficient to comprehend how viewers are implicated in the texts they encounter. Politically, this model left no space of manoeuvre for television consumers. They are implicitly conceived as "prisoners" of the text. It is against this background that Morley decided to undertake an empirical investigation of how groups of viewers with different social positions read or interpret one particular text: an episode of the television program *Nationwide*. One of the most important motivations of Morley's intervention, then, was to overcome the theoreticism of *Screen* theory's discourse, in which the relation of text and subject is dealt with "as an [*a*] *priori* question to be deduced from a theory of the ideal spectator 'inscribed' in the text."[10] By looking at how one text could be decoded in different ways by different groups of social subjects, Morley intended, and succeeded, to demonstrate that encounters between texts and viewers are far more complex than the theory would suggest; they are overdetermined by the operation of a multiplicity of forces – certain historical and social structures, but also other texts – that simultaneously act upon the subjects concerned.[11] Principally, what *The "Nationwide" Audience* explores is the notion that the moment of decoding should be considered as a relatively autonomous process in which a constant struggle over the meaning of the text is fought out. Textual meanings do not reside in the texts themselves: a certain text can come to mean different things depending on the interdiscursive context in which viewers interpret it.

The meaning and politics of Morley's turn toward empirical research of the television audience should be assessed against this critical background. It is first of all a procedure that is aimed at opening up a space in which watching television can begin to be understood as a complex cultural practice full of dialogical negotiations and contestations, rather than as a singular occurrence whose meaning can be determined once and for all in the abstract. Doing empirical research then is here used as a strategy to break out of a hermetically closed theoreticism in which an absolute certainty about the ideological effectivity of television is presumed. Thus, when Morley says that the relation of an audience to television "remains an empirical question," what he is basically aiming at is to open up critical discourse on television audiences, and to sensitize it for the possibility of struggle in the field of television consumption – a struggle whose outcome cannot be known in advance, for the simple reason that encounters between television and audiences are always historically specific and context-bound.

Academic convergence?

The "Nationwide" Audience has generally been received as an innovative departure within cultural studies, both theoretically and methodologically. If *Screen* theory can be diagnosed as one instance in which critical discourse on television suffered from the problem of the "disappearing audience,"[12] Morley's project is an indication of a growing acknowledgment within cultural studies that television viewing is a practice that involves the active production of meanings by viewers.

But the book has also been welcomed by some adherents of the influential uses and gratifications approach, who see it as an important step on the part of "critical" scholars in their direction, that is as an acceptance of, and possible contribution to, a refinement of their own basic axiomatic commitment to "the active audience." On the other hand, some uses and gratifications researchers, for their part, have begun to take over semiologically informed cultural studies concepts such as "text" and "reader," thereby indicating an acknowledgment of the symbolic nature of negotiations between media texts and their readers which they, in their functionalist interest for the multiple relationships between audience gratifications and media "uses," had previously all but ignored.[13]

On top of this conceptual rapprochement, these social scientists have also expressed their delight in noticing a methodological "concession" among "critical" scholars: finally, so it is argued, some "critical" scholars at least have dropped their suspicion of doing empirical research. In a benevolent, rather fatherly tone, three senior ambassadors of the uses and gratifications approach, Blumler, Gurevitch, and Katz, have thus proclaimed a gesture of "reaching out" to the other "camp," calling for incorporating some of the insights developed within the "critical" perspective into their own paradigm.[14] Evoked then is the prospect of merging the two approaches, to the point that they may ultimately fuse into a happy common project in which the perceived hostility between the two "camps" will have been unmasked as academic "pseudo-conflicts." As one leading gratifications researcher, Rosengren, optimistically predicts: "To the extent that the same problematics are empirically studied by members of various schools, the present sharp differences of opinion will gradually diminish and be replaced by a growing convergence of perspectives."[15]

However, to interpret these recent developments in audience studies in terms of such a convergence is to simplify and even misconceive the issues at stake. For one thing, I would argue that the two perspectives only superficially share "the same problematics," and that what separates a "critical" from a "mainstream" perspective is more than merely some "differences of opinion," sharp or otherwise: it concerns fundamental differences not only in epistemological, but also in theoretical and political attitudes toward the aim and status of doing empirical research as such.

The academic idealization of joining forces in pursuit of a supposedly common goal as if it were a neutral, scientific project is a particularly depoliticizing strategy, because it tends to neutralize all difference and disagreement in favor of a forced consensus. If I am cautious about this euphoria around the prospect of academic convergence, it is not my intention to impose a rigid and absolute eternal dichotomy between "critical" and "mainstream" research. Nor would I want to assert that Morley's project is entirely "critical" and the uses and gratifications approach completely "mainstream." As I have noted before, the relationship between "critical" and "mainstream" is not a fixed one; it does not concern two mutually exclusive, antagonistic sets of knowledge, as some observers would imply by talking in terms of "schools" or "paradigms." In fact, many assumptions and ideas do not intrinsically belong to one or the other perspective. For example, the basic assumption that the television audience is "active" (rather than passive) and that watching television is a social (rather than an individual) practice is currently accepted in both perspectives. There is nothing spectacular about that.[16] Also, I would suggest that the idea that texts can generate multiple meanings, and that the text/reader relationship takes the form of negotiations, is not in itself a sufficient condition for the declared convergence.[17]

In other words, in evaluating whether we can really speak of convergence, it is not enough to establish similar research questions, or to identify a common acknowledgment of the usefulness of certain methods of inquiry. Of course, such commonalities are interesting enough and it would be nonsense to discard them categorically. I do think it is important to get rid of any dogmatism or antagonism-for-the-sake-of-it, and to try to learn from others wherever that is possible. But at the same time we should not lose sight of the fact that any call for convergence itself is not an innocent gesture. It tends to be done from a certain point of view and therefore inevitably involves a selection process in which certain issues and themes are highlighted and others suppressed. And it is my contention that an all too hasty declaration of convergence could lead to neglecting some of the most important distinctive features of cultural studies as a critical intellectual enterprise.

A difference in conceptualizing the object of study is a first issue that needs to be discussed here. Thus, to take the common interest in "audience activity" as an example in a cultural studies perspective, "audience activity" cannot and should not be studied in isolation. Rather than dissecting "audience activity" into variables and categories in order to be able to study them one by one, so that we could ultimately have a complete and generalizable formal "map" of all dimensions of "audience activity," which seems to be the drive behind the uses and gratifications project,[18] the aim of cultural studies, as I see it, is to arrive at a more historicized insight into the ways in which "audience activity" is related to social and political structures and processes. In other words, what is at stake is not the understanding of "audience activity" as such as an isolated and isolable phenomenon and object of research, but the embeddedness of "audience activity" in a network of ongoing cultural practices and relationships.

As a result, an audience researcher working within a cultural studies sensibility cannot restrict herself or himself to "just" studying audiences and their activities (and, for that matter, relating those activities with other variables such as gratifications sought or obtained, dependencies, effects, and so on). She or he will also engage with the structural and cultural processes through which the audiences she or he is studying are constituted and being constituted. Thus, one essential theoretical point of the cultural studies approach to the television audience is its foregrounding of the notion that the dynamics of watching television, no matter how heterogeneous and seemingly free it is, is always related to the operations of forms of social power. It is in this light that we should see Morley's decision to do research on viewers' decodings: it was first of all motivated by an interest in what he – in the quote at the beginning of this chapter – calls "the ideological operations of television."

It is important then to emphasize that the term "active audience" does not occupy the same symbolic status in the two approaches. From a cultural studies point of view, evidence that audiences are "active" cannot simply be equated with the rather triumphant, liberal-pluralist conclusion, often expressed by gratificationists, that media consumers are "free" or even "powerful" – a conclusion which allegedly undercuts the idea of "media hegemony." The question for cultural studies is not simply one of "where the power lies in media systems" (i.e. with the audience or with the media producers),[19] but rather how relations of power are organized within the heterogeneous practices of media consumption. In other words, rather than constructing an opposition between "the" media and "the" audience, as if these were separate ontological entities, and, along with it, the application of a distributional theory of power (that is, power is a property that can be attributed to either side of the opposing entities), cultural studies scholars are interested in understanding media consumption as a site of cultural struggle, in which a variety of forms of power are exercised, with different sorts of effects.[20] Thus if, as Morley's study has shown, viewers can decode a text in different ways and sometimes even give oppositional meanings to it, this should not be conceived as an example of "audience freedom," but as a moment in that cultural struggle, an ongoing struggle over meaning and pleasure which is central to the fabric(ation) of everyday life.

I hope to have made clear by now that in evaluating the possibility or even desirability of convergence, it is important to look at how "audience activity" is theorized or interpreted, and how research "findings" are placed in a wider theoretical framework. So, if one type of "audience activity" which has received much attention in both approaches recently has been the interpretative strategies used by audiences to read media texts (conceptualized in terms of decoding structures, interpretative communities, patterns of involvement, and so on), how are we to make sense of those interpretative strategies? The task of the cultural studies researcher, I would suggest, is to develop *strategic interpretations* of them, different not only in form and content, but also in scope and intent, from those offered in more "mainstream"-oriented accounts.[21] I will return to this central issue of interpretation.

Beyond methodology

A troubling aspect about the idea of (and desire for) convergence, then, is that it tends to be conceptualized as an exclusively "scientific" enterprise. Echoing the tenets of positivism, its aim seems to be the gradual accumulation of scientifically confirmed "findings." It is propelled by the hope that by seeking a shared agreement on what is relevant and by developing shared methodological skills the final scientific account of "the audience" can eventually be achieved. In this framework, audience studies are defined as just another branch of an academic discipline (i.e. mass communication), in which it is unproblematically assumed that "the audience" is a proper object of study whose characteristics can be ever more accurately observed, described, categorized, systematized, and explained, until the whole picture is "filled in." In principle (if not in practice), this scientific project implicitly claims to be able to produce total knowledge, to reveal the full and objective "truth" about "the audience." Audience here is imagined as and turned into an object with researchable attributes and features (be it described in terms of arrays of preferences, decodings, uses, effects, or whatever) that could be definitively established – if only researchers of different breeding would stop quarreling with each other and unite to work harmoniously together to accomplish the task.[22]

From such an academic point of view, the question of methodology becomes a central issue. After all, rigor of method has traditionally been seen as the guarantee *par excellence* for the "scientific" status of knowledge. In positivist social science, the hypothetico-deductive testing of theory through empirical research, quantitative in form, is cherished as the cornerstone of the production of "scientific" knowledge. Theory that is not empirically tested, or that is too complex to be molded into empirically testable hypotheses, is dismissed as "unscientific." These assumptions, which are central to the dominant version of the uses and gratifications approach as it was established in the 1970s, are now contested by a growing number of researchers who claim that reality cannot be grasped and explained through quantitative methods alone. Furthermore, they forcefully assert that to capture the multidimensionality and complexity of audience activity the use of qualitative methods – and thus a move towards the "ethnographic" – is desperately called for.[23]

From an academic point of view, it is this methodological challenge that forms the condition of possibility of the perceived convergence. However, although I think that the struggle for legitimization of qualitative research is a very important one, I do believe that it is not the central point for critical cultural studies. This is because the struggle is cast primarily in methodological terms, and therefore its relevance is confined to the development of audience research as an *academic* enterprise. Given the decade-long hegemony of positivism and the quantifying attitude in audience research, this development is a significant one indeed. Unfortunately, however, many discussions about the usefulness of qualitative methods still do not question the epistemological distinction between science and common sense that lies at the heart of positivism. The aim is still the isolation of a body of knowledge that can be recognized as "scientific" (in its broadest meaning), the orientation is toward the advancement of an academic discipline, and concomitantly, the technical improvement of its instruments of analysis.

A cultural studies perspective on audience research cannot stop short at this level of debate. For a critical cultural studies, it is not questions of methodology or academic struggle as such that prevail. On the contrary, we should relativize the academic commitment to increasing knowledge for its own sake and resist the temptation to what Stuart Hall has called the "codification" of cultural studies into a stable realm of established theories and canonized methodologies.[24] In this respect, the territorial conflict between "mainstream" and "critical," quantitative and qualitative, humanistic and social scientific, and so on, should perhaps not bother us too much at all in the first place. As James Carey once remarked, "perhaps all the talk about theory, method, and other such things prevents us from raising or permits us to avoid raising, deeper and disquieting questions about the purposes of our scholarship."[25] And indeed: why are we so interested in knowing about audiences in the first place? In empirical audience research, especially, it is important to reflect upon the status of the knowledge produced. After all, scrutinizing media audiences is not an innocent practice. It does not take place in a social and political vacuum. Historically, the hidden agenda of audience research, even when it presents itself as pure and objective, has all too often been its commercial or political usefulness. In other words, what we should reflect upon is the *political* interventions we make when talking about audiences – political not only in the sense of some distant societal goal, but, more importantly, in that we cannot afford ignoring the political dimensions of the *process* and practice of knowledge production itself. What does it mean to subject audiences to the researcher's gaze? How can we develop insights that do not reproduce the kind of objectified knowledge served up by, say, market research or empiricist effects research? How is it possible to do audience research which is "on the side" of the audience?[26] These are nagging political questions which cannot be smoothed out by the comforting canons of epistemology, methodology, and "science."

Of course, it is not easy to pin down what such considerations would imply in concrete terms. But it could at least be said that we should try to avoid a stance in which "the audience" is relegated to the status of exotic "other" – merely interesting in so far as "we," as researchers, can turn "them" into "objects" of study, and about whom "we" have the privileged position to acquire "objective" knowledge.[27] To begin with, I think, critical audience studies should not strive and pretend to tell "the truth" about "the audience." Its ambitions should be much more modest. As Lawrence Grossberg has suggested, "the goal of [critical research] is to offer not a polished representation of the truth, but simply a little help in our efforts to better understand the world."[28] This modesty does not have so much to do with some sort of false humility as with the basic acknowledgment that every research practice unavoidably takes place in a particular historical situation, and is therefore principally of a partial nature. As Hammersley and Atkinson have provocatively put it, "all social research takes the form of participant observation: it involves participating in the social world, in whatever role, and reflecting on the products of that participation."[29] The collection of data, either quantitative or qualitative in form, can never be separated from their interpretation; it is only through practices of interpretative theorizing that unruly social experiences and events related to media consumption become established as meaningful "facts" about audiences. Understanding "audience activity" is thus caught up in the discursive representation, not the transparent reflection, of realities having to do with audiences.

These considerations lead to another, more politicized conception of doing research. It is not the search for (objective, scientific) knowledge in which the researcher is engaged, but the construction of *interpretations*, of certain ways of understanding the world, always historically located, subjective, and relative. It is the decisive importance of this interpretative moment that I would like to highlight in exploring the possibilities of critical audience studies.[30]

In positivism, interpretation is assigned a marginal place: as a result of its emphasis on the empirical testing of theory, interpretation is assumed to follow rather automatically from the so-called "findings." Achieved then is an apparent innocence of interpretation, one that is seemingly grounded in "objective social reality" itself. In fact, the term "interpretation" itself would seem to have definite negative connotations for positivists because of its connection with "subjectivism." And even within those social science approaches in which the interpretative act of the researcher – not only at the moment of data analysis, but also at that of data collection – is taken more seriously, interpretation is more often than not problematized as a methodical rather than a political matter, defined in terms of careful inference making rather than in terms of discursive constructions of reality.

It should be recognized, however, that because interpretations always inevitably involve the construction of certain representations of reality (and not others), they can never be "neutral" and merely "descriptive." After all, the "empirical," captured in either quantitative or qualitative form, does not yield self-evident meanings; it is only through the interpretative framework constructed by the researcher that understandings of the "empirical" come about. The choice of empirical methods of investigation is only one part of a double venture: it is in the dialectic between the empirical and the theoretical, between experience and explanation, that forms of knowledge, that is interpretations, are constructed. Here then the thoroughly political nature of any research manifests itself. What is at stake is a *politics of interpretation*: "to advance an interpretation is to insert it into a network of power relations."[31]

This also implies a shift in the position of the researcher. She or he is no longer a bearer of truth, but occupies a "partial" position in two senses of the word. On the one hand, she or he is no longer the neutral observer, but is someone whose job it is to produce historically and culturally specific knowledges that are the result of equally specific discursive encounters between researcher and informants, in which the subjectivity of the researcher is not separated from the "object" s/he is studying. The interpretations that are produced in the process can never claim to be definitive: on the contrary, they are necessarily incomplete (for they always involve simplification, selection, and exclusion) and temporary. "If neither history nor politics ever comes to an end, then theory (as well as research) is never completed and our accounts can never be closed or totalized."[32] And on the other hand, and even more important, the position of the researcher is also more than that of the professional scholar: beyond a capable interpreter, she or he is also inherently a political and moral subject. She or he is an intellectual who is not only responsible to the Academy, but to the social world she or he lives in as well. It is at the interface of "ethics" and "scholarship" that the researcher's interpretations take on their distinctive political edge.[33]

Of course, all this entails a different status for empirical research. Material obtained by ethnographic fieldwork or depth-interviews with audience members cannot simply be treated as natural "data." Viewers' statements about their relation to television cannot be regarded as self-evident facts. Nor are they immediate, transparent reflections of those viewers' "lived realities" that can speak for themselves. What is of critical importance, therefore, is the way in which those statements are made sense of, that is interpreted. Here lies the ultimate political responsibility of the researcher. The comfortable assumption that it is the reliability and accuracy of the methodologies being used that will ascertain the validity of the outcomes of research, thereby reducing the researcher's responsibility to a technical matter, is rejected. In short, to return to Morley's opening statement, audience ethnographies are undertaken because the relation between television and viewers is an empirical *question*. But the empirical is not the privileged domain of the *answers*, as the positivist would have it. Answers (temporary ones, to be sure) are to be constructed, in the form of interpretations.[34]

Towards interpretative ethnography

I would now like to return to David Morley's work, and evaluate its place in the research field in the light of the foregoing reflections. To be sure, Morley himself situates his work firmly within the academic context. And parallel to the recent calls for convergence and cross-fertilization of diverse perspectives, Morley seems to have dropped his original antagonistic posture. For example, while in *The "Nationwide" Audience* he emphasizes that "we need to break fundamentally with the 'uses and gratifications' approach,"[35] in his most recent book, *Family Television: Cultural Power and Domestic Leisure*, he simply states that this new piece of research draws "upon some of the insights of this very approach."[36] The latter book is also in a more general sense set in a less polemical tone than the first one: rather than taking up a dissident's stance against other theoretical perspectives, which is a central attribute of *The "Nationwide" Audience*, *Family Television* is explicitly presented as a study that aims to combine the perspectives of separate traditions in order to overcome what Morley calls an "unproductive form of segregation."[37] Furthermore, both books are written in a markedly conventional style of academic social science, structured according to a narrative line which starts out with their contextualization within related academic research trends, followed by a methodological exposition and a description of the findings, and rounded off with a chapter containing an interpretation of the results and some more general conclusions. In both books Morley's voice is exclusively that of the earnest researcher; the writer's I, almost completely eliminated from the surface of the text, is apparently a disembodied subject solely driven by a disinterested wish to contribute to "scientific progress."[38]

Morley's academistic inclination tends to result in a lack of clarity as to the political thrust of his analyses. For example, the relevance of *Family Television* as a project designed to investigate at the same time two different types of questions – questions of television use on the one hand, and questions of textual interpretation on the other – is simply asserted by the statement that these are "urgent questions about the television audience."[39] But why? What kind of urgency is being referred to here? Morley goes on to say that it is the analysis of the domestic viewing context as such which is his main interest, and that he wishes to identify the multiple meanings hidden behind the catch-all phrase "watching television." Indeed, central to *Family Television's* discourse are, as Stuart Hall remarks in his introduction to the book, the notions of variability, diversity, and difference:

> We are all, in our heads, several different audiences at once, and can be constituted as such by different programmes. We have the capacity to deploy different levels and modes of attention, to mobilise different competences in our viewing. At different times of the day, for different family members, different patterns of viewing have different "saliences."[40]

Yet, when taken in an unqualified manner, it is exactly this stress on difference that essentially connects Morley's project with the preoccupations of the uses and gratifications research. After all, it is their self-declared distinctive mission to get to grips with "the gamut of audience experience."[41] For them too, the idea of plurality and diversity is pre-eminently the guiding principle for research. A convergence of perspectives after all?

Despite all the agreements that are certainly there, a closer look at the ramifications of Morley's undertaking reveals other concerns than merely the characterization and categorizing of varieties within viewers' readings and uses of television. Ultimately, it is not difference as such that is of main interest in Morley's work. To be sure, differences are not just simple facts that emerge more or less spontaneously from the empirical interview material; it is a matter of interpretation what are established as *significant* differences.[42] In cultural studies, then, it is the meanings of differences that matter – something that can only be grasped, interpretatively, by looking at their contexts, social and cultural bases, and impacts. Thus, rather than the classification of differences and varieties in all sorts of typologies, which is a major preoccupation of a lot of uses and gratifications work, cultural studies would be oriented toward a detailed understanding of how and why varieties in experience occur – a venture, to be sure, that is a closer approach to the ethnographic spirit.

In *Family Television*, for example, Morley has chosen to foreground the pattern of differences in viewing habits that are articulated with gender. What Morley emphasizes is that men and women clearly relate in contrasting ways to television, not only as to program preferences, but also in, for example, viewing styles. The wives interviewed by Morley tend to watch television less attentively, at the same time doing other things such as talking or housework. The husbands, in contrast, state a clear preference for viewing attentively, in silence, without interruption "in order not to miss anything."[43] These differences are substantiated and highlighted by Morley's research as empirical facts, but he is careful to avoid considering these as *essential* differences between men and women. As Charlotte Brunsdon has noted, it seems possible "to differentiate a male – fixed, controlling, uninterruptible gaze – and a female – distracted, obscured, already busy – manner of watching television. There is some empirical truth in these characterizations, but to take this empirical truth for explanation leads to a theoretical short-circuit."[44] Indeed, in mainstream sociological accounts, gender would probably be treated as a self-evident pregiven factor that can be used as "independent variable" to explain these differences. Male and female modes of watching television would then be constituted as two separate, discrete types of experience, clearly defined, fixed, static "objects" in themselves as it were.[45] Such an empiricist account not only essentializes gender differences, but also fails to offer an understanding of how and why differentiations along gender lines take the very forms they do.

In contrast to this, both Morley and Brunsdon start out to construct a tentative interpretation which does not take the difference between male and female relations to television as an empirical given. Neither do they take recourse to psychological notions such as "needs" or "socialization" – as is often done in accounts of gender differences, as well as in uses and gratifications research – to try to understand why men and women tend to watch and talk about television in the disparate ways that they do. In their interpretative work Morley and Brunsdon accentuate the structure of domestic power relations as constitutive for the differences concerned. The home generally has different meanings for men and women living in nuclear family arrangements: for husbands it is the site of leisure, for wives it is the site of work. Therefore, television as a domestic cultural form tends to be invested with different meanings for men and women. Television has for men become a central symbol for relaxation; women's relation to television, on the other hand, is much more contradictory. Thus asserts Brunsdon, in commenting on Morley's research:

> The social relations between men and women appear to work in such a way that although the men feel ok about imposing their choice of viewing on the whole of the family, the women do not. The women have developed all sorts of strategies to cope with television viewing they don't particularly like. The

men in most cases appear to feel it would be literally unmanning for them to sit quiet during the women's programmes. However, the women in general seem to find it almost impossible to switch into the silent communion with the television set that characterises so much male viewing.[46]

Women's distracted mode of watching television thus does not have something to do with some essential femininity, but is a result of a complex of cultural and social arrangements which makes it difficult for them to do otherwise, even though they often express a longing to be able to watch their favorite programs without being disturbed. Men, on the other hand, can watch television in a concentrated manner because they control the conditions to do so. Their way of watching television, Brunsdon concludes, "seems not so much a masculine mode, but a mode of power."[47]

What clearly emerges here is the beginning of an interpretative framework in which differences in television viewing practices are not just seen as expressions of different needs, uses, or readings, but are connected with the way in which historical subjects are structurally positioned in relation to each other. Women's viewing patterns can only be understood in relation to men's patterns; the two are in a sense constitutive of each other. Thus, if watching television is a social and even collective practice, it is not a harmonious practice.[48] Because subjects are positioned in different ways toward the set, they engage in a continuing struggle over program choice and program interpretation, style of viewing, and textual pleasure. What kind of viewer they become can be seen as the outcome of this struggle, an outcome, however, that is never definitive because it can always be contested and subverted. What we call "viewing habits" are thus not a more or less static set of characteristics inhabited by an individual or group of individuals; rather they are the temporary result of a never-ending, dynamic, and conflict-ridden process in which "the fine-grained interrelationships between meaning, pleasure, use and choice" are shaped.[49]

Morley's empirical findings, then, acquire their relevance and critical value in the context of this emerging theoretical framework. And of course it could only have been carried out from a specific interpretative point of view. Needless to say that the point of view taken up by Morley and Brunsdon is a feminist one, that is, a position that is sensitive to the fact that male/female relationships are always informed by power, contradiction, and struggle. Television consumption, so we begin to understand, contributes to the everyday contruction of male and female subjectivities. At this point, we can also see how Morley's research enables us to begin to conceive of "the ideological operations of television" in a much more radical way than has hitherto been done.[50] The relation between television and audiences is not just a matter of "negotiations" between texts and viewers. The process of television consumption, and the cultural positioning of television as such, have created new areas of constraints and possibilities for structuring social relationships, identities, and desires. If television is an "ideological apparatus," to use that old fashioned-sounding term, this is not so much because its texts transmit certain "messages" as because it is a cultural form through which those constraints are negotiated and those possibilities take shape.

But, one might ask, do we need empirical research or, more specifically, audience ethnographies to arrive at such theoretical understandings? Why approach audiences empirically at all?[51] I would like to make one last comment on Morley's work here. Due to his academistic posture Morley has not deemed it necessary to reflect upon his own position as a researcher. We do not get to know how he found and got on with his interviewees, nor are we informed about the way in which the interviews themselves took place. One of the very few things we learn about this in *Family Television* is that he gave up interviewing the adults and the young children at the same time, reportedly "because after an initial period of fascination the young children quite quickly got bored"![52] But what about the adults? What were the reasons for their willingness to talk at such length to an outsider (or was David Morley not an outsider to them)? And how did the specific power relationship pervading the interview situation affect not only the families, but also the researcher himself? These are problems inherent in conducting ethnographic research that are difficult to unravel. But that does not mean that audience researchers should not confront them, and, eventually, draw the radical and no doubt uncomfortable conclusions that will emerge from that confrontation.[53]

Meanwhile, I do think that, in the ever-expanding field of audience studies, an ethnographic approach can and does have a distinct critical value. Ethnographic work, in the sense of drawing on what we can perceive and experience in everyday settings, acquires its critical mark when it functions as a reminder that reality is always more complicated and diversified than our theories can represent, and that there is no such thing as "audience" whose characteristics can be set once and for all.[54] The critical promise of the ethnographic attitude resides in its potential to make and keep our interpretations sensitive to concrete specificities, to the unexpected, to history; it is a commitment to submit ourselves to the possibility of, in Paul Willis' words, "being 'surprised,' of reaching knowledge not prefigured in one's starting paradigm."[55] What matters is not the certainty of knowledge about audiences, but an ongoing critical and intellectual engagement with the multifarious ways in which we constitute ourselves through media consumption. Or, as in the words of Stuart Hall: "I am not interested in Theory, I am interested in going on theorizing."[56]

Notes

1 David Morley, *The "Nationwide" Audience: Structure and Decoding* (London: British Film Institute, 1980), p. 162.

2 David Morley, "'The *Nationwide* Audience' – A Critical Postscript," *Screen Education* 39 (summer 1981): 13. It should be noted, however, that the term "ethnographic" is somewhat misplaced in this context. Within anthropology, ethnography refers to an in-depth field study of a culture and its inhabitants in their natural location, which would require the researcher to spend a fair amount

of time in that location, allowing her/him to acquire a nuanced and comprehensive insight into the dynamics of the social relationships in the culture under study, and enabling her/him to produce a "thick description" of it. Most qualitative studies of media audiences do not meet these requirements. In Morley's *Nationwide* study, for example, the informants were extracted from their natural viewing environment and interviewed in groups that were put together according to socio-economic criteria. In a looser sense, however, the use of the term "ethnographic" could be justified here in so far as the approach is aimed at getting a thorough insight into the "lived experience" of media consumption. For a useful introduction to the principles of ethnography as an instance of social research, see Martyn Hammersley and Paul Atkinson, *Ethnography: Principles in Practice* (London and New York: Tavistock, 1983).

3   See, for example, Dorothy Hobson, "Housewives and the Mass Media," in Stuart Hall, Dorothy Hobson, Andrew Lowe, and Paul Willis (eds) *Culture, Media, Language* (London: Hutchinson, 1980), pp. 105-14; and Dorothy Hobson, *"Crossroads": The Drama of a Soap Opera* (London: Methuen, 1982); Janice Radway, *Reading the Romance: Women, Patriarchy, and Popular Literature* (Chapel Hill: University of North Carolina Press, 1984); Ien Ang, *Watching "Dallas". Soap Opera and the Melodramatic Imagination* (London and New York: Methuen, 1985); James Lull, "The Social Uses of Television," in *Human Communications Research* 6, no.3 (1980): 198-209; Elihu Katz and Tamar Liebes, "Mutual Aid in the Decoding of *Dallas*: Preliminary Notes from a Cross-Cultural Study," in Phillip Drummond and Richard Paterson (eds) *Television in Transition* (London: British Film Institute, 1985), pp. 187-98; Tamar Liebes and Elihu Katz, "Patterns of Involvement in Television Fiction: A Comparative Analysis," *European Journal of Communication* 1 (1986): 151-71; Klaus Bruhn Jensen, *Making Sense of the News* (Ahrhus: University of Ahrhus Press, 1986); Thomas Lindlof (ed.) *Natural Audiences: Qualitative Research and Media Uses and Effects* (Norwood, NJ: Ablex Publishing Company, 1987); James Lull (ed.) *World Families Watch Television* (Newbury Park, Calif.: Sage, 1988).

4   C. Wright Mills, *The Sociological Imagination* (Harmondsworth: Penguin, 1970), chapter 3.

5   Lawrence Grossberg, "Critical Theory and the Politics of Empirical Research," in Michael Gurevitch and Mark R. Levy (eds) *Mass Communication Review Yearbook,*vol. 6 (Newbury Park, Calif.: Sage, 1986), pp. 86-106.

6   It should be stressed, however, that the "critical" tradition is not a monolithic whole: there is not one "critical theory" with generally shared axioms, but many different, and often conflicting "critical perspectives," e.g. political economy and cultural studies.

7   Thus, I take issue with the conceptualization of recent debates in communication studies in terms of a dichotomization of "critical" and "empirical" schools, as is done in some contributions to the *Ferment in the Field* issue of the *Journal of Communication* 33, no.3 (1983).

8   For an overview of the media studies work of the Centre, see Hall *et al.*, *Culture, Media, Language*. For an introduction to the cultural studies approach, see e.g. Thomas Streeter, "An Alternative Approach to Television Research: Developments in British Cultural Studies in Birmingham," in Willard D. Rowland, Jr. and Bruce Watkins (eds) *Interpreting Television: Current Research Perspectives* (Beverly Hills, Calif.: Sage, 1984), pp. 74-97; John Fiske, "British Cultural Studies and Television," in Robert C. Allen (ed.) *Channels of Discourse* (Chapel Hill: University of North Carolina Press, 1987), pp. 254-69.

9   Morley, *The "Nationwide" Audience*, p. 161; Steve Neale, "Propaganda," *Screen*, 18, no.3 (1977).

10 Morley, *The "Nationwide" Audience*, p. 162.

11 The direct theoretical inspiration of Morley's research was the so-called encoding/decoding model launched by Stuart Hall, which presented a theoretical intervention against *"Screen* theory." See his "Encoding/Decoding" in Hall *et al., Culture, Media, Language*, pp. 128-38, and also, in the same volume, Stuart Hall, "Recent Developments in Theories of Language and Ideology: A Critical Note," pp. 157-62. Morley himself elaborated on the "interdiscursive" nature of encounters between text and subjects in "Texts, Readers, Subjects," in *Culture, Media, Language*, pp. 163-73.

12 See Fred Feyes, "Critical Communications Research and Media Effects: The Problem of the Disappearing Audience," *Media, Culture, and Society 6 (1984): 219-32.*

13 "Gratifications researchers, in their paradigmatic personae, have lost sight of what the media are purveying, in part because of an overcommitment to the endless freedom of the audience to reinvent the text, in part because of a too rapid leap to mega-functions, such as surveillance or self-identity."

> (Jay G. Blumler, Michael Gurevitch, and Elihu Katz, "Reaching Out: A Future for Gratifications Research," in K.E. Rosengren, L.A. Wenner, and Ph. Palmgreen (eds) *Media Gratifications Research: Current Perspectives* (Beverly Hills, Calif.: Sage, 1985), p. 272)

14 ibid.

15 Karl Erik Rosengren, "Communication Research: One Paradigm, or Four?" *Journal of Communication* 33 (1983): 203; also Tamar Liebes, "On the Convergence of Theories of Mass Communication and Literature Regarding the Role of the Reader" (paper presented to the Conference on Culture and Communication, 1986); and Kim Christian Schroder, "Convergence of Antagonistic Traditions? The Case of Audience Research," *European Journal of Communication* 2 (1987): 7-31. Such an insistence upon convergence is not new among "mainstream" communication researchers. For example, Jennifer Daryl Slack and Martin Allor have recalled how in the late 1930s Lazarsfeld hired Adorno in the expectation that the latter's critical theory could be used to "revitalize" American empiricist research by supplying it with "new research ideas." The collaboration ended only one year later because it proved to be impossible to translate Adorno's critical analysis into the methods and goals of Lazarsfeld's project. Lazarsfeld has never given up the idea of a convergence, however. See Jennifer Daryl Slack and Martin Allor, "The Political and Epistemological Constituents of Critical Communication Research," *Journal of Communication* 33 (1983): 210.

16 Note, for instance, the striking similarities between the following two sentences, one from a uses and gratifications source, the other from a cultural studies one: "There seems to be growing support for that branch of communications research which asserts that television viewing is an active and social process" (Katz and Liebes, "Mutual Aid," p. 187); "Television viewing, the choices which shape it and the many social uses to which we put it, now turn out to be irrevocably active and social processes" (Stuart Hall, "Introduction," in David Morley, *Family Television. Cultural Power and Domestic Leisure* (London: Comedia, 1986), p. 8).

17 Tamar Liebes suggests that "the focus of the convergence is on the idea that the interaction between messages and receivers takes on the form of negotiation, and is not predetermined" ("On the Convergence," p. 1). However, as I will try to show, what makes all the difference in the theoretical and political thrust of

ethnographic audience studies is the way in which "negotiation" is conceived. Furthermore, "not predetermined" does not mean "undetermined," – and how (complex, structural, conjunctural) determinations should be conceived remains an important point of divergence between "critical" and "mainstream" studies. It is also noteworthy to point out that, while uses and gratifications researchers now seem to be "rediscovering the text," researchers working within a cultural studies perspective seem to be moving away from the text. This is very clear in Morley's second book, *Family Television*, on which I will comment later in this chapter. In fact, it becomes more and more difficult to delineate what "the television text" is.

18 See, for example, M. R. Levy and S. Windahl, "Audience Activity and Gratifications: A Conceptual Clarification and Exploration," in Rosengren *et al.*, *Media Gratifications Research*, pp. 109-22.

19 Blumler *et al.*, "Reaching Out," p. 260.

20 In stating this I do not want to suggest that cultural studies is a closed paradigm, or that all cultural studies scholars share one – say, Foucaultian – conception of power. Thus, the Birmingham version of cultural studies, with its distinctly Gramscian inflection, is criticized by Lawrence Grossberg for its lack of a theory of pleasure. An alternative, postmodernist perspective on cultural studies is developed by Grossberg in his "Cultural Studies Revisited and Revised," in Mary S. Mander (ed.) *Communications in Transition* (New York: Praeger, 1983), pp. 39-70.

21 Strategic interpretations, that is interpretations that are "political" in the sense that they are aware of the fact that interpretations are always concrete interventions into an already existing discursive field. They are therefore always partial in both senses of the word, and involved in making sense of the world in specific, power-laden ways. See Mary Louise Pratt, "Interpretive Strategies/Strategic Interpretations: On Anglo-American Reader-Response Criticism," in Jonathan Arac (ed.) *Postmodernism and Politics*, (Minneapolis: University of Minnesota Press, 1986), pp. 26-54.

22 Rosengren expresses this view in very clear cut terms, when he reduces the existence of disagreements between "critical" and "mainstream" researchers to "psychological reasons" ("Communication Research: One Paradigm, or Four?," p. 191).

23 Cf. James Lull, "The Naturalistic Study of Media Use and Youth Culture," in Rosengren *et al.*, *Media Gratifications Research*, pp. 209-24; Klaus Bruhn Jensen, "Qualitative Audience Research: Towards an Integrative Approach to Reception," *Critical Studies in Mass Communication* 4 (1987): 21-36; Thomas R. Lindlof and Timothy P. Meyer, "Mediated Communications as Ways of Seeing, Acting and Constructing Culture: The Tools and Foundations of Qualitative Research," in Lindlof, *Natural Audiences*, pp. 1-30.

24 Lawrence Grossberg (ed.) "On Postmodernism and Articulation: An Interview with Stuart Hall," *Journal of Communication Inquiry* 10, no.2 (summer 1986): 59.

25 James Carey, "Introduction," in Mander *Communications in Transition*, p. 5.

26 I borrowed this formulation from Virginia Nightingale, "What's Happening to Audience Research?," *Media Information Australia* 39 (February 1986): 21-2. Nightingale remarks that audience research has generally been "on the side" of those with vested interests in influencing the organization of the mass media in society, and that it is important to develop a research perspective that is "on the side" of the audience. However, it is far from simple to work out exactly what such a perspective would mean. The notion of the "active audience," for example, often put forward by uses and gratifications researchers to mark the distinctive identity of the "paradigm," is not in itself a guarantee for a stance "on the side

of the audience." In fact, the whole passive/active dichotomy in accounts of audiences has now become so ideologized that it all too often serves as a mystification of the real commitments behind the research at stake.

27 Reflections on the predicaments and politics of research on and with living historical subjects have already played an important role in, for example, feminist studies and anthropology, particularly ethnography. At least two problems are highlighted in these reflections. First, there is the rather awkward but seldom discussed concrete relation between researcher and researched as human beings occupying certain positions invested with power; second, there is the problem of the discursive form in which the cultures of "others" can be represented in non-objectifying (or better, less objectifying) ways. See, for example, Angela McRobbie, "The Politics of Feminist Research," *Feminist Review* 12 (October 1982): 46-57; James Clifford, "On Ethnographic Authority," *Representations* 1, no. 2 (1983): 118-46; James Clifford and George E. Marcus (eds) *Writing Culture. The Poetics and Politics of Ethnography* (Berkeley, Los Angeles, London: University of California Press, 1986). Researchers of media audiences have, as far as I know, generally been silent about these issues. However, for a perceptive and thought-provoking engagement with the problem, see Valerie Walkerdine, "Video Replay: Families, Films and Fantasy," in Victor Burgin, James Donald and Cora Kaplan (eds) *Formations of Fantasy* (London and New York: Methuen, 1986), pp. 167-99.

28 Grossberg, "Critical Theory," p. 89.

29 Hammersley and Atkinson, *Ethnography*, p. 16.

30 For a general overview of the interpretative or hermeneutic turn in the social sciences, see Paul Rabinow and William M. Sullivan (eds) *Interpretive Social Science* (Berkeley, Los Angeles, London: University of California Press, 1979). A more radical conception of what they call "interpretive analytics" is developed by Hubert Dreyfuss and Paul Rabinow in their *Michel Foucault: Beyond Structuralism and Hermeneutics* (Chicago, Ill.: University of Chicago Press, 1982).

31 Pratt, "Interpretive Strategies/Strategic Interpretations," p. 52.

32 Grossberg, "Critical Theory," p. 89.

33 Cf. Paul Rabinow, "Representations Are Social Facts: Modernity and Post-Modernity in Anthropology," in Clifford and Marcus, *Writing Culture*, pp. 234-61.

34 A more general, lucid criticism of empiricist mass communications research is offered by Robert C. Allen in his *Speaking of Soap Operas* (Chapel Hill and London: University of North Carolina Press, 1985), chapter 2.

35 Morley, *The "Nationwide" Audience*, p. 14. Morley's main objection to the uses and gratifications approach concerns "its psychologistic problematic and its emphasis on individual differences of interpretation." At another place, Morley even more emphatically expresses his distance from the uses and gratifications approach: "Any superficial resemblance between this study of television audience and the 'uses and gratifications' perspective in media research is misleading" (David Morley, "Cultural Transformations: The Politics of Resistance," in Howard Davis and Paul Walton (eds) *Language, Image, Media* (Oxford: Basil Blackwell, 1983), p. 117).

36 Morley, *Family Television*, p. 15.

37 ibid., p. 13.

38 Note that in positivist epistemology intersubjectivity is considered as one of the main criteria for scientific "objectivity." One of the myths by which the institution of Science establishes itself is that of scientific discourse as a process without a

subject. Hence the normative rule that the concrete historical subject of science, the researcher, should be interchangeable with any other so as to erase all marks of idiosyncratic subjectivity.

39   Morley, *Family Television*, p. 13.
40   ibid., p. 10.
41   Blumler *et al.*, "Reaching Out," p. 271.
42   It goes without saying that we are *not* speaking about significant differences in the quantified, statistical sense here.
43   Morley, *Family Television*, chapter 6.
44   Charlotte Brunsdon, "Women Watching Television," *MedieKultur* 4 (1986): 105; also quoted in Morley, *Family Television*, p. 147.
45   All sorts of cautious qualifications as to the generalizability of such "findings," so routinely put forward in research reports that the validity of the given typifications are said to be limited to certain demographic or subcultural categories (e.g. the urban working class), do not principally affect this reification of experential structures.
46   Brunsdon, "Women Watching Television," p. 104.
47   ibid., p. 106.
48   An image of the television audience as consisting of harmonious collectivities is suggested by Elihu Katz and Tamar Liebes when they describe the social process of decoding a television programme as an activity of "mutual aid." See Katz and Liebes, "Mutual Aid."
49   Hall, "Introduction," in Morley, *Family Television*, p. 10.
50   In contrast to his later *Family Television, The "Nationwide" Audience* focused on the ideological operations of the television medium itself.
51   Some critical scholars still dismiss the idea of doing empirical audience research altogether, because, so they argue, it would necessarily implicate the researcher with the strategies and aims of capitalist culture industry. See, for example, Tania Modleski, "Introduction," in Tania Modleski (ed.) *Studies in Entertainment. Critical Approaches to Mass Culture* (Bloomington Ind.: Indiana University Press, 1986), pp. xi-xii.
52   Morley, *Family Television*, p. 174.
53   Cf. Walkerdine, "Video Replay": "Much has been written about the activity of watching films in terms of scopophilia. But what of that other activity . . . this activity of research, of trying so hard to understand what people see in films? Might we not call this the most perverse voyeurism?" (p. 166).
54   This is not the place to go into the more radical, metatheoretical attempts to deconstruct the concept of audience as a useful starting point of research and analysis. The future of audience studies, however, cannot afford not to reflect on the consequences of such basic, radical critiques. See Briankle G. Chang, "Deconstructing the Audience: Who Are They and What Do We Know About Them?" in Margaret L. McLaughlin (ed.) *Communication Yearbook* 10, (Beverly Hills, Calif.: Sage, 1987), pp. 649-65; Martin Allor, "Relocating the Site of the Audience: Reconstructive Theory and the Social Subject," *Critical Studies in Mass Communication* 5 (1988): 217-33.
55   Paul Willis, "Notes on Method," in Hall *et al.*, *Culture, Media, Language*, p. 90.
56   Grossberg (ed.), "On Postmodernism and Articulation," p. 60.

Chapter six

Text and audience

Charlotte Brunsdon

Preliminary: Soap opera and good television

The serial form has an international, multi-media history. Television serials, distinguished internationally by their viewer loyalty, have proved themselves an indispensable element in most broadcasting economies. Soap opera, in Britain, has, as a genre, a very powerful metaphorical existence, even though we have no equivalent of daytime North American soaps. To say something is soap opera is to say that, minimally, it is bad drama. Frequently, it is to say that the drama is slackly written, cheaply produced, poorly acted. Perhaps more significantly, it is to imply cliché, banality, and bathos. It is never a term of approbation. This meaning of the term "soap opera" is imbricated with another, more general meaning. In this usage, the term "soap opera," with all the evaluative weighing I have described, is used metonymically to refer to television itself. Thus reference is made to a low-prestige leisure activity, engaged in thoughtlessly by those who do not have the inner resources to do anything else.

In Britain, with its long tradition of audience-improving public service broadcasting, this accretion round the term "soap opera" is particularly resonant, condensing as it does an opposition between good television and popular television. Good television in Great Britain generally draws its legitimation from other, already validated art forms: theater, literature, music. That is to say, television is good when it brings to a wider audience already legitimated high- and middle-brow culture. In this mode, television can be good as a potentially democratic, or socially extensive, transmitter.

The other mode of legitimation, or set of discourses within which television is allowed to be "good," poses a privileged relation to the real. Although this mode does reference specific qualities of broadcast media, the qualities concerned – those facilitating the transmission of reports of live events – are precisely self-negating. Thus sport, public events, current affairs, wild life programs, are "good television" if we seem to get unmediated access to the real world, and are not distracted by thinking about television *as television*.

The other term, that is constructed in opposition to "good television," is not bad television; it is popular or commercial television, and its origin, in Britain, is usually, casually, dated to 1955, and the start of commercial broadcasting. This bad television, which is where we find, and indeed what is meant by the term, soap opera, has another name, and that is "American series." Dick Hebdige has discussed the subcultural significance of "the American," and particularly of the discriminations made about design details like streamlining among British working-class youth in the 1950s.[1] Ien Ang points to the significant anti-American element in what she refers to as the "ideology of mass culture."[2] I want at this stage merely to reference these and other discussions in pointing to a little connotational string: soap opera – television – commercial – American.

We can see these wider, connotational meanings of soap opera when fears about satellite television are expressed in terms of the specter of "Wall to wall *Dallas*,"[3] and in the terminological wriggling conducted by the production companies of British soap operas. Granada, which produces the long-running *Coronation Street,* is notoriously resistant to the idea that the serial should be referred to as a soap, and when the BBC announced that a new continuing serial was in production (*EastEnders*), early newspaper coverage was sensitive to the *frisson* of incompatibility between the meanings "BBC" and "soap opera" ("The BBC prefers to call it 'a folk opera.' But that's splitting hairs."[4]) The implication of this comment is useful to us here. Inside commercial, mass produced soap, there is a traditional authentic community waiting to get out.

But television, producer of images in the age of electronic, rather than mechanical, reproduction, is of course, *par excellence*, the medium without authenticity. This founding lack of authenticity has two consequences which should concern us: first, in the relation between the lack of authenticity and the absence of a specifically televisual aesthetic, and second, in the way we understand some of the approaches to the television audience.

The absence of authenticity creates a founding lack in any relation television might have to already existent aesthetic discourse. Aesthetic discourses have been traditionally and historically organized partly through notions of "the real" and "the authentic," and the search for criteria which can identify and establish these and other categories, such as "the beautiful" and "the good." As I have observed, in British critical discourse about television, "the good" is precisely constructed through reference to that which is other than television – already existing and validated art forms, or "the real." It may be pertinent to note Bourdieu's observation that the aesthetic gaze is constructed in and through an opposition to the naïve gaze.[5] In much contemporary cultural discourse, television is the object of the naïve gaze against which the aesthetic gaze is constructed. Thus bad cinema or theater is designated soap opera, while video art barely makes it to the arts pages of newspapers. This constitution of television as the bad cultural object creates a critical abyss when we try to shift the gaze, to look at television, not through it to the Real or High Art. To echo a formulation which has a different political and historical resonance to my own project, there is almost no elaborated discourse of quality, judgment, and value which is specific to television, and which is not derived from production practices or professional ideologies.[6]

Horace Newcomb, writing in 1974, has argued for the use of criteria of intimacy, continuity, and history in a television aesthetic, and has also argued for the importance of soap opera in the development of television drama.[7] Intimacy and continuity do seem important elements in characterizing what is specific to television in certain textual modes. They are also, of course, characteristic of certain ways of watching television. The challenge of an adequate television aesthetic (if this is indeed what we should wish to call it) is that it must not only take a position on the relationship(s) between what we might call the institutional and the program components of televisual discourse, but it must also address extremely variable and diverse ways of watching television.

By the former, I mean to indicate the critical and analytical importance granted to what we might temporarily call the television-ness of television, which can be taken as the dominant focus for analysis, as opposed to the more traditional concentration on single programs. The classical site within British cultural theory for discussion of how the television text can be constituted as an object of study is Raymond Williams' formulation of "flow," taken up by John Caughie in his analysis of "the world" of television, and John Ellis with the notion of the segment.[8] In North America, "the viewing-strip" was proposed as the relevant unit by Newcomb and Hirsch in their 1983 essay.[9] These attempts to theorize how we may both grasp the continuousness of television and integrate the experience of viewing into analysis, can, I think, be most usefully supplemented by the deployment of the notion of "mode of address," which allows us to specify, at a formal level, the way in which the television text is always constructed as continuously there for someone. The differing identities posed in these interpellations (child, citizen, hobby enthusiast, consumer, etc.), and the overlapping and contradictory ways in which we are called to watch, form one of many sites for further research.[10] An insistence on the analytic importance of these moments – continuousness and mode of address – gives us some access to the inscription of television's institutional basis in its formal operation.

Among commentators less sympathetic to the pleasures of popular television viewing there is also a stress on the television-ness of television. Here though, the attention to the institutional aspects of television viewing is not motivated by the need to specify the modes of existence of a cultural form in order to lay the foundation for further analysis, but to argue that the "television-ness" of television viewing overwhelms any specific contents the medium may offer. Particularly for those concerned with children and adolescent viewers, watching television is often *per se* a bad thing, and thus program differentiation is of limited interest. Attention is instead focused on children's absorption in the screen and their inability to concentrate for longer than the length of a commercial.[11] A rather ironic advertisement on North American television at present (1987) addresses the viewer as concerned parent: "Are your kids spellbound?" over an image of a white male child glued to the box. The answer to television addiction turns out to be a video game called *Videosmarts* which will transform the TV zombie into an active and engaged spectator.[12]

The difficulty of defining or constituting the television text is accentuated by the privacy of television usage and the absence of an academy concerned to regulate the production and consumption of television.[13] These factors tend to privilege the perception of diverse modes of engagement with the television text as a specific and defining feature of television viewing. There are two problems with this view. First, as Paddy Scannell has argued, this is surely a feature of broadcast media, rather than television as such.[14] Second, we should not forget that people have always engaged very variously with all forms of cultural texts. Many books bought are not read, many paintings in art galleries not looked at, much music used as background, but the institutions of high culture, the academy, the museum, patronage, the auction room, have historically codified, both explicitly and implicitly, the proper mode of engagement with the text – be it a (sublime) mountain view or a lyric poem. Although many people may not engage in these proper ways, critical and aesthetic discussion is usually conducted on the assumption – or negotiation – of this type of engagement.

This is not to polemicize for and against particular ways of watching television. It is to point out that although historical research such as that of William Boddy and Lynn Spigel shows us that there was originally considerable uncertainty on how to understand the place of television in the home, the institutions of television are primarily concerned with maximizing audiences and revenue, not with the codifying of proper ways to watch.[15] Thus the discovery, by scholars who have to some extent historically defined themselves against the older traditions of "uses and gratifications" research, of the existence of diverse listening and viewing strategies, may seem to point us to defining features of broadcast media, but these are, in a tautological manner, only defining if we choose not to pay attention to what is on the screen.

An aesthetic of television would thus, in some ways, have to be an anti-aesthetic to be adequate to its object and the practices constituting it. Most interestingly, in relation to the question of an aesthetic, we have the question of function. People do turn on the television to watch specific programs, but they also put it on for company, to make the house feel lived in, to see if there's anything on. People do lots of different things with television and partly judge it accordingly. There is also evidence of a perpetual collection and classifying of material related to favorite programs. Everyday, in workplaces and homes, the previous night's viewing is sifted over and sorted, organized into categories which could form one basis for a popular aesthetic.

It is here, with the audience, that we find television's only possible moment of authenticity (and I do not propose authenticity as a desirable or necessary quality of a medium). The audience is, of course, economically necessary to the continuing profitability (existence) of the television companies which form just one part of the combines which contribute to the expansion of multinational leisure industries. But it is the symbolic necessity of the audience, its varied inscription throughout the television text, with which I want to work here. From audience as addressee of continuity announcements; laughing, gasping, and participating in situation comedies and game shows; making purchase choices from the address to the consumer in commercials; to audience as vox pop commentator on newsworthy events, the audience is called on, and constructed by television, as its main source of legitimation.

We can see this if we consider the connotational work done by the frequently repeated phrase: "taped before a live studio audience." The show that can claim this is, precisely, more authentic – more real, more natural, less manipulative, less televisual – than the show with canned laughter. Similarly the nervous, often emotional "person in the street" who comments, seemingly without rehearsal or editing, on a news event, lends realism, a guarantee of authenticity, to the awesome technological possibilities of electronic news-gathering services. Television is not just a popular medium because lots of people watch it. Television is a medium which constantly inscribes its own popularity into its programming in the way in which it displays its ability to mobilize all different kinds of people to participate, and thus to legitimate it, as *the* popular form.

We can see this in the institution's insatiable hunger for "real people." Jane Root quotes the producer of *The Price is Right*, William G. Stewart, making an illuminating comment about the search for authenticity:

> I wouldn't pick someone to be a contestant who would attempt to be a star. I want nice ordinary people who just come along for a bit of fun: some of them are so ordinary they are surprised to be chosen.[16]

In its most self-referential form, we see this hunger given expression in the range of television trivia games, in which families compete with each other to demonstrate the compatibility of their viewing habits and the totality of their recall. It is, however, not only the institution of television which has an insatiable hunger for nice ordinary people. As John Caughie has pointed out, "writing about pleasure on television frequently seems to be about other people's pleasure."[17] Academic television researchers are also caught in this search for the authentic response. We too are looking for folk, not soap, opera. I think it is arguable that essential questions about the differentiation of television's output – about the text – are being displaced on to questions about how television is watched. It is this process of displacement which I wish to trace in the second part of this chapter.

The modes of dispersal of the television text

I wish here to examine what has happened to the television text as an object of study in recent years. I want to trace, very schematically, the different ways in which the television text as an object of study has been under assault, and to argue for the importance of retaining the notion of text as an analytic category.

1. My first starting point is institutional, and consists of some observations of trends at the two International Television Studies Conferences held in London in 1984 and 1986.[18] There are, of course, always on-going debates in particular intellectual fields, which sometimes get into apparently obvious sets of issues and concerns at particular historical moments in the academy. There are also always more and less fashionable and attractive areas for research. Although not the only shift in parameters of debate, there was, between the 1984 and 1986 conferences, a clear move in interest from what is happening on the screen to what is happening in front of it – from text to audience.

This is not in any way to underestimate the amount of research that has already been conducted into the behavior and readings of the audience, both in Britain/Europe and in the United States. It is to suggest that the 1986 conference provides a convenient, if arbitrary, way of marking the entry of new and different interests into audience research. The 1984 conference took place just at the very end of a period of ten years or so of British culturalist analyses of popular film and television texts.

These analyses had, in the main, what one could call a political motivation. For a range of quite complexly articulated reasons, including the (semi-) institutionalization of Film, Television, and Cultural Studies within the academy, the rightward shift in the British political scene, the ageing of the generation radicalized in 1968, not to mention the institutional convenience of textual analysis, we had in Britain the burgeoning of academic analyses of popular texts and pastimes which sought to discredit both the left-pessimist despair over and the high-cultural dismissal of mass and popular cultures. From the mid-1970s onwards, "progressive" academics in the cultural fields became increasingly involved in the production of what could be termed "the redemptive reading." *Film noir*, 1950s color melodrama, television programs such as *The Sweeney*, *Coronation Street* and *Crossroads* were among the many texts addressed.[19]

The point about the "redemptive reading" is that it is not a simple populist embrace of the entertainment forms of late capitalism. The purely populist moment – although of course there has always been a straightforwardly populist strain contributing to the arguments for this sort of work – comes at the end of this period, roughly contemporary with the shift to the audience which I am describing, and, in popular cultural terms, with Madonna's rise to stardom.[20] The redemptive reading is not populist in that it starts with an acceptance of the uncongenial politics of whatever cultural text – for it is primarily a political reading – and then finds, at the least, incoherences and contradiction, and at the most fully articulated subtexts of revolt. Partly because of the centrality of Hollywood to the constitution of Film Studies as a discipline, it is here that this form of critical practice is at its most sophisticated and elaborated. The notorious category "e" of *Cahiers du Cinema* ("films which seem at first sight to belong firmly within the ideology and to be completely under its sway, but which turn out to be so only in an ambiguous manner"[21]) is of course a category of reception ("If one reads the film obliquely, looking for symptoms "[22]), unlike all the other categories in their influential 1969 taxonomy. The famous account of *Young Mr Lincoln* reveals what was at stake for cinephiles when ideological correctness became the principal critical criterion. The loved object, Hollywood cinema, which would have had to be jettisoned under the regime of the right-on, could be retrieved if its textual (here standing for ideological) coherence could be demonstrated to be only apparent. [23]

The redemptive reading frequently meets with a certain skepticism, a doubt that real readers really read like that. The 1984 International Television Studies Conference (ITSC) marked a suitable final appearance for the dominance of this type of textual analysis – the theoretical position had now to be supported by research into how non-academic readers read. In the 1984 ITSC, the conference strand that was bulging at the seams was that of "textual analysis." In 1986, submissions to this area were radically reduced and there was increased evidence of qualitative audience research. This "new" audience work, which comes partly from the necessity of testing the type of textual hypotheses referred to in the last paragraph, and which is often influenced by the ascendancy of reception theory in Literary Studies, met, often in ignorance, the older, more quantitative traditions of Mass Communications research. As Jane Feuer observed in her 1986 paper, the television text has been displaced by the text of audience – a much more various and diverse text – and the enormous conceptual and methodological problems entailed.[24]

I won't rehearse the problems of audience research here. It is, however, undoubtedly the case that we are beginning to see a whole new body of research into how people view television, and this research functions to disperse further the Text as an analytic category. We can now, following the work of, for example, Peter Collett, Ann Gray, Dorothy Hobson and David Morley (to take British examples), only argue that people watch television in extremely heterogeneous ways. People watch alone, with intimates, with strangers. They watch while they are doing something else, even when they are in another room. The notion of "flow," made less harmonious through practices such as channel zapping, has to be supplemented by the major variable of audience-presence-for-the-text. But how can we theorize this in a way which allows us to do more than accumulate an ethnography of particular practices?

2. The second way in which we lose the text is through the proliferation, across different media, of potential textual sites. At one level, this is a phenomenon of marketing and product licensing, and of the international character of image markets, to paraphrase Mattelart *et al.*;[25] at another, of the deep penetration television has in our daily lives. Thus we can buy videos of early episodes of *Coronation Street*, read novels based on any of the soaps, etc., but we can also overhear – and join in – conversations about soap characters, and read about predicted narrative events in newspapers.[26] Again, though, what is posed for us is the question of how we organize our perception of these issues, rather than the self-evident textual destruction that some have found.

Tony Bennett and Janet Woollacott have done exemplary work on what they call "the Bond phenomenon," in which they examine the many moments, textual existences, and transformations of James Bond. They set out "to demonstrate, in a practical way rather than just theoretically, that 'the text itself' is an inconceivable object."[27] Their achievement, I think, is not to prove that the text itself is an inconceivable object, but that the choice of what is recognized as constituting "a" text, consciously or not, is a political as well as a critical matter. It is around this issue that the contemporary struggles to dominate the critical field will be fought.

Literary analysis has as one of its specialisms the identification of reference and allusion. Modernism was partly modern in its use of quotation and the assumed knowledge of other texts. But the intertextuality of television is in some ways more radical, without the central organizing drive of the author, or, as I have argued, the specific hierarchies of form given by an established aesthetic. This quality, the promiscuous and nearly parodic self-referentiality of television, is not quite specific to television in a way that could define the medium. It is a quality – along with others also attributable to television – seen as characteristic of a postmodern era.[28] It is essential that we recognize the fact that television, and video, (along with the computer), are major agents in our understanding of contemporary time and space, and they contribute to the trans- formation of these categories in everyday life. This insight is potentially more useful than the analysis of single programs as if they were poems. But I'm not sure that this perception requires that we throw up our hands and say: "But it's all so ephemeral/pastichey/without reference/depthless/intertextual that there's nothing to analyse."

3. The third type of textual dispersal can be traced to feminist critical initiatives. This is of particular relevance because women have historically figured as preferred objects (I use the term advisedly) of audience research. Women soap opera viewers and listeners have proved particularly attractive to both commercial and academic researchers in ways which are I think relevant to us here.

If we accept that soap opera is in some ways the paradigmatic television genre (domestic, continuous, contemporary, episodic, repetitive, fragmented, and aural) we have also to ask why it has had until recently so little serious critical attention. The first part of the answer comes from the little connotational set I outlined earlier (soap opera – television – commercial – American). Soap opera has had little attention, except, ironically, in terms of the investigation of its effects on audiences, because it has not been considered textually worthy. Robert Allen puts this nicely when he writes of soap opera viewers not being granted the capacity of aesthetic distance from the text.[29] A range of critics have also pointed to the key significance of the social status of soap opera fans in determining the aesthetic status of the form. Feminist critics in the 1970s added vehemence to the general rejection of the genre, but have subsequently, in two slightly different ways, contributed to the revaluation of the role of the listener/viewer.

First, in a relatively short period, feminist criticism has moved from its initial repudiation of women's genres to the analysis and defense of traditionally feminine forms such as soap opera, melodrama, and romance.[30] This process, as I have argued at greater length elsewhere, has necessarily involved the attempt to analyse and enter imaginatively into the pleasures of the audiences for these forms.[31] Sometimes motivated by a desire to defend the audience and its pleasures, sometimes concerned principally to use cultural texts as sites where the constitution of contemporary femininities can be analysed, this work necessarily demands the investigation of the responses of audiences/ readers/viewers to the relevant texts. Thus much of the new audience research that I have already referred to has been specifically concerned with "feminine" texts, female audiences, and feminist methodologies.

It is the notion of feminist methodology which points to the other important element contributed by feminist criticism. This is the use of autobiographical data, and the validation of the use of "I" in academic discourse. I am of course simplifying and generalizing to make my point – the "I" also enters academic discourse through other routes, and the exploration of subjectivities constituted in subordination has been essential to groups other than women, and fragments the simple gender category. Here, however, the point is that the particular value set on the recounting and exploration of personal experience within second wave feminism, and the recognition of the extremely contradictory nature of experience and identity, have worked to construct autobiographical data as "proper" data. Thus, in addition to the audience studies of Janice Radway, Ien Ang, Dorothy Hobson, and Ann Gray, in which the focus is on other women, we also have Jo Spence's autobiographical photographic projects and the outstanding cultural analyses of Judith Williamson and Rosalind Coward who both work explicitly with their own histories.[32] Because the definition of feminist methodology frequently involves particular political understandings of the way in which the researcher herself inhabits the gender category woman, we have, in much feminist research, a certain fluidity of pronouns, a blurring of the separation of the object and the subject of research. This blurring is of course a feature of some sociologies – what I wish to do here is to point to the peculiar force that the first-person pronoun has in feminist discourse, a force which often has the resonance of "authenticity."

This "I" of some feminist discourse is a rather complicated affair in terms of whom it speaks to and for. Sometimes we have the simple use of autobiographical data, which is not explicitly articulated with either the assumed, or researched, experiences of "other women." Sometimes we have an "I the researcher," who sees herself as part of a larger category, "we women," on whose behalf, for whose good, and to whom she will, at different moments and simultaneously, speak. There will thus be the validation of autobiographical material and a feminine "I" over and above any unitary and inherent meaning of the text, but the status and identity of this reader/writer validated over the text fluctuates.

For our purposes, the point could be seen as a paradoxical one, in that feminist intervention in a particular academic field turns out to reproduce exactly the existing structure or patterning of the field. The traditional approach to soap opera within media research was to focus on audience rather than text. Although differently motivated, and ascribing different moral qualities to the two terms, text and audience, feminist research too has moved from the "bad" text to the "good" audience.

To conclude

I am not trying to argue for the reinstatement of what we might call the pre-audience text. Through the different routes which I have tried to outline, I think we can see some of the reasons for the growth in audience research projects. The discrediting of a simple cross/tick political aesthetic of popular texts, as if that is all they merit, was overdue. The investigation of the activities of viewers reveals the variety of contexts and modes of viewing which prevent the television text ever being, in any way, a simple, self-evident object for analysis. Similarly, we have to accept the potentially infinite number/flow of textual sites. Together, I think these recognitions begin to lead us to the postmodern haven of insignificance, and I have, in this context, characterized the pursuit of the audience as a search for authenticity, for an anchoring moment in a sea of signification.

So first, I want to argue that, difficult as it may be, we have to retain a notion of the television text. That is, without the guarantees of common sense or the authority of a political teleology with the recognition of the potentially infinite proliferation of textual sites, and the agency of the always already social reader, in a range of contexts, it is still necessary – and possible – to construct a televisual object of study – and judgment.

Here, I think we can most usefully learn from the practices of television itself. The broadcast world is structured through regularity and repetition. Time shift video recording alters the viewer's position in relation to this regularity and repetition, but I am not sure that it fundamentally transforms the broadcast structure of the day and week. Although it is tempting to start with a distinction between viewing alone and viewing with others, and recent research suggests that this might be particularly important in relation to understanding women's pleasures, the primary distinction seems to be between modes of viewing which are repeated on a regular basis and uncommon or unfamiliar modes of viewing (it thus incorporates the solitary/in company distinction).[33]

The need to specify context and mode of viewing in any textual discussion, and the awareness that these factors may be more determining of the experience of a text than any textual feature, do not, in and of themselves, either eliminate the text as a meaningful category, or render all texts the same. I may normally watch *Brookside* with one other person, and indeed prefer watching it in this familiar way, but I can still recognize the program when alone or with a large group doing something else. The fact that the text is only and always realized in historically and contextually situated practices of reading does not demand that we collapse these categories into each other.

Second, I do want to raise questions about the overall political shape, or weighing, of this concentration on the newly found audience. Although frequently informed by a desire to investigate, rather than judge, other people's pleasures, this very avoidance of judgment seems somehow to recreate the old patterns of aesthetic domination and subordination, and to pathologize the audience. Because issues of judgment are never brought out into the open, but always kept, as it were, under the seminar table, criteria involved can never be interrogated. It is for this reason that I wish to retain/construct the analytic category of the television text, for if we dissolve this category into the audience, we further inhibit the development of a useful television criticism and a television aesthetic. This is quite difficult enough without collapsing bad programs into bad audiences. I do not wish to argue that television studies should be devoted to discriminating between "good" and "bad" programs – but I do want to insist that most academics involved in audience studies are using qualitative criteria, however expressed or repressed, and that the constitution of the criteria involved should be the subject of explicit debate.

What we find, very frequently, in audience data, is that the audience is making the best of a bad job. The problem of working always with what people are, of necessity, watching, is that we don't really ever address that something else – what people might like to watch (and I don't mean to imply that these other desires simply exist without an object, but that is another whole paper at least). The recognition of the creativity of the audience, must, I think, be mobilized back into relation to the television text, and the demands that are made on program makers for a diverse and plural programming which is adequate to the needs, desires and pleasures of these audiences. Otherwise, however well intentioned, our work reproduces and elaborates the dominant paradigm in which the popular is the devalued term.

A later version of this paper entitled 'Television: Problems of aesthetics and audiences' was presented to a conference on television held at the Centre of Twentieth Century Studies, the University of Wisconsin-Milwaukee in April 1988.

Notes

1 Dick Hebdige, "Towards a Cartography of Taste," *Block* 4 (1981): 39-56.
2 Ien Ang, *Watching "Dallas" : Soap Opera and the Melodramatic Imagination* (London: Methuen, 1985).
3 Christopher Dunkley, television critic of the *Financial Times* used this phrase in the title of his book on the future of television, *Television Today and Tomorrow: Wall to Wall Dallas?* (Harmondsworth: Penguin, 1985).

4   Geoff Baker, "Queens of the East End," *Daily Star*, February 13, 1985.

5   Pierre Bourdieu, "The Aristocracy of Culture," in *Distinction: A Social Critique of the Judgment of Taste*, trans. Richard Nice (London: Routledge & Kegan Paul, 1984), pp. 11-57.

6   Robert Sklar opens his essay on television criticism: "This is an essay about a subject that does not exist: television criticism" (*Prime-Time America* (New York: Oxford University Press, 1980), p. 143). The following provide useful surveys of television criticism in Britain and the USA: Mike Poole, "The Cult of the Generalist: British Television Criticism 1936-83," *Screen* 25, no. 2 (March-April 1984): 41-62; John Caughie, "Television Criticism: 'A Discourse in Search of an Object,'" *Screen* 25, nos. 4-5 (July-October 1984): 109-20; Horace Newcomb, "American Television Criticism, 1970-1985," *Critical Studies in Communication* 3, no.2 (June 1986): 217-28.

7   Horace Newcomb, *Television: The Most Popular Art* (New York: Anchor, 1974), particularly chapter 10. Robert Allen has argued that Newcomb is overdependent on British television to exemplify his point. This would be significant in the context of my argument because of the way in which the art/entertainment axis is inscribed over British/American television. Robert C. Allen, *Speaking of Soap Operas* (Chapel Hill: University of North Carolina Press, 1985), pp. 222-3. See also chapter 4 of Allen's book.

8   Raymond Williams, *Television: Technology and Cultural Form* (London: Fontana, 1974); John Ellis, *Visible Fictions: Television Video Cinema* (London: Routledge & Kegan Paul, 1982); John Caughie, "The 'World' of Television," in Claire Johnston (ed.) *History, Production, Memory*, (Edinburgh: Edinburgh Film Festival Magazine, 1977), pp. 72-83.

9   Horace Newcomb and Paul Hirsch, "Television as a Cultural Forum," *Quarterly Review of Film Studies* 8, no.3 (summer 1983): 45-56, reprinted in Horace Newcomb (ed.) *Television - The Critical View*, (New York: Oxford University Press, 1987). This essay offers one formulation of the agency of the viewer in the constitution of the television text:

Using the viewing "strip" as the appropriate text of television, and recognizing that it is filled with varied topics and approaches to these topics, we begin to think of the television viewer as a bricoleur who matches the creator in the making of meanings. Bringing values and attitudes, a universe of personal experiences and concerns, to the texts, the viewer selects, examines, acknowledges and makes texts of his or her own.

(Television, p. 467)

10   The 1982 British Film Institute Summer School "Who Does Television Think You Are?" co-ordinated by David Lusted and held at Stirling University, attempted to work through some of the issues involved in conceptualizing television through notions of mode of address.

11   See, for example, Marie Winn, *The Plug-In Drug* (New York: Viking, 1977).

12   Philip Simpson (ed.) *Parents Talking Television* (London: Routledge & Kegan Paul 1987) provides a basis for a less paranoid discussion of children and television.

13   I do not want to underestimate the role of industry spectaculars, Emmy nights, etc., but in Britain at least these are radically separate from any type of endorsement of television as "legitimate" culture – that one can, for example, gain instruction in at universities. The more practice- and industry-oriented courses in broadcast media at North American universities may make generalization about this point quite improper.

14   Paddy Scannell, "*Radio Times*: The Temporal Arrangements of Broadcasting in the Modern World" (paper presented at the International Television Studies Conference, London, 1986). See also Simon Frith's discussion of the making of BBC light entertainment: "The Pleasures of the Hearth," in *Formations of Pleasure* (London: Routledge & Kegan Paul, 1983), pp. 101-23.

15   William Boddy, "'The Shining Centre of the Home': Ontologies of Television in the 'Golden Age,'" in Phillip Drummond and Richard Paterson (eds) *Television in Transition* (London: British Film Institute, 1985), pp. 125-34. Lynn Spigel, "Ambiguity and Hesitation: Discourses on Television and the Housewife in Women's Home Magazines 1948-1955" (paper presented at the International Television Studies Conference, London, 1986).

16   Jane Root, *Open the Box* (London: Comedia, 1986), p. 98.

17   Caughie, "The 'World' of Television," p. 116.

18   I was a member of the organizing committee of the 1986 International Television Studies Conference, and a discussant in 1984.

19   E. Ann Kaplan (ed.) *Women in Film Noir* (London: British Film Institute, 1978); Geoffrey Nowell-Smith, "Minelli and Melodrama," *Screen* 18, no.2 (summer 1977): 113-18; *Screen Education* 20 (autumn 1976), a special issue on *The Sweeney*; Richard Dyer, Christine Geraghty, Marion Jordan, Terry Lovell, Richard Paterson, and John Stewart (eds) *"Coronation Street"* (London: British Film Institute, 1981).

20   Madonna occasioned an absolute flurry of approving leftist and feminist review articles in Britain – in, for example, *Marxism Today*, *New Socialist*, and *Women's Review*. (This was the cover story for the March 1986 issue of *Women's Review*. The byline on the contents page read "Madonna – how Sheryl Garratt learned to stop worrying and to love her.") The *New Internationalist* currently advertises for subscribers with the slogan "From Mao to Madonna." E. Ann Kaplan discusses one of her videos from a rather different perspective in *Rocking Around the Clock* (London: Methuen, 1987), and Madonna also pops up on the cover of Robert C. Allen's collection of essays on television, *Channels of Discourse* (Chapel Hill: University of North Carolina Press, 1987).

21   Jean-Louis Comolli and Jean Narboni, "Cinema/Ideology/Criticism," *Cahiers du Cinéma* 216 (October 1969), reprinted in translation in Bill Nichols (ed.) *Movies and Methods I* (Berkeley and Los Angeles: University of California Press, 1976), pp. 22-30.

22   Nichols, *Movies and Methods*, p. 26.

23   The Editors of *Cahiers du Cinéma*, "John Ford's *Young Mr Lincoln*," *Cahiers du Cinéma* 223 (1970), reprinted in translation in Nichols, *Movies and Methods*, pp. 493-529.

24   Jane Feuer, "Reading *Dynasty*: Television and Reception Theory" (paper presented at the International Television Studies Conference, London, 1986).

25   A. Mattelart, X. Delcourt, and M. Mattelart, *International Image Markets* (London: Comedia, 1984).

26   Rosalind Brunt, "Street Credibility," *Marxism Today* (December 1983): 38-9.

27   Tony Bennett and Janet Woollacott, *Bond and Beyond: The Political Career of a Popular Hero* (Basingstoke and London: Macmillan Education, 1987), p. 7.

28   Fredric Jameson, "Postmodernism, or, The Cultural Logic of Late Capitalism," *New Left Review* 196 (July/August 1984): 53-92.

29   Allen, *Speaking of Soap Operas,* pp. 28f. Allen also provides an extensive bibliography.

30   A restricted set of references here would include: Ellen Seiter, "Eco's TV Guide:
      The Soaps," *Tabloid* 5 (1982): 35-43; Dorothy Hobson, *"Crossroads" : The
      Drama of a Soap Opera* (London: Methuen, 1982); Charlotte Brunsdon,
      "Crossroads: Notes on Soap Opera," *Screen* 22, no.4 (1981): 32-37; Dyer *et al.*,
      "Coronation Street"; Ang, *Watching "Dallas"*; Christine Gledhill (ed.) *Home Is
      Where the Heart Is: Melodrama and the Women's Picture* (London: British Film
      Institute, 1987); Janice Radway, *Reading the Romance: Women, Patriarchy, and
      Popular Literature* (Chapel Hill: University of North Carolina Press, 1984); Jean
      Radford (ed.) *The Progress of Romance* (London: Routledge & Kegan Paul, 1986).
31   Charlotte Brunsdon, "Women Watching Television," *MedieKultur* 4 (November
      1986): 100-12. See also Ien Ang, "Feminist Desire and Female Pleasure," *Camera
      Obscura* 16 (1988).
32   Dorothy Hobson, "Housewives and the Mass Media," in Stuart Hall, Dorothy
      Hobson, Andrew Lowe, and Paul Willis (eds) *Culture, Media, Language*
      (London: Hutchinson, 1980), pp. 105-14; Ann Gray, "Behind Closed Doors:
      Video Recorders in the Home," in Helen Baehr and Gillian Dyer (eds) *Boxed In:
      Women and Television,* (New York and London: Pandora Press, 1987), pp. 38-54.
      An example of Coward and Spence's work can be found in a piece they did
      together: "Body Talk," in Patricia Holland, Jo Spence, and Simon Watney (eds)
      Photography/Politics: Two (London: Comedia, 1986), pp. 24-39; see also Sarah
      McCarthy's "Autobiographies," pp. 134-41 in the same volume; and Judith
      Williamson, *Consuming Passions* (London: Marion Boyars, 1986).
33   David Morley, *Family Television: Cultural Power and Domestic Leisure*
      (London: Comedia, 1986); Gray, "Behind Closed Doors."

Chapter seven

Out of the mainstream:

Sexual minorities and the mass media

Larry Gross

In a society dominated by centralized sources of information and imagery, in which economic imperatives and pervasive values promote the search for large, common-denominator audiences, what is the fate of those groups who for one or another reason find themselves outside the mainstream? Briefly, and it is hardly a novel observation, such groups share a common fate of relative invisibility and demeaning stereotypes. But there are differences as well as similarities in the ways various minorities (racial, ethnic, sexual, religious, political) are treated by the mass media. And, given important differences in their life situations, members of such groups experience varying consequences of their mediated images.

In this chapter I will discuss the general question of minority perspectives applied to the study of mass media content and effects, and I will elaborate in greater detail the situation of sexual minorities (lesbian women and gay men) as members of the mass media audience.

Sexual minorities differ in important ways from the "traditional" racial and ethnic minorities; they are, in an interesting sense, akin to political minorities (so-called radicals and "fringe" groups). In both cases their members typically are self-identified at some point in their lives, usually in adolescence or later, and they are not necessarily easily identifiable by others. These two groups also constitute by their very existence a presumed threat to the "natural" (sexual and/or political) order of things, and thus they are inherently problematic and controversial for the mass media. These characteristics can be seen to affect the way members of such groups are depicted in the media (when they do appear), and also suggest ways to think about the effects of such depictions on the images held by society at large and by members of these minority groups.

Before turning to the discussion of minority audience perspectives, it would be helpful to characterize briefly the role of the mass media, television in particular, in our society.

The system is the message

First, the economic, political, and social integration of modern industrial society allows few communities or individuals to maintain an independent integrity. We

130

are parts of a Leviathan, like it or not, and its nervous system is telecommunications. Our knowledge of the "wide world" is what this nervous system
transmits to us. The mass media provide the chief common ground among
the different groups that make up a heterogeneous national community. Never
before have all classes and groups (as well as ages) shared so much of the
same culture and the same perspectives while having so little to do with their
creation.

Second, representation in the mediated "reality" of our mass culture is in itself
power; certainly it is the case that non-representation maintains the powerless
status of groups that do not possess significant material or political power bases.
That is, while the holders of real power – the ruling class – do not require (or
seek) mediated visibility, those who are at the bottom of the various power
hierarchies will be kept in their places in part through their relative invisibility.
This is a form of what Gerbner and I have termed symbolic annihilation.[1] Not all
interests or points of view are equal; judgments are made constantly about
exclusions and inclusions and these judgments broaden or narrow (mostly
narrow) the spectrum of views presented.

Third, when groups or perspectives do attain visibility, the manner of that
representation will itself reflect the biases and interests of those elites who define
the public agenda. And these elites are (mostly) white, (mostly) middle-aged,
(mostly) male, (mostly) middle and upper-middle class, and entirely heterosexual
(at least in public).

Fourth, we should not take too seriously the presumed differences between the
various categories of media messages – particularly in the case of television.
News, drama, quiz shows, sports,and commercials share underlying similarities
of theme, emphasis, and value. Even the most widely accepted distinctions (i.e.
news vs. fiction programs vs. commercials) are easily blurred. Decisions about
which events are newsworthy and about how to present them are heavily
influenced by considerations of dramatic form and content (e.g. conflict and
resolution) that are drawn from fictional archetypes; and the polished
mini-dramas of many commercials reveal a sophisticated mastery of fictional
conventions, just as dramatic programs promote a style of consumption and
living that is quite in tune with their neighboring commercial messages. More
important, the blending of stylistic conventions allows for greater efficacy and
mutual support in packaging and diffusing common values.

Fifth, the dominant conventions of our mass media are those of "realism" and
psychologically grounded naturalism. Despite a limited degree of reflexivity
which occasionally crops up, mainstream film and television are nearly always
presented as transparent mediators of reality which can and do show us how
people and places look, how institutions operate; in short, the way it is. These
depictions of the way things are, and why, are personified through dramatic plots
and characterizations which take us behind the scenes to the otherwise
inaccessible backstages of individual motivation, organizational performance,
and subcultural life.

Normal adult viewers, to be sure, are aware of the fictiveness of media drama: no one calls the police when a character on television is shot. But we may still wonder how often and to what extent viewers suspend their disbelief in the persuasive realism of the fictional worlds of television and film drama. Even the most sophisticated among us can find many components of our "knowledge" of the real world which derive wholly or in part from fictional representations. And, in a society which spans a continent, in a cosmopolitan culture which spans much of the globe, television and film provide the broadest common background of assumptions about what things are, how they work (or should work), and why.

Finally, the contributions of the mass media are likely to be most powerful in cultivating images of groups and phenomena about which there is little first-hand opportunity for learning; particularly when such images are not contradicted by other established beliefs and ideologies. By definition, portrayals of minority groups and "deviants" will be relatively distant from the real lives of a large majority of viewers.

Television as the mainstream

The average American adult spends several hours each day in this television world, children spend even more of their lives immersed in its "fictional reality." As I have already suggested, the mass media, and television foremost among them, have become the primary sources of the common information and images that create and maintain a world view and a value system. In a word, the mass media have become central agents of enculturation. In the Cultural Indicators Project we have used the concept of "cultivation" to describe the influence of television on viewers' conceptions of social reality.[2]

On issue after issue we find that assumptions, beliefs, and values of heavy viewers of television differ systematically from those of light viewers in the same demographic groups. Sometimes these differences appear as overall, main effects, whereby those who watch more television are more likely – in all groups – to give what we call "television answers" to our questions. But in many cases the patterns are more complex. We have found that television viewing, not surprisingly, serves as a stable factor differentially integrated into and interacting with different groups' life situations and world views. In our recent work we have isolated a consistent pattern which we have termed "mainstreaming."[3]

The mainstream can be thought of as a relative commonality of outlooks and values that television tends to cultivate in viewers. By mainstreaming we mean the sharing of that commonality among heavy viewers in those demographic groups whose light viewers hold divergent positions. In other words, differences deriving from other factors and social forces – differences that may appear in the responses of light viewers in various groups – may be diminished or even absent when the heavy viewers in these same groups are compared. Overall, television viewing appears to signal a convergence of outlooks rather than absolute, across-the-board increments in all groups.

Choices or echoes?

The mainstream which we have identified as the embodiment of a dominant ideology, cultivated through the repetition of stable patterns across the illusory boundaries of media and genre, and absorbed by otherwise diverse segments of the population, nevertheless has to contend with the possibility of oppositional perspectives and interpretations. What options and opportunities are available to those groups whose concerns, values and even very existence are belittled, subverted, and denied by the mainstream? Can the power of the mass media's central tendencies be resisted? Can one avoid being swept into the mainstream? The answers to such questions depend in large part on which group or segment we are discussing; while many minorities are similarly ignored or distorted by the mass media, not all have the same options for resistance and the development of alternative channels.

In general the opportunities for organized opposition are greatest when there is a visible and even organized group which can provide solidarity and institutional means for creating and disseminating alternative messages. There are numerous examples of groupings that have sprung up, as it were, along the right bank of the mainstream. Most organized and visible among these are the Christian fundamentalist syndicated television programs. These programs provide their (generally older and less educated) viewers with an array of programs, from news to talk shows to soap operas to church services and sermons, all reflecting perspectives and values that they quite correctly feel are not represented in mainstream, prime-time television or in the movies.[4] As one of Hoover's conservative, religious respondents put it, in discussing network television:

> I think a good deal of it is written by very liberal, immoral people . . . Some of the comedies, the weekly things that go on every week, they make extramarital affairs, and sex before marriage an everyday thing like everybody should accept it . . . and they present it in a comic situation, a situation that looks like it could be fun and a good deal of these weekly shows I don't like go for that.[5]

The religious sponsoring and producing organizations are not merely engaged in meeting their audiences' previously unmet needs for a symbolic environment in which they feel at home; they are also attempting to translate the (usually exaggerated) numbers of their audiences and their (constantly solicited) financial contributions into a power base from which they can exert pressure to alter the channel of the mainstream and bring it even closer to where they now reside, up on the right bank.

At the moment, and for the foreseeable future in the United States, at least, there is no comparable settlement on the left bank of the mainstream. There are many reasons why the organized left has been unable to match the right's success in harnessing the available resources of media technology. It is not hard to see that some minority perspectives are in fact supportive of the dominant ideology, however much the media's need for massive audiences might sacrifice or offend their interests, while other minority values are truly incompatible with the basic power relationships embodied in that mainstream.

Minority positions and interests which present radical challenges to the established order will not only be ignored, they will be discredited. Those who benefit from the status quo present their position as the moderate center, balanced between equal and opposing "extremes" – thus the American news media's cult of "objectivity," achieved through a "balance" which reflects an invisible, taken-for-granted ideology. As a CBS spokesman explained it, when dismissing attempts by Jesse Helms and Ted Turner to take over the network:

> Anyone ... who buys a media company for ideological reasons must be prepared to pay dearly for that conviction. The right-wingers and the left-wingers in this country are vociferous but small in number compared to the ordinary citizen, who, when it comes down to it, is a centrist.[6]

The fatal flaw in the credo of centrism and moderation is that how one defines the "responsible" extremes will determine where the center will fall. In the United States the mass media-legitimated spectrum runs a lot further right than it does left, which puts the "objectively balanced" mainstream clearly to the right of center. Jesse Helms can be elected and re-elected to the Senate and can embark on a public campaign to take over CBS; his opposite number on the left, whoever that might be, couldn't conceivably claim or receive that degree of visibility, power, and legitimacy.

Yet, in the final analysis, neither flank can avoid serving in one way or another to buttress the ramparts of the status quo, and to keep the truly oppositional from being taken seriously. American presidential politics recently featured a matched pair of Christian candidates, but neither the minister of the left, Jesse Jackson, nor the minister of the right, Pat Robertson, could hope to do more than exert some small pressure on their respective branches of the Property Party, whose two official divisions – the Democrats and the Republicans – offer an illusion of choice within the political mainstream.

Homosexuals and television: fear and loathing

Close to the heart of our cultural and political system is the pattern of roles associated with sexual identity: our conceptions of masculinity and femininity, of the "normal" and "natural" attributes and responsibilities of men and women. And, as with other pillars of our moral order, these definitions of what is normal and natural serve to support the existing social power hierarchy.

The maintenance of the "normal" gender role system requires that children be socialized – and adults retained – within a set of images and expectations which limit and channel their conceptions of what is possible and proper for men and for women. The gender system is supported by the mass media treatment of sexual minorities. Mostly, they are ignored or denied – symbolically annihilated;

when they do appear they do so in order to play a supportive role for the natural order and are thus narrowly and negatively stereotyped. Sexual minorities are not, of course, unique in this regard.[7] However, lesbians and gay men are unusually vulnerable to mass media power; even more so than blacks, national minorities, and women. Of all social groups (except perhaps communists), we are probably the least permitted to speak for ourselves in the mass media. We are also the only group (again, except for communists and, currently, Arab "terrorists") whose enemies are generally uninhibited by the consensus of "good taste" which protects most minorities from the more public displays of bigotry.

The reason for this vulnerability lies in large part in our initial isolation and invisibility. The process of identity formation for lesbian women and gay men requires the strength and determination to swim against the stream. A baby is born and immediately classified as male or female, white or black, and is treated as such from that moment, for better or worse. That baby is also defined as heterosexual and treated as such. It is made clear throughout the process of socialization – a process in which the mass media play a major role – that one will grow up, marry, have children and live in nuclear familial bliss, sanctified by religion and licensed by the state. Women are surrounded by other women, people of color by other people of color, etc., and can observe the variety of choices and fates that befall those who are like them. Mass media stereotypes selectively feature and reinforce some of the available roles and images for women, national minorities, people of color, etc.; but they operate under constraints imposed by the audiences' immediate environment.

Lesbians and gay men, conversely, are a self-identifying minority. We are assumed (with few exceptions, and these – the "obviously" effeminate man or masculine woman – may not even be homosexual) to be straight, and are treated as such, until we begin to recognize that we are not what we have been told we are, that we are different. But how are we to understand, define, and deal with that difference? Here we generally have little to go on beyond very limited direct experience with those individuals who are close enough to the accepted stereotypes to be labeled publicly as queers, faggots, dykes, etc. And we have the mass media.

The mass media play a major role in this process of social definition, and rarely a positive one. In the absence of adequate information in their immediate environment, most people, gay or straight, have little choice other than to accept the narrow and negative stereotypes they encounter as being representative of gay people. The mass media have rarely presented portrayals which counter or extend the prevalent images. On the contrary, they take advantage of them. Typically, media characterizations use popular stereotypes as a code which they know will be readily understood by the audience, thus further reinforcing the presumption of verisimilitude while remaining "officially" innocent of dealing with a sensitive subject.

But there is more to it than stereotyping. For the most part gay people have been simply invisible in the media. The few exceptions were almost invariably either victims – of violence or ridicule – or villains. As Vito Russo noted recently, "it is not insignificant that out of 32 films with major homosexual characters from 1961 through 1976, 13 feature gays who commit suicide and 18 have the homosexual murdered by another character."[8] Even this minimal and slanted presence, however, seems to be so threatening to the "industry" that gay characterizations and plot elements always come accompanied by pressbook qualifications and backpedaling. In his survey of the treatment of gay people in American film,[9] Russo presents a sample of the predictable distancing that gay themes evoke from directors (*"The Children's Hour* is not about lesbianism, it's about the power of lies to destroy people's lives," William Wyler, 1962; *"Sunday, Bloody Sunday* is not about the sexuality of these people, it's about human loneliness," John Schlesinger, 1972; *"Windows* is not about homosexuality, it's about insanity," Gordon Willis, 1979), and actors (*"The Sergeant* is not about homosexuality, it's about loneliness," Rod Steiger, 1968; *"Staircase* is not about homosexuality, it's about loneliness," Rex Harrison, 1971). It is easy to imagine how comforting these explanations must have been to lesbian and gay audience members looking for some reflection of their lives in the media. But it is not only the audiences who appear to require protective distancing from gay characters and themes. We are frequently treated to showbiz gossip intended to convey the heterosexual bona fides of any actor cast in a gay role, as when the actor playing the swish drag queen Albin in the stage version of *La Cage aux folles* told several interviewers that he had consulted with his wife and children before accepting the role.

The gay liberation movement emerged in the late 1960s in the United States, spurred by the examples of the black and feminist movements. Consequently, media attention to gay people and gay issues increased in the early 1970s, much of it positive (at least in comparison with previous and continuing heterosexist depictions and discussions), culminating (in the sense of greater media attention – in the pre-AIDS era) in 1973, with the decision by the American Psychiatric Association to delete homosexuality from its "official" list of mental diseases. By the middle 1970s, however, a backlash against the successes of the gay movement began to be felt around the country, most visibly in Anita Bryant's successful campaign to repeal a gay rights ordinance in Dade County, Florida, in 1977. Since then the gay movement and its enemies, mostly among the "new right," have been constant antagonists (right-wing fund-raisers acknowledge that anti-homosexual material is their best bet to get money from supporters), and television has often figured in the struggle. But, although the right wing has attacked the networks for what they consider to be overly favorable attention to homosexuals, in fact gay people are usually portrayed and used in news and dramatic media in ways that serve to reinforce rather than challenge the prevailing images.

Kathleen Montgomery observed the efforts of the organized gay movement to improve the ways network programmers handle gay characters and themes. In particular she describes the writing and production of a made-for-television network movie that had a gay-related theme, and involved consultation with representatives of gay organizations. And the result?

> Throughout the process all the decisions affecting the portrayal of gay life were influenced by the constraints which commercial television as a mass medium imposes upon the creation of its content. The fundamental goal of garnering the largest possible audience necessitated that (a) the program be placed in a familiar and successful television genre – the crime-drama; (b) the story focus upon the heterosexual male lead character and his reactions to the gay characters rather than upon the homosexual characters themselves; and (c) the film avoid any overt display of affection which might be offensive to certain segments of the audience. These requirements served as a filter through which the issue of homosexuality was processed, resulting in a televised picture of gay life designed to be acceptable to the gay community and still palatable to a mass audience.[10]

Acceptability to the gay community, in this case, means that the movie was not an attack on our character and a denial of our basic humanity; it could not be mistaken for an expression of our values or perspectives. But of course they were not aiming at us, either; they were merely trying to avoid arguing with us afterwards. In Vito Russo's words, "mainstream films about homosexuals are not for homosexuals. They address themselves exclusively to the majority."[11] However, there will inevitably be a great many lesbians and gay men in the audience.

The rules of the mass media game have a double impact on gay people: not only do they mostly show us as weak and silly, or evil and corrupt, but they exclude and deny the existence of normal, unexceptional as well as exceptional lesbians and gay men. Hardly ever shown in the media are just plain gay folks, used in roles which do not center on their deviance as a threat to the moral order which must be countered through ridicule or physical violence. Television drama in particular reflects the deliberate use of clichéed casting strategies which preclude such daring innovations.

The stereotypic depiction of lesbians and gay men as abnormal, and the suppression of positive or even "unexceptional" portrayals, serve to maintain and police the boundaries of the moral order. It encourages the majority to stay on their gender-defined reservation, and tries to keep the minority quietly hidden out of sight. For the visible presence of healthy, non-stereotypic lesbians and gay men does pose a serious threat: it undermines the unquestioned normalcy of the status quo, and it opens up the possibility of making choices to people who might never otherwise have considered or understood that such choices could be made.

The situation has only been worsened by the AIDS epidemic. By 1983 nearly all mass media attention to gay men was in the context of AIDS-related stories, and because this coverage seems to have exhausted the media's limited interest in gay people, lesbians became even less visible than before (if possible). AIDS reinvigorated the two major mass media "roles" for gay people: victim and villain. Already treated as an important medical topic, AIDS moved up to the status of "front page" news after Rock Hudson emerged as the most famous person with the disease. At present AIDS stories appear daily in print and broadcast news – often with little or no new or important content – and the public image of gay men has been inescapably linked with the specter of plague. Television dramatists have presented the plight of (white, middle-class) gay men with AIDS, but their particular concern is the agony of the families/friends who have to face the awful truth: their son (brother, boyfriend, husband, etc.) is, gasp, gay! But, even with AIDS, not too gay, mind you. In the major network made-for-television movie on AIDS, NBC's *An Early Frost*, a young, rich, white, handsome lawyer is forced out of the closet by AIDS. "We know he is gay because he tells his disbelieving parents so, but his lack of a gay sensibility, politics and sense of community make him one of those homosexuals heterosexuals love."[12]

An Early Frost is thus another example of the pattern discerned by Montgomery: although this time the familiar and successful genre is family- not crime-drama, the focus is still on the heterosexual characters and their reactions. As William Henry notes in a recent overview of television's treatment of gays (or lack of same) during the past fifteen years,

> when TV does deal with gays it typically takes the point of view of straights struggling to understand. The central action is the progress of acceptance – not self-acceptance by the homosexual, but grief-stricken resignation to fate by his straight loved ones, who serve as surrogates for the audience. Homosexuality thus becomes not a fact of life, but a moral issue on which everyone in earshot is expected to voice some vehement opinion. Just as black characters were long expected to talk almost exclusively about being black, and handicapped characters (when seen at all) were expected to talk chiefly about their disabilities, so homosexual characters have been defined almost entirely by their "problem."[13]

Being defined by their "problem," it is no surprise therefore that gay characters have mostly been confined to television's favorite problem-of-the-week genre, the made-for-television movie, with a very occasional one-shot appearance of a gay character on a dramatic series (examples include episodes of *Lou Grant, Medical Center* and *St. Elsewhere*). Continuing gay characters tend to be so subtle as to be readily misunderstood by the innocent (as in the case of Sidney in *Love, Sidney*, whose homosexuality seemed to consist entirely of crying at the movies and having a photo of his dead lover on the mantelpiece), or confused about their sexuality and never seen in an ongoing romantic relationship (as in the case of the off-again-on-again Steven Carrington in *Dynasty*, whose lovers have an unfortunate tendency to get killed).

Despite their greater freedom from the competition for massive mainstream audiences – perhaps because of their need to compete for the primary audience of teens and young adults – commercial films are no more welcoming to gay characters than television. In fact, as Vito Russo shows in the revised edition of his 1981 study, *The Celluloid Closet* (1987), recent films are awash with gay villains and victims once more:

> The use of the word faggot has become almost mandatory. Outright slurs that would never be tolerated in reference to any other group of people are commonly used onscreen against homosexuals. . . . Anti-gay dialogue is most often given to the very characters with whom the audience is supposed to identify.[14]

Films offer their makers a degree of license which isn't available to television producers – an opportunity to use language and depictions of sexuality that go far beyond the limits imposed on television – but as far as gay people are concerned, this mostly serves as a hunting license.

Colonization: the straight gay

There are several categories of response to the mainstream media's treatment of minorities; among them are internalization, subversion, secession, and resistance. To begin with, as we have already noted, we are all colonized by the majority culture. Those of us who belong to a minority group may nevertheless have absorbed the values of the dominant culture, even if these exclude or diminish us. We are all aware of the privileging of male-identified attributes in our patriarchal culture, and the dominance of the male perspective in the construction of mass-mediated realities. Similarly, the US media offer a white-angled view of the world which is shared with people of color everywhere. In a study of Venezuelan children in which they were asked to describe their heroes, the hero was North American in 86 per cent of the cases and Venezuelan in only 8 per cent; English-speaking in 82 per cent and Spanish-speaking in 15 per cent; white heroes outnumbered black heroes 11 to 1; and heroes were wealthy in 72 per cent of the cases.[15]

Sexual minorities are among the most susceptible to internalizing the dominant culture's values because the process of labelling generally occurs in isolation and because:

> We learn to loathe homosexuality before it becomes necessary to acknowledge our own. . . . Never having been offered *positive* attitudes to homosexuality, we inevitably adopt *negative* ones, and it is from these that all our values flow.[16]

Internalization and colonization can also result in the adoption of assimilationist strategies which promise upward (or centerward) mobility, although at the cost of cutting off one's "roots." Gay people by and large know how to "pass"; after all, it's what they have been doing most of their lives. But the security attained is fragile and often illusory, and certainly will not provide support in resisting the inferiorizing pressures of the straight culture they attempt to blend into. And all too often, there really isn't any resistance anyway, as the process of internalization has achieved the desired goal. The Zionist polemicist Ahad Ha-Am drew on a biblical analogy to describe this phenomenon, in his essay on Moses: "Pharaoh is gone, but his work remains; the master has ceased to be master, but the slaves have not ceased to be slaves."[17]

The supposedly liberal and tolerant domain of the media does not necessarily permit homosexuals (or other minorities) to overcome the burdens of self-oppression:

> When it comes to keeping minorities in their place, the entertainment industry continues to divide and conquer. For all the organizing that women have done, for instance, in their attempts to break down the barriers, well-placed women executives say they've received very little mutual support from their equally well-placed peers. The old-boy network rules, and the individual women, gays, blacks, or hispanics who attain some degree of success usually have to camouflage themselves in the trappings of their masters.[18]

Similarly, gay writer Merle Miller recalled that, "as editor of a city newspaper, he indulged in 'queer-baiting' to conceal his own homosexuality."[19] Openly gay actor Michael Kearns speaks of "a gay agent who makes it a habit to tell 'fag jokes' at the close of interviews with new actors. If an actor laughs, he's signed up; if he doesn't, he isn't."[20] Working backstage, it would seem, does not exempt one from falling under the spell of the hegemonic values cultivated and reflected by the media. However, as Raymond Williams has suggested, hegemony "is never either total or exclusive. At any time, forms of alternative or directly oppositional politics and culture exist as significant elements in the society."[21]

Resistance and opposition

The most obvious form of resistance, but possibly the most difficult, would be simply to ignore the mass media, and refuse to be insulted or injured by their derogation and denial of one's identity and integrity as a member of a minority group. Unfortunately, although some of us can personally secede from the mass-mediated mainstream, or sample from it with great care and selectivity, we cannot thereby counter its effect on our fellow citizens. We cannot even prevent our fellow minority-group members from attending to messages which we feel are hostile to their interests (this is, of course, a familiar dilemma for parents who feel that commercial television is not in the best interests of their children). Given the generally high levels of television viewing at the lower rungs of the socio-economic ladder, it can be expected that large segments of the population consume media fare that serves to maintain their subordinate status. In the United States, black households are disproportionately heavy television consumers: "Black households, which represented about 9 percent of all television households surveyed, accounted for about 14 percent of all household viewing. According to the United States Census Bureau, blacks constituted 12 percent of the population last year."[22]

We might expect self-identified ideological minorities to be better able to resist the siren's song of the mass media; and we have noted that the religious right has developed alternative channels to provide their adherents with a source of value-congruent media fare. We've also noted the absence of equivalent programming on the left bank of the mainstream. Leftists, it seems, are faced with fewer choices, and they experience the ambivalence of being aware of the central role the media play in consensualizing a dominant ideology and yet not wanting (or being able) to pull completely out of the mainstream themselves. In an ongoing study of American leftists' relationships to the mass media, Eugene Michaud has encountered many expressions of such hostility and ambivalence, despite which the respondents interviewed continue to watch television:

"Frankly, I detest TV. It's the source of many family disputes. I really find TV obnoxious and really intrusive on whatever you're trying to do. . . .For most people, I think TV is a way of relaxing – it's a distraction . . . life is hard – so it's very easy to watch TV." (Male, 36)

"I have a lot of trouble with the TV news. I get upset and I want to run away. Or I get obnoxious and start sneering at it, and my wife gets upset because she's trying to listen. . . . I realize that there's this vast treasure trove of ideas and images from TV which most people are plugged into." (Male, 44)

"I hate watching the TV news and having someone give me the straight administration line. . . . The way I watch TV is if I don't have anything else to do and I'm bored." (Female, 32)

"We watch network news sometimes, but I feel like it's junkfood news. I find it very frustrating. They never analyse anything. . . . It's also so easy to turn on TV, and there's all this visual stuff. It's so effortless." (Female, 32)

"I do watch *Nightline*, but it pisses me off to no end . . . the way they manipulate things to put forth a certain point-of-view. It's a total set-up." (Male, 32)[23]

Observers of the current television scene will not be surprised to learn that there are one or two shows that do manage to appeal to Michaud's leftist respondents. Most frequently praised is *Hill Street Blues*, although it's generally judged to have declined after its first few seasons. Its spin-off, *St. Elsewhere*, receives similar reviews. The decline is often interpreted in ideological terms:

"I used to watch *Hill Street Blues* regularly, but I mostly don't bother any more . . . it used to try to demonstrate the ambiguity people felt towards each other and towards their work. Now, it's just the traditional good guys against the bad guys. I think it's a reflection of the Reagan era." (Female, 34)

The ratings smash hit *Cosby Show* is popular among some leftists, despite its up-scale values, because it features a black family and because "there's a lot of love, which is appealing, and it does capture the real dynamics of family life in a funny way" (Male, 30).

Lesbian women and gay men do not constitute an ideological minority in the same way that American leftists do (although those gay people who are part of the "movement" certainly tend to be left-identified), and they are less likely to condemn the mass media in the way the left does. However, few lesbian women and gay men could remain unaware of how they are treated in the media – when their existence is even acknowledged – and their relationship to the media is likely to be colored by this awareness. Just as racial and ethnic minority groups pay close attention to programs which feature their members, so too gay people will tune in regularly to any program which promises an openly or explicitly lesbian or gay character (or even a favorite performer assumed to be gay). The images and messages they will encounter will not, as we have already noted, provide them with much comfort or support. More typically, they will again be marginalized, trivialized, and insulted.

While working on this paper I went to see the latest film written and directed by Woody Allen, *Radio Days*, and was irritated, though not surprised, by the inclusion of a gay character whose only function is to evoke a laugh at his own expense, and to further underline the hopelessness of a woman who would fall in love with him. My irritation was caused not only by Woody Allen's gratuitous insult – I've come to expect these from him – but also by the hilarity it produced among the audience. The experience of having one's status as "fair game" emphasized in this graphic fashion while sitting in a movie theater is familiar to gay people, just as it is to people of color and to women. Even when a gay characterization is intended to be sympathetic (as in the wildly successful *La Cage aux folles*), the gay members of the audience may wince at the falsity of the image, and find themselves laughing at different times from the straight audience. There can be a perverse pleasure in this perception – Elizabeth Ellsworth describes lesbian feminist reviewers of *Personal Best* (a film written and directed by a straight man, which includes a lesbian relationship as a central theme, despite the usual pressbook obfuscation) who "expressed pleasure in watching the dominant media 'get it wrong' in watching it attempt, but fail, to colonize 'real' lesbian space."[24]

It can be argued that the best stance for gay people to adopt *vis-à-vis* the mass media would be to repay them with the same indifference and contempt they reveal toward us. Unfortunately, while this might be a gratifying and appropriate individual solution, it is not realistic as a general strategy. One may be able to reduce one's own irritation by ignoring the media, but their insidious impact is not so easily avoided. What cannot be avoided, however, can be better understood, and studies of lesbian and gay audiences and their responses should be included in the emerging research agenda.

Subversion

A second oppositional strategy is the subversion and appropriation of mainstream media, as well as the occasionally successful infiltration. The classic gay (male) strategy of subversion is camp – an ironic stance toward the straight world rooted in a gay sensibility:

> a creative energy reflecting a consciousness that is different from the mainstream; a heightened awareness of certain human complications of feeling that spring from the fact of social oppression; in short, a perception of the world which is coloured, shaped, directed and defined by the fact of one's gayness.[25]

This characterization would, of course, also fit many other minorities who experience oppression, but the gay sensibility differs in that we encounter and develop it at a later stage in our lives; it is nobody's native tongue. Moreover, while sharing much with other minority perspectives, camp is notably marked by irony and a theatrical perspective on the world which can be traced to the particular realities of gay experience:

> The stigma of gayness is unique insofar as it is not immediately apparent either to ourselves or to others. Upon discovery of our gayness, however, we are confronted with the possibility of avoiding the negative sanctions attached to our supposed failing by concealing information (i.e. signs which other people take for gay) from the rest of the world. This crucial fact of our existence is called *passing for straight*, a phenomenon generally defined in the metaphor of theatre, that is, playing a role: pretending to be something one is not; or, to shift the motive somewhat, to camouflage our gayness by withholding facts about ourselves which might lead others to the correct conclusion about our sexual orientation.[26]

Camp offers a subversive response to mainstream culture, and provides both in-group solidarity and an opportunity to express distance from and disdain for the roles most gay people play most of the time. Exchanged in private settings, camp is a mechanism of oppositional solidarity which repairs the damage inflicted by the majority and prepares us for further onslaughts. As a restricted code used in public settings, camp can be a way to identify and communicate with other "club members" under the unknowing eyes of the straight world – in itself an act of subversive solidarity (as well as self-protection). Camp can also be a form of public defiance, and a risky expression of a difference which dares to show its face.

Camp is also the quintessentially gay strategy for undermining the hegemonic power of media images.[27] The sting can be taken out of oppressive characterizations and the hot air balloons of official morality can be burst with the ironic prick of camp humor. Most importantly, by self-consciously taking up a position outside the mainstream, if only in order to look back at it, camp cultivates a sense of detachment from the dominant ideology.

> The sense of being different ... made me feel myself as "outside" the mainstream in fundamental ways – and this does give you a kind of knowledge

of the mainstream you cannot have if you are immersed in it. I do not necessarily mean a truer perspective, so much as an awareness of the mainstream as a mainstream, and not just the way everything and everybody inevitably are; in other words, it denaturalizes normality. This knowledge is the foundation of camp.[28]

Camp can also be seen in the appropriation of mainstream figures and products when they are adopted as "cult" objects by marginal groups. Camp cult favorites are often women film stars who can be seen as standing up to the pressures of a male-dominated movie industry and despite all travails remaining in command of their careers (Bette Davis, Joan Crawford, Mae West), or at least struggling back from defeat (Judy Garland[29]).

Cult movies like *The Rocky Horror Picture Show* provide occasions for meeting others with the same perspective, and turning a media product into the pretext for communal interaction. In a study of patrons waiting to see *Rocky Horror* outside a Rochester, NY, movie theater, it was learned that, excluding the first-timers, the mean number of times respondents had seen the movie was eleven.[30] The audience members are there to participate in a ritual and a social event which create and reinforce a solidarity of non-mainstream identification. The *Rocky Horror* cult has served all over the United States as an opportunity for lesbian and gay teenagers to meet and support each other in the coming-out process.

In our own voice

The most effective form of resistance to the hegemonic force of the dominant media is to speak for oneself. At one level this means attempting to be included in the category of recognized positions and groupings acknowledged by the mass media. Achieving this degree of legitimation is not a negligible accomplishment, and it is not to be despised or rejected as an important minority goal. The success of various minorities in exerting pressure on the media can be seen in the care with which images of these groups are balanced and presented. In fact, the television networks have taken to complaining about the difficulties they face in finding acceptable villains.

> "In their desire to avoid stereotyping, I think broadcast standards and practices sometimes goes to an absurd extreme," said Bruce J. Sallan, ABC's vice president in charge of motion pictures on television. "There are almost no ethnic villains on television. We can't do a Mafia picture at ABC, because broadcast standards won't let us deal with Italians involved in organized crime."[31]

A recent ABC-TV film, *The Children of Times Square*, was allowed to have a black villain after he was balanced by sympathetic black characters: "We had instructions from the network that if a black is shown in a bad light, we must also show a black in a good light."[32]

Gay people have not yet achieved the degree of social power and legitimacy which would permit them to demand the same self-censorship on the part of the media, and consequently we are still treated to gay villains and victims unbalanced by gay heroes or even just plain gay folks. As we have seen from Kathleen Montgomery's research, gay pressure can hope at most for a limited success: a story which offends neither minority nor mainstream sensibilities too much. Could we hope for much more? Probably not, since the numbers simply are not there to put sufficient pressure on the media – and numbers are the bottom line. We might exact concessions along the way, forcing some respect for our humanity, but we cannot expect the media to tell our stories for us, or allow us to do so through their channels.

The ultimate expression of independence for a minority audience struggling to free itself from the dominant culture's hegemony is to become the creators and not merely the consumers of media images. In recent years lesbian women and gay men have begun – although with difficulty – to gather the necessary resources with which to tell our own stories.

There have always been minority media in the United States; various immigrant groups supported newspapers, books, theater and occasionally movies in their native languages. But these immigrant voices were stilled as succeeding generations were assimilated into mainstream culture, losing touch with the language and culture of their grandparents. The black press has survived and occasionally flourished alongside the mainstream media, and black culture (music and dance in particular) has been the source of much inspiration and talent which have crossed over into the mainstream (sometimes in whiteface).

Since the 1970s a lesbian and gay alternative culture has offered a range of media sources and products – press, music, theater, pornography – which are unmistakably the product of gay people's sensibility. Here, too, there is the occasional cross-over, as when Harvey Fierstein's *Torch Song Trilogy* wound its way from off-off-Broadway to a Tony Award for best play on Broadway. But crossing-over is no guarantee of protection from the dominant culture. Even speaking in his own voice – quite literally, as when Fierstein starred in his play – the gay author may find that straight audiences do not see beyond their preconceptions. *Torch Song Trilogy* was reviewed in the *New York Times* by Walter Kerr, the "dean" of Broadway theater critics, and the review is both patronizing and simply wrong.[33] Much of the action in the third act centers on the fact that Arnold, the protagonist, has adopted a gay teenager, and on the "return" of his former lover who is in the process of leaving his wife. The play ends with clear intimations of an emerging gay "nuclear family" – with Arnold as mother, his returned lover as daddy, and their adopted gay son. What does Walter Kerr do with this? He misunderstands – or at least misrepresents – it so badly that I must assume bigotry blinded him to plot details so obvious no tyro critic could miss them. He implies that the adopted son is a "kept" boy Arnold has picked up. The former lover is described as "also sharing the flat, though not yet the boy." When the boy tells the former lover, "I'd be proud to call you daddy," Kerr detects "possible betrayal, sensual shiftings" – that is, he thinks the boy is seducing the man!

One clue to Kerr's stupidity – astounding in so veteran a critic – may be found in his comment about "this rambling and, because it can only move in circles, repetitive plot." Why, we might ask, can it only move in circles? The answer is not to be found in the theory of drama, but in the tired homophobic clichés of psychiatric theories about gay people. Kerr "knows" that we are all caught up in narcissistic repetition compulsions. The truth is, of course, that Kerr is the one who is handicapped by a repetition compulsion, sitting there on the aisle wrapped in the old miasmal mist.

When mainstream critics do not blame gay artists for things which they have themselves misread into the works they are reviewing, they may still find fault with them for not rising above their parochial concerns, that is, for addressing themselves to the concerns of their fellow gay people. In a letter to the *New York Times Book Review*,[34] justifying his negative review of Edmund White's *States of Desire: Travels in Gay America*, Paul Cowan assures us that,

> it's crucial to communicate across tribal lines. Good literature has always done that – it has transformed a particular subject into something universal. Mr. White didn't do that: in my opinion it's one of the reasons he failed to write a good book.

I'm tempted to say, aha, the old universalism ploy! Perhaps good literature has always transformed a particular subject into something universal. But, of course, there's always a double standard in the application of the universalism criterion.

In an essay entitled "Colonialist Criticism," the Nigerian writer Chinua Achebe decries those western critics who evaluate African literature on the basis of whether it overcomes "parochialism" and "achieves universality":

> It would never occur to them to doubt the universality of their own literature. In the nature of things, the work of a Western writer is automatically informed by universality. It is only others who must strive to achieve it.[35]

In the past decade lesbian and gay film makers have been able, with difficulty, to raise the money needed to produce independent documentaries and fictional films which have inaugurated a true alternative channel in the crucial media of movies and television. The pioneering documentary *Word is Out* (1977), and the more recent Oscar-winning *Life and Times of Harvey Milk*, among others, represent authentic examples of gay people speaking for ourselves, in our own words; although even here there have been compromises in order to meet the demands of the Public Broadcasting System – the only viable channel for independent documentaries in the United States.[36] And, even more recently and tentatively, there are the stirrings of lesbian and gay fiction films exhibited through mainstream (art) theaters and becoming accessible to a nationwide gay audience.

146

There is, alternatively, a homosexual cinema. It neither concerns itself overtly with issues of gay politics nor does it present gay sexuality as society's perennial dirty secret. The key to gay films, whether they are made by heterosexuals or homosexuals, is that they do not view the existence of gay people as controversial. ... These films may reflect the fear, agitation, and bigotry of a society confronted with such truth, but it is not their view that such emotions are rational or even important to explore.[37]

The products of the nascent lesbian/gay cinema find a powerful response among their primary audience, and can easily become cult films of a different sort from the midnight orphans of the mainstream industry. *Desert Hearts* is such a film. Made on a small budget collected in two and a half years of arduous grass-roots fund raising and based on a novel by lesbian author Jane Rule, *Desert Hearts* achieved both cross-over box-office success and a cult following among lesbians.

"I've waited 25 years for this movie," says Pat, a 47-year-old secretary in San Francisco, California. "I'm sick of seeing only heterosexual love stories. *Desert Hearts* is a movie I can finally identify with. It's like when I was little, we only had 'white dolls' to play with, as if all babies were white. Movie makers have done the same thing; they've generally ignored gays until the last few years. This movie is a positive step in making lesbian movies more acceptable to the general public. I've seen it 22 times and am still not tired of it."

"I think that women are drawn to it, lesbians are drawn to it in the same way that black people were drawn to *Superfly*. It isn't so much the content. It's a matter of the identification with it and the way it's been presented," says screenplay writer Natalie Cooper. "I'm glad that it served – for anyone – no matter how small, something that could make people feel okay, instead of feeling peripheral or put down. Just to say, 'Hey, I dig it and I love it; I do that, too.' They can say, 'This is our movie, this is our thing.' It makes them feel, dare I say maybe, not proud but viable."[38]

Finally, then, the answer to the plight of the marginalized minority audience would seem to lie in the cultivation of alternative channels, even while we continue to press upon the media our claims for equitable and respectful treatment. But neither goal can be easily achieved, and each will require overcoming formidable obstacles.

Notes

1   George Gerbner and Larry Gross, "Living with Television," *Journal of Communication* 26, no.2 (1976): 182.
2   George Gerbner, Larry Gross, Michael Morgan, and Nancy Signorielli, "Living with Television: The Dynamics of the Cultivation Process," in Jennings Bryant and Dolf Zillmann (eds.) *Perspectives on Media Effects* (Hillsdale, NJ: Lawrence Erlbaum Associates, 1986), pp. 17-40.

3   George Gerbner, Larry Gross, Michael Morgan, and Nancy Signorielli, "The 'Mainstreaming' of America," *Journal of Communication* 30, no.3 (1980): 10-29; George Gerbner, Larry Gross, Michael Morgan, and Nancy Signorielli, "Charting the Mainstream: Television's Contributions to Political Orientations," *Journal of Communication* 32, no.2 (1982): 100-27; and Gerbner *et al.*, "Living with Television" (1986).

4   See George Gerbner, Larry Gross, Stewart Hoover, Michael Morgan, Nancy Signorielli, Harry Cotugno, and Robert Wuthnow, *Religion and Television* (University of Pennsylvania: The Annenberg School of Communications, 1984); and Stewart Hoover, "The 700 Club as Religion and as Television," unpublished Ph.D. dissertation, University of Pennsylvania, 1985.

5   Hoover, "The 700 Club," pp. 382f.

6   Murray Roth, "CBS Evaluates Turner Takeover: 'Not a Snowball's Chance . . .',", *Variety*, April 24, 1985, p. 163.

7   See Larry Gross, "The Cultivation of Intolerance," in G. Melischek *et al.* (eds) *Cultural Indicators: An International Symposium* (Vienna: Austrian Academy of Sciences, 1984), pp. 345-63.

8   Vito Russo, "A State of Being," *Film Comment* (April 1986): 32.

9   Vito Russo, *The Celluloid Closet: Homosexuality in the Movies* (New York: Harper & Row, 1981).

10   Kathleen Montgomery, "Gay Activists and the Networks," *Journal of Communication* 31, no.3 (1981): 49-57.

11   Russo, "A State of Being," p. 32.

12   Andrea Weiss, "From the Margins: New Images of Gays in the Cinema," *Cineaste* (1986): 4-8.

13   William Henry, "That Certain Subject," *Channels* (April 1987): 43f.

14   Russo, *The Celluloid Closet*, p. 251.

15   Antonio Pasquali, "Latin America: Our Image or Theirs?", in *Getting the Message Across* (no editor listed) (Paris: The UNESCO Press, 1975), pp. 62f.

16   Andrew Hodges and David Hutter, *With Downcast Gays: Aspects of Homosexual Self-Oppression* (Toronto: Pink Triangle Press, 1977), p. 4.

17   Ahad Ha-Am (Asher Ginzberg), "Moses," in *Selected Essays of Ahad Ha-Am*, ed. Leon Simon (New York: Atheneum, 1970), p. 320.

18   Gregg Kilday, "Hollywood's Homosexuals," *Film Comment* (April 1986): 40.

19   Barry Adam, *The Survival of Domination: Inferiorization and Everyday Life* (New York: Elsevier, 1978), p. 89.

20   Samir Hachem, "Inside the Tinseled Closet," *The Advocate*, March 17, 1987, p. 48.

21   Raymond Williams, *Marxism and Literature* (Oxford: Oxford University Press, 1977), p. 111.

22   Thomas Morgan, "The Black Viewers' New Allure for the Networks," *New York Times*, December 1, 1986.

23   Eugene Michaud, "The Whole Left Is Watching," Ph.D. dissertation in progress, University of Pennsylvania, 1987 (personal communication).

24   Elizabeth Ellsworth, "Illicit Pleasures: Feminist Spectators and *Personal Best*," *Wide Angle* 8, no.2 (1986): 54.

25   Jack Babuscio, "Camp and the Gay Sensibility," in Richard Dyer (ed.) *Gays and Film* (London: British Film Institute, 1977), p. 40.

26   ibid., p. 45.

27   See ibid.; also Richard Dyer, *Heavenly Bodies: Film Stars and Society* (London: British Film Institute/Macmillan, 1987).

28 Derek Cohen and Richard Dyer, "The Politics of Gay Culture," in Gay Left
    Collective (eds) *Homosexuality: Power and Politics* (London: Allison & Busby,
    1980), pp. 177f.
29 See Dyer, *Heavenly Bodies*.
30 Bruce Austin, "Portrait of a Cult Film Audience: *The Rocky Horror Picture
    Show*," *Journal of Communication* 31, no.2 (1981): 47.
31 Stephen Farber, "Minority Villains Are Touchy Network Topic," *New York
    Times*, February 29, 1985.
32 ibid.
33 *New York Times*, June 27, 1982.
34 *New York Times Book Review*, September 3, 1980.
35 Chinua Achebe, "Colonialist Criticism," in *Morning Yet on Creation Day* (New
    York: Anchor Books, 1976), p. 11.
36 See Thomas Waugh, "Minority Self-Imaging in Oppositional Film Practice:
    Lesbian and Gay Documentary," in Larry Gross *et al.*, (eds) *Image Ethics* (New
    York: Oxford University Press, 1988).
37 Russo, "A State of Being," p. 34.
38 Jan Huston, "Fans Make *Desert Hearts* a Cult Classic," *Gay Community News*,
    January 25, 1987, p. 8.

Chapter eight

Soap operas at work

Dorothy Hobson

It's like Gail in *Coronation Street*. I only watch *Coronation Street* so I can only talk about it – it's almost as if you know her so I think "I wonder what she'll do about this baby" – almost like someone you work with in the office.

Soap operas, British, American, Australian, are part of the everyday lives of their audience. They depict everyday happenings and they also form part of the cultural exchanges which go on in both the home and the workplace. A large part of the enjoyment which is derived from watching soap operas is talking about them with other people. Television may be viewed in the home and research has examined this aspect of the viewing experience but the talk about television also happens some time after the program has been viewed. Often this takes place outside the home with friends, at school, at work, or at leisure. This is also true for other television programs and the completion of the process of communication is extended to the pleasure which is derived from exchanging views and opinions with friends and colleagues about the programs which have been seen.

Talking about soap operas forms part of the everyday work culture of both men and women. It is fitted in around their working time or in lunch breaks. The process takes the form of storytelling, commenting on the stories, relating the incidents and assessing them for realism, and moving from the drama to discussing the incidents which are happening in the "real world," as reported in the media.

The process of watching soap operas is in no way a passive operation and it continues after the viewing time and is extended into other areas of everyday life. This chapter begins to look at the way that serials are incorporated into the lives of viewers outside the home, at their workplace. It also explores the way that fiction is interwoven with events in the "real" world – both those directly experienced by the viewers and those which they have heard reported in the media.

"Let's meet at Tressines" – methodology

This chapter is based specifically on research which was conducted during the week February 2-7, 1987. It was designed to find how much soap operas in general fitted into the everyday cultural environment of work. The research method involved an interview and "just talking" about the serials. The research is based on an interview with a group of six women, all of whom work for Birmingham City Council in one of the departments responsible for running the city's public education system.

Contact was made through a friend of mine who works in the same office and had told me that the "girls" (sic) in her office talked about soap operas at work. I told her that I needed to talk to some women about soap operas and she then asked them if they would talk to me. They agreed to meet me, and sent a message – "We'll meet you in Tressines." We arranged a mutually convenient time. This was during their lunch hour and since they worked "flexitime" there was the possibility that they could stay longer, although this would actually be costing them money. The lunch hour also gave them the opportunity to leave after the first hour if they wanted. Four of them stayed for over two hours and the other two had to return to relieve those still back in the office. It was not possible or desirable to meet at their office – partly because this would have only been feasible with local authority approval but also because an informal setting is more conducive to free conversation. I met them at Tressines, a city center night-club a few minutes' walk from their office. A conventional club disco at night, Tressines opens at midday – between 12 and 3 – for drinks and lunches. It was an interesting location in which to conduct the interviews. Dimly lit, with restrained flashing disco lighting and music, food and wine – generally relaxed and informal. We sat around on low sofas with a table between and they ate their lunch and drank wine.

I recorded the interviews and my secretary came with me to take notes, particularly on who was speaking to ease identification when transcribing the tape. What I found surprising was that there were many more women there than men; and, amazingly, there were young women with babies in buggies visiting their friends, or just simply stopping for a lunchtime break. They knew the night-club as an evening venue and had extended it to being a predominantly female meeting place at lunchtime.

"The group"

The women I interviewed were all employed in various positions in the local authority office. Their job involved the staffing of schools in the public education system in the City of Birmingham. They advertised for teachers, auxiliary workers, laboratory technicians, and secretarial staff. Working in clerical jobs, they were responsible for the hiring and administration of all school employees. Their qualifications ranged from O levels to, in one case, a university degree. However, the degree reflected not the needs of the job but the fact that in a decreasing job market many people are over-qualified for their jobs. They were not of equal status: Diane and Wendy were Section Leaders – designated staffing officers – and all the others were clerical assistants. Their ages ranged from 23 to 35. Their personal details are shown in Figure 8.1:

Figure 8.1

Name	Age	Marital status	Occupa-tion	Qualifications	How many TVs	Whom do you watch with	Favorite programs
Vijya	23	separated	Clerical Assistant	3 O levels	3	family/alone	EastEnders, Colbys, Dallas, Catch Phrase (Q), Blind Date (LE), Dynasty
Susan	24	single	Clerical Assistant	12 O levels 4 A levels B.Sc. Mathematics	2	boyfriend/alone	Crossroads, Coronation Street, Dynasty, East-Enders, Sons & Daughters, Randall & Hopkirk (Deceased) (DS), horror films
Gill	33	married	Clerical Assistant	O levels	1	husband	EastEnders, Howard's Way (D), Ever Decreasing Circles (SC), Brookside
Wendy	29	married	Staffing Officer	O levels	1	husband/alone	Coronation Street, Dallas, Yesterday's Dreams (DS), Howard's Way (DS), nature programs
Mary	35	married	Office Clerk	O levels	1	husband	Films, comedies, documentaries
Diane	27	married	Staffing Officer	O levels	2	husband	Brookside, soaps, comedies, documentaries

Key to programs: (DS) drama series
(LE) light entertainment
(Q) quiz show
(SC) situation comedy

Bland facts or statistics give only a limited picture of any group of people. Additional descriptive material adds to the information and builds up a picture of the group. As well as working together, the women do spend some of their social time together. They would go out for meals in the evenings, visit each other, and occasionally go together to visit the theater to see a play or a show. They are a work group who have a bond of friendship formed through their work; their ease with each other was reflected in the way they talked freely about the television programs and their own feelings about television, and the relation of those thoughts and feelings to their own lives. Their work situation is unstructured and they can plan their work processes and fit them in around their social intercourse.

Any researcher entering a group in order to study it and its opinions is unaware of the group dynamics which already exist within it and the way that its normal ways of operating will affect how the members talk to a researcher. My belief has always been that the group dynamics which have already been established will continue to operate in any group discussion. Of course, there are exceptions, as when someone in the group has greater knowledge about a subject than the others. In this discussion it became evident when Vijya was talking about Asian culture as represented in *EastEnders* that her superior knowledge meant that she took the leading role. During the rest of the discussion she was relatively quiet.

Since my knowledge of the group was limited to the meeting which I had with them, I used my contact, who was not at the discussion (since she did not watch soap operas), to find out more about the women, to validate or contradict the impression which I had of them. I asked a simple question, "Of the group of women who would you have expected would have said the most or led the discussion?" Her answer confirmed the exact way that the interview and discussion had gone, even though she had no knowledge of what they had said.

"Well, Wendy and Diane would have plenty to say and they are definitely more intelligent than the others. Diane is the one who is the most intelligent and what she says is usually worth listening to. Mary says a lot, but sometimes she rambles on and gets off the point, but she would also have plenty to say. Gill is much quieter and although she would have opinions she tends to say less or is less forceful. However, that may be because she is not so much part of the group as the others. Vijya's quite quiet as well but she is an Indian girl who had an arranged marriage which didn't work out and she now lives with her parents and is much more westernized and goes out with the girls. We all spend a certain amount of time together outside work and apart from Sue, who is rather younger than the others, they would go out for meals, to each other's houses and to the theater. Everyone is happy in each other's company."

The closeness of the group of women had an effect not only on the free way that they spoke about the television programs which they viewed and these programs' relation to their own lives, but also on the actual mode of discourse in which they operated. They interrupted each other, finished each other's sentences, and presented the same word in unison to respond to something which someone had said. An example was when Gill was talking about *Brookside*. "There are certain ones in there that get on your nerves. . . ." "The Corkhills!" she was interrupted in unison by all the women. They were so aware of what they all thought that their responses were simultaneous. Their comments came quickly on the heels of each other. They were often talking amongst themselves rather than answering questions which I had asked. I might ask the first question but they would move on to other topics as they took the discussion to areas which they would discuss naturally amongst themselves.

A brief guide to soaps on British television

As the British soap operas which are discussed in this article may be unfamiliar to some readers, I have given a very brief introduction to the characteristics of the series which are mentioned.

Coronation Street, first transmitted December 1960, ITV. Set in the north of England in a working class area with terraced houses, a local pub 'The Rover's Return,' and a corner shop, all of which feature in the series. Reflects the northern working-class values and way of life. The mother of British soaps and the one to which all others paid deference. Wide range of strong, interesting women characters spanning all ages.

Crossroads, first transmitted November 1964, ITV. Set in the Midlands around Birmingham. Originally set in a motel to reflect the growth of motorways and motels in the 1960s. One of the top-rated series for many years but also the butt of all the jokes about soap operas and bad acting, etc. Much changed from its original form with an almost complete change of cast. Now axed and last episode transmitted in spring 1988.

Brookside, first transmitted 1982, Channel 4. The serial that extended the genre. Set on a real housing estate in Liverpool. Features the lives of the people who live in the houses. Families represent all social classes in Britain. Acclaimed for its realism of production methods and inclusion of contemporary social issues, although often criticized for the latter.

EastEnders, 1985, BBC. Set in Albert Square in the East End of London (actually at Elstree Studios). The BBC's blockbuster series – massive support and publicity from BBC. Life of families in the 1980s in the East End of London – working class, ethnic, different social classes including invading Yuppies. Top of ratings – innovative in content, form, and scheduling.

Sons and Daughters, ITV. Imported Australian soap.

Chateauvallon, Channel 4. French soap shown in French language version and English subtitles, also in dubbed version.

Why do we watch soap operas?

The first question, which puzzles critics and fans of soap operas alike, is why do people watch? They watch for the stories, the characters, the entertainment value, and because the program-makers structure the series in such a way that everyone wants to know what happens next.

The following comments perhaps sum up the reasons for the popularity of soap operas:

DH   Why do you actually like soap operas?
Di   Easy to watch.
V   I quite like the story.
Di   Yea, you get involved.

In this interview the women refer to British and American serials, but clearly differentiate between the two examples of the genre.

M   I think some are more down to earth than others.

Di   The fantasy Americans and that, you can't relate to. I mean they're on a different planet really.

M   But they're nice to watch because of the clothes and their houses, and, etc.

DH   And what about the characters in the American soaps? I mean why do you like them or don't you really like them and do you feel you can identify with any of them?

?   No. [Laughter]

M   I don't think you can relate to them in that respect, no.

DH   And is it mainly the women or the male characters that you think are more interesting in the American soaps?

All   The women really.

M   The females really, in *Dallas*. I like to watch Bobby.

W   I like J. R. though. When he's sort of scheming and he'll sort of turn his back on whoever he's playing up and this smile comes on his face and I think, Ooh, he's at it again, you know.

DH   Why do you like people like J. R.?

W   Well he's a very clever bloke, isn't he?

V   He's very crafty.

Di   You've got to admire him though, the way he – he knows his business, sort of thing. He knows.

W   And it's sort of the power that money can have, you know, that really comes across. He'll say, "It don't matter what the price is, I'll pay it but you do your job." And I respect the way he says, "I want a good job done," you know. I just like him.

Di   I suppose most people want to stand up to people in their life but they haven't got the power that he has, have they?

DH   Do you think the women in *Dallas* are weak?

All   They all are.

M   They are really.

Di   If J. R. was my husband I wouldn't marry him again. That sort of thing . . . .

DH   But you just said you find his portrayal of power is quite attractive.

Di   Yea, on the telly but I don't think I'd like to be married to him. [Laughter]

M   But perhaps she means to other people and not necessarily to whatsername –

Di   Sue Ellen.

M   I don't think she comes out very well in it, she's a bit of a cry-baby really, isn't she, she's always. . . .

DH	What about the men in the American soaps?
V	Geoff in the *Colbys*. I quite like Miles as well.
W	I quite liked Jack Ewing.
?	Something attractive about him – sort of roguish. Joan Collins'... I don't know his name.
?	Dexter.
W	He wasn't too bad – had a nice body. [Chorus of ooh's]
G	Last week he was showing his body so you couldn't help see it.
?	But I mean even in *Dallas* when it gets on to the technical side I can carry on with me knitting but when it gets to scandal and gossip – the knitting goes down – you start watching.
DH	So that when they go into business parts you think that's a bit boring.
M	If I tape *Dallas* I fast forward that bit – not that important to the plot.

This exchange begins to differentiate between the British and American soap operas. The first distinction is definitely in terms of categorizing British soaps as "down to earth" and the Americans as "fantasy," "on a different planet really!" Their saving grace is the pleasure derived from the clothes and the nice houses. What British viewers never know is whether *Dallas* and *Dynasty* are fantasy for American viewers as well. Fantasy or reality – it is the characters who really hold the appeal for viewers. The women interviewed were unanimous when they said in unison that it was the women who were the most interesting characters in the American soaps. However, after being unanimous in supporting the women the group then went on to discuss the devilish attraction of J. R. and the magnetism of power, the physical attractions of Bobby and Jack Ewing, Geoff Colby, and Dex's body. Sue Ellen is categorized as a cry-baby and no other women get mentioned!

This extract summarizes J. R.'s attraction. He is a good character within a soap opera but certainly not one to be desired in real life. Similarly the other men are admired by some for their attractive or just plain sexy qualities but neither are they fantasies which anyone would like to bring over into everyday life. The lives of soap opera men at work are boring and the blessing of a recording means you can fast forward past the work bits!

Even the glamor of living in an American soap holds little appeal for the women. I broached with them the subject of whether they were affected by watching too much glamor – did it make them envious?

DH	When critics interview me they always say, but surely its wrong for people to see programs with so much glamor and money and it must make people envious. What do you think, how would you answer, if they said that to you?
M	It doesn't make me envious but it's nice to see how the other half lives.

Di	It's fantasy though, isn't it?
?	Yea, yea.
DH	But does it relate – do you think, "Is this realistic or not?" Or does that not enter into it when you watch a program like that?
M	When you look at the plots I think, "That's not very realistic." Or I can imagine that happening but I don't think I could live like them anyway.
W	I wouldn't like to live in the same house as my mother-in-law [laughter] and all my brothers and sisters, you know. The bedrooms are just sort of down one corridor. It's not that big. And you're dolled up as though you're going out for an evening meal at breakfast, you know. I just couldn't live like that. But I like to watch it. I think there must be people who live like this.

The prospect of living at Southfork does not appear to be the fantasy of British soap viewers, at least not if they would have to live with their in-laws. There is no envy and certainly no wish to have a similar life-style. Clearly, the Englishwoman's home is still her castle, especially if she doesn't have to share it with her family or her mother-in-law.

Even the American soap "queens" come in for criticism.

DH	Do you talk about the clothes?
M	Comment about something that caught your eye.
W	It's like the hair. You think, "What's she done?"
Di	Only about the women.
M	Men look the same all the time.
V	Joan Collins' outfits are funny and strange – looked like a clown. Big shoulder pads and you think how's she going to get through the door? Krystal is better dressed.
DH	They are not young.
V	Quite ancient.

Again, the actresses may be beautiful but the audience is still critical. "What has she done to her hair?" they ask – and the "cruelty of youth" is clear when 23-year-old Vijya describes them as "quite ancient."

British realism

If American soaps represent fantasy, then British soaps are definitely judged for their realism. The subject is one about which the audience is very knowledgeable and they make judgments to decide how well the production has represented the fiction and its characters. The characters in the British soap opera *EastEnders* are either conventional East End working class or the ever-emerging Yuppies who now star as the fantasy of the British television and advertising executive. Most of the rest of the population have only seen or heard of the species through the media! The recognition that it is the women characters who are the strongest in the series is one which is common to audience reactions to British soaps. The women characters who are seen as the most popular are those who have to struggle against the vicissitudes of life. It is their ability to "cope" which is seen as admirable and women's behavior was not expected to be "wimpish." Even within the fantasy of American soaps, these women saw Sue Ellen as a "cry-baby." If the characters are seen as keeping on top of their own lives that is judged as admirable and only in extreme cases does the audience excuse lapses in strength from the women in the soap operas.

DH   What about the English soaps then? What do you think about the characters in those?

M   They're very realistic.

Di   Women seem to be much stronger in them, don't they.

DH   Who do you think are strong characters in British soaps?

Di   Well, in *EastEnders* it's Pauline.

M   What's his name's wife at the caff.

W   Sue, Sue.

Di   She seems to moan a lot but I mean she doesn't get any results, does she? She was looking for his brother the other night.

When I went to get more wine the conversation continued and when I returned they brought me up to date. The discussion had moved to the physical appearance of the characters and a clear distinction is made between the actress and the character she plays. Since the BBC has a tendency to promote *EastEnders* through other programs, its stars regularly appear as themselves on chat shows and in charity events and major variety programs. In fact, many of the stars now appear regularly on television. There is no confusion for viewers who know, for example, that Wendy Richards is playing a "role" when she appears looking "old and awful" in *EastEnders*.

Di   While you were up the bar we was talking about Pauline in *EastEnders* and said doesn't she look old – look awful.

DH   You mean as actress or character?

Di   Character – looks old – not the glamor part, is it.

DH   Is anybody glamorous in British soaps?

Di   Don't watch *Crossroads* regularly but Nicola Freeman, she's attractive in a funny sort of way.

?   Which one's that?

Di   The boss at *Crossroads*. Yes, she's attractive.

DH   What about the men – are they attractive?

Di   In *Brookside* they are all right.

DH   Who?

Di   The young ones.

G   They are not as classy.

Di   Perhaps that's part of the character.

Not only characters are judged for realism, the events in their everyday life also have to conform to an expectation which the audience has about the way that they would behave. However, as Mary says, it is how she would "imagine" that part of London to be. The only person who can really judge the realism of a soap are those in the region in which the soap is set.

DH   Do you think characters in British soaps show realistic pictures of life in the areas where they are supposed to be?

M   Fairly. How I would imagine that part of London to be in say *EastEnders*.

V   Dr Legg's always in the pub and visiting homes.

Di   That's what I don't like about *EastEnders* and *Coronation Street*. A lot of it is round the pub.

V   If you want a cup of tea you go up to the café.

G   Now *Brookside* there isn't a pub, is there?

M   I'm referring to the bits at allotments, that sort of bits are fairly realistic – not all of it though – the bar and the caff – no.

Di   In *EastEnders* they go to the caff when they live over the road.

M   You wouldn't spend money on a cup of tea if you were unemployed and sometimes they walk in, say something and they're off again.

Di   Another time they don't pay for what they have.

The expectations of realism are not confined to the level of cups of tea and having a chat. These women expected a level of realism which incorporated the basic necessities of everyday living.

W   Never go to the toilet.

Di   Hilda cleans the toilet every morning and nobody uses them.

DH   Would you want them to go? If somebody suddenly said I've just got to go to the loo – does anybody go to the loo in anything on television?

All   No.

V   Except in comedy programs, then they laugh at them.

W   If they do, it's only ever the men who are sort of stood there.

?   I don't think its necessary to film 'em in there.

W   In *Minder* – they go to the loo.

Di   A lot of the police ones, they do. It's sort of undercover and it's a place to have a chat.

These comments reveal not only the level of realism which the women would expect in a serial, but also the way in which they widen the conversation to include other program genres. They oscillate between a criticism of the lack of reality when toilets are not included and then criticize their appearance in other series. Interestingly, none of the police film series which they cite is included in their favorite television programs. In the earlier extract when they comment on the fact that "Dr Legg's always in the pub and visiting homes," they are making a comparison with their own experience of "reality" when doctors are not known to socialize with patients and they certainly do not sit in local pubs.

Pleasure at work

One of the areas of particular interest to me was the way in which soap operas and, indeed, television in general is discussed by women at their workplace and the way that they bring the interests of the private sphere into the public domain. Indeed it is the fusion of the two areas which characterized much of the discussion which we had.

DH   So how, in what, how does television in general come into your conversation at work?

M   It's almost every morning, isn't it really. We tend to say, "Did you see such and such last night?" It depends on the plot in the program at the time.

Di   If it's been a gripping episode then even those who haven't seen it talk about it.

M   The Michelle and Lofty episode was quite a talking point.

Di   But also we come in when we miss one and say, "What's happened?"

DH   What do you do if you miss something – do you ask at work the next day?

M   Yes.

Di   But whether that's because of the way we are, the way the office is set up. We get on with our work but we've got a relationship where we can and do talk about these sort of things. The general banter going on in the office that allows us to be able to do that.

M   Whether you'd get that similar situation elsewhere I'm not sure.

DH   If you are at work you're talking about other things as well. You are saying that your work enables you to chat at the same time as you work.

M   No, you fit it in.

Di   It's the way we can get on with our work.

M   It may be in between phone calls. If someone rings. It can go dead for half an hour – if the phone rings you say "Hang on a minute – don't say any more."

Di   Conversation might take all morning.

M   You stop, then when you put the phone down you start again and someone else's phone will go and you stop again.

This extract indicates the way that these women are able to discuss what happened the previous evening and carry on with their work. They do not talk while they are working, but rather they carry on the general conversations about the soaps in between their work. The storytelling carries on with breaks while they take and make telephone calls.

They also told how people who have not seen an episode and have recorded it are "protected" from hearing what has happened. How do they all know how much of a story they can tell?

Di   Well, say like we're talking now and say we are talking about *Dallas*, someone will say "Sh! don't tell me," and then we'll say after "Have you watched it?" and then we'll talk about it.

The group respects the wishes of the person who has missed an episode and if she has recorded it, waits until it has been watched before talking about it in the office. But not all missed episodes are recorded and it is then that "catching up on the stories" happens at work. It is clear that the soap producers are served exceptionally well by their viewers because they act as the bridge between episodes. This is beneficial to the producers and the television company because it helps to ensure that the viewers do not lose interest and stop watching a series because they have missed what is going on.

Soap operas depend on the audience following the stories and need their audience to be loyal and watch regularly. Built into the structure of the programs are devices which enable the viewers to keep up to date. If viewers miss an episode such devices help them to catch up and to be ready to see the next episode. The storytelling within the serials is reproduced outside when the stories are retold for friends and colleagues. In one sense retelling soap opera stories gives everyone the opportunity to be a storyteller without the necessity to be able to create their own storylines. In some instances it is the talking about soap operas at work or among families and friends that determines whether someone begins watching the series in the first place. When a storyline is so strong that it is a main topic of conversation it is reason enough to get someone watching so as not to be left out of the conversation which takes place at work.

The famous storyline in *EastEnders* of the Michelle-Lofty, will-she-won't-she, on-off marriage became such a talking point that it made Mary start watching the program.

Di   But Mary never watched *EastEnders* until she heard us all talking at work about what is going to happen.

M   But my sister she was always going, "You must watch it," or if I was on the phone to her and it was two minutes to half past, then she'd say "I'll have to go."

The myth of the passive viewer

One of the most fallacious myths to have grown up about watching television is that of the passive viewer. According to the theory, widely held by newspaper television critics and interviewers on television current affairs shows, the viewer is a cultural and economic hermaphrodite of indeterminate age, who watches all television programs from a slumped position, having switched off their brain before they fell into the chair. Viewers lose all critical faculties, including the ability to distinguish between fact and fiction, to know whether they are being preached at or manipulated and to make intelligent judgments about the programs which they are watching.

The only people I ever met who have been confused about the difference between fact and fiction on television have been television critics. In fact, they are not confused themselves but they fear for the rest of the audience. Their fears are misguided. Criticism of the soap operas takes place while people are watching them and when they talk about them afterwards.

As well as telling the story of the missed episodes the conversation which takes place at work is critical of the programs. Exchanges take place which indicate that far from accepting everything that is shown, viewers heavily criticize the soaps. The following is a selection of criticisms from the women to whom I spoke. Each serial comes in for light-hearted attack.

American Soaps:

DH   So which would you say is your actual favorite soap?
?   Well any one really – *Dallas*.
G   That's gone off.
M   Oh, it has gone off, definitely.
Di   That's gone on for too long without the storyline being changed. The British soaps, OK, they've been going on but storylines have progressed on.
M   *Dallas* seems to have gone back rather than on, but I will have to watch it. I wouldn't have said there was a lot to choose between *Dallas* and *The Colbys* either, they're the same sort of. . . .

And on to *Crossroads*:

M   Well they used to. I haven't watched it since – I used to watch that every night, *Crossroads*, for a long long time but I haven't watched it for about three or four years and I don't miss it at all. I thought I would but I don't, I find it dreadful to watch now. Very amateurish, isn't it, when you look back now.
Di   When you compare it with others.

Chateauvallon:

?   I don't like that new French one they've put on.
DH   *Chateauvallon*.

?	No because you know, it's all out of sync.
G	It's like an amateur film, it's all dubbed.
DH	Have you not seen it with the subtitles?
G	No, no.
DH	Would you think you'd prefer it with sub-titles?
?	I don't know whether to read or look at the pictures.
M	I prefer dubbed I think.
G	At least you haven't got to concentrate on the writing – voices don't match with the person.
M	But at least you can hear even though it's not synchronized.

Brookside:

DH	Can we talk specifically about *Brookside* and *EastEnders* – what do you think of *Brookside*?
Di	I like *Brookside* but – I watch it every week but some of the things that have happened there in one close – I mean if I lived there I'd move. I mean murders, rape.
?	I don't watch so I don't know.
G	There are certain ones in there that get on your nerves.
All	The Corkhills.
Di	The Corkhills are, I mean they're awful. And Bobby Grant, I hate him.
W	He's not the same character that he used to be.
DH	What do you think is wrong with him?
Di	He's stroppy with everyone and every situation that occurs, and I mean he was never like that at one time.
G	He's such a know-all. . . .
Di	. . . change a job.

EastEnders:

DH	What about *EastEnders*?
Di	Has its ups and downs. I enjoy – I watch it but some weeks I find . . .
M	Patchy, isn't it really? I mean I know people are addicted to it.

All the soaps came in for criticism. The comments speak for themselves but do indicate that viewers are not sitting passively watching in an uncritical manner. They are always making judgments on the serials both within the truth of the fiction and by comparing the serials with "real" life.

Another way in which the mingling of fiction and reality goes on in the telling of the stories is when viewers discuss the way that a storyline has been developed and decided. They make assessments of the validity of what happens in the soap opera and compare it with what they believe the character would do; but they also comment on what they would do if they were in the same position.

During the week of the interviews the main talking point about soaps with the women I interviewed was the story of Gail and her baby. This story in *Coronation Street* had been running since the previous summer when Gail Tilsley, a young working-class wife and mother, had been experiencing difficulties with her marriage. Her husband Brian, who had been a local Romeo both before and since his marriage, had become completely engrossed in his own car repair business and had taken to spending too much time with his business colleagues and neglecting his wife. Gail repeatedly tried to regain his attention, to no avail, and at the low point in the marriage, Brian's cousin Ian arrives from Australia on a visit and becomes very attracted to her, and she becomes attracted to him. A relationship develops and, against her better judgment, Gail sleeps with Ian while Brian is away. In due course, Gail finds that she is pregnant and, much against the wise advice of her mother, she tells Brian that the baby might not be his. Her marriage breaks up and eventually Ian returns to England and asks her to go back to Australia with him. Ian has a blood test at the hospital which proves that the baby is not his and so supposedly is Brian's after all. Gail asks him not to tell anyone what he has found out as she does not want Brian to come back to her for the reason that he is the father. During the interview week this was where the story had reached and was the main talking point in all discussions about soap storylines for that week. The women talked about the way that Gail was handling the situation. I asked them what was the secret of soap operas.

W	It's entertainment. The key thing is to entertain those watching.
M	Why do you keep watching?
Di	Because you get involved in the characters. As though living their lives. Almost become. . . .
W	Like Gail in *Coronation Street*. I only watch *Coronation Street*, that's why I can only talk about that, it's almost as if you know her so I think I wonder what she'll do about this baby – almost someone you work with in the office.
M	Or is it because you think would you make the same decision in that position? Would you do the same? The other night and she had had the baby and was in hospital and the Aussie was outside waiting to see her. Now he was standing outside and I was thinking will she let him in or won't she? She didn't in the end. I was thinking, well, I would have let him in.
W	You think, Oh, he's been standing there all that time.
M	You think in that situation would you do the same.
Di	You get involved.
DH	Did you think it was in her character that she didn't let him in?
Di	Yes, 'cos she's quite strong-minded, isn't she.
W	Has she always been? She hasn't.
M	No, she was weak. It's only recently that she's built up. When I first used to watch it was fairly weak. Brian walked all over her.

W	Only since she had this fling with Ian that character has built up. At first when she said, he knew he wasn't the father and she said don't tell anyone. At first I couldn't make out why. I thought she was going to tell Brian and then I realized she wants Brian to go back because he wants her and not just because he knows the baby's his. She's quite good really.
Di	You're thinking about it, getting involved in the character.
M	Is that why you watch it though?
W	Yes – I think it is. I've got to watch again to find out, you know, what is going to happen, what's she gonna do, is Brian gonna go back, and I hate it when you read in the paper if they put it in before it happens.

It is clear from this extract that the women have a strong affinity with the character and have made no moralistic judgments about her behavior. They even see the character as having a stronger will than they might have had in the circumstances. They are also making critical judgments of the program in terms of reality and what they see as true to the character. It shows the complex interpretations which are at work in the watching of soaps and indicates how far from correct are those who see soap audiences as passive sponges for the messages of drama. The comments show an interweaving of fact and fiction in the commentary upon the television program and events in everyday life. However, there is no confusion of fact and fantasy and each area is kept separate in the discourse. There is a complex linguistic movement between subjects and there is no need to signal that people are talking about different topics. Because the subject matter of the soap operas is so familiar to the viewers there can be a free exchange of information.

A special knowledge – Asian culture

One of the women in the group, Vijya, was Asian and she had a specific knowledge of the culture which was represented in the series *EastEnders*. The fiction did not satisfy her ideas of the way that her people should be portrayed.

As the discussion progressed the other women began asking Vijya what she thought of the storyline which is currently running. The character Naima did not get on with her husband from the arranged marriage and she stayed on in England while he returned to Bangladesh. Her family have kept a check on her and they have now sent her cousin to take control of the shop and ultimately to marry her.

V	Naima's cousin – don't know his character – so demanding.
W	Wants everything his way.
DH	Is that realistic?
V	No. It's Naima's shop and she would say, "That's my shop and everything goes where I say."
DH	I wondered, is that realistic?

V   They are trying to arrange a marriage but it wouldn't work. They wouldn't send him round and try to fix them up together like that. It wouldn't work like that.

DH   Do you mean that he wouldn't be sent there to live or it wouldn't be to do with a marriage?

Di   Knowing what Naima's family are like, would she be allowed to keep the shop?

V   Well, she's got the shop and I think she's doing everything against her parents.

Di   But you never see her parents. In real life surely her parents would be there. Are they supposed to be here or in Bangladesh?

?   In Bangladesh. She came over with her husband and they have gone back.

V   So really she hasn't any family to say "Don't do this!"

DH   She would be allowed to be left here, she wouldn't have to go back?

V   She could stay – I don't know.

Di   Would her family disown her because, knowing how they are, because she hasn't gone back, been all independent?

V   When she started in *EastEnders* she was very, very Indian and then she changed herself and became more westernized. To her she belongs to this country. She thinks, I don't need to go back, don't need to listen to my parents. Her husband didn't respect her, they weren't getting on, she didn't have the freedom.

Vijya's knowledge of the culture was far greater than anything which the other women knew and they asked her about the reality of the storyline. Her analysis was that it was not realistic but when I talked to my friend after the interviews she said that Vijya had had an arranged marriage herself the previous August and it had not worked out and her husband had returned to Bangladesh while she had returned to live with her parents. Her assessment was based on her knowledge of the culture and of her own experiences: a nice example of the way that the knowledge of the audience is always at work when they are making readings of television texts. It was also a subtle way for the other women to find out about the situation in which Vijya found herself.

Conclusion

This chapter has attempted to discuss the way that talking about soap operas and television has fitted into the working life of one group of women. Most of what they say will be familiar to anyone who has done research about audiences and particularly to those involved with research into soap operas. The findings are not invalidated by this similarity to earlier findings; rather, they confirm that whenever and wherever audiences discuss programs they come up with similar conclusions.

They discuss the events on television in relation to the fiction, the accuracy of the fictional representation, and also in relation to criteria within the "real world." There is no confusion, only an interweaving. They compare events in soaps with events which have happened in their own experiences and those of people they know. The findings add to the body of research which is now accumulating on this genre and also belies the myth that soap opera viewers are passive.

Soap opera is a genre where the viewer is always in a superior position to the producers, because the topic is the everyday life of the characters. If the producer makes a mistake or the actor or actress behaves differently from how viewers think he or she should behave, then they have the superior feeling that they know best. They can excuse the mistakes because of the innocence or the ignorance of the production, and their own views are discussed and revised with their colleagues and friends when they talk about the soaps at work or at home the next day.

The process of television communication is recognized as not being complete until it is perceived and understood by the viewer. A program is made by its production team, exists as a physical entity on tape or film – but only exists as a means of communication or cultural form when it is transmitted and received by the viewers. But the way that audiences talk about the viewing of soap operas and other forms of popular television programs indicates that a further stage of communication takes place when they talk about the programs in a context completely removed from the viewing situation. It is the talk about television programs and often the relating of those programs to the everyday life of the viewers that move television into a further dimension from that which ends with the viewing moment. Indeed, talking about television programs and what has happened in them is essential to making a program popular and part of the cultural capital of general discourse.

Chapter nine

The media in everyday family life:

Some biographical and typological aspects

Jan-Uwe Rogge

It is a Sunday afternoon like any other in the Smith family: Robert Smith, aged 45, a truck driver; his wife Mary Smith, aged 40; and their three children Uwe, aged 5, Anna, aged 7, and Petra, aged 9. The family lives in a three-bedroom apartment.

I met Anna while doing some field research at a kindergarten. The children were asked to draw a picture portraying Sunday afternoon at home. The focal point in Anna's picture was the dominant father, sitting next to mother on the sofa with the three children in front of him, pressed up against his knees. On the table was the Sunday "coffee and cake," and in the background, out of perspective, a television set showing *Pinocchio* could be seen. In the left-hand corner of the picture was a window, through which the outlines of a truck could be recognized.

The room in the picture exuded an atmosphere of security, warmth and intimacy. When I showed it to the mother, she made the following comments:

"Yes, that's the way things are in the afternoon at our place. Anna has certainly caught the mood. But what else can we do? Things are not so easy for us with my husband on the road all the time. Sunday is the only time we have to spend together. My husband doesn't want to go out, he wants something to take his mind off things because he has to be off again early on Monday morning."

In a talk I had later with Mr Smith, he also confirmed that Sunday afternoons in the Smith family are usually devoted to the same routine, which he unquestioningly accepts as normal, namely to media activities. However, he did add in a tone of resignation: "Well, I know we should try to do something different really, in fact, we do now and then." To this Mrs Smith remarked: "The last time we did something different was four months ago."

On the whole, they talk very little. Mrs Smith is responsible for bringing up the children. Robert Smith has a lot of time for his own thoughts when he is on the road. "You see, you tend to do a lot of thinking to yourself and forget what it's like to talk to other people. It's a good thing we manage to get by without too much talking."

Sunday afternoon presents no problem for the children. Here is what Petra has to say:

"We have enough time for playing during the week . . . . If we go out Daddy is always so jumpy. It's better at home. There we can have him all to ourselves . . . . It doesn't really matter what's on on TV. The main thing is that Daddy's home."

Later on, Anna adds:

"It does matter. When *Pinocchio's* on, I get all excited and nervous, and when I can feel Daddy there things are not half as bad as they would be if I had to go through all that on my own."

These extracts from my interviews with the Smith family may be used to illustrate some aspects which highlight the subjective significance which media activities have for the Smith family. The media have a definite place in the family interaction pattern. They structure the framework of family life, the external milieu, the demands imposed by the world of work, etc. When examining a family's media activities it is therefore not sufficient just to ask the usual questions, like "What effect do the media have on families?" or "How do families use the media?"

The way in which families use the media points, rather, in a different direction: it highlights two aspects of a family's way of negotiating their contact with the media, one that has to do with content and another that has to do with function. From the point of view of content, media activities can be understood as an attempt to construct a meaningful relationship between the media program and reality as actually experienced. Conscious, subconscious, or preconscious wishes play an important role in the way people use the media. The media are interpreted against the background of everyday life as it is lived and experienced, they are used to cope with everyday problems. The media are unquestioningly accepted as normal, they are something completely familiar. Their general ubiquity causes them to be allocated certain functions in people's everyday lives. The media form a part of the family system, a part many can no longer imagine living without. This is one of the principal reasons why media activities are characterized by emotional familiarity. People seek contact with the media because the media appeal and give access to feelings such as pleasure, fear, joy, and insecurity. The situations in which the media are used also have a high emotional value. The media provide remedies for loneliness, they are used to create "good" feelings or to define human relationships.

For this reason, everyday media activities within the family context cannot be reduced to a simple medium-receiver relationship. To ascertain the motivating factors of media use in everyday life, it is necessary, rather, to examine what significance is given and what functions are allocated to the media. It is also important to understand and record the needs and motivations of all members of a family. I should like to illustrate this by referring to the Smith family once more. Their media activities quite clearly reveal their wishes, value systems, upbringing methods, and everyday knowledge. They further show how difficult it is to alter unsatisfactory situations, especially when the objective structures hinder rather than encourage alternatives. Media activities and their possible alternatives cannot, therefore, be seen in isolation from the exigencies of the world of work and a family's concrete circumstances of life. It is equally important to take into account the communicative climate in the day-to-day life of a family or at the place of work. Also, the psycho-social, economic, and ecological background of a family's use of the media must enter into the analysis.

Thus, as a first point, we can ascertain that there is, in families, a connection between and a close interweaving of the need for communication and media activities at any given time. However, when establishing such homologies, it is essential not to overlook another aspect which I would now like to draw attention to. The word "new" now seems to be undergoing a kind of inflation in connection with the discussion of changes in information and communication technology. Media activities in families consist of the use of old and new media. To view the phenomenon solely from the point of view of change is to reduce illegitimately the complexity of everyday human activity, for if we take a closer look at the way families negotiate their contact with the media in their day-to-day lives it is obvious that their activities are characterized by permanence in change. In other words, it is not only the momentary need for communication that determines the everyday media routine, but also past experiences which extend their influence into present media activities. Let me illustrate this with an excerpt from an interview.

Helga Peters is aged 58, a secondary-school teacher, married with two children, aged 26 and 28. Both children have left home. In this part of the interview, Mrs Peters tells me about her contact with the media during her youth and childhood. For her there were only books, reading material of the more demanding type, visits to the theater, and concert-going. The cinema, popular magazines, and radio music were all frowned upon:

> "This continual search for merit, this concentration on educative material has been the dominating trend throughout my whole life and, although I now see it as a bad thing, it strongly influenced the way I brought up my children. I passed on the values my father drilled into me. . . . Of course, it wasn't so easy to do this with my children as it had been with me, they broke out far more often than I had ever been able to, or dared to."

The media habits Mrs Peters had acquired and lived during her youth and childhood also continued into the early years of her marriage:

> "Take the cinema, for example. It's only in the last few years that my husband and I have taken to going to the cinema because it gives us pleasure and enjoyment and now it annoys me to see how much I've been missing. . . . It's exactly the same with television, radio, and books, this step away from having to find a justification for everything, away from this consumption of education and culture, to be able to admit to oneself that something was great and not to

always ask like a little teacher — so, what beneficial effect did that have on us
. . . ? There are some things that never even occurred to me until a couple of
years ago, after the children had left home, but it was still a big step to take
from thinking about a thing to actually doing it, and I haven't completely got
out of my old habits and don't want to either because there are still a lot of
things that were good . . . I was much more conscious of the ways I received
what was offered. . . . Today, people tend more to just consume things, but on
the other hand, I think that the pretentious attitude is just as bad."

I would like to discuss this interview excerpt in terms of the change and
continuity aspect. The way people use the media is something that is acquired
during the course of an individual biography; it is the result of a long socialization
in the family. A person's early experiences with the media, therefore, have a
decisive influence on the way he/she negotiates his/her contact with the media
later in life. Each person has a certain number of "media careers" in the course of
a lifetime, e.g. in early childhood, during the school years, the beginning of
adolescence, the first months in the first job or at college, the early years of
marriage, etc. When looked at from the point of view of media careers, media
activities can be seen to have two aspects: one which is dynamic and subject to
change and one which stresses the permanent and more stubborn qualities of a
person's behavior.

At this point, it is perhaps necessary to make some basic comments on the state
of research into media activities in families. I would like to touch upon five main
aspects. The two interviews from which I have quoted so far clearly indicate the
complex nature of media activities. It quite often happens, however, that this
many-sided phenomenon is collapsed into a linear model operating with concepts
of effect or reward (What effect do the media have? or: how do people use the
media?). Such models fail to account for the great differences in the way a
program like *Dallas* or a quiz show is used as far as viewing and communication
needs are concerned.

This leads us on to a further gap in current research. There has not been
sufficient investigation into the areas of everyday life (particularly family life) in
which the media make their influence felt. There has been much facile talk about
families, about youth and children, but little attention has been paid to families'
strategies of action or their ways of thinking. The theories they develop for
coming to terms with everyday life and the knowledge they possess based on
everyday common sense have not really been accounted for in audience research.
Equally little regard has been paid to the close interrelationship between the work
situation, leisure-time possibilities, socio-ecological determining factors, and the
routines established in contact with the media. This complexity has not only been
overlooked, but all too often completely ignored. It is therefore easy to
understand why the research has by and large been restricted to a reduced way of
seeing the phenomenon, namely as a situation in which families are threatened by
the media. But anyone who wishes to describe changes in family life (due to

whatever influences) must take into account the results of research into the sociology and psychology of the family. Only by integrating such data and the relevant research methods into our methodological approach are we able to do justice to the multidimensional problem we're facing.

Let me add a final point of criticism that pertains in particular to the dramatic changes we're witnessing in communication technology today. I pointed out that some of the research in this area has been too quick to argue with abstract typologies, assuming a theoretical "average viewer." Anyone who asserts that TV consumption is on the rise in households with cable television is arguing both in the abstract and without making sufficient differentiation. Only when such trends are examined in relation to educational background, social class, conditions of work and living, to the psycho-social situation and the emotional climate, to the family history and the methods of upbringing adopted is it possible to make statements which approximate the actual changes in patterns of television consumption, and only on this basis can we develop more concrete pedagogic strategies which are in closer touch with day-to-day existence.

The attempt to develop an approach appropriate both to the methodological complexity of the problem and to the new conditions brought about by the advances in communication technology was made in the context of two research projects carried out between 1981 and 1986 at the University of Tübingen's Ludwig Uhland Institute for Empirical Cultural Studies, under Klaus Jensen's and my direction. In both projects our central concern was the changes in everyday family life brought about by the media. Within the framework of this overall objective, we attempted to provide as detailed an account as possible of everyday media use in the family unit. At the same time and on the basis of an adequate understanding of the new ways which families are developing for their media use, we also aimed at an accurate description of the more traditional structures of everyday media behavior.

Any understanding of individual and familial activities with regard to the media must be based on an interpretative paradigm which emphasizes the dynamic aspect of social situations and human actions. By employing such an approach we were able to account for the ambivalences and complexities of social reality, and to offer evaluations of the different meanings given to specific situations by our informants. Only by concentrating on an individual's strategies of meaning construction and rituals of action, i.e. the structural moments of subjective media reality, are we in a position to isolate certain interpretations as adequate out of the almost inexhaustible spectrum of possible ones. For the perceived meaning of a given object (and this includes media messages) can be conceived of as a point of intersection between a person's individual and social, biographical and contemporary situational contexts.

In order to do justice to the complexity of human actions in relation to the media, we need a method of hermeneutic interpretation. Applying such a method to the family in its specific set up as well as its broader social conditions enables us to describe those structural aspects which are relevant to the family's everyday media-related activities. Such an approach may be called hermeneutic and interpretative because it does not lose sight of the actual living situations. Rather, it relates media use to the concrete everyday world of a given family.

It is of course trivial to state that the family as such simply does not exist. Factors such as the material resources available or the kinds of occupations held by family members vary considerably from family to family. Another criterion for distinguishing between families is the family biography (e.g. its specific cultural traditions, communicative competence, emotional climate) which is unique in each case. At the same time, each family undergoes different cycles of development. Such cycles are characterized by continuity and change in communication and media habits. Taking all of this into account it stands to reason that an essential prerequisite for an adequate explanation of the everyday use of the media is an approach to the family that is based on system theory.

By family system I mean that all events and all activities (including those that have to do with television or the media) have a systematic character, that is all members of a family participate in these events with differing degrees of involvement. Examples are easy to find: the father who reads the newspaper at the breakfast table, ignoring the other members of the family; the mother who does not allow her children to watch television, but whose order is boycotted by her husband; the sports program on a Saturday which causes the family to postpone their evening meal together; the resulting discord; the television set running in the background to enforce silence or to make the stillness easier to bear.

By everyday family life I mean the familiar world of a family's experience, the world in which it lives. It is a world unquestioningly accepted as normal, a world whose general framework is taken for granted. This everyday life is not static, as is often assumed, but possesses a dynamic character. It encompasses the past, the present, and the future, as becomes apparent from the two concepts, family biography and family cycle. Everyday life is lived out in a field of tension formed by individual and family biographies, socio-cultural and social structures, and socio-historical processes of development.

This means that everyday knowledge (e.g. knowledge about the media) is never complete, although it is not something that can simply be changed at will. Thus, a new media program is interpreted against the background of existing opinions and a new family serial is compared with what is known about past serials of this type. I have thus alluded to a third concept. Each family constructs its own media world. This includes knowing about the media, for example which programs are available, how genres influence and affect each other. Media worlds are the product of meaning-making within a family. This alone is sufficient reason for looking at media activities and everyday family life from the point of view of the families themselves. In such a perspective, the media not only appear different from how they do to the researcher or the educator, they actually are different.

In the two projects above, we interviewed a total of 420 families. Even though our research emphasized the everyday use of the media in different types of households, our research design did not overlook the fact that the media-related activities of families are not only determined by the specifics of the family system, but also by other subsystems such as the world of work, club memberships, activities in organizations, kinship relations, circles of friends, etc. Our concentration on families did not preclude taking into account other social relationships or social factors. Rather, it provided the necessary focus, a focus which promised to yield insights into the integration and effect of transcendent structures. This means that the methodological design the two projects employed called for a multiple-level analysis. Therefore, the guiding principle of the narrative family interviews was to address the multiple aspects of concrete living situations and other realms of everyday life. Such a procedure and the data it yielded allowed us, during the interpretation phase, to bring to bear the different sets of data on a single family member and his/her biographical as well as present situation – a strategy which also helped to preserve the uniformity of our data material.

In sum, our approach may be described as qualitatively oriented field work, a type of research which relies on direct or indirect, systematic or unsystematic participant observation as well as on structured or unstructured narrative interviewing. In concrete terms, our methodology employed four separate components: the standardized questionnaire, the qualitative interview, participant observation, and, finally, a media journal (which I cannot comment on here). The questionnaire was handed out to each member of a given household; it served to generate basic statistical data. The qualitative interviews were done, as far as possible, with the entire family, for the presence of all household members during the interview yielded initial insights into the family's communication structures. Open questions encouraged the informants to supply specific information on their everyday lives. Asking precise questions and close observation allowed us to explore concrete behavioral patterns and concomitant cognitive-emotional styles which people have developed for their media use. It further helped us to understand how the use of the media intersects with other everyday activities and life-styles, which interactions predominate during the process of media assimilation, which media supplies are subjectively most important.

The overall objective of our data gathering was of course to subject linguistic utterances and observed behavior to interpretation in order to arrive at general statements about the structures of everyday behavior. Interpretation was, and this is important to emphasize, not limited to an individual and "unmediated" experience of the media. Rather, it was always directed at establishing links and connections between the individual phenomenon and the fundamental structure.

The cases I am now about to mention will help clarify the relevance and scope of the concepts I have just outlined. In these case studies I have tried to work toward establishing qualitative links between day-to-day life and a family's use of the media. Case studies are indispensable at this point in audience scholarship because they allow for the multilevel analysis I have just outlined, and because it is of course too early to make statistically relevant statements about the relationships between media-related actions and the various aspects of people's everyday worlds. The case studies have been selected out of a large number of families in order to illustrate typical trends.

Sandra Higgs, aged 31, is employed full-time at the public library. Peter Higgs, 35 years old, had a post as a civil engineer "before the firm went bankrupt." They have two children, Harry and Heather, aged 7 and 5. The unemployment of Mr Higgs has its effects on all members of the household. These effects can be described by the terms "restructuring," "reorientation," and "functional change." First of all, magazines "that were just bought on the side" are no longer read. The same applies to books: "Now I borrow more books from the library and don't buy so many for the kids. But they don't really miss that because I can always manage to borrow something," comments Mrs Higgs when describing the change in the situation. A more noticeable change is the import- ance that television has now assumed for the members of the family. Before Mr Higgs became unemployed they had a very consistent attitude toward using the media, an attitude that tried to achieve a balance between educational and entertainment programs. Now "the box," to use the words of Peter Higgs, has become increasingly important to compensate for boredom, dissatisfaction, stress, and tensions.

> "I'm gradually getting to notice how much more important the box is becoming for me. It's not that I'm watching that much more TV now, it's the kind of things I watch and the eagerness I lap them up with. Before, that would never have entered my mind. . . . What worries me is the way the box is beginning to occupy my thoughts so much . . . I would never have thought how quickly such a thing can get a grip on you without you realizing it. . . . Yes, and how difficult it is to get out of the habit again once you've got used to it . . . and then, of course there are the children who used to watch very little television. You should see the way they watch TV now – three months and you've got kids who are always glued to the box because you're always glued to it yourself."

The two children were also torn out of their accustomed rhythm but they have now adapted to the new situation. Harry says: "Now I am allowed to watch more telly in the evenings too. Mum lets me." But he also thinks that "Mum gets cross more than she used to. She loses her temper more," which makes him feel sad.

Sandra Higgs has also observed the change in herself and has noticed that her daughter, on these occasions, becomes intimidated and withdraws to her room, sits down in her "cosy corner" and listens to her cassettes: "She obviously needs to retreat like that and probably feels quite OK. That's what I think, anyway. She knows that I love her."

Mrs Higgs has also noticed something else:

"Lately Heather has only been listening to those daft programs, dreadful I would say. But of course I don't say it, but she rejects outright anything that is in any way linked with problems. Yes, and then sometimes she will just burst into tears when she's watching or reading something that's quite harmless. She has become a lot more unstable. That's her way of reacting to everything."

Harry, too, increasingly tends to avoid anything in the media that is problem- or reality-oriented. According to Sandra Higgs, he uses the television "to kill the time." Harry and Heather have developed an attitude that is geared toward compensation in their use of the media.

Unemployment changes the media routines, as far as both the quality and quantity of media activities are concerned. Media activities in the home, especially, assume a more central position. The television slips into the role of sole entertainer. To use the media increasingly means to relax and switch off, to escape depression and ward off boredom. The psycho-social and psychological strain which is a concomitant factor of unemployment hampers communication within the family and allocates a special entertainment function to the media. The dwindling of interpersonal communication which then follows is an expression of a lack of orientation, of discouragement, self-doubt, uncertainty and isolation.

Wendy Rees lives with her three children (aged 6, 11, and 15) in an old block of tenements in the center of a big city. She has a two-bedroom apartment, has been separated from her husband for many years, and has an afternoon job as a cashier, which means that she does not arrive home from work until eight o'clock in the evening. "Irene, my eldest, looks after the children until then," says Mrs Rees. In the mornings she carves wooden pendants for a boutique and works at home. "I need that," she explains, "otherwise things would get me down." When she is doing this work she listens to the radio,

"folk music or pop, then you don't feel so alone. Oh yes, and the news. I must always listen to the news, to see if anything has happened. Then I have to see the same thing on the telly or read about it in the papers. I'm a real catastrophe Jane."

She laughs, but seems sad at the same time.

"Take the police report, for example. I think Irene should start to look at that, too. I always get shivers down my spine when I'm watching that. Yes, it really gives me the shivers. I don't think I could face watching that if I was on my own. But you don't mind the bit of fear when there are two of you."

The Reeses not only watch a lot of television; they also own a video-recorder. Irene comments:

"If the weather is bad or in winter or when there's nothing else to do, then the children already start watching the video in the afternoon, they look at those slushy, sentimental films or plenty of adventure films. Sometimes they will watch one after the other."

Mrs Rees tries to persuade herself that this is nothing to worry about. She remarks: "I still think that's better than them hanging around doing nothing. Anyway, what else is there for them?"

Sometimes she punishes the children, especially John and Jimmy, by forbidding them to watch the television or the video. "But then, neither of them will talk to me. They've really got me where they want me. They know I don't like being on my own. I nearly always give in." It's the same with the evening meal, which is nearly always eaten in front of the television when the evening news is on: "I think that's good for them. They can learn something from that."

Mrs Rees tries to draw her children's attention in particular to catastrophes and accidents or to suffering and need.

"Sometime they've got to learn to take care and they should learn to realize that we don't have it all that bad. When we are all sitting there together nice and cosy, I feel like we're a real little clique."

The way Mrs Rees uses the media, using them for her own particular needs and to define her relationship to the children, also became apparent in two other situations. She makes her children stay seated a long time at the table, showing them how much importance she attributes to the media in this situation. The television situation creates a bond between the children, induces an enforced intimacy and imposes a feeling of community with no words being spoken. John and Jimmy, in particular, have seen through their mother's rituals and have used them for implementing their own strategies for coping with everyday life. The children know that their mother cannot be consistent in carrying through her prohibition of the media.

Late in the evening, Wendy Rees watches her daily "video weepy": "Then I can forget everything, but I have to be completely on my own, otherwise I can't really get into it."

A few interpretative comments are in order here. In this case it is not the quantity but the quality of the media activities which is the problem. Television rituals mean not speaking, an enforced community; the television routine suppresses real conflicts or offers a superficial harmony. The example of the Rees family also illustrates how media programs compensate for emotional deficits and can act as a substitute for real experience; it shows how television is used to give expression to ideas of intimacy and closeness. There is also another important point to be made. The discussions on the new media have caused many of the older media to be forced into the background and disregarded. This, for example, is true of radio, which still plays an important part as far as quantity is concerned. From the point of view of the user, it often serves the purpose of offering a constant flow of background noise, helping him/her to avoid negative, depressive moods, and providing contact to the world outside the home, or replacing real communication partners. This is also true of other media. They are used to bring relief, but this superficial and short-term relief causes further problems because the silent community, thus engendered, veils the real problems and their resolution through dialogue. It thus hampers and finally cripples such dialogue.

At the outset I mentioned two levels of approach: the level of objective media reality, i.e. the significance the media have in everyday family life, and the level of subjective media reality, i.e. the fact that families structure their everyday lives on the basis of greatly varying ideas. In conclusion, I would like to highlight some trends issuing from the individual cases, thereby commenting on the level of objective media reality.

The mass media, with the rhythms and the weekly and daily schedules peculiar to them, have a formative influence on lifestyles and patterns of communication. But households and household members never make use of the whole media spectrum. Rather, they select, from the totality available, their own program which has its special significance for them. Here parental influence largely determines the genre preferences and media styles of children. Styles of media are not merely current styles, but are always biographically determined. A sediment of acquired knowledge helps structure the way in which the media are perceived in the present. The situations in which the media are received are generally characterized by ambiguity. Thus for one particular family, watching a detective program can mean entertainment and excitement, for another this experience can promote a group feeling, while for a third it can be used to compensate for an inner vacuum, stress situations, or feelings of loneliness. Media entertainment is also used for the sake of the alternatives it would seem to offer to mundane reality, for the space it provides for phantasies and daydreams.

I should now like to turn to the second level of analysis: subjective media reality. This has mainly to do with people's everyday knowledge about the media, the patterns of behavior adopted. They show the interrelation between individual day-to-day experiences and patterns of using the media. Here it is possible to pick out three trends that can be generalized: parents have opinions about the media, for example about the disadvantages of television or the merits of books, they have experiences with genres ("Sport is exciting," "*Dallas* is wonderfully feeble-minded"). They understand the significance of the media in stress situations ("Just switch on the TV, then switch off yourself. Empty your mind"). Such conceptions are learned from early childhood, especially when the example of the parents shows them to be appropriate for coping with everyday life. Another aspect of subjective media reality is knowing about the significance the media have in day-to-day life; perhaps the television set is used as an instrument of power to assert certain needs and interests; films and music are used to compensate for loneliness, programs are seen to hide real conflicts. Media activities have long established themselves as a routine, a ritual, there is something typical, something ever-recurring about them: tuning into a certain radio station first thing in the morning, getting used to being given the time, reading strategies for newspapers and magazines, listening to the radio on the way to work, switching on the TV after returning from work, watching the evening news, *Dallas* on a Tuesday, the sports program on Saturdays, etc.

Thus, subjective media reality has many facets: on the one hand, the form taken by media activities expresses cultural orientation and day-to-day life-styles. Media activities can be defined as part of a way of life. On the other, media contact defines interpersonal relationships and the emotional and communicative climate in a family. Certain aspects of media use can illuminate defects or even skills in negotiating everyday family life. Finally, media activities can be seen as a fusion of the intentions behind the programs of the media and the experiences of the user.

The preceding is of course only a rough outline of the two research projects dealing with everyday family life and the mass media. Probably the most important insight we had in the course of our work on these projects was to realize that audience scholarship currently needs to press on with a medium-range theory which is able to link basic theoretical insights and practical field work in its analysis of media influences on society and families.

Chapter ten

Approaching the audience:

The elderly

John Tulloch

Recent work I have done with the sicence fiction audience provides a point of departure for analysing the characteristics of elderly television audiences. The elderly soap viewer differs from the younger science fiction fan in a number of ways. First, he or she is unlikely to be part of an organized audience community, and so is much less likely to adopt a position of discursive power in relation to an interviewer. *Doctor Who* fans have regular conferences where episodes from the archives are rescreened, and where knock-out quizzes based on intensive knowledge of the minutiae of the program's history produce a confident understanding of what the show is "about." In interview situations this intensive history dominates, and except where called into discussion the interviewer ceases to exist to a degree I have not experienced in any other audience group.[1] The elderly I interviewed, in contrast to the science fiction fans, are isolated in small domestic units, have fewer opportunities for group conversation about their favorite shows, and (when confident about the interviewer) will want to talk (often during the show you are watching with them). Often they will call the interviewer back later on to say something they had forgotten to say on the first occasion.

Second, then, the elderly are particularly keen to discuss their favorite shows, not only having fewer community gatherings, but also far less space in general where they can engage with television, unlike children who may act out their favorite soap in the playground, talk about it in the classroom, write fan letters to stars, discuss it at fan clubs, and so on. Writing to the producers of the show is one of the few ways in which the elderly do engage with the show, and analysis of these letters indicates that they regard the show just as much as theirs as do the young science fiction fans, though in a different way, with references out to their own experience rather than inwards to the show's mythography. Here, for instance, is a letter from an elderly English viewer of *A Country Practice*:

> How I enjoy it! I feel I've got to know all of you now, as I must not miss it. It's cold here now, and getting dark between 3 pm and 4 pm when I switch on to look at you all. I am a widowed pensioner and have been enjoying each programme as I sit in my comfy armchair (with my knitting) and prepare to be

wafted away to the other side of the world. My husband would like to have come over to Australia way back in 1945 to start a new life after "the War." We had lost everything, house, all possessions and I was evacuated to a safe part of Britain with our baby son only 3 months of age. Having seen our home in ruins and loss of near and dear neighbours my husband was all for us going, but I was afraid of the uncertainty. No job, no home and a baby so we never came. Our son is 38 now and although buying his own house 50 miles away is kind and attentive to me. I get lonely as I've been alone now for 9 years. My darling died very quickly aged 57 & he knew how I loved TV although he was a Radio Ham enthusiast in touch with many countries and Radio Stations. Must finish off now as I'm apt to go on and on (even talk to myself). I'm happy to see you all and thought I'd let you know. Hope you get this alright. Good health.[2]

In addition to this personal memory emphasis, letters from the elderly to JNP (the production company of *A Country Practice*) tend to underline the "clean" and "nice" aspects of the show in contrast to the "constant obscenities, cruelty and violence" seen on television generally. In these letters, the producers are asked to

please keep this show as nice as it mostly is, then you will never get complaints – only commendations. Please do not try to make our littlies "grow up" too quickly – let them know instead what nice things are on offer in this world. Knowledge should be kept for those mature enough to bear it.[3]

Sometimes commendation of the show for its wholesomeness comes with implied threats of discontinuing viewing, as in the case of the viewer who had read in a newspaper that the young romantic leads, Simon and Vicky, would get divorced:

I am one who hopes that the marriage doesn't end in divorce, mainly because this seems to happen so often in "Soapies." ... Marriage is damned hard work and each partner has to learn to give as well as to take. One only gets out of a marriage what one puts into it. I don't usually write letters like this but I feel so strongly about T.V. shows where marriage usually ends in divorce. I only hope this one will not go that way. I feel I write on behalf of a lot of viewers.[4]

Quite explicit in this elderly woman viewer's letter is the opinion that fans have earned the right, through their loyalty to the show, to expect the marriage to last. Their investment of time and emotion has made it their show, to the degree of asking the producers to ensure the stability of marriage. Here the words "I feel I write on behalf of a lot of viewers" is an attempt to mobilize a collectivity of viewers out of a disparate and isolated viewing situation. Unlike science fiction fans who orchestrate the media and organize massive letter-writing campaigns when there is a threat of their show being taken off, the elderly soap viewer has little power; and is doubly weak in that whereas science fiction is a mega-buck, currently "in" genre with the advertiser-desired younger audience, shows liked primarily by older audiences are constantly under threat. Feuer, for instance, talks of the network war for young adult demographics in the US in the early 1970s leading to the cancellation of "demographically impoverished" shows that appealed to the elderly;[5] and in Australia *Carson's Law*, a period soap with a strong older audience but few younger viewers, was taken off, while *A Country Practice* (which also appealed to the elderly but was protected by broad audience demographics) continued.

Further, where elderly people's favorite shows are protected in this way by broad demographics, there is yet another threat. Under ratings pressure (for instance when a number of major stars leave the show, as happened with *A Country Practice*), there may be a new narrative shift toward the younger viewer. As the executive producer told me, at these times (when other channels mount a campaign to attack a top-rating show at its moment of weakness), the program gives the committed older viewer "enough to keep them happy" and "concentrates on the swinging voter."[6] "Young people's themes" (teenage sexuality, drugs, etc.) are introduced quite consciously, and these may disturb the older viewer's comfortable relationship with the show. A number of elderly viewers, for instance, told me that they were disturbed by the English soap *EastEnders* (which they originally liked) introducing "punk" and teenage sex themes.

However, in the case of *A Country Practice* it seems that this emphasis on young people and "romance" is contained successfully for the elderly within the rhythm of the show. The executive producer spoke of the way in which Vicky and Simon were

> originally brought . . . into the show as young romantic leads, but you can't stay a young romantic lead. You have to develop the characters. After two years they got married, and after another year they had children, and after another year they were written out. So we have to replace the romantic stream. We are going back to the early . . . situation and starting again.[7]

Provided that they were written out together (i.e. are not divorced) most elderly people I spoke with were sorry but not distressed; as one said, it is like "normal family life" where the young grow up and leave home.

Far more disturbing to elderly viewers was when their favorite soaps dispensed with older characters; in interview after interview they said that *Crossroads*, *Coronation Street*, *Emmerdale Farm*, *The Sullivans* had "gone off" since the older regulars died or left. To some extent this was a reminder of their own lives and mortality:

> "It's strange when they all start dying, one starts going, then another."
> "Well, actually, when you come to work it out, they become part of your life. They're in your room."

In particular, they valued the family, and the role of the mother in holding the family together. When the mother in *The Sullivans* died:

> "There's no story there now, really. She kept it together."
>
> "She reminded me of normal family life. The family drift apart when the mother dies."

In one case, an elderly viewer, thinking I had some power to influence what happened in Australian soaps, tried to mobilize the interview situation to change things:

> "I watch *The Sullivans* which I like very, very much – I really do. The wife, she was supposed to be killed, isn't she, in England in the war, and I would like her, really, to come back, only she had sort of lost her memory and in hospital or whatever, and then to come back into the series when she had regained her memory. I'd like that, because I thought she was a very good actress and it makes a very startling thing to bring in another character again, and it would be nice for the father. I think the father is so nice that he's not complete without a wife really, and it might make a bit of a surprise if she came back that way. People during the war did lose their memories, they *were* dug out, and for some time didn't regain it, and when they did it was possible to pick up the old traces."

This elderly woman had not been included in my original schedule of interviews, had waylaid me in the corridor on the way to another flat, drew me into her unit, and began with the comments just quoted. Then, after discussing her likes and dislikes generally, she returned to the same theme as I left, calling for the reinstatement of *The Sullivans'* mother.

The elderly, I am arguing, have neither the formal spaces for wide discussion of their favorite shows, nor the economic resources to control television's direction and future. But they often generate what public discourse they can, either in letters to the production house, or, when the situation arises, in enthusiastic discussion with researchers.

The Bournemouth study

My approach to the elderly in Bournemouth (England) was not designed as an ethnographic study in itself. I had been researching and co-writing a study of *A Country Practice*, which included an audience section. Here we examined the show "at home," "at school," and "at work," covering all the broadly targeted audiences except the elderly.[8] We tried (by publicity in the press and by personal visits to social events for elderly people at a shopping center) to get access to elderly people at home. The press publicity (in a widely read article about the show) attracted only one letter, that of an 80-year-old lady who excused herself on the grounds of "old age and dilatoriness" from responding further. In addition,

I don't feel that I could undertake to watch any programme on a commercial channel regularly, as I find the interruptions so irritating – I should say *maddening* ... I am really more interested in radio than TV, both classical music and talks and commentaries, and have a *few* TV programmes which I follow.

Obviously our publicity had not attracted even one regular *A Country Practice* viewer. At the shopping center there were many *A Country Practice* viewers, but none was prepared to invite us home as researchers. They were "frightened of strangers" and their rooms were "too small." Our attempt to find out about their "other family" of soap opera was threatening the very same domestic world of closeness and security which the program generated.

During the time of the research, *A Country Practice* (together with other Australian soaps – *Sons and Daughters*, *The Young Doctors*, *The Sullivans*, and later *Neighbors*) began to screen regularly in England. Bournemouth is an English town noted for its elderly population (as a southern seaside town with a mild climate). My own elderly family lived there, and my uncle and aunt (both in their late seventies) lived in a Shaftesbury Home, which catered solely for the elderly, with a live-in warden and custom-designed facilities for the physically handicapped. Its residents would see it as one cut above the town's "old people's homes."

I chose this particular home for a reason. Ien Ang has usefully questioned the positivist tendency of relegating the audience "to the status of exotic 'other' – merely interesting in so far as 'we' as researchers use 'them' as 'objects' of study, and about whom 'we' have the privileged position to know the perfect truth."[9] In the Bournemouth study, neither I nor the elderly audience was "other" in this way. My uncle arranged the majority of the interviews among people he knew; I was first of all "Douglas' nephew" to the old people I spoke with, and second "an Australian researcher about television." And my intention was to share, as far as possible, the "mutual knowledge" about television of these old people, a task made easier by many years of sharing television with my own elderly family and relatives in Bournemouth.

The first set of interviews (with the twenty elderly people who consented to be interviewed) took place in November 1985 during a short research trip to England, and consisted of my visiting people (introduced by my uncle) in their flats and discussing with them over the space of one to two hours their television likes and dislikes, their viewing habits, daily routine, and a little of their past background. The second set of interviews took place in November 1986, during which time I sat with each set of interviewees for a couple of hours on a Wednesday evening, noting (and taping) their reactions to television shows, their choices of show, their conversation, and talking with them when they wanted to. There were fewer groups this time; one couple were too sick to see me, one old man had died, and others I had interviewed the first time who did not, by and large, watch television were not relevant to this stage of the research.

I began by asking them about Australian soaps, then broadened out to include English and US soaps and other genres. All the elderly people who watched soaps were very forthcoming (they all especially liked the Australian soaps). Those who did not watch soaps were also very revealing, elaborating without prompting on their daily activities and leisure pursuits, and on why they did not watch soaps.

On the second visit, I chose the evening when *Dallas* was screening, because it had been the focus of most recent soap/audience research, and I was interested in comparing these findings where the major emphasis was on younger women and homemakers, with my work on the elderly.[10] In fact, too few watched *Dallas* for me to make any systematic comments about this age group; however, some meaningful responses (in terms of gender and class) did emerge, which I will discuss later.

The elderly: Habits of viewing

For some old people, who live alone in specially designed, labor-saving units, and have little to fill their time, the preoccupation with soap opera characters is both intense and catholic, as with Mrs McLaughlan who "likes them all":

"I have *The Sullivans* at 12.30 – I switch the set on for that. And then I have the news, and I've just had cookery and . . . short story. . . . And now it's *Take the High Road* – I always watch that, the Scottish one. I like that one as well because it's a family, and I love Scotland, it's partly my home. Then we go on to *Young Doctors* today. Well, then, when that one finishes at 4 o'clock . . . I switch off and I go on again for, like yesterday, *Sons and Daughters*. . . . And most of the evening I have it on, after that."

But other old people in the same units see things differently. Miss Harring (an elderly lady who is physically handicapped and confined to a wheelchair) responded similarly to the 80-year-old who wrote to us in Australia:

"I normally don't watch the television in the daytime hardly at all, unless there's something like a coronation or a royal wedding or something special. . . . When you get to this stage, you're so slow about everything that, you know, there are priorities. And I never have really been a great television fan. I think there's a lot on it now that is good; more the documentaries I suppose. And I do, I'm afraid, fall for it occasionally. I watch it from bed at night. I go to bed early and watch it, and sometimes – I'm either waiting for something I want to come on and there is some other basically rubbishy stuff, and I sort of put up with it. And occasionally I fall for it afterwards. But I usually put it on at six for the news. . . . That's on BBC. . . . I can't stand ITV, basically because I cannot bear being interrupted constantly by these adverts. The first time I ever saw ITV I was very untelevision-minded. This is going back twenty years, and

I went to stay with friends who put on the television . . . on ITV. . . . Suddenly it seemed to sort of not make sense. . . . We'd gone into an advert and I hadn't realized it."

This difference between Mrs McLaughlan and Miss Harring, a continuous and a "discriminating" viewer, matches closely Nancy Wood Bliese's experience of the elderly. "Some older persons, like Sarah, are so busy that they do not have much time for television or other media use; others, especially the homebound, used media to fill time."[11] Sarah

> has little time for television. She usually watches one or two programs a day, which she chooses for their informative or cultural enrichment characteristics. She . . . is too busy to bother watching "trash" programs. . . . She has a very busy schedule of volunteer work during the day and her evenings are spent catching up on correspondence with friends, doing necessary housework, engaging in her hobby of needlepoint, or curling up with a good book.[12]

My experience with the Bournemouth elderly suggests it is "high culture" values rather than not being homebound which determines the "continuous versus discriminating" distinction. Miss Harring, for instance, is seriously disabled and confined indoors to a wheelchair. Yet, when friends rented a television set for her one Christmas, Miss Harring

> was furious. I didn't want the beastly thing, and for some little time when I first had it, rather than keep switching it on and off, I put it on so that I would know what was coming on and what wasn't, and covered it up with a teatowel. I used to go and lift it now and again and have a peek, you know. But back in those days I wasn't so pushed for time, and I'm bound to say I did get hooked on things like *Z-Cars* and even *Dr Kildare*. . . . Cliff Michelmore used to do a thing in the early evening, *Tonight*.

Int.:   Why did you say, "even" *Dr Kildare*?

Miss H: Pretty grotty, isn't it, really? I mean, it's terribly sort of – it's not getting you any further, is it? I mean, quite honestly – and this sounds priggish – but I haven't really got time to spare to sit here and simply amuse myself. I've got more than enough to do. I write umpteen letters. I've got many, many interests . . . which I haven't got time to pursue. I don't even read much in the daytime at all; any reading I do is done in bed. I do lie down in the afternoons, and if I don't fall asleep, I read then. But I suppose really, when it comes down to it, I've got a vast number of friends and I love to write letters and I love to receive letters. That takes a lot of time because my letters stretch into small books. And I'm constantly sort of stirring up trouble, like "Save the Children" and that sort of thing, and all these things, they take a lot of time.

It was in writing and receiving letters that Miss Harring "purchased" that need which other old people describe as "knowing another family" via soaps. The interpersonal relationships that one old person uses soap operas for, another constructs by way of letters. These daily "books" were, in a sense, Miss Harring's own soap opera. As for television, it had its place only when this important task of relating to friends was done, and then she would watch news and current aff- airs, but never *Coronation Street*, *EastEnders* or things "I cannot waste time on."

Bliese rests content with using her example of Sarah to challenge the stereotype of the elderly as "passive" consumers of media. In fact, the difference in television viewing habits between Mrs McLaughlan and Miss Harring is worth exploring further. Miss Harring's use of television, and her preferences, were very similar to another Bournemouth pair, mother and daughter, Eileen and Judith Oldfellow. Judith suffers from an unknown virus with similar effects to MS and, in middle age, is looked after by her mother. Like Miss Harring, the Oldfellows are too busy to be "drawn into these love affairs that are going on all the time, everywhere" in soaps. Again:

"The trouble is, we can't really sit for long enough. Unless there's something very interesting that holds us there, we're finding something else to do. Writing letters, or reading."

"We go abroad quite a lot. But I don't know, there's so much to see if you look. But a lot of people don't look, do they? And we go off up to the forest."

"RSPB, bird watching."

"And also for the disabled club."

"Yes. Access to various places. We spent a few days on the Isle of Wight, surveying . . . toilets . . . to see what access is like. . . . We had two community nurses with us who we met by accident; they didn't have a clue. They said, 'Oh well, a wheelchair can get into that toilet,' and it was only across a field and up a step! . . . Even with people on sticks, or frail people, you see: how do they get in and out of these places? . . ."

"We don't just sit and watch anything."

"You see, some people have television on all day, don't they?"

"It's a time waster."

"Yes, it is."

"But it's good for people who are shut in."

"And you do learn, certain things."

For the Oldfellows "learning certain things" depended on watching programs based on "fact": "News, current affairs, and travel," and they were disappointed that the Australian dramas don't show a lot "about Australia: Australian life. . . . The way they live . . . the customs. . . . We like things like that, interesting." As for television dramas, they were prepared to give *A Country Practice* a try when they heard it had stories about MS and mentally handicapped children (Judith works voluntarily at a mentally handicapped children's school); and they liked *Tenko*:

"Again, it was based on fact."

"That happened."

"Yes, it did happen unfortunately. I knew several women who came home from these camps in Burma, and they said it was absolutely true to life. And *The Flame Trees of Thika*; anything that's based on fact, I like. I don't like – fantasy; perhaps we don't need it."

For these women *Tenko* and *The Flame Trees of Thika* combined their search for "facts, interesting things" with travel and knowledge of other cultures. Clearly there was an important class element in this; the Oldfellows were well enough placed financially to "travel a lot," and so be able to speak knowledgeably about Canadian, Dutch, and Italian television. Similarly, Miss Harring's put-down of soaps and "rather grotty" serials was from a high-culture position.

Yet, Miss Harring's account of a program she particularly liked revealed areas where she, too, had been disadvantaged: as a woman.

"I've tried to watch *Triumph of the West*. I only understand about half of it, but at least I'm sort of trying to understand it. . . . It's about how the development of the western civilization has sort of taken over – it's become so powerful. Going right back – the Christian wars and all that sort of thing, bringing it right up to date. I must say, it does make one feel rather ashamed, the way we have behaved. But it's really a little bit beyond me. I want to go on a bit or something. . . . *I am basically extremely ignorant. . . . I had a nicely private education*, where I was taught deportment more than anything else, you know. . . . And I think perhaps I'm missing out on it now."

Clearly, these texts (*Tenko, Triumph of the West, The Flame Trees of Thika*) had some continuity of information content, in that they were all about the interaction of western with eastern or so-called "primitive" cultures. There were also differences between them in the degree to which they problematized the meaning of this interaction in terms of western imperialism. However, for Miss Harring, such texts operated by way of a more personal meaning, which had to do with her own condition of disability and exploitation as reader of the text. Not any text would do (as all these non-regular television watchers insisted), and certainly the influence of the aesthetic and academic discourses that Robert Allen, Ien Ang, and others have described seemed clear in these women's definition of the "grotty" and the "waste of time." Nevertheless, their pleasures in television drama were no less functions of their daily routines than those who watched soaps all afternoon and evening.

Miss Harring's account of how she actually did get "hooked" on a soap – the radio serial, *The Archers* – is an interesting example of the complexity of "needs" that are part of the social experience of the audience.

Miss H: There was a time, and it was only for a spell of two or three years, I used to listen to *The Archers*. Before that I couldn't have bothered with *The Archers*, then suddenly I must have listened to it a bit and enjoyed it, and I went on for quite a long time. But I never listen to it now."

Int.:   Why do you think you actually got into it?

Miss H: I think probably because at that time I used to stand up on calipers to eat my lunch at the sink . . . because it was not wasting time doing two things at once, and I used to have the wireless on while I was doing that.

Int.:   So you mean it could have been anything?

Miss H: I suppose it could, but I did get that I wanted to put it on the next day to see what happened.

The Archers was, like *A Country Practice*, an "information" and "country issues"-oriented drama, which might account for why Miss Harring listened to it long enough to "want to put it on the next day to see what happened." But even for people stridently opposed to it as a "waste of time" like Miss Harring, soap opera clearly can have, as Cassata and Skill point out, "the uncanny ability to create characters and situations which hook the viewer into a willing complicity in the life that it offers."[13] How is this?

I want to suggest that there are at least two important reasons for this willing complicity. The first has to do with the enormous shared knowledge that regular soap viewers quickly build up; the second, with the interaction between soap text and the viewer's practical consciousness.[14]

Shared knowledge and paradigmatic complexity

Robert Allen argues that the high degree of narrative redundancy in soaps invokes a "paradigmatic network." Whereas "high culture" viewers see this as "an endless string of excruciatingly retarded subplots," to "the experienced reader . . . soap opera's distinctive networks of character relationships open up major sources of signifying potential that are simply unreadable to the naïve reader."[15] It is the lack of appropriate cultural capital to enter and use soaps (to compare and contrast, with the minutest discrimination) which leads the naïve reader to say she "can't get into it," is "sort of out of the picture," and complain of an episode of *A Country Practice* that

"There's nothing going on, excepting a whole bunch of people talking on here and there yesterday. We saw one man in one bed in a room, and he had his brother there. He'd had an accident – and that is all. And then we saw the two doctors – they were off duty – sitting in their canteen, having tea. And we saw another one at the end, just came in, put his coat on, off he went."

Naïve readers, by the way, are not necessarily "high-culture" ones; the elderly lady quoted here was in fact an avid watcher of other soaps. But it is high-culture readers who habitually make their criticism visibly discursive (in "quality" newspapers, university literature courses, etc.), and place that criticism (legitimated by talk about cardboard stereotypes and banality) within the discourse of "mass culture" ideology.[16]

It is because of its syntagmatic redundancy that critics who want their television to connect them very directly with the real world, like Miss Harring, complain that soap isn't "getting you any further, is it?" And it is because of its paradigmatic complexity that viewers who, like the Oldfellows and Miss Harring, "can't really sit still for long enough" to watch it (and so are unable to acquire the cultural capital to make fine distinctions of character and place) define soaps as "these love affairs, that's going on all the time everywhere." But, when for very specific experiential reasons (such as Miss Harring's disability and daily routine) the critic becomes the fan, aesthetic complaints about soap redundancy turn into narrative urgency: "I did get that I wanted to put it on the next day to see what happened."

Soaps and practical consciousness

In the case of one elderly woman (who had an extremely poor short-term memory but a good long-term one) afternoon soaps seemed to give her the focus on her daily affairs that was otherwise lacking. Her memory was too poor to complete efficiently household tasks like cooking (her husband did that); instead she sat in her chair watching each soap opera in turn, whistling or humming the signature tune of each one, and smiling a lot at the storylines. Sitting in her familiar room, among familiar characters and tunes, she more confidently organized her day; in the evenings she frequently organized it differently, recalling in detail her family past.

To take the question of the relationship between soap pleasures and practical consciousness further, consider the daily routine of a couple who, like the McLaughlans, were "continuous" television viewers. Mr and Mrs Mallard's preference for medical soaps illustrates how television drama is part of a daily life pattern, and how this routine is determined by ageing.

Mr Mallard enjoys *A Country Practice* "because I've got diabetes, and on there they talk about it"; for Mrs Mallard "it's our favorite" because there is a close parallel between the caring nature of people in the show and her own daily routine. She described how she would nurse her husband, lying awake between his prescribed 9 o'clock bedtime and 10 o'clock Complan, reading (usually a medical biography); and how she would organize people to take her shopping in accordance with the needs of her husband and timing of her favorite "medical" soap.

> "And then we come back, because the bus only runs every hour. . . . And when I come back on Tuesday, *A Country Practice* is on, so I'm back in time for that. . . . I have to get back for lunchtime because Harry has to have his meals at certain times every day, so we get back in time for that."

"Getting back in time for that" refers to both Harry Mallard's special lunch and *A Country Practice*. It is not simply that television watching has to be carefully positioned by elderly people who cannot afford VCRs and are reliant on other people to take them shopping (I heard frequent comments that an elderly woman couldn't watch *The Sullivans* or *A Country Practice* because she was preparing the lunch, or *Sons and Daughters* because she was preparing tea). It is also that the themes of some soaps are part of the daily experience of the elderly. For these old people soaps were firmly placed within a routine of organization and caring – by the center's warden, by younger family and friends with cars, by Mrs Mallard herself; similarly their favorite programs were about professional organization and caring. In that sense, soaps became part of their practical consciousness, their competence in caring or being cared for. These things were of no less life-and-death significance than the information on the news (which the Mallards disliked); they were simply more manageable, and became part of their day in an experiential way. In an important sense, soaps are generically defined by these old people as the non-news, non-current affairs (and therefore more manageable) world of daily living and dying.[17]

Television drama texts are defined as much by the regime of watching as by their conditions of production, and have effect as part of the domestic routine. As Fiske says, "such texts not only *mean* but *do*," and he draws on Barthes' metaphor of the economy of the text "by which he refers to the text's function, not meaning, and this function is as a coin of exchange by which the reader purchases something which he or she needs as part of his/her cultural identity."[18] This places Terry Lovell's notion of the use value of the text within the daily routine of its audience.[19] For the Mallards, medical soaps (and books) were used and gave pleasure within the "care" routine of the elderly.

The main emphasis of the first phase of my interviews with the elderly was to examine television (and non-television) use as part of daily routine. Here I was allowing them to tell me their story, and afterwards place it in a critical perspective. In the second phase I spent more time with elderly people whom I had interviewed the year before, whom I either already knew or whom, through their friendship patterns, I came to know better. In this stage of analysis I wanted to go further into mutual knowledge, and also to take more account of my position as interviewer.

Case studies: Generational values

In her "uses and functions" approach to media and the elderly, Nancy Wood Bliese points to the fact that the "range of types of media used, functions of those uses, and amount of usage seems to be very similar to the range for all adults over thirty-five," although there may be more intense use of particular media forms by the elderly because of problems of eyesight or budget.[20] Thus, for instance, I found much less negotiation about, and pre-planning of, the week's television than Morley did in his home audience study.[21] Many of the elderly could not afford the *TV Times*, and so would use that day's newspaper to decide what to view, or, alternatively, would simply leave the television switched on, remembering the day and channel of their favorite programs. In the Gilroys' home the newspaper was used to check memory rather than to pre-plan, and the television set was left running.

Mr G: We watch quite a lot, you know – things we get talking about.
Mrs G: At our ages there's nothing else to do, is there? Let's be fair.

Far from this continuous flow of television being used to "disengage" or "substitute" for reality, however, it was used actively and with discrimination. In the first place, even in the smallest flats, where the television was running constantly, the elderly would vote with their feet or with their attention.

Mrs S: He usually lets me have what I want on. Or if there's a clash I go
          over to my friends across the road, and he watches what he wants
          . . . 'cause he likes cowboys and that, and I won't watch 'em.

A common practice in my parents' home would be for my father (who, unusually among the elderly I observed, has always done most of the cooking) to potter around in the kitchen whenever soaps come on, with the stern instruction to "call me for the news." When his brother visited, they would stand talking (usually about politics) in the kitchen even if there was no cooking or washing up to be done. When the situation was reversed, in my uncle's smaller flat, they would stay in the living-room talking, while my aunt would place her chair close to the television set, intermittently watching it while the soaps were on. Similarly, my uncle (who doesn't cook) would play the "male" host role when visitors (including myself as interviewer) came, pottering in and out of the kitchen with beer or Scotch. As he told me, "I can't stick *Coronation Street* – I mean, I look at it sometimes, but, you know, when it comes on think 'Oh law,' and I go into the kitchen to wash up."

Second, even when sitting still in front of the screen, the elderly actively engage with it; my father and uncle vent their anti-trade union anger consistently during the news – which they watch so ritually (every news broadcast on BBC radio and television during the day and evening) and with so much irritation as to constitute one of the main means of regulating their day and the tenor of their emotions. In this case their main engagement is with the screen; no one in the room normally discusses their comments about unions.

In other cases, criticism arising from a show is more personal, and more amenable to negotiation. Bliese is right to argue that the elderly particularly enjoy game shows for the intellectual stimulation and challenge. This in itself is a matter for discussion, which they flesh out with the personalities of the contestants and the jokes of the quiz master. The Savages had a quite precise set of distinctions for quiz celebrities they liked "as a laugh" or thought were "too noisy and over the top"; and they would engage in their own character hermeneutic running parallel to the fortunes of the game show itself. The night I watched *Strike It Lucky* with them, for instance, one of the female contestants wore an outrageously tight dress to draw attention to her breasts and figure, so that it was difficult for her to walk comfortably up the steps to her position in front of the boxes.

Mrs S:	If she knew what she looked like.
Int.:	I think she does, doesn't she?
Quiz master:	A food processor – you don't really need it to get out of that. . .
Mrs S:	She couldn't have that frock much tighter, could she? Look!
Quiz master:	. . .dress better.
Mrs S:	He's taking the rise out of her. Look at it!
Quiz master:	A knitting machine!

Bliese noted that 29 per cent of her sample of elderly people mentioned watching specific programs that their friends also watched so that they could use the program as a topic for conversation. This "interpersonal interaction" use of television is, in fact, prepared for by ongoing comment and discussion between an elderly couple during a program, to the extent that they find no difficulty at all in airing their views with an interviewer. The only problem, Mr Gilroy felt, was remembering everything he wanted to say during the space of the interview; and he was one of the people who called for me to come back so that he could say some more.

What is particularly noticeable with the elderly as a group is the way in which they engage with television (and the interviewer) in terms of "their generation's values." Watching television with the Savages, for instance, was to hear constantly about "the older people." We were watching *This Is Your Life*:

Mr S:	When you see young kids on there, *This Is Your Life*, it's wrong. How can it be their lives?
Mrs S:	Someone that's getting on and done something really well. . . .
Mr S:	When we did get the older people on, the people that have *lived* their life more or less, it shows more. . . . The other week it was – even a chap like Bob Geldof – they haven't lived, have they? He's only young.
Mrs S:	I know he'd done good and all that, but. . .
Mr S:	They haven't lived a life.
Mrs S:	It can't be *"This" Is Your Life*, can it?
Mr S:	Today's chap's got something to say, hasn't he? – He's got about eighty years of it.

Again, they mentioned enjoying "the Royal Variety Performance this time. . . . Nearly all old stars. Vera Lynn was on it"; and also *Name That Tune* for "its memories."

I have argued elsewhere that the elderly, deprived through their low appeal to advertisers of programs of their own choice, "must carve out their pleasure as a kind of guerilla activity, weaving together another temporal zone out of genres as different (or even apparently opposed) as *Name That Tune*, *Minder*, and *Till Death Us Do Part*,"[22] and further that sitcoms are enduringly popular because structured in terms of the comedy of generational difference. As such, they help center for the elderly their memories, their "other" maps of place, time, language, and value. Soap opera helps do this in a different way, since, as one elderly man said of the older characters in *A Country Practice*, "things are centered round them. Because no matter what happens, it always seems more or less to come back to them – Frank and Shirley."

> "I think it would be more of a problem if Frank and Shirl left than the younger ones. That would spoil it. It's like *Crossroads* – we used to love that, but I can't get so interested in it now that it's changed like that . . . because we lost two good older characters."[23]

I found no case of the elderly complaining about the portrayal of older people in soaps, as Bliese did for commercials and other programs.[24] The elderly see older people in soaps as a privileged point of narrative transmission; it is only when they die or disappear that they switch off.

The working-class Savages focused this most clearly in terms of being comfortable with characters and places.

Mrs S: *Crossroads* – that's not the same as it used to be since they've modernized it all up as they have. . . . Made it into a leisure center.
Mr S: They've had quite a few new people come in and had the whole hotel done up – swimming pool and everything else in it.
Mrs S: Really poshed it up. . . . It's not so homely as it was. . . . They're trying to bring it too much up to date. I wouldn't like to go there. If I had to go there I don't think I'd be comfortable in a place like that. It's the way it's done now. When she moved out, they sacked her, didn't they, that Meg – it seemed to go downhill from then I think.

The kind of "guerilla activity" I'm describing is the selecting out from different programs, different narratives, a particular space for "older people" – pleasure as a *bricolage* of generic appropriations. And frequently the principle of selection for this *bricolage* is a mix of gender and class as well as age. As the Savages told me, the genre which they (and most old people they talk to) particularly like is quiz shows "because the majority of them are down to our level." Similarly, soaps work "at our level," while the news carries a degree of violence that is frightening because "beyond us. We've reached a stage now where it sickens us. It's not our way of life, so obviously we don't want to know about it."

Bliese links her "functions" of media usage among the elderly loosely to television genres. For instance: "For intellectual stimulation and challenge (e.g., game shows). As a less costly substitute for other media (e.g., television news

194

instead of a newspaper). . . . For self-improvement (e.g., exercise programs, language lessons).[25] In contrast, other uses and gratifications approaches found that various television genres could fulfill most of the "needs" analysed, to different degrees among different people.[26] My point, though, is not to legislate between different uses and gratifications conclusions, but rather to criticize the approach generally on the grounds (familiar enough within cultural studies) that it is altogether too atomistic and psychologistic in its approach to the elderly. It ignores subcultural difference (the elderly are very articulate about their generational difference, as we have seen), and within this generational set of likes and dislikes, it ignores the different ways in which members of the same elderly cohort sharing different class and gender positions will interpret a set of messages differently.

By and large, the gender differences I found tended to support what other theorists have already described;[27] the old people themselves were particularly clear about these differences between "male" genres (news, "cowboys') and "female" ones ("I like a good romance"),[28] though in some cases elderly men had begun to "not want to know" about the news. However, I also found that class patterns related to gender in complex experiential ways. I describe elsewhere how generational memory (and perceptions of "the real") relate to class differences;[29] here I will conclude by looking briefly at class/gender differences I found by contrasting two families (the upper middle-class Tollards and working-class Gilroys) as an indication of the kind of analysis available to ethnographic research, while still taking account of the role of the interviewer. It is perhaps important to mention here my observation that the power exchange in the Tollard interview seemed less that between interviewer and respondents than between husband (using the interview as a chance to criticize soaps) and wife. The man who always went into the kitchen when *Coronation Street* was on was only too keen to interrupt my discussion with his wife of her favorite soaps with "I don't know if you're interested in what I have to say." He then proceeded to dominate the conversation.

Prior to this I had observed Mrs Tollard watching television, choosing each soap opera as it came on – *Crossroads, Coronation Street, Dallas* – with considerable enjoyment. Her laughter with favorite characters while watching was in marked contrast to her more muted "Well, I do like them" at the beginning of the interview, and her "Well, it's a bit common, isn't it?" after her husband's attack on *Coronation Street*. Within the extended and acutely class-conscious Tollard family, Mrs Tollard had never been recognized as "of the same class" as her husband, and it seemed that in her almost private communication with *Coronation Street* (her chair pulled close to the screen while Mr Tollard pottered in and out of the kitchen) she was enjoying that "vicarious, evanescent . . . alternative reality" that James Lull describes as part of television's function in "helping married couples maintain satisfactory relationships."[30] As such, it was an almost silent alternative world except for Mrs Tollard's laughter. In the interpersonal situation of the interview she avoided dramatizing her alternative world since this might well have caused conflict with her husband. Instead, she mediated her view in terms of her husband's class values, playing a conciliatory role which recognized his competence and dominance, while ensuring their solidarity as a couple. This negotiation was particularly marked when, after Mr Tollard railed against a strike in *Crossroads* as both "unreal" and the sort of thing "I can't stand," she tried to fill out the causes of the strike, finishing (when he was still unsatisfied) with "still, it's all over now, isn't it?"

Mr Tollard was one who consistently mobilized "my generation" in his discussion of television programs that he liked or disliked. His sense of current television drama is that it consistently "knocked down" his class, its heroes and values. He disliked *Coronation Street* as typical "working-class" fare ("why can't they have something that is middle class, that is decent English?"); and he hated people who promoted strikes in *Coronation Street* and *Crossroads*, fearing they were more in tune with the present than he was. "Our world was a different world. We can't adjust ourselves, the other people can."

In contrast to the Tollards whose family had been "officers and gentlemen" in the British Raj for over 200 years, the Gilroys were working class; and clear class and gender differences were apparent both in their television pleasures and in their interpersonal interaction around the television set. Mr Gilroy, a Cockney, had been forced on to the streets early as a barrow boy. "The only way I knew how to eat was to go out and try and earn it. I played truant from school and never went at all – just to eat." Becoming a bookie, Mr Gilroy was "a very quick learner, I was quick at anything. I used to get in with people, like millionaires although I never had tuppence." Some of these were in organized crime, like the Kray twins, and Mr Gilroy (who particularly liked boxing on television) discussed the shooting of former world light-heavyweight boxing champion Freddy Mills in relation to this: "I knew that feller, he was an angel of a man . . . wouldn't hurt a soul. . . . Somebody shot him, put the gun inside the car and said he'd shot himself."

Unlike Mr Tollard who disliked *Dallas* ("all they can think about is parties and sex. . . . And of course it's the same with everything now practically. . . . Not only television, it's life itself"), Mr Gilroy liked it, because he saw the big-money characters in *Dallas* as similar to people he had known. But he told the Freddy Mills story to distinguish the ones "on the fiddle" whom he approved of from those whom he didn't.

In contrast to Mrs Tollard, Mrs Gilroy was not at all self-conscious about her watching of soaps. Like her husband, she wove current pleasures through her past. She argued that Mr Gilroy liked soaps where people were "fiddling the money," such as *EastEnders* and *Dallas*, because he would dearly like to go from the world of one to the other. "You like the richness of *Dallas*, which you'll never have." He didn't, she said, like any soaps "in the middle – like *Sons and Daughters*," whereas she did because of the "everybody knows everybody" gossip they contained. "This is more the story of my life. I was brought up in Bournemouth, and this place was a little village when I was born you see. This is how we lived, all sort of everybody knew everybody, all intertwined."

Characteristically her discussion of Freddy Mills was as someone who was part of her close-knit Bournemouth community.

"Freddy was my age, near enough. . . . He came from here, I call him a local boy. See, Chrissie his sister's still alive. I know her. With Freddy and Chrissie and all them lot I went to school. . . . But them Londoners, they're terrible – I think they're a cruel lot."

It is clear from this discussion that the Gilroys had a perfectly clear understanding of their likes and dislikes, and a way of "making sense" of it within their own cultural space. They used shows like *Dallas*, *EastEnders*, *Sons and Daughters* (as well as boxing heroes) to understand their past and present difference (as between London and Bournemouth working class). Both class and gender differences were mobilized in their discussion with me to explain their preferences; and there was no sense here, as there was in Mrs Tollard's case, of a pleasure that was acceptable only as long as it was not discussed. Mrs Gilroy regarded her television pleasures as of equal status with those of her husband.

My role as interviewer was partly to try to understand and so share this mutual knowledge, partly to make it discursive. In doing so I was inevitably at times bringing my own "second-order" concepts to the situation, through questions like: "So maybe the big-money characters in things like *Dallas* are a bit like, but on a bigger scale, people you did know?" But these were questions which derived from mutual knowledge they were sharing with me, and the questions could then be accepted and elaborated, disagreed with, or modified. In this case, my question generated the discussion about Freddy Mills, and their different discursive positioning of this "star." This then led on to Mrs Gilroy's thoughts about "roughness," and the difference of positioning between herself (as small-community "local") and her husband (as "rough" Londoner) in relation to television soaps.

My point is that there is no objectively neutral way for an observer or interviewer to gain understanding from an audience; he or she is part of the process of "making meaning," of making practical consciousness discursive, of "getting to know what actors already know, and have to know, to 'go on' in the daily activities of social life." The division between practical and discursive consciousness (the difference between the Gilroys' perhaps non-conscious grounding of their pleasures in different social experience and their discussion of it with me) can be altered by all kinds of learning experience, including in this case the research process itself. There is nothing artificial about this; equally it might have occurred over drinks with their friends, the Tollards. It is the way all living proceeds.[31]

Approaching the observer[32]

I have described two phases of my audience research with the elderly, the first stage concerned with questions of daily routine and practical consciousness, the second trying to draw out the relationship of interviewer to the (practical and discursive) consciousness of the audience. There is a third phase of research still to be done. I want to describe briefly here what its parameters will be.

As I said before, a major focus of old people's negotiation of television is via generational memory. In his discussion of memory, Giddens argues:

> Discursive consciousness connotes those forms of recall which the actor is able to express verbally. Practical consciousness involves recall to which the agent has access in the durée of action without being able to express what he or she thereby "knows." The unconscious refers to modes of recall to which the agent does not have direct access because there is a negative "bar" of some kind inhibiting its unmediated incorporation within the reflexive monitoring of conduct and, more particularly, within discursive consciousness.[33]

I have not examined unconscious "memory" in this paper. I have emphasized instead the relationship of practical to discursive consciousness (and of both to memory) because of their significance to ethnographic research, in so far as practical consciousness consists of that active "knowing" of the rules and procedures which constitute daily social life (of which television watching is part); and discursive consciousness is the daily process of recalling that "knowing" in words (a process of which the interviewer is part). Also, I agree with Giddens that recent psychoanalytical theories which have tried to show the foundation of institutions in the unconscious are guilty of two forms of reductionism, failing to take serious account of the operation of historical social forces and of the reflexive control (at both practical and discursive levels) that agents have over their conduct. This double reductionism has led psychoanalytically inspired film theory that is concerned with the "positioning of the subject" to leave us with the sense of a determined and passive audience. Consequently, it is not surprising that ethnographically oriented research concerned with the culturally active agent has tended to ignore the unconscious.

Nevertheless, the relationship of discursive consciousness, practical consciousness, and unconscious is a crucial one for current social theory, replacing, as Giddens says, that older psychoanalytical triad of ego, super-ego, and id.[34] Just as important as the discursive relationship between interviewer and audience is the unconscious one. Valerie Walkerdine (in the best analysis of this relationship that I know[35]) speaks of the "voyeurism of the theorist" in her discussion of her experience of watching a working-class family watch a video of *Rocky II*.

In the first step of her analysis, Walkerdine relates *their* voyeurism (of violence) to class and gender patterns within the family, in particular to the fantasy of the working-class male.

> The fantasy of the fighter is the fantasy of a working-class male omnipotence over the forces of humiliating oppression which mutilate and break the body

in *manual* labor . . . Mr Cole is a very small man. Fighting is a way of gaining power, of celebrating . . . that which is constituent of oppression.[36]

As a conscious "fighter" for his class Mr Cole is quite discursive, urging his children to fight against both middle-class teachers and their peers. However,

latent beneath Mr Cole's conscious self-identification as a fighter may lurk the fear of a small man whose greatest fear is his cowardice and his femininity. It is this which has to be displaced by projection on to, and investment in, others (his wife, Joanne) who can be the objects of his protection and for whom he fights.[37]

His daughter Joanne ("Dodo") is stretched across this world of conscious struggle and unconscious fear and fantasy: encouraged as a "tomboy" to fight like her brother, she is also infantilized by her father's nickname and his determination to be "her Other – the big man, the protector." The gender positioning within their practice of television/video viewing thus "reveals the complexity of his identification with, and investment in, her as he makes her simultaneously his feminine ward to be protected . . . and his masculinized working-class fighter, like her brothers."[38]

In the second step, Walkerdine relates *her* voyeurism (as the observer who was initially shocked and disgusted at working-class "violence" and "sexism" as Mr Cole replayed the most brutal boxing sequence again and again) to the history of her own subjectivity. This included her relationship with her own working-class father as "Other, his forbidden femininity, the powerless child;"[39] her experiential desire to "*be* that fairy – small, protected, adored and never growing up;"[40] and her ability to use her mind rather than body (unlike Mr Cole) to "fight" out of the working class and become, as academic, a "Surveillant Other" in her turn.

The great value of Walkerdine's analysis is in relating psychoanalysis to ethnographic work by rejecting the quest for the unobtrusive observer, and instead foregrounding the social regulatory power of intellectualization. On the one hand there is the "will to truth" that "designates the social scientist as an expert in the bourgeois order which produces this intellectuality." This is the role of "theorist/voyeur" (which was Walkerdine's position at the start of the research) who "expresses shame and disgust at the 'animal passions' which have to be monitored and regulated."[41] On the other hand there is the observer's movement toward knowledge by way of recognizing her own fantasies.

I wanted to use my own fantasied position within those practices as a way of engaging with their unconscious and conscious relations of desire and the plays of anxiety and meaning. Often when interviewing the participants I felt that I "knew what they meant," that I recognized how the practices were regulated or that I understood what it was like to be a participant.[42]

Walkerdine became aware of the relation (in class, gender, and interviewer/interviewee terms) between Mr Cole's "desperate retreat to the body" and her own desperate retreat to the mind – both as ways to "become bourgeois."[43]

My study of the elderly audience in Bournemouth was not designed to examine the kinds of problem that Walkerdine poses: a much more focused analysis of individual television programs and individual viewer responses than I had time for would be required. Walkerdine herself only examines one film text (*Rocky II*) and one family watching it on one occasion. Moreover, her class, age, and gender relationship with her audience was very different from mine, generating quite different possibilities of "mutuality." Unlike her, I was a male interviewer, and much younger than my (mixed working- and middle-class) audience group. I was also (unlike Walkerdine) middle class by birth as well as by academic aspiration. My "memories" (unconscious, practical, and discursive) are very different from hers. How then to understand my positioning as observer in (to use Walkerdine's words) that "fantasy space" which constitutes knowledge of my audience? As I have said, this requires a third phase of research not yet done; but in concluding I briefly want to indicate the direction this kind of analysis could take.

It would start with my uncle: the point of mediation between the elderly people and me, their "observer" and "young friend." While discussing (and criticizing) the "realism" of television drama during the second period of interviews, he mentioned his strong dislike of socialist playwright Trevor Griffiths' recent demystification of the "Scott of the Antarctic" legend in the series *The Last Place on Earth*; adding: "I would never follow a man like that. Whereas the Scott that I imagine would be rather like your uncle Cromarty, whom one would follow – at least, I would."

My uncle here was putting together a personal and a public history. Indeed, several histories intersected in his words:[44] Trevor Griffiths' own critique in the series of the conventional empiricism of television historiography; the intertextual history of the Scott family's rebuttal (as circulated very visibly in newspaper previews) of *The Last Place on Earth*, with particular emphasis on Lord Kennet's words, "no such man as that portrayed here could have held a polar expedition together"; my uncle's own history as the youngest, least sporting, least "macho" brother in a proud imperialist family, in which his brother Cromarty (holder, like me, of the sign of our history – a family name traceable to the fourteenth century) was supreme emblem; my uncle's positioning (while at his exclusive English public school) within the history of a *Boy's Own* reading formation that did so much to generate, circulate, and refurbish the Scott myth; my own history as the first generation to "fail" the family by going to a state secondary school, partially recuperated in my uncle's eyes through my studying history at Cambridge, and later lost to him again through the experience of May '68 and radical sociology; my very recent history as an academic, talking with Trevor Griffiths and watching him at work making a film with Ken Loach.

In my interviews with Griffiths a particular history (and mutuality) was mobilized; in my interview with my uncle quite another. Yet that engagement I had with Griffiths (via a post-'68 radical social theory) was one which, in a very different form, my uncle (as the "soft," non-colonist "intellectual" of the family) had had with Sydney and Beatrice Webb and then with the perceptions of 1930s Russia (Stalin was one of the "heroes" whom, together with Scott and Churchill, he didn't want knocked). In my own case, too, going to university, "staying with the schoolbooks" and so not being "out in the real world," was regarded ambivalently within the family. So both he and I carried with us a set of desires (to understand beyond our family colonist order) and anxieties (as "soft" near-outsiders to that order) which, as they intersected, became discursive around the discussion of Scott – a mutuality which was at the same time a profound opposition worked through different historical positions (the 1930s, the 1960s).

How this relates to that academic dominance of "Surveillant Other" in the interview discussion of Griffiths is an interesting question; so too are the representations of our relationship that my uncle carried forward to the other elderly people I interviewed. Different fantasies, different desires, different anxieties, different recognitions and memories were made to work with and against each other as I moved, as interviewer, from Trevor Griffiths one week to my uncle in Bournemouth the next, and from my uncle (by way of his mediation) to the Gilroys, the Savages and the Mallards. As interviewing subject I was positioned in multiple sites (as were my elderly audience). A reflexive understanding of that positioning is crucial if we are to avoid what Walkerdine rightly calls the fantasy of intellectualization – a regulatory process that produces audiences as "other" in our quest for knowledge-as-power.

Notes

1   See John Tulloch and Manuel Alvarado, *"Doctor Who" : The Unfolding Text* (Basingstoke: Macmillan, 1983). Other audience groups examined included mothers and pre-school children, primary and secondary schoolchildren, university students, and others targeted by the show.
2   John Tulloch and Albert Moran, *"A Country Practice" : 'Quality Soap'* (Sydney: Currency, 1986), pp. 228-9.
3   ibid., p. 229.
4   ibid., p. 233.
5   See Jane Feuer, "MTM Enterprises: An Overview," in Jane Feuer, Paul Kerr, and Tise Vahimagi (eds) *MTM: "Quality Television"* (London: British Film Institute, 1984), pp. 4ff.
6   See John Tulloch, *Television Drama: Agency, Audience and Myth* (London: Routledge, forthcoming).
7   James Davern, interviewed in 1986.
8   See Tulloch and Moran, *"A Country Practice,"* chapters 15 and 16.
9   See Ien Ang's chapter in this volume, pp. 96–115.
10   See for instance Ien Ang, *Watching "Dallas" : Soap Opera and the Melodramatic Imagination* (London and New York: Methuen, 1985) and the chapter by Seiter *et al.* in this volume, pp. 223–47.
11   Nancy Wood Bliese, "Media in the Rocking Chair: Media Uses and Functions Among the Elderly," in Gary Gumpert and Robert Cathcart (eds) *Inter/Media:*

Inter-Personal Communication in a Media World (New York: Oxford University Press, 1986), p. 575.

12   ibid., p. 573.

13   Mary Cassata and Thomas Skill, *Life On Daytime Television: Tuning-In American Serial Drama* (Norwood, NJ: Ablex, 1983), p. 169.

14   Practical consciousness: "What actors know (believe) about social conditions, including especially the conditions of their own action, but cannot express discursively" (Anthony Giddens, *The Constitution of Society* (Cambridge: Polity Press, 1984), p. 375).

15   Robert C. Allen, *Speaking of Soap Operas* (Chapel Hill and London: University of North Carolina Press, 1985), p. 71.

16   For further discussion of soap opera and "mass culture" ideology, see Ang, *Watching "Dallas"*, pp. 86-116.

17   See Tulloch, *Television Drama*.

18   John Fiske, "Television, Culture and Communication" (paper presented at the Australian Communication Association Conference, August 1985), p. 20.

19   For an elaboration of notions of exchange and use value in relation to soap opera, see Terry Lovell, *Pictures of Reality: Aesthetics, Politics and Pleasure* (London: British Film Institute, 1980).

20   Bliese, "Media in the Rocking Chair," p.575.

21   David Morley, *Family Television: Cultural Power and Domestic Leisure* (London: Comedia, 1986).

22   Tulloch, *Television Drama*.

23   Tulloch and Moran, *"A Country Practice"*, p. 290.

24   Cassata, Anderson, and Skill note the positive, "stable emotional," "highly respected" and "opinion leader" qualities of the older soap opera inhabitant when "compared to the overall depiction of the older adult in television as a whole," projecting "an almost unrealistically 'good' image of the older person" (Mary Cassata, Patricia Anderson, and Thomas Skill, "Images of Old Age on Daytime," in Cassata and Skill, *Life on Daytime Television*, p. 43).

25   Bliese, "Media in the Rocking Chair," p. 575.

26   For instance, see Denis McQuail, Jay Blumler, and J. R. Brown, "The Television Audience: A Revised Perspective," in Denis McQuail (ed.) *Sociology of Mass Communications* (Harmondsworth: Penguin, 1972), p. 153.

27   While the competences necessary for reading soap opera are most likely to have been acquired by those persons culturally constructed through discourses of femininity, the competences necessary for reading current affairs TV are most likely to have been acquired by those persons culturally constructed through discourses of masculinity.

> (David Morley, "'The *Nationwide* Audience' – A Critical Postscript," *Screen Education* 39 (summer 1981): 13)

28   For instance, Mrs Gilroy:

> "'Course women are different to men – we like a good searching soul story ... *Thornbirds* for instance. ... *Dallas* is not a man's scene. It's got too many Joan Collins types and all this business. It's all right for the women, with the dresses and the glamor and the beautiful hair."

29   John Tulloch, "The TV Audience: Generational Memory and 'the Real'" (unpublished paper, 1987).

30   James Lull, "The Social Uses of Television," *Human Communication Research* 6, no.3 (spring 1980): 204. This is part of the "Affiliation/Avoidance" relational use of television; other relational uses which Lull isolates are "Communication/

Facilitation," "Social Learning," and "Competence/Dominance," all of which, in different mixes, are useful in understanding television viewing practices.

31 For a full account of theories of human agency and social structure, see Giddens, *Constitution of Society*.

32 A longer theoretical section at the beginning of my paper in which I explained the ethnographic approach in my study had to be omitted for publishing reasons.

33 Giddens, *Constitution of Society*, p. 49.

34 ibid., p. 7.

35 Valerie Walkerdine, "Video Replay: Families, Films and Fantasy," in Victor Burgin, James Donald, and Cora Kaplan (eds) *Formations of Fantasy* (London: Methuen, 1986), pp. 167-99.

36 ibid., pp. 173, 182.

37 ibid., p. 183.

38 ibid., p. 188.

39 ibid., p. 186.

40 ibid., p. 187.

41 ibid., p. 194.

42 ibid., p. 191.

43 ibid., p. 181.

44 This analysis will be elaborated in my forthcoming book, *Television Drama*.

Chapter eleven

On the critical abilities of television viewers

Tamar Liebes and Elihu Katz

The status of the viewer has been upgraded regularly during the course of communications research. In the early days, both major schools of research – the dominant, so-called, and the critical – saw the viewer as powerless, and vulnerable to the agencies of commerce and ideology. Gradually, the viewer – and indeed, the reader and the listener – were accorded more power. With the rise of gratifications research, the viewer began to be seen as more selective and more active than was originally supposed, at least in the sense of exercising choice in the search for satisfaction, and less isolated.[1] The new-Marxists, for their part, have recently acknowledged that the media can be consumed oppositionally or in a mediated sense and not only hegemonically, thereby adding the notion of conscious decoding to counter the instrumental and even intuitive matching implicit in gratifications.[2] It appears that recent literary theory has followed a similar course, abandoning the idea of readers uniformly fashioned by the text in favor of readers as members of interpretative communities that are in active "negotiation" with the text, both aesthetically and ideologically.[3] Although it may seem that the reader posited by gratificationists is most powerful of all because s/he is free to bend the text in any way s/he sees fit – indeed, virtually to abolish the text – the fact is that her or his seeking is determined by her or his needs, and these needs – so the critics say – may well be determined by the media.[4]

In short, the reader/listener/viewer of communications theory has been granted critical ability. The legendary mental age of 12 which American broadcasters are said to have attributed to their viewers may, in fact, be wrong. Dumb genres may not necessarily imply dumb viewers, or, in other words, there are creative options within formulaic popular culture which may challenge both producers and readers.[5]

Empirical evidence for critical ability is still very sparse: Neuman and Himmelweit have made a start toward classifying viewers' reactions to programs and their critical vocabularies.[6] So far, one can say only that there is a growing consensus among these and other scholars that the operational definition of "critical" coincides with an ability to discuss programs as "art" or constructions, that is to recognize or define their genres, formulas, conventions, narrative schemes, etc. We would give equal credit for critical ability to viewers who are able to perceive a "theme" or "message" or even an "issue" in a fictional narrative, such as the message "there is room at the top," for example.[7] We would code such a generalization as critical, all the more so if it takes a more complex form such as "the program says that mobility is possible because this is what the producers have been paid to tell us." We would also credit as critical viewers who are aware that they themselves are using analytic criteria – such as "schemes," "scripts," "frames," "roles," and other notions of viewer processing and involvement in their own responses to the program.

Two of these categories relate to the viewer's awareness of the text as a construction either in its *semantic* aspect – themes, messages, etc. – or in its *syntactic* aspect – genre, formulas, etc. The third category relates to the viewer's awareness of the processing of the program by her or his cognitive, affective and social self. This third form of criticism, we shall call *pragmatic*.

We attempted to identify these three categories of criticism in viewers' reactions to the television series *Dallas*. Our data consist of some sixty-five focus-group discussions of an episode of *Dallas* among three married couples who are friends or neighbors and who share the same ethnic background. Four of the ethnic communities are Israeli – Arabs, recent Jewish immigrants from Russia, Moroccan Jews, and second-generation kibbutz members; a fifth is second-generation Americans in Los Angeles; a sixth consists of Japanese in Tokyo where *Dallas* badly failed.[8]

The Israeli groups – some ten from each one of the four communities – were assembled by asking a host couple to invite two other couples from their intimate circle to view an episode of *Dallas* together, at home, at the time of its broadcast on Israeli television. The serial is subtitled both in Hebrew and in Arabic and broadcast with the original English-language soundtrack. An interviewer and a technical assistant joined the group to make notes on the interaction during the viewing, and to conduct and tape the post-viewing discussion which lasted approximately one hour. Interviews were conducted over a period of four weekly episodes; ten to twelve groups, from each ethnic community, saw one of the episodes.

The ten American groups were recruited in similar fashion and similarly interviewed, except that they were shown tapes of the same episodes that were seen off-the-air by the Israelis. Since the American *Dallas* was two seasons ahead of the Israeli *Dallas*, we chose to show the Americans the same episodes, even if many of them had seen them before.

An effort was made to achieve ethnic homogeneity within each group, and on the whole this was successful, partly because of a tendency to ethnic homogeneity within neighborhoods, partly because of the natural tendency to ethnic friendships, partly because the person who contacted the host couple made clear that the discussion would be conducted in the shared language of the group. Thus, the Russians and the Arabs were interviewed in their native languages; the Moroccans and the kibbutz members were interviewed in Hebrew. A similar effort was made to achieve homogeneity with respect to age and secondary-school education, since the aim of the study was to compare *cultural* differences in reaction to the program. This was intrinsically more difficult, however, given the real-world variations among groups as to education level. Accordingly, in order to make certain that the differences we attribute to ethnicity are not better explained by education, we have double-checked our conclusions by introducing rough statistical controls for educational level.

The Japanese, of course, were in an entirely different situation. Since *Dallas* survived only for a few months on one of the private television networks in Japan, and almost none of the focus-group members had seen it, it hardly made sense to show them the episodes that the other groups had seen; instead they were shown the very first episode of the serial, dubbed for broadcast in Japanese.

It should be noted that each of the ethnic groups uses the program more referentially – as a connection to real life, including their own lives – than they use it critically or, in Jakobson's sense,[9] metalinguistically. Overall, referential statements exceed critical statements by a ratio of more than 3:1. The ethnic communities, however, vary considerably in this regard. About 30 per cent of the framing statements made by western groups – Russians, Americans, and kibbutz members – are critical, compared with only 10 per cent of the framing statements made by Arabs and Moroccans. This difference holds even after educational differences are accounted for; indeed, among the lower-educated, the *only* metalinguistic statements are made by the more western groups.[10] Japanese viewers made, proportionately, the most critical statements of all.

If most referential statements are "hot," by our definition, most critical statements may be considered "cool." But just as we find "cool" involvements in the referential frame – in playful responses to the reality of the program, for example – so we find "hot" involvements in the critical frame. These "hot" responses concentrate in the semantic realm, as we shall see.

Using an altogether different coding method, we attempted to validate this pattern by analysing replies to the more specific question: "Why all the fuss about babies?"[11] Some participants told us that the program dotes on babies "because they are needed by dynasties as heirs" – a statement we coded as referential. Others told us that babies are good for soap operas because they permit parents to fight over them – a statement we coded as critical, or metalinguistic. Consider the following quotes, illustrative of referential or metalinguistic "babies," respectively:

Luba The emphasis on the issue of babies in the family shows the importance of babies in a monarchy. They cannot risk [the possibility] that the empire they have built would vanish with their death; continuity is important. (Russian Group #62)

Ahavon-
chitz There are a lot of problems around babies in such a family – the real identity of the baby, sicknesses, kidnappings – which provide a lot

of possibilities for the writer of the series in constructing the plotline. (Kibbutz Group #81)

Table 11.1 Function of babies

	Americans	Moroccans	Arabs (percentages)	Russians	Kibbutz
Story babies:					
for the characters	14	19	24	16	16
Real babies:					
for people ("life")	58	75	74	67	66
Dramatic babies:					
for the producers	28	5	1	15	19
Total statements					
(= 100%)	(120)	(175)	(68)	(82)	(61)

Table 11.1 reports on these differences in relating to babies. The referential divides in two: statements which speak of the function of babies for "life," and statements which speak of the function of babies for the characters in the story, as if they were real. Metalinguistic babies speak of the function of babies for the producers and writers.

In the analysis of these data, the three western groups again exceeded the others in their use of critical explanations, but the Americans this time showed a marked preference for this kind of framing; they made almost twice as many critical statements as the Russians and the kibbutzniks and six times as many as the Moroccans. The Arabs gave almost no metalinguistic explanations for the fuss about babies. Further examination of these data by educational level (of the group) shows that the higher educated make most of the critical statements, but that the ethnic differences persist.

The higher rate of making critical statements about television programs among the western groups may reflect their greater experience with the medium, or their greater training in criticism, or perhaps their greater familiarity with the society being portrayed. That the Americans are strikingly more critical in response to the more specific question about babies suggests that they do, after all, have more experience with television genres and their production than even the other western groups. The Americans seem especially able to respond to specific questions of this kind, although we do not know why. Thus, in the discussion of babies, they seem to be aware of the difference between the function of a baby for the story (whether it is seen or only talked about) and its appearance on the screen – both critical framings.[12] They are also the only ones who sometimes perceive a demographic message in the appearance of babies, apparently because Americans are having to struggle between the ethic of self-fulfillment vs. the ethic of altruism.

Table 11.2 Critical statements, semantic and syntactic

	Americans	Moroccans	Arabs (percentages)	Russians	Kibbutz
Syntactic statements					
Genre, formula	48	43	20	49	48
Dramatic function	40	25	35	12	21
Semantic statements					
Themes, ideology,					
message	21	31	44	38	31
Total critical statements					
(= 100%)	(80)	(28)	(20)	(86)	(52)

With this basic distinction in mind, we devote the rest of the paper to analysis of the critical realm. As stated at the outset, the critical involves awareness either of the semantic elements of the text and/or of the roles of the reader as processor of the text. Accordingly, what follows is a discussion of the critical statements of *Dallas* viewers in each of these realms. Obviously, the analysis must focus disproportionately on the three western groups who participate most in the metalinguistic realm, but it is important to bear in mind that most of the statements of these viewers, too, fall into the referential realm, and thus that the sophisticated viewer should be seen as a commuter between the referential and the critical, and not just as one or the other.[13]

We now consider these critical categories, illustrating each by reference to viewers' statements. The critical categories employed by the Japanese groups are included here as well, at which point it should be noted that the Japanese have hardly any referential statements at all since they had no opportunity to get "into" the program.[14]

Most of what we want to say is illustrative. We wish to show how ordinary viewers frame everyday television critically, or metalinguistically, and to map the several ways in which they subdivide the frame. We draw on three different data-sets to provide an overall context to what is primarily a qualitative analysis. First, in Table 11.2, we present a glimpse of differences among the ethnic communities (the four Israeli groups and the Americans) in their use of the semantic and the syntactic, that is in the proportion of their critical statements about content and form. A second set of data, to be introduced as Table 11.3, is based on a reanalysis of the critical realm, in order to compare the critical statements of the Japanese with those of the others, and, while we were at it, in order to operationalize the critical categories we had developed in the course of the qualitative analysis presented in this paper.

A glance at Table 11.2 suggests that the several communities differ in the target of their critical statements. The Arabs and the Russians give greater emphasis to the semantic – to the thematics of the program, its ideology, and its message – while the Americans concentrate on statements about form.[15] The Americans (and the Arabs, although the absolute number is small) give rather more emphasis to statements about the functions of characters in the dramatic construction, showing awareness of the dimensions in terms of which the characters are polarized (good–bad, strong–weak, etc.).[16]

Semantic criticism

Theme

The form of criticism closest to the acritical referential realm is the ability to discern and generalize the *theme* of the narrative. Viewers who say that the program reflects the egoism of the modern world are taking a first step away from the referential where they would say: "J.R. tricks people. This is interesting because it is the only way to succeed. I, for instance, am going to do the same thing myself. I am going to accumulate money, acquire land and use my cunning" (Arab Group #46). As hegemonic theorists would expect, the referential viewer takes for granted that J.R. is real, and speaks as if *Dallas* were some sort of documentary. The critical viewer – even at this elementary level – shows awareness of the program as separate from reality and is concerned with the accuracy of the relationship. In this realm, there are notable similarities between Arabs and Russians who see the program as representing "moral degeneracy" or "rotten capitalism," although the Russians somewhat more than the Arabs question the accuracy of the representation.

The Arabs are more likely to blame moral degeneracy for the ills of modern society, whereas the Russians see more political causes. But it is often very difficult to separate the two; indeed, several (four of ten) of the Arab focus groups employ Marxist rhetoric to assert that the program reveals that capitalism is to blame for the moral and political degeneration of the west. For example:

Anise   "[*Dallas*] embodies western capitalism and shows that the more freedom there is for people, it becomes too much because it has already led to anarchy". (Arab Group #43)

A possible explanation of the high sensitivity of Arabs in Israel to the dangers of western culture is offered by Samooha who claims that (1) Israeli Arabs are at a different stage in the modernization process (with respect to the status of women); (2) western culture is associated with the colonial administration under which they suffered, and which, in their opinion, favored the Jews over the Arabs; (3) even after the withdrawal of colonialism, western culture continued to be associated with it, and Israel itself is considered a present-day colonial power; (4) capitalism is perceived as a threat to the traditional social system.[17] Arabs therefore have more reason than others to dissociate themselves from the culture of *Dallas*.

Some of the Japanese viewers claim that *Dallas* is compatible with a sense of a creeping recession. In an America which has come to realize that it is past its prime, "bitter," unhappy, unharmonious dramas express the *Zeitgeist*. Put differently, one Japanese participant sees the adventures of the Ewings as demonstrative of the end of the era of the American rich (Group #5). Indeed, some of the Russian groups go so far as to wonder whether the text is not itself critical of western society and its economic and moral order, reminding us of Fiedler's contention that the best of popular culture is subversive.[18] Hanna, a member of one of the Russian groups (#68), claimed that *Dallas* is a "socialist text."

Messages

These discussions of theme may appear either as inferences of the viewers or as intentions – "messages" – ascribed by the viewer to the producers. Thus, the most frequent theme perceived in *Dallas* – that the rich are unhappy – may be mentioned as the viewers' own conclusion or may be thought to be what the producers are trying to teach us. Yet a further step – one particularly characteristic of the Russians – is not only to ascribe intent to the producers but to ascribe manipulative intent, in the sense that the producers are telling us something they want us to believe but do not necessarily believe themselves. For example:

Alona   I started to wonder why the series is so popular. What happens there? Why does it attract the middle-class person that much? It's nice for him to know that the millionaires are more miserable than himself. Sure, a miserable millionaire is a nice thing because everyone within himself wants a millionaire to be poor, and nevertheless, he himself wants to be a millionaire. Here he sees the millionaires portrayed as if they were real. (Russian Group #62)

Thus, we are dealing here in three levels of thematics – the elementary, the one closest to the referential, in which viewers make an inference about the theme of the program; a second level in which viewers make an assumption about the producer's didactic aims in introducing the theme ("message"); and a third level, in which viewers suspect the producer of trickery, even if they themselves see through the trick. Some of these statements are as "hot" as many referential statements are. In other words, critical statements are not simply "cool" and contemplative, but can express intense feelings.

Our coding of "messages" does not permit us to distinguish easily between "the program teaches us" and "the producers are trying to tell us," although we did code manipulative intent separately.[19] Messages, like themes, are sprinkled throughout the discussions, although many are concentrated in reply to our explicit question: "What is the program/the producer trying to say?" Nevertheless, it is interesting to note that the Russians and the kibbutzniks (to a lesser extent) are most active in spotting messages, anticipating our explicit question long before it was asked. As Table 11.2 shows, the Arabs and Moroccans – not the Americans – follow the Russians and kibbutzniks in the frequency of themes and messages, although most of their replies are in answer to the explicit question. From the nature of these replies – Arabs give particular emphasis to the theme "the Americans are immoral" more than to the theme "the rich are unhappy" – it seems safe to infer that the Arabs are responding in the realm of themes rather than intentional messages.

But what happened to the Americans this time? In the domain of messages, the Americans tend to be resistant. Not only do they offer fewer messages than any of the other ethnic groups, they also protest that *Dallas* can have no message for them since it is just entertainment, only escape. Paralleling their playful statements in the referential, the Americans refuse to acknowledge that there can be anything serious about *Dallas*. When the Americans do acknowledge a theme or a message, they tend to say that the message will be so perceived by foreign viewers who do not know that the program is just escape, and not about anything real. When the Americans perceive messages for themselves – and this is relatively rare – they ascribe didactic and meliorist intent to the producers; e.g. the producers think that it is important to have a strong father figure in society, or that babies are a good thing after all, and that one can have babies and go on being egoistic.[20] In this realm, at least, the Americans are surely less critical than the others, and thus perhaps more vulnerable to manipulation. They believe that the producers do good homework, and that they have a sense of responsibility on which the viewer can count.

Archetypes

A higher level of thematic criticism might be labeled archetypical in that generalization about the narrative is based on the perception of an underlying theme that unites a class of texts or performances. The image of the good sheriff entering the enemy camp unarmed and staring the villain into surrender to justice and civilization is equally applicable to the classic western movie, President Sadat's heroic visit to Jerusalem, and an American detective shaming a mafioso off his private island.[21] The essence of this form of criticism is intertextual, revealing an awareness of similar dynamics among different texts; at its most classic, it is archetypical in the same way as Oedipus, or Joseph, or Cain and Abel. This form is not very frequent in our data, although the occasional archetypical allusions are dramatic indeed. Thus, we heard J.R. compared to Arab sheikhs in the Persian Gulf, and – by both Arabs and kibbutzniks – to General Sharon. Of course, the reference to classic sibling rivalries in a dynastic context is much more frequent, although most of these do not make explicit mention of the various pairs of biblical brothers.[22] A Japanese viewer notes that the image of an ancestral father bestowing his blessing on that son who will deliver a first heir also figures in Japanese stories of dynastic intrigue.

At the extreme of archetypical themes, the viewer is saying in effect that the theme must have influenced the narrative, consciously or not. Semioticians sometimes speak as if the writer or producer is merely an instrument through which these classic stories retell themselves. This structural aspect of storytelling, therefore, stands on the borderline between semantic and syntactic criticism: in so far as it deals with themes, it belongs in the domain of the semantic; in so far as it alludes to a classic sequence of actions or to themes that are elements of an identifiable narrative genre, it belongs in the domain of the syntactic, to which we now turn.

Syntactic criticism

Critical ability in the syntactic domain reveals an understanding of the component elements of a genre or formula and the nature of the connections among these elements. Almost two-thirds of the critical statements of each of the four Israeli groups are of this character – relating either to *Dallas* as a soap opera, or to a comparison of *Dallas* and other genres, or to the rules of storytelling which dictate the behavior of characters and the sequence of events in the corpus of *Dallas* episodes. An even larger proportion of the critical statements made by Americans are of this type but rather than be impressed by this syntactic ability of the Americans one should be impressed by the high level of similar ability shown by the non-Americans who are far less experienced with the regularities of American television drama. It should be noted, in this connection, that Israel has never seen a proper soap opera; *Dallas* is the closest they have come.

Genre

Nevertheless, Israeli viewers often volunteer quite precise definitions of what we would recognize as soap opera even when they cannot name the genre. Consider the following examples from two members of kibbutz groups:

Orly Every week the program focuses on the story of one of the stars. Every now and then they move from one to another and succeed in showing a few minutes of each star, to show that the story progresses a little bit . . . and they've introduced a new character, that is the daughter of the mother, and they leave us with some line of thought about each one – what will happen between her and what's-his-name. (Kibbutz Group #80)

Ze'ev It's impossible to achieve one's goal in this series; I'll tell you why. It's what they call a "soap opera" in the States. Are you familiar with this term? It's a series that goes on for years on end, and in order to get the audience to stay with it, it ends in the middle. The audience hopes the missing end will be told next week, but it never is. They always manage to get to another scene that won't be completed either. That's the way they hold the audience for years, endlessly. If they get to some ending, if everybody gets what he wants the following week, nobody will view. (Kibbutz Group #81)

In Japan, on the other hand, viewers say that they will stay with a series only if all the characters are reasonably satisfied at the end of the episode. In comparing the formula of American soaps to the brand they themselves produce, viewers claim that, unlike *Dallas* – where an episode races at a fast tempo to end at the height of conflict after fifty minutes – the Japanese "home drama" goes on for two hours, at a much slower pace, ending on a note of harmony. According to the discussants, Japanese cannot bear family conflict to drag on from one week to the next as this would spoil "the mood of relaxing" at home. This incompatibility between the formula and viewers' expectations gives a clue to the reason why American family dramas have failed in Japan.

It is interesting to compare these statements with Thorburn's analysis of the television melodrama which argues that since the story's end is never in sight the dramatic tension inheres in the short conversational segments with their heavy emotional loading.[23] The steady barrage of these crises is what makes for the melodrama. Members of a kibbutz group and a Russian group put it rather similarly:

Ze'ev   I don't remember one scene which did not consist of a conversation between a man and a woman, not necessarily married. He talks to that one, then they change the scene and she talks to that other one. There is a lot of tension in these conversations, actually in every scene. There is no sex in the program but the relationships between the sexes are very prominent. (Kibbutz Group #81)

Sasha   Normally, the series of events would be sufficient for a hundred families; suddenly everything fell on the family. . . . We forgive Katzman [the series' producer]. It's true he has to hold the audience, to drag the time. (Russian Group #63)

Attention is also given to the repetitiveness of the story. The point that the story is always the same was proposed in one of our Moroccan groups. Thus, Yossi (#20) counters the interviewer's request that the group relate the story by saying "the same as last week; believe me, [they are] the same faces." But the group ignores him in favor of a detailed discussion of what the story is about. The Americans, on the other hand, are much more insistent about the formulaic aspect of the story; they point out that J.R. has a weekly trick with somebody as his intended victim.

Mich   Well, it's very well written though they'll always let you hang, you know, at the end of the program and you, well, like we say, we got to tune in and see what happened – to so-and-so and so-and-so from the episode.

Deana   And two years ago they ended the season when J.R. got shot and we
         had to wait a couple of months to find out who shot him, and this
         year they had the big fire and now you're going to have to wait for a
         couple of months to find out what happened. (American Group #8)

Apart from identifying *Dallas* as a soap opera, there is occasional awareness of
the way in which *Dallas* is not a soap opera. The Americans specialize in these
nuances, emphasizing that *Dallas* is in prime time, and that the leading character,
in his devil-like surrealism, is somehow different from soap opera characters.
"Without J.R.," someone says, "the rest of it is soap garbage" (Group #14).
Comparisons are made between *Dallas* and successors such as *Dynasty*, in
character delineation, geographic location, dramatic inventions and rhythm.[24]

Sometimes *Dallas* is perceived as belonging to less obvious genres. A number
of comments compare *Dallas* to Godfather stories, noting the similarity to the
adventures of a family mafia, just as Mary Mander does in her academic analysis
of the program.[25] Japanese viewers prove more familiar with American culture
than Israelis, and several of them join Michael Arlen in associating the Ewings
with the legendary oil dynasty of Edna Ferber's *Giant*.[26] Made famous in its
Hollywood film version, this saga depicts intrigue and sibling rivalry of a wealthy
family living in an isolated, large, gloomy ancestral mansion. One Japanese
discussant recalls *Gone With the Wind*, describing the attachment of southern
gentry to Tara and the land.

Many comments compare *Dallas* to the genres of their own cultures,
emphasizing differences. The Russians, in particular, make pejorative
comparisons to the family sagas of Pushkin and Tolstoy for example, while
Japanese also make analogies to the family dramas of Chekhov, defining *Dallas*
as a "family collapse story," molded on the pattern of *The Cherry Orchard*.
Americans mention *The Forsyte Saga* and *The Brothers*, pointing out that the
stories of these families, unlike that of the Ewings, are interwoven with political
and historical process. *Dallas* characters are afloat in space and time. They do not
even age. Comparing *Dallas* with *Forsyte*, an American group member remarks:

Norman   If you watched it [*Forsyte*] for six to eight weeks, and you started
         when they were twenty and you ended when they were sixty, the
         whole life went through what was happening in the country at the
         same time – the strikes in 1926 and so forth. Here, nothing. I mean
         the atom bomb could be blown up somewhere and the people in
         Dallas wouldn't care. (American Group #4)

The syntactic critics see the program as a story of endless turn-taking between the
good guy and the bad guy rather than as a developing narrative. Indeed, one
American went so far as to say that it is not so much a moral struggle as amoral
entertainment, like wrestling, he says.

Greg   When I watch it sometimes I feel like I'm just about watching
         wrestling tape team matches or something like that. The bad guys

keep squashing the good guys, using all the dirty tricks and then every once in a while some good guy will resort to the bad guys' tricks and, you know, stomp on the bad guy for a while and all the crowd will go, yeh, yeh, yeh, and then the next week, the bad guys are on top again squashing the good guys. (American Group #3)

Dramatic Function

Analysis of the dramatic functions of the characters is part and parcel of the same kind of critical ability. Earlier we reported on the response to our question, "Why all the fuss about babies?" by which the three western groups — but especially the Americans – revealed an awareness of how babies propel the story along, in generating conflict, for example. The Americans are aware, further, that the babies need not even be seen on the screen; all they need to do is to be present in the minds of the others. In this connection it is interesting to note that some Japanese viewers – it will be recalled that they are not acquainted with the serial – retell the first episode in terms of the potential dramatic function of the two persons perceived as the central characters.[27] Thus, the two "keys" to how the narrative will continue are identified as an internal and an external force. From within the family, they predict, J.R. will move the story along by virtue of being a trickster while as an outsider, Pamela, the newcomer wife, will advance the story through her love for Bobby, thus to break the vicious pattern of the rival families' feuds, to transform Bobby and make the newly wed couple into the spiritual, if not material, winners. One of the Japanese viewers speculates on the delicate balance between the central characters needed to make the story interesting: "If Pamela is going to control J.R., the program won't be interesting because what is interesting is J.R.'s tricks."

The obvious references to the personification of good and evil, or to the function of the minor strands of the story in providing tension release, are further examples of sophistication about how stories are constructed and punctuated.

Carol   "They kind of use [Ray] as a fill-in . . . I seem to focus on the hard core stuff and every time they show Ray in there it is just like a side-track when you go and get a cup of coffee" (American Group #16).

Business

The Americans, again, are the most sophisticated about that other set of building blocks of television narrative, namely the business behind the box. Their critical statements show keen awareness that characters come and go not only as a function of the needs of the story but as a function of the deals they strike with producers and of the accident rate on the Santa Monica Freeway. Two of the

215

American groups contemplate the possibility that Pamela's attempted suicide may be related to her contractual state. The similarities in the narrative of *Dallas* and *Dynasty* are also remarked upon and attributed to the "invisible college" of writers and producers. Consistent with such economic and/or gossipy framing, Americans – when asked by us how the serial can ever end – tend to say "by catastrophe," as if to say that only some *deus ex machina* can do it. This is in contrast to other groups who say – when asked the same question about how to end the story – either that there will be a happy end for everybody, or that the good and bad will be appropriately rewarded. These latter endings are consistent either with a more referential view of the characters as real or with a metalinguistic view of a traditional story. By their catastrophic ending, the Americans seem to be saying that the story cannot be stopped by inherent or conventional means, and that only radical external intervention will do. The Americans also note that the great climaxes at the end of the season create a tension strong enough to hold the viewer through the summer months, and that the best programs are broadcast during the semi-annual special ratings ("sweeps").[28]

While far less knowledgeable than the Americans about what goes on behind the scenes, the Russians know, nevertheless, that "something" is going on. They are interested, however, not in contractual relations at the level of actors but in the business of buying and selling audiences, and in the suspicion of ideological control of the program by elites. Indeed, the Russians, curiously, are the only ones who take the credits seriously. They know the names of the producers, speculate on what motivates them, and sometimes believe that they are being manipulated from on high, and that producers are propaganda mongers.[29]

There is no question that the Americans are far ahead of the others in the making of metalinguistic statements of all kinds. They are the only ones who show awareness or interest in the business aspect; they are the most sensitive of all groups about the nuances of genre and why *Dallas* is and is not a soap opera, and how and why it compares with its several spin-offs. The Russians also show a high level of syntactic awareness but their emphasis is rather more on the formulaic aspects of the story and its valuelessness as literature; they are also more likely to suspect that some sort of propaganda is at work. Kibbutzniks tend to pay more attention to the segmental structure of the program as a sequence of two- and three-person conversations interwoven through the episode and its never-endingness.

Pragmatic criticism

Awareness of the nature and causes of involvement in the semantics and syntactics is what we call "pragmatic criticism." Some groups express this awareness with respect to the nature of their involvement in characters and themes; others are aware of the ways in which the structure of the program captures and occupies their imagination.

The naturalness of the characters is remarked by a number of discussants, particularly Americans. It is the awareness that the characters are acting "themselves" – that it is very difficult to separate character from actor in the ubiquitous genre of soap opera – that puts people in this particular kind of critical mood. For example:

Janet   This guy is such a jerk I really get mad. You know I always thought
        that these women that saw actors and actresses in airports and called
        them by their stage names or whatever was the last part they played
        . . . but I honestly feel that if I saw this guy in the airport – I would
        be tempted to tell him off – even knowing actually that this is a part
        I would really like to ram him hard. (American Group #9)

Viewers are also aware of the way in which their involvement may result from the similarities between family problems in the story and family problems of their own. For example:

Eitan   I would say that somehow we enjoy it because the problems the
        Ewings have evoke some of the dark secrets which exist in every
        family. I used to say that my family was a zoo until I discovered
        that every family has different animals but everybody has a zoo at
        home.

Helen   If you will take your own family and create a series for us every
        week . . . I would not like to hurt you.

Eitan   No, you don't hurt me. I agree with you, this is my own family zoo,
        but I think every family has such zoos. (Kibbutz Group #80)

The genre, too, is recognized as a source of involvement. A number of discussants mention the built-in compulsion to find out what will happen next week or, better, to spend the week inventing possible solutions to last week's problems or to next week's continuation. This participatory function is well known from the earliest research on radio soap opera and, indeed, from literary research on novels published in installments in popular magazines, such as Dickens.[30]

Altogether, the point of this pragmatic criticism is that it connects reflexively between the text and the readers' definition of their own experiences or of their roles. Thus, the ludic viewer fancies himself in the role of putative writer as well as reader, or of a sports spectator placing bets on likely outcomes. Indeed, one viewer called *Dallas* a game of "risk" and another called it a wrestling match.

More traditional viewers refuse to play games and insist that they are viewing – licentiously perhaps – as persons with moral convictions that predetermine their response to the program. The Arab groups, for example, regularly speak of the program in terms of "we" and "they," and although this polarity is by no means metalinguistic, it does imply a self-consciousness about the "role of the reader." The following quote from Machluf makes the same point:

Machluf You see I'm a Jew wearing a skullcap and I learned from this film
          to say [quoting from Psalms] "Happy is our lot" that we're Jewish.
          Everything about J.R. and his baby, who has maybe four or five
          fathers, I don't know . . . I see that they're all bastards. (Moroccan
          Group #20)

The Japanese also explain their non-involvement in the program in terms of the
difference between the two cultures and in terms of their attitude toward
American society;[31] indeed, the incompatibility they experienced was enough to
dissuade them from viewing. As one non-viewer claims, the Japanese could have
been affected by the series "some years ago [when] Japanese had admired
American life and society." Now that they are more critical of the Americans they
see beyond the glamor into the violence within the family, and it only makes them
wary.

By contrast, the Russian and American viewers show their self-awareness in
the viewer role by explicitly excluding themselves from the kinds of effects that
they attribute to others. In pointing out the ideological manipulation they
perceive in the story, the Russians are saying that others, not themselves, will be
affected. Similarly, the Americans who insist that the program has no message or
moral for them are equally insistent that the rest of the world will misread *Dallas*
as an America full of neurotic people walking on streets paved with gold.

Conclusions

It should be reiterated, in conclusion, that these types of critical statements about
Dallas emerged in the course of focus-group conversations that did not require
discussants to use the critical register.[32] Indeed, the two more traditional groups
in our study volunteered only a small number of the sort of metalinguistic
statements we have analysed in this paper, and all six ethnic groups excepting the
Japanese talked more referentially than critically. It is important to note that even
the most critical groups speak referentially as well.

Critical reactions do not necessarily imply distance; indeed, some of them are
genuinely "hot" in the intensity of their involvement and, sometimes, outrage.
Indeed, the "coolest" kinds of critical framing – the syntactic statements – may
lower the barrier to the penetration of unchallenged messages. In this sense, the
Arabs and Russians are better "protected" than the Americans. When the Arab
groups speak critically, they express awareness of the politics of the program and
of a theme or message to which they are opposed; this parallels the "normative
opposition" of Arabs and Moroccans in the referential realm. Some Russian
groups go even further and perceive conspiracy; they think the producers may be
willfully distorting reality in order to influence us.

The Russians also reject the program on aesthetic grounds, by comparison
with the literary genres with which they are familiar. This "aesthetic opposition"
takes its place alongside "normative opposition."

Table 11.3 Forms of opposition

	Referential	Critical
"Hot"	moral	ideological
"Cool"	ludic	aesthetic

It is worth noting, again, that the forms of opposition are diverse. Thus, moral opposition may be either referential – when it accepts the message as reality, gives it "standing," and argues with it – or it may be critical, when it betrays an awareness of the (manipulative) construction of an ideological message. Indeed, all critical statements – certainly including "aesthetic opposition" – may be deemed oppositional in the sense of rejecting the referential reading.[33] This may clarify a confusion in some of the literature on oppositional readings.[34]

The types of opposition may be presented schematically, by cross tabulating the hot/cool dimension with the referential/critical. Thus, Table 11.3 shows that the combination referential/hot may produce "moral opposition" to the content of the programs while critical/hot, through awareness of the manipulative construction of the message, may produce what we have called "ideological opposition." Within the cool mode, referential/cool is associated with the ludic, and critical/cool may produce "aesthetic opposition." Each of these forms of opposition, as we have said, constitutes a different kind of "defense" against the message of the program, and, by implication, as we have also noted, a different form of vulnerability.

We have said at various points that each type of "opposition" may both defend a viewer and cause her or him to be open to influence. Thus, moral defense is based on giving a program standing, and so deeming it worthy of argument. Ideological defense is vulnerable because it is based on automatic transformations, as if to say that the opposite of the message *is* the truth. Aesthetic defense risks letting the ideological message slip by, while the playful escape of ludic defense may fail to bring one back to earth.

We wish to thank the Annenberg Schools, Inc. and the Hoso Bunka Foundation for their support of this project. Professor Sumiko Iwao collaborated in collection and analysis of the Japanese data, parts of which are included here.

Notes

1   See Elihu Katz, "Communications Research Since Lazarsfeld," *Public Opinion Quarterly* 51, no. 4; part 2 (winter 1987): S25-S45.
2   R. Parkin, *Class, Inequality and Political Order* (London: MacGibbon & Kee, 1971); Stuart Hall, "Encoding and Decoding in the Television Discourse," in Stuart Hall, Dorothy Hobson, Andrew Lowe, and Paul Willis (eds) *Culture, Media, Language* (London: Hutchinson, 1980), pp. 128-38; and David Morley, *The "Nationwide" Audience: Structure and Decoding (London: British Film Institute, 1980).*

3   Stanley Fish, *Is There a Text in This Class? The Authority of Interpretive Communities* (Cambridge, Mass.: Harvard University Press, 1980); and Janice Radway, *Reading the Romance. Women, Patriarchy and Popular Literature* (Chapel Hill: University of North Carolina Press, 1984).

4   Philip Elliott, "Uses and Gratifications Research: A Critique and a Sociological Alternative," in J. Blumler and E. Katz (eds) *The Uses of Mass Communication* (Beverly Hills, Calif.: Sage, 1974), pp. 249-68.

5   Umberto Eco, "Innovation and Repetition," *Daedalus* 114, no. 40 (fall 1985): 161-84.

6   W.R. Neuman, "Television and American Culture: The Mass Medium and the Pluralist Audience," *Public Opinion Quarterly* 46 (1982): 471-87; and Hilde Himmelweit, Betty Swift, and Marianne E. Jaeger, "The Audience as Critic," in P. H. Tannenbaum (ed.), *Entertainment Functions of Television* (Hillsdale, NJ: Erlbaum, 1983), pp. 67-106.

7   Sari Thomas and Brian P. Callahan, "Allocating Happiness: TV Families and Social Class," *Journal of Communication* 32 (1982): 184-90.

8   The sample is in no sense "representative." It is too small, for one thing, and not random in any formal sense. Informally, however, one can make a good case that these are bona fide members of their respective subcultures.

9   Roman Jakobson, "Linguistics and Poetics," in DeGeorge and DeGeorge (eds) *The Structuralists: From Marx to Levi-Strauss* (New York: Anchor Books, 1980), pp. 85-122.

10 Tamar Liebes and Elihu Katz, "Patterns of Involvement in Television Fiction: A Comparative Analysis," *European Journal of Communication* 1, no. 2 (1986): 151-72.

11 We coded every reply to the question "Why all the fuss about babies?" in terms of types of babies ("story," "real," "dramatic") and types of functions ("inheritors," "pleasure-givers," "tension-creators," etc.), paraphrasing statements or parts of statements in the form of codeable nuclear sentences. Thus, the statement: "There are a lot of problems around babies in such a family: the real identity of the baby, sicknesses, kidnapping. Therefore around them there is a lot of scope for the writer to build up a plot." This is coded: *Drama babies* function *for producers* as *conflict.* The average group provided some ten codeable replies. Japanese groups could not be expected to answer questions about babies since they viewed only the first episode, where the problem of babies does not yet exist.

12 As in the following example (American Group #4):

    Donna   Kids don't play an important *part*. The only time when you ever see them is when the maid is carrying the baby off.

    Sandi   The babies play important *roles* only because of what revolves around them.

13 Empirical observations lead us to this conclusion, which reinforces the idea that sophistication may be defined as observation of one's more naïve self. Eco, in "Innovation and Repetition," in our opinion, makes too sharp a distinction between the naïve and the sophisticated.

14 We omit here the pragmatic domain, because our original coding was based only on the semantic and the syntactic.

15 The semantic statements are "hotter" as we shall note again, and sometimes include negative evaluations of the ideology of the theme or message, paralleling the statements of normative opposition to the Ewings in the referential. The former qualify as critical because of their explicit recognition that the program has a theme or message.

16 For an analysis of these dimensions from the viewers' perspective see Sonia

Livingstone, "Viewers' Interpretations of Soap Opera: The Role of Gender, Power and Morality" (paper presented at the International Television Studies Conference, London, 1986).

17 See Sammy Samooha, "Between Two Cultures: How Jews and Arabs in Israel Perceive Their Own Culture and Each Other's Culture" (paper presented at the conference "Attitudes to Western Culture," The Van Leer Institute, Jerusalem, 1984).

18 Leslie Fiedler, *What Was Literature? Mass Culture and Mass Society* (New York: Simon & Schuster, 1982).

19 We coded all statements beginning with "the program/the story teaches us" or "they – the writers/producers – are trying to show/tell us" as messages and marked whether this message was manipulative or not.

20 Greg They [the producers] are trying to show a family; a family needs a strong father image. Some of the programs they show today, so many today, are without fathers anymore. That is not good for family entertainment, we need a strong father figure holding everyone together. (American Group #16)

    Janet Maybe they are trying to relate to the young people of today, who many of them don't want children because it interferes with their selfish lives, to put across that it is OK to want children, to say that you can care about yourself and be selfish but you can have a child also. (American Group #3)

21 For an analysis of Sadat's televised visit to Jerusalem see Elihu Katz, Daniel Dayan, and Pierre Motyl, "Television Diplomacy: Sadat in Jerusalem," in G. Gerbner and M. Seifert (eds) *World Communications* (New York: Longmans, 1980), pp. 127-36; also Tamar Liebes, "Shades of Meaning in President Sadat's Knesset Speech," *Semiotica* 48, no. 3/4 (1984): 229-65. For an analysis of an American detective as the lone hero of a western, see BBC, *Violence on Television: Programme Content and Viewer Perception* (London: BBC Audience Research, 1972).

22 Biblical themes in the *Dallas* stories are discussed in Tamar Liebes and Elihu Katz, "*Dallas* and Genesis: Primordiality and Seriality in Television Fiction," in James Carey (ed.) *Communications and Culture* (Newbury Park, Calif.: Sage, 1988), pp. 113-25.

23 David Thorburn, "Television Melodrama," in Horace Newcomb (ed.) *Television – The Critical View*, (New York and Oxford: Oxford University Press, 1982, 3rd edn.), pp. 529–46.

24 Robin *Dynasty*, which I watch a lot of now, moves a little bit slower. You know, with this one, if you really miss an episode you've got to try and figure out what happened in between – unless you're able to talk to someone else, 'cause there always is something going on, and *Dynasty* in comparison the show moves a lot slower. (American Group #4).

25 Mary Mander, "*Dallas*: The Mythology of Crime and the Moral Occult," *Journal of Popular Culture* 171 (fall 1980): 44-8.

26 Michael J. Arlen, "Smooth Pebbles at Southfork," in his *Camera Age: Essays on Television* (New York: Farrar, Straus & Giroux, 1980), pp. 38-50.

27 As *Dallas* is not broadcast in Japan, our Japanese participants were shown the first episode of the series in which Bobby brings Pamela to Southfork after having married her in secret. The new wife happens to be the daughter of the Barnes family, the enemies of the Ewings.

28 Lynn They seem to have certain shows that are preliminary to other shows. I guess they save the better shows until rating time (American Group #16).

29 The Russians are "literate." They read the title of the episode, for example, and ask whether it is a good name for the story.

30   Herta Herzog, "What Do We Really Know About Daytime Serial Listeners?" in
      Paul F. Lazarsfeld and Frank Stanton (eds) *Radio Research 1942-1943* (New
      York: Duell, Sloan & Pearce, 1944), pp. 3-33; Wolfgang Iser, *The Act of Reading:
      A Theory of Aesthetic Response* (London: Routledge & Kegan Paul, 1978).

31   As Kyoko puts it, "it might be the difference between meat-eating people and
      grass-eating people. Europeans and Americans are war-like."

32   Except for "messages," which we decided to include, belatedly, among the critical
      categories. But, as we have noted, the coding permits us to distinguish between
      messages supplied in answer to our explicit query and those volunteered prior to
      our putting of this question.

33   We note again that we are discussing statements, not people. Almost everybody
      who makes oppositional statements in the critical frame also makes referential
      ones.

34   In *The "Nationwide" Audience*, Morley makes the point, which we make in this
      chapter, that his focus-group discussions of a television newsmagazine accepted
      the ideology of the program even while they were critical of its aesthetics. Others
      opposed the ideology while remaining uncritical of the construction. Morley was
      thus surprised to learn that critical readings do not necessarily constitute a defense
      against ideology.

Chapter twelve

"Don't treat us like we're so stupid and naïve":

Toward an ethnography of soap opera viewers

Ellen Seiter, Hans Borchers, Gabriele Kreutzner,
and Eva-Maria Warth

During the summer of 1986, the Tübingen Soap Opera Project team conducted twenty-six ethnographic interviews with viewers in western Oregon. The first part of this paper places our study within the context of recent ethnographic work on particular social audiences of popular texts and describes our research design. The second part gives a preliminary report of our analyses and is divided into three sections: 1) soap operas in the context of everyday life for women working in the home; 2) how viewers construct the soap opera as a text; and 3) a feminist approach to the issue of gender and genre. Finally, we take a discursive approach to the interviews conducted by Kreutzner, Warth, and Seiter in all-female groups in our postscript on gendered discourse.

The ethnography of reading

Our study of Oregon soap opera viewers is indebted to recent work in the "ethnography" of reading that has been done by David Morley and Janice Radway. In *The "Nationwide" Audience*, Morley proposes a model for the interaction of viewer and television text which challenges both the uses and gratifications model, with its unlimited possibilities for individual responses to the media, and the hypodermic needle theory of mass culture, with its ideological overdetermination.[1] In "A Critical Postscript" to *The "Nationwide" Audience*, published in 1981, Morley raises a number of issues pertinent to our own study.[2] Whereas the *"Nationwide"* study emphasized the influence of class as a parameter of cultural decodings, the postscript draws attention to the investigation of sex/gender as a crucial aspect in the production of meaning. As the work of Charlotte Brunsdon suggests, the social category of gender is essential to an understanding of the specific relationship between a generic form and gender-specific cultural competences of viewers.[3] Morley's critical reassessment of *"Nationwide"* also points to theoretical problems raised by fictional texts. The concept of "preferred reading," which has been developed in the context of news and current affairs television, raises a number of problems when applied to fictional forms. The hierarchy of discourses in television's fictional texts tends to be more ambiguous, preventing narrative closure on all levels of the text, and thus rendering the text more open to divergent meanings.

Another point of departure from *Nationwide* lies in Morley's reformulation of the notion of decoding, which is no longer conceived of as a single act of reading, but also as "a set of processes – of attentiveness, recognition of relevance, of comprehension, and of interpretation and response."[4] This conceptual shift is closely related to a stronger emphasis on respondents' actual interlocutions as primary "data" rather than, as in *Nationwide*, dealing only with the substance of the viewers' responses. Morley suggests that specific meaning constructions can only be accounted for by close attention to the linguistic form in which they are expressed. In conclusion, Morley proposes an "ethnography of reading" which would account for the cultural rules organizing individual diversities of a basically social phenomenon.[5]

Janice Radway's study of forty-two American women who are avid readers of romances, *Reading the Romance: Women, Patriarchy, and Popular Literature*, starts from the premise that the popular appeal of a fictional text depends on the recognition of its genre attributes. Radway sets out to "represent schematically the geography of the genre as it is surveyed, articulated, and described by the women themselves."[6] By relying on empirical work – questionnaire responses and intensive interviews – Radway avoids the pitfalls both of an older type of formula criticism developed within popular culture studies and of the theoretical assumption of the implied reader as used in models of reader-response criticism. The value of this approach lies in its capacity to account for the affinities and correspondences between a certain narrative style and the cultural competences of a particular group of readers.

Conceived of as an ethnography, Radway's book is not limited to the exploration of text and genre. Locating her findings within the theoretical frameworks furnished by feminist sociologist Nancy Chodorow and Marxist critic Fredric Jameson, she concludes that women who purchase and read romances use the act of reading to create their own space in the confining routines of their daily lives as wives and mothers. Thus, reading romances provides the women relief from the seemingly endless demands on them as nurturers. In more general terms, the reading of romances implies a gesture of protest against the strictures of their everyday lives within a patriarchal society. Radway's decision to shift the emphasis of inquiry from the text itself to the social event of reading, and to investigate this event through the application of ethnographic methods, were influential on the design of our own research project. Like David Morley's recent work on television in the familial context, *Family Television*, Radway offers the insight that in order to understand the meaning of popular culture, one has to ask what it is that people are doing when they read or watch, and how they themselves understand these activities.

In adapting Morley's and Radway's work to a study of the soap opera, our work focuses on a privileged object within television research. The genre's special status has a number of rather different sources. Thus the first empirical broadcast media audience study, Herta Herzog's pioneer article "On Borrowed Experience," investigated soap opera listeners.[7] Textual analyses have frequently centered on soap operas, which attract scholarly interest because of their comparatively long history, their proliferation, and the special problems posed by seriality and melodrama. Because they are broadcast daily, soap operas lend themselves to an investigation of television in the context of the everyday. Since the genre has been associated with an audience of women, it has attracted the attention of feminist critics. This body of work has attempted to theorize the construction of gender within the text and within the audience. Finally, prime-time serials such as *Dallas* and *Dynasty* have become symbols of US cultural imperialism, and the subject of study outside the United States. Within the context of the problematic of culture and ideology, empirical audience studies on US prime-time soap operas in other countries have attempted to come to terms with cross-cultural readings of these shows.

The Oregon audience study

All of the interviews took place in the Eugene/Springfield metropolitan area of western Oregon. The area is characterized by high unemployment (9.5 per cent during the summer of 1986), relatively low per capita income ($7,302 per year), and a predominantly white population (blacks making up only 1,618 of a county population of 275,226; other minorities, mostly Chicanos (Hispanic-Americans), Asians, and Indians, make up about 3 per cent of the total population). The largest employer in Eugene is the University of Oregon; in Springfield it is the Weyerhauser lumber mill, where the workers were on strike during most of the interview period (a strike which ended with the workers giving up about $4 an hour in wages and fringe benefits). Like the entire state of Oregon, Eugene/Springfield has suffered from serious economic depression since the 1970s, due to its reliance on the lumber industry (which suffered from a drastic fall in housing starts) and tourism (which suffered from the rise in gasoline prices).

Between July 21 and August 16, 1986, we conducted a total of twenty-six interviews. Each interview was carried out by two scholars of whom at least one was German. Fifteen all-women groups were visited by a female research team. All of our informants were white. Among the sixty-four participants were fifteen men. Eleven informants were unemployed at the time of the interview. The large number of unemployed men and women in our pool reflects our technique for contacting informants – to run an ad. in the Help Wanted section of the Eugene newspaper – and also reflects the economic depression which characterizes the region. Because of the tendency in this kind of academic research to deal predominantly with middle-class informants, and because of our interest in working-class readings of soap operas, we welcomed this composition of our informant pool. We judge our failure to contact any women or men of color for the interviews, however, as a serious limitation of the study.

The text of our ad. ran, under the bold print headline **SOAP OPERAS**, as follows: "We are writing a book and need to talk to people about soap operas. If you and your family/friends watch them, we would like to interview you as a group at your home ($5/hour per person). Please contact us at. . . ." The advertisement ran for three days; we were flooded with telephone calls. We asked the callers what programs they were interested in, where they lived, and how many friends or family members were available for an interview. Appointments were arranged with callers, giving preference to those who could promise large groups for the interview, to older respondents, and to callers who lived outside the university area.

The groups ranged in size from two to nine participants. The interviews took place at one informant's home and in the company of friends and family members she had chosen for the purpose of the interview. While some audience studies hire interviewers who are not involved later in the analysis of the transcripts and tapes, we remained within the boundaries of the ethnographic method in that all of the interviews were carried out by the four primary researchers on the project.

The informants impressed us as remarkably open and secure in the uncontested and undisparaged status of their knowledge about soap operas. The location of the interviews – the home of the informant who initially answered our advertisement in the newspaper – added to the sense of comfort. This also allowed us to gather more information about the informants by observing the domestic surroundings, which were carefully noted immediately after the interview. The ethnographic concern with speech was facilitated by the cultural difference between informants and interviewers (since at least one of the two interviewers was German). The definition of slang expressions, the identity of characters and actors, the description of the shows, and reviews of past plot events could be elicited from a believable (and often factual) non-initiate position that created less defensiveness from the informants, who were in a position, as members of the culture and authorities on US television, to speak to the 'foreigners' with competence and expertise.

In the first minutes of each interview we explained that US prime-time shows such as *Dallas* or *Dynasty*, but no daytime soap operas, are shown on German television, and that the goal for the German members of the team was to learn about soap operas while visiting the United States. The informants usually were not at all surprised to hear about the success of *Dallas* or *Dynasty* in West Germany, but frequently expressed some pity for German viewers deprived of daytime soap operas.[8] Most of our informants assumed from our ad. that we were interested in talking about daytime programs, and hesitated to discuss prime-time serials until they were assured of our interest.

Questions of methodology

The author of the leading textbook on ethnographic methods defines ethnography as "the work of describing a culture."[9] Ethnographers working within anthropology emphasize "the native point of view" or the "ideational orientation," that is "the importance of understanding any given group's lifeways by discovering the learned systems of meaning by which it is structured."[10]

Television audience studies, even when they use ethnographic or qualitative methods, have not satisfied the requirements of ethnography proper, and our own study is no exception. While ethnographies are based on long-term and in-depth field work, most television audience studies have involved only brief periods of contact, in some cases less than one hour, with the informants. Also, while ethnographic methods have traditionally been used to study culture as a whole, television researchers study only one aspect of a culture when using this method and attempt to relate it to social identity.[11] Ethnographic audience studies share, however, ethnography's basic interest in an empirical investigation of cultural practices as lived experiences.

Recently, hermeneutic and discursive approaches to the study of culture have led to a fundamental critique of the epistemological, theoretical, and political assumptions implied in the concept of ethnography as "the work of describing a culture." As the title of James Clifford's seminal article indicates, "ethnographic authority" has increasingly come under scrutiny.[12] Of particular importance in our context is the critical challenge to traditional ethnography's implicit insistence on scholarly experience as an unproblematic source and ultimate guarantee of knowledge about a specific culture or cultural process. Today, there is an increasing tendency within ethnography to reject "colonial representations," i.e. "discourses that portray the cultural reality of other peoples without placing their own reality into jeopardy."[13] Such a position does not only apply to ethnographic accounts of "other" cultures, but is also significant on an intracultural level. Audience studies are carried out by academics with specific social and cultural backgrounds, who "go out in the field" to learn about the uses and understandings of groups of viewers with social and (sub)cultural backgrounds usually different from their own. This means that the differences and similarities between participants and scholars in terms of class, gender, race, culture or subculture, educational background, age, etc. have to be reflected. These aspects will inevitably be at work in the exchange between interviewer and interviewee, and, as we shall try to show, they will shape the understandings and meanings produced in this situation.[14]

The following sections of our chapter present preliminary reports on our analyses of the interviews.[15] In the first section, "Soap operas and everyday life," Eva-Maria Warth describes the way soap operas serve to organize time in the context of everyday life, especially housework. In the second section, "Text and genre," Hans Borchers discusses the various ways in which viewers define and describe the soap opera as text and as genre. Ellen Seiter and Gabriele Kreutzner, in "Resisting the place of the ideal mother," compare women's readings of the soap opera with the feminine subject position which critics see "inscribed" in the soap opera text.

Soap operas and everyday life
(Eva-Maria Warth)

It was above all the work performed at the Centre for Contemporary Cultural Studies at Birmingham and by Hermann Bausinger at the Department for Empirical Cultural Studies at the University of Tübingen which drew attention to the necessity of analysing media experience in its social context. According to this approach, the construction of the meaning of television and its programs is a social process that occurs within the everyday interactions of the home and the workplace. The question of how the media take part in structuring and organizing everyday life is inextricably related to the question of what meaning viewers give to a certain media product, in our case, the soap opera. What is important here, however, is the relationship between the levels of the general and the concrete: while soap operas certainly do belong to everyday life for those who watch them, individual routines differ remarkably according to class, gender, and age.

This section concentrates on the ways in which soap operas intersect with the everyday lives of women working in the home. While our study turned out to be rich in material on the interrelationship between the social condition of house-wives and the soap opera discourse, this section focuses mainly on how our informants describe the ways in which media schedules influence and intersect with the temporal organization of their work. We will begin with a brief historical outline of the mass media's implications for the organization of time in the domestic sphere. The media's function in the context of the rationalization of housework will then serve as a backdrop for our informants' accounts of how their viewing is fitted in between the demands of housework and their need for leisure.

In his influential study "Time, Work-Discipline, and Industrial Capitalism," E. P. Thompson proposes that temporal organization must be analysed historically in terms of its relation to the production process.[16] His study shows that the revolution in the experience of time in the nineteenth century was not limited to the production process proper, but rather influenced all aspects of life. Training in time discipline was reinforced by rationalization efforts in the industry at the beginning of this century, which also produced changes in the time organization of the domestic sphere. The subjugation of the sphere of reproduction to time patterns similar to those of the production sphere resulted in a rigidity typical of the workplace.

These changes were of special importance for women, for whom the home primarily represents a place of work rather than a sphere of leisure, as it usually is for men. Despite the interdependency of the spheres of production and reproduction, housework is still surrounded by a discourse of naturalness, which renders it universal and timeless. In this context, housework is theorized as determined by natural time cycles, as a sphere of autonomy which resists industrial time economy.

It is the achievement of Gisela Bock and Barbara Duden to have countered such ideologies of naturalness by theorizing housework in economic and historical terms.[17] They show how Taylorism, which initiated the rationalization process in the US in the 1920s, grew to encompass the sphere of reproduction as well. This extension of rationalization to the home was seen as a prerequisite for workplace efficiency. According to the new principles of scientific management, housework appeared irrational and unstructured. The separation of planning and execution of daily work was seen as the most important requirement in the process of restructuring. Housework was no longer theorized as relying on the natural skills of women, but was conceived of as a "science" which needed to be studied. If on the one hand this implied an upgrading of housework, it simultaneously surrendered housework to a male discourse, which from then on was assigned final authority in questions of child rearing and household management. Radio, and especially daytime soap operas, which were designed for a specifically female audience in the 1930s, played a vital part in this process. Informative programs on household management as well as other women's programs such as the soap opera dealt, respectively, with practical and emotional problems encountered by women working in the home. In addition, the regularity of the broadcast supported the efforts toward efficiency and rationalization which were introduced via daily schedules, e.g. distinct time structures which were modelled in accordance with the production process. The schedules of radio and television were not arbitrary, but were designed in accordance with certain structures created by housework itself. The schedules thereby became synchronized and tied into a well-defined and "universal" schedule. Lesley Johnson describes this process:

> In the promotion of radio as the constant companion to the housewife, programmers had adapted their timetables to the imagined patterns of a woman's life. Through this process radio stations set out to regulate the work and rhythms of daily life of all women to this pattern. So similarly did radio strive to control the domestic lives of all members of the community in the attempt to time-table their listening according to strict, reliable schedules.[18]

Although the hour or two of soap opera watching represents a fixed point in the daily schedule for most of our informants, there were significant differences in the way women reconciled this fixed pattern to their obligations and needs.

Soap opera viewing raises the problem of female pleasure and its place in women's lives. Housewives especially are not usually granted a right to relaxation, since housework is constructed as a potentially endless task. Nancy Chodorow has drawn attention to the "fundamental asymmetry in daily reproduction. Men are socially and psychologically reproduced by women, but women are reproduced (or not) largely by themselves."[19] The problem of women's reproduction is aggravated by the fact, noted by Ann Gray, that "the domestic sphere is increasingly becoming defined as their only leisure space."[20] The lack of a clear spatial demarcation between work and leisure therefore makes it even more complicated for women to assign a comfortable space for themselves and to reconcile their own needs with the needs of others.

For women in the home, leisure activities such as watching television must be viewed as complementary to work. The practices of soap opera viewing and their evaluation may be seen as women's attempts to resolve contradictions inherent in domestic work. In this context, television reveals the constraints of housework as unpaid labor (which accounts for the absence of regulated leisure time).

In our study we observed significant differences in our informants' patterns of soap opera engagement and their evaluation of viewing as a habit. These differences seem to be closely connected to the way in which the organization of their work allows for or excludes the possibility of leisure time. These organizational patterns correspond closely to Ann Oakley's findings in her seminal study, *The Sociology of Housework*.[21] Oakley differentiates between women who perform their household duties according to set standards and routines and those who do not. The work patterns of the first group show the effects of the industrialization of "domestic" time in the attempt to impose a sense of rationality, efficiency, and security on a potentially endless and typically frustrating activity. Those of our informants who fit this first category used soap operas as a fixed point in time around which daily tasks are organized: "I schedule all my activities in the morning so that I'm home in the afternoon to watch my shows." Household duties are planned and timed according to the television schedule: "I go out and fix casseroles for supper and throw them in the oven between two and three o'clock, you know, so I don't miss them [the soaps]."

In the context of this kind of household management, which is subjected to norms of efficiency and rational organization, soap operas may be more easily regarded as a reward, as a well-earned moment of leisure which is enjoyed without guilt:

SS   What I try to do is get everything I want to do done before that time. Then I don't feel guilty if I sit down and watch them. . . . I like to get up in the morning and get done what I figure I should do and then that's my relaxing time. It's just to sit down for a few hours.

One woman in her fifties very self-confidently described the way she defends her soap opera pleasure against social obligations and the needs of others:

MD   People know not to call me between 12.30 and 3.00 unless it's a dire emergency. If it's really something, they can call me at 1.30. Cause *Capitol* is on and I don't really watch it. . . . All of my friends know, do not call at that time. My husband . . . if he comes in he's very quiet and just goes right on out.

The pleasure of undistracted and concentrated viewing, which Charlotte Brunsdon has described as a mode of viewing associated with power (and thus with male viewing patterns) is made possible for these women by adapting their work to principles associated with the sphere of production and thus paid for by a submission to the norms of male discourse.

While most of our informants would consider undivided viewing the ideal mode of soap opera reception, the women who belong to the second group – those who do not adhere to a strict routine – experience this pleasure only as a rare luxury. One of these informants could afford a soap opera "treat" only during a time which for many women is associated with guilt-free indulgence: "I used to sit, especially when I was pregnant, to sit three hours and watch TV. . . . I can't do that any more." The women who do not tightly structure their housework, either because domestic circumstances do not allow it (e.g. the presence of small children in the household) or because it is not their style, must constantly struggle to reconcile their need for leisure with conflicting obligations: "I turn it on when I can, if I'm in the kitchen, I turn the TV on . . . I'm usually cooking dinner or making the kids' lunch or something."

If soap operas cannot be aligned with special household chores demanding little concentration, the soap opera text becomes reduced to what can be heard while working in different parts of the house: "I *listen* to them, honest to God, I never sit! The voices . . . I keep it punched [keep the volume up]." Viewing in this case becomes highly selective and is restricted to moments of high dramatic impact, as the following quote from another viewer suggests:

RG   I'll clean, but I'll have the TV on so I can hear it . . . if you can hear
      what's going on . . . like, you know, if there is a good fight or
      something going on, I always run in here and turn off the water and
      then sit in here and watch what's going on.

The conflict between household demands and the pleasures of soap opera viewing is one aspect which may account for the ambivalent attitude some of these women have toward their habit of viewing. The underlying sense of guilt ("I realized that I'm not getting anything done") which accompanies viewing for women in the second group may have contributed to the different kinds of relationships they established with us as interviewers compared to the first group. Those women who presented themselves as untroubled by conflicts over housework tended to remain rather formal and distant in the interview situation and tended to address us mainly in terms of our roles as academics. In contrast to this attitude, the informants belonging to the second group often quickly transformed the interview into the scenario of an intimate confession. We were frequently treated as confidantes, with the expectation that we would be sympathetic to the pleasures of soap opera viewing and understanding of the troublesome consequences these pleasures were reported to have in terms of neglected household work.

These differences in viewing behavior suggest that the conditions under which soap operas are watched differ even for women in similar situations, i.e. those working in the home, and they have considerable influence over selectivity, attention, and involvement with soap opera programs.

Text and genre
(Hans Borchers)

The decision to do an audience study pertaining to an entire genre of television programming distinguishes our approach from other soap opera audience studies which focus on a specific show or a single episode. Examples of this type of research are the studies of Ien Ang and of Elihu Katz and Tamar Liebes. Ang's *Watching "Dallas"* was inspired by the reception of the prime-time soap opera in Holland. Apart from her concentration on one show, Ang's approach differs methodologically from ours. Ang did not actually see and interview her inform-ants, instead she used letters from viewers, written in response to an ad. in a women's magazine. The audience research done by Katz and Liebes focuses on a single episode.[22] Their interview sessions were centered on the showing of this episode which the authors then encouraged their informants to discuss. The project's concern with specific decoding processes of different cultural groups necessitated the restriction to one episode in order to allow for comparison. Using only a "slice of the text" as the basis of their investigation does not, however, provide insights into the specific nature of the reception of a potentially endless serial program.

In contrast to the work of Katz and Liebes, our research emphasizes meaning negotiations and specific forms of interaction generated by soap operas as a genre *per se*; a restriction of the textual base would have been a serious limitation. Therefore we did not rely on reactions to one episode, but rather identified the text with the experience of soap operas as our viewers described it on the basis of their individual exposure to the genre (length of viewing period, regularity, choice of programs, etc.). This approach allowed for the determination of the text from the perspective of the viewer, who tends to discuss soap opera narratives in terms of plotlines, rather than in terms of individual episodes. The narrative material resulting from the interviews therefore provides insights into the way selections are made during the interaction with the genre in its entirety. While our approach is less often revelatory of the meanings attributed to smaller segments of text, it generates a great deal of information on how viewers perceive the soap opera generically.

It is in terms of such a comprehensive understanding of the soap opera text that our interview material bears on recent theoretical studies. One of the most significant points such studies have made is the identification of the soap opera text as a fictional narrative governed by certain aesthetic and generic rules. Robert C. Allen's book *Speaking of Soap Operas* is exemplary of this approach in that it develops a strong argument against the notion that soap operas are representations of real life. Allen emphasizes the form's textuality, its identity as a fictional and narrative construct, and hence its inherent similarity to literary and film genres. One major consequence of addressing the soap opera as an aesthetic construct is to take its full dimensions into account, to acknowledge it as a "huge meta-text," a saga which, in some cases, has taken shape over the course of several decades.[23]

No television critic can possibly claim to be in control of this kind of text – as opposed to the literary or film critic whose texts tend to be much more manageable. The soap opera viewer's position in relation to the text is similar to the critic's but not identical with it. Although the textual knowledge and genre competence of the habitual viewer are, generally speaking, of a higher order than those of the television scholar, her or his reading will remain at best an approximation of the total text. The point is that the nature of soap operas as "huge meta-texts" necessitates, be it in smaller or in larger measure, selectivity.

If the awareness of one's necessarily fragmentary actualization of the text is a groundrule for watching soap operas, the question arises: how do people cope with the soap opera text's gigantic dimensions and characteristic elusiveness? Our informants were aware of the impossibility for a single person to grasp fully the text of a soap opera. They freely admitted that, for one reason or another, their readings were incomplete; they even took this incompleteness for granted. A woman who no longer owns a television set told us: "Now, see, I don't even have a TV. I haven't watched for two months, three months, and I still know what's going on." Such a claim shows that the concept of text entertained by viewers differs to a remarkable degree from what the standards of a traditionally print-oriented culture tend to define as "the text." Because of the vicissitudes of their personal circumstances, working careers, and everyday lives, even the most loyal fans are perfectly aware that at best they only have a very sketchy notion of the text in its totality.

What we found in our interviews over and over again was that soap opera texts are the products not of individual and isolated readings but of collective constructions – collaborative readings, as it were, of small social groups such as families, friends, and neighbors, or people sharing an apartment. Most viewers report that they have made it a habit to rely on other people in order to compensate for gaps in their comprehension. One woman admitted she usually falls asleep during her soap opera hour. She can afford to because her daughter, who watches the show with her, will be there to tell her about the episode when she wakes up at the end of the hour: "I feel like all I've got to do if I want to know something is ask Shauna and she'll fill me in." Another woman reported that she called a friend in Los Angeles to tell her about the love-affair between Victor and Nicki in *The Young and the Restless*. Sometimes women watch the show together over the phone: "I'll call Christie, the other girl who watches it [*All My Children*] and we'll sit on the phone and watch it together and talk about everything as it's happening."

Since viewing a soap opera is an activity which often extends over many years, relying on another, more experienced viewer becomes standard practice for the neophyte. Those informants who talked about their earliest encounters with soap operas very often conceived of this process in terms of an initiation they underwent under the supervision of a more knowledgeable viewer, usually their mothers. Here is a typical version of this initiation story:

LMo My mother is the one that got me hooked on soap operas. It was a long time ago. She used to watch them as a kid, when she was in college. And so a long time ago, when I was at home, helping to take care of my younger brother, and she'd be home sometime during the day, working, and she'd turn on the soap operas and so I'd ask her who these people were. And she can give me a whole run-down history twenty years ago.

If calling upon the familial and social networks for support in the formidable task of keeping track and making sense of their shows is one way of coping with the text, the strategy of a deliberately selective reading is another. Since our lack of familiarity with some of the shows quickly became obvious to our informants, they often volunteered to give plot summaries. What these summaries reveal is the soap opera viewer's ability to discriminate between subjectively attractive and unattractive storylines, and to concentrate on those segments of the text which they find personally most satisfying. A 34-year-old woman was very outspoken in describing her technique of separating, as she put it, the fillers from the meat:

LMa They introduce like maybe three plotlines, and then, usually there is one that thrills, you know, you're dying to find out what's going on, and the other two are fillers, and I'll skip through the conversation ones. I do that a lot on *Santa Barbara*. Like, "OK, come on, let's just . . .," you know. I'll skip to the meat, you know.

Many of our informants mentioned this habit of focusing on a particular storyline instead of attempting to keep abreast of the whole complicated plot structure of a soap opera. Some reported using video recorders for the express purpose of cutting out segments they classified as unexciting or meaningless. A 24-year-old college student told us that he regularly watched four soap operas and that in order to keep track of all the stories, he would borrow a tape from his next-door neighbor whenever he couldn't watch his shows in the afternoon:

MM So I can just go over at night if I want to time it. You can watch a whole show in a half an hour, easy. Oh yeah! Zap through all the commercials, zap through all the meaningless scenes where nothing happens or no dialogue.

Assembling a condensed version of the text requires, of course, a thorough and sophisticated knowledge of the genre. We found that our viewers not only possessed expert textual knowledge, they were also very much aware of the poetic and generic rules that govern soap opera programs. Often informants explained to us the basic elements of the genre as well as the precise manner in which these elements are introduced and orchestrated, as in the following account:

234

RG   They'll have one group of people that's really suspenseful . . . like a murder that's going on and they're investigating it . . . or there's some juicy affair. . . . And they're always introducing people that have got a deep secret. And you want to find out what the hell the secret is. . . .They always introduce new characters, you know, like somebody new comes to town and somebody else is all upset about it and they go "but why?" and then all of a sudden that son comes along that's illegitimate, that so and so doesn't know about, and that kind of stuff.

Generally speaking, we found that viewers have a strong sense of the constructedness of soap operas, of the essential artificiality of their favorite program. Not only did viewers frequently talk about and criticize the people who make soap operas (especially writers), they also commented on the conventions that rule and structure the shows. Their genre competence comes in many disguises. It was apparent in the complaint that writers cancel and replace characters too facilely, in the sober assessment of the cycles soap opera plots go through in the course of a year relative to the ratings sweeps weeks, as well as in the often-reported practice of predicting future plot developments – what Charlotte Brunsdon has called, "the pleasure of hermeneutic speculation."[24]

Another aspect of their generic competence was the informed and mostly negative opinion the majority of our interviewees expressed about prime-time soap operas. Since we encouraged them to talk about prime-time television, they offered a whole assortment of critiques of *Dallas*, *Dynasty*, *Knots Landing*, and other prime-time shows. With the exception of a few viewers who voiced their impatience with a certain dragging on of storylines on daytime soaps, the large majority expressed their preference for the daytime variety of the genre. Prime-time soap operas were judged as too glittery and expensive-looking; our informants complained that they don't deal with "the normalcy of people." Others resented the rich veneer of prime-time soaps, their "mega-buck characters," especially the actress Joan Collins ("She makes more in one day than I've made in my whole life"). For many, prime-time soap operas belong to a different category altogether. One viewer said he likes "the soaps better than *Dallas* and *Falcon Crest*"; another told us that "the soaps are more laid back, they're not made for nights," and a third viewer remarked that although she watches daytime and prime-time soaps, the prime-time variety is "not as hooky." Most of our viewers expressed their loyalty to the daytime soaps and tended to be very conscious of the differences between the original thing and the spin-off.

Alongside their generic expertise, their discrimination and critical distance, our informants also evinced the seemingly contradictory impulse to permit the fiction to spill over into their real lives and social worlds. Most of them told us they were bound to the characters on their show by feelings of intimacy. They sometimes referred to them as friends with whom they talked, laughed, cried, and suffered. Here is a young woman who resented her boyfriend's lack of understanding when she cries over the characters on her show:

DL   Yeah, and the old man comes home and he'll say: "God, why do you get so involved with it. It's just TV!" [Changes her voice] "Yeah, but you don't know them like I do, you know, they're like my friends." He don't understand.

Another woman, who lives with her ageing mother, took the trouble of typing out an account of the two "most memorable, moving scenes I've seen on soap operas," in response to our post-interview questionnaire. Her account amounts to a highly personal reaction to the deaths of two characters on *Days of Our Lives* and *Another World*.

The pleasure our viewers derive from their appreciation of the text's fictionality does not prevent them from getting personally involved in the text – and, by extension, from experiencing soap operas as texts which are relevant to social reality. Our interview with a group of four viewers provided an example of the coexistence of both attitudes toward the soap opera text. While one group member argued that a soap opera is "just a TV show," another claimed that "they do set moral standards" and that "there are people that really do believe those things." He continued to substantiate his point by establishing an analogy between Phoebe's disapproval of Tad and Hilary's affair on *All My Children* and his own great aunt's severe standards in sexual matters – standards from which he himself and his girlfriend had suffered.

It seems, then, that the soap opera text, not least because of the strong need it creates for collaborative readings, has considerable potential for reaching out into the real world of the viewers. It enables them to evaluate their own experiences as well as the norms and values they live by in terms of the relationship patterns and social blueprints the show presents. It is important to remember, however, that this is only one side of the text's appeal. Our women informants appreciated the notorious Erica Kane of *All My Children* because of the remarkable success she enjoys in her personal life and her career, and it became clear that they tend to see her as a model applicable to their own private situations and to the social roles they were themselves involved in. At the same time, they took great pleasure in the very unreality and fictional constructedness of the storylines Erica was often a part of. When a particularly outlandish turn in the plot required Erica to walk through the jungle for three days, they commented: "It's unreal that she would look like that after three days of not washing her hair and. . . . But they had her that way so . . . it was kind of funny! That's part of it, that it's fun to watch that!"

Our viewers' appreciation of both aspects of the Erica Kane character points to the divergent ways in which the soap opera text may elicit gratification. It also testifies to the ability of experienced viewers to commute with considerable ease between a referential and a purely fictional reading – even if these readings appear to be mutually exclusive. The evidence our interview material contains leads us to conclude that, while the text has the potential of addressing its readers on a level of social engagement, its principal appeal is undoubtedly to their genre competence, sense of critical distance, and enjoyment of the sheer playfulness of fiction.

Resisting the place of the "ideal mother"
(Ellen Seiter and Gabriele Kreutzner)

In her influential analysis of the daytime soap opera, Tania Modleski describes the woman's position as a reader inscribed in the text in these terms:

> The subject/spectator of soap operas, it could be said, is constituted as a sort of ideal mother, a person who possesses greater wisdom than all her children, whose sympathy is large enough to encompass the conflicting claims of her family (she identifies with them all), and who has no demands or claims of her own (she identifies with no one character exclusively).[25]

The soap opera villainess may make it difficult for viewers to assume this female position comfortably, for they may find that she acts out their own, largely hidden, desires for power although at the same time they feel they must condemn and despise her. The model Modleski uses is Freudian: "The extreme delight viewers apparently take in despising the villainess testifies to the enormous amount of energy involved in the spectator's repression and to her (albeit unconscious) resentment at being constituted as an egoless receptacle for the suffering of others."[26]

Modleski offers no possibility for *conscious* resistance to the soap opera text: the spectator position is conceived of in terms of a perfectly "successful" gender socialization entirely in keeping with a middle-class (and white) feminine ideal. The desire to watch soap operas comes from a kind of repetition compulsion brought about by the conflict between the ideal mother position of feminine passivity and the villainess's expression of real but hidden fantasies of power. Robert C. Allen has suggested that this work poses a problem in that "although Modleski seems to present the mother/reader as a textually inscribed position to be taken up by whoever the actual reader happens to be, she comes close at times to conflating the two."[27]

In our description of those Oregon interviews conducted within all-female groups, we would like to take Modleski's concept of the textual position offered by the soap operas as a starting point. While this position was partially taken up by some of our middle-class, college-educated informants, it was consciously resisted and vehemently rejected by most of the women we interviewed, especially by working-class women. The relationship between viewer and character more typically involved hostility – in the case of some of the presumably sympathetic characters – as well as fond admiration – for the supposedly despised villainesses.

Strongly held preferences for individual characters and dislikes for others prevented the ideal mother position as Modleski describes it from ever being fully taken up. Sympathy for characters was mentioned only rarely, while outrage, anger, criticism, or a refusal to accept a character's problems was frequently expressed. The women we interviewed showed a conscious, full-fledged refusal of the narrative's demand for sympathy and understanding. This refusal was fueled by the recognition of a gaping class difference between the comfortable professional lives of the television characters and the difficult financial situations in which many of our informants often find themselves. The fact that women characters on soap operas usually bear no visible responsibility for childcare and housework increased this resentment. It is not the villainess whom these working-class informants despise – it is the woman who suffers despite her middle-class privileges, a character type they call the "whiner," or the "wimpy woman."

The "whiner" came up repeatedly in our interviews with a group of six women, the mother MP, her three daughters, and their female room-mates, all of whom lived next door to each other in Springfield, worked at minimum-wage jobs (newspaper delivery, bartending) and helped operate M's home telephone answering service. What is most irritating and infuriating about the "whiner" is her passivity, her dependence on men, her failure to take care of herself. While reconstructing the storyline around the character of Rick Webber, one of *General Hospital*'s doctors, his wife, television journalist Jeannie Webber, was discussed by the group:

DI   And now he married Jeannie and all she does is cry and whimper, that's all she does.

MT   I don't like her either!

DI   She don't do nothing! I mean she cries about her son, she cries about her job, she cries about her baby, she cries about everything.

MT   She cries when she makes love, I think.

DI   She cries all the time! She's a wimpy woman!

Both   They can take her off! She's a wimpy woman!

Among a group of middle-class women in their fifties who worked at home, we found another hostile rejection of a sympathetic character who herself acts like an ideal mother:

MD   Like Karen on *Knots Landing*, the neighbor that you'd like to choke. I mean she's a little busybody. She's always going around and telling everyone what to do and what they should do. And sympathizing.

This remark is especially interesting because Karen comes under attack specifically for her feminine qualities, such as sympathizing with others.

In a group consisting of a woman in her thirties, JS, and her mother-in-law, two foster-daughters, a cousin, and a friend and neighbor, the women discussed their feelings for the villainesses on their favorite shows. All of the women commented on their preference of strong villainesses; the younger respondents expressed their pleasure in and admiration for the powerful female characters who were also discussed in terms of transgressing the boundaries of a traditional pattern of resistance for women within patriarchy. The pattern here of finishing each other's sentences was typical of many of our interviews with all-female groups:

LD   Yeah, they can be very vicious [Laughs] – the females can be very vicious . . .

JS   Seems like females have more of an impact than the males.

SW   . . . and they have such a . . .

TM   . . . conniving . . .

SW   . . . brain! Yeah! [Laughter]

LD   They're sneaky!!! Yeah!

SW   They use their brain more . . . [Laughter] instead of their body! They manipulate, you know!

Tania Modleski's work suggests that the only outlet for female aggression and anger on the soap opera is the character of the villainess. Drawing on psychoanalytic theory, Modleski argues that female aggression is repressed and is symbolically taken up, played out, and neutralized in the character of the villainess. Our respondents, however, expressed love and admiration for these powerful female transgressors. For them, one of the pleasures of soap opera viewing consists in targeting certain characters as objects of their own verbal aggressions. KK and JH, two college-educated women sharing a house and making their living from organizing adult education courses, put it this way:

JH   A lot of times we just get caught up in it, and [we go] "Oh you bitch" or something . . .

KK   Yeah, it's a good cathartic kind of thing, you know, because, we can just kind . . . one creep Waide comes on, you know, and we go: "Yeah, I hate you, this is stupid," you know, so we get out a lot of stuff . . .

These women explained their own viewing in terms of their interest in eastern philosophy and psychotherapeutic work. The pleasure in working out aggressions, however, seemed to be extremely important for many of our viewers. In another interview, KH, a 35-year-old woman employed doing clerical work for a cottage-industry record business expressed her enjoyment in taking unrestricted aggression toward a male character:

KH   We should have Jodie here, she's fourteen years old, and she and I just get so excited talking about *One Life to Live* . . .

DH   Yeah, Jodie yells at them, I don't. [Turns to KH] You sit there and yell at them!

KH   Oh, I do! . . . Especially when that ugly guy was on *General Hospital*, and he played two parts . . .

DH   Oh, Grant!

KH   Grant and somebody . . . who was his own twin . . .

DH   She hated Grant!

KH   And I hated him! I hated him, the original one, and then when they came up with a twin, and I had to see him again, in another part, I just screamed at him: "Where's your forehead," you know, I just hated him!

DH   . . . and he was . . . he was in Eugene, and a friend of hers saw him and she wanted to run out and say: "Please, can I have your autograph, my friend hates you!" I love that! Isn't that great?

Aggression was not limited to the actors, but extended to the scriptwriters as well, for slowing down the storylines and underestimating the viewer's intelligence, as MT expressed it: "just don't drag them out and don't treat us like we're so stupid and naïve, you know! Like I said: I don't like to figure out stuff myself: keep me hanging, too."

Most women have an ambivalent relationship to the narratives: enjoying the suspense but conscious of being manipulated by the story, made to wait for plot developments. And while some women enjoyed successfully predicting plot developments, for MT (who works for minimum wage), scriptwriters have a job to do, one they get paid a lot of money for, and they should be better at it than she is, i.e. able to provide her with surprises. Like MT, a number of women felt they could write soap operas themselves, if given a chance.

In our interviews, female anger was far less repressed than the Freudian model of the feminine subject or Modleski's textual position allows for. In their interaction with the fictional world of the soap opera, women openly and enthusiastically admitted their delight in following soap operas as stories of female transgressions which destroy the ideological nucleus of the text – the sacredness of the family. In a follow-up interview with JS and SW, both expressed their partisanship for female transgressions of the holy law of marriage in cases where the (fictitious) situation seemed to become unbearable for the female character. Both said their husbands disapproved of this attitude:

SW   But there's lots of times where you want the person to dump the husband and go on with this . . .

JS   Oh, Bruce [her husband] gets so angry with me when I'm watching the show and they're married and I'm all for the affair. [Laughter] It's like, it's like [Voice changes to imitate Bruce]: "I don't like this, I don't know about you" [Laughter] . . . [and I say] "Dump him !!!"

Both women explained to us that they strongly favored the breakup of soap opera marriages in cases where the husband neglected the wife, and drew explicit connections to their own situations:

SW   He gets mad at me, but . . . it does justify the reason for her [if the husband neglects the wife], I'm all for it . . . think where you're saying: pay more attention!

JS   Right! See, this happens to you if you don't pay attention to me!

These quotations indicate a vast gap between the model of the passive feminine subject inscribed in the text and our women viewers who fail to assume the position of the all-understanding (and therefore powerless) spectators of textual construction. The "successful" production of the (abstract and "ideal") feminine subject is restricted and altered by the contradictions of women's own experiences. Class, among other factors, plays a major role in how our respondents make sense of the text. The experience of working-class women clearly conflicts in substantial ways with the soap opera's representation of a woman's problems, problems some women identified as upper or middle-class. This makes the limitless sympathy that Modleski's textual position demands impossible for them. The class discrepancy between textual representation and their personal experience constituted the primary criticism of the programs. Let's return to our conversation with MP and her daughters:

MP   The one thing I guess I don't really care about in the soaps is that . . . they're playing all the women as being career-oriented and, ah, making lots of money, they are not . . . they are not bringing other people . . . you know, not every woman is making a good income.

DI   Asa's wife doesn't. Asa's wife, she's not . . .

MP   Yeah, but she's not working, she's a staying-home wife. They need to bring in a few single mothers that are trying to . . .

DI   Make and take on five an hour.

MP   Yeah, right, trying to juggle the books and find a baby sitter . . .

MT   . . . deliver newspapers at one o'clock in the morning, working there until . . .

MP   They don't need too many of them, 'cause there is a lot of women that, you know, don't want that, they need escape to what it would be like when they're rich, but once in a while they should bring that in, 'cause . . . it shows: "Hey, this is what it's really like!"

DI   Say, wake up and . . .

MT   That's why you want them to escape, cause after three hours you turn them off and you might return to your three thirty-five job.

MP   Yeah, I know, but if that's all you see, then, it'll . . . you'll lose your interest.

One of the problems with the spectator position described by Modleski is that the "ideal mother" implies a specific social identity – that of a middle-class woman, most likely with a husband who earns a family wage. This textual position is not easily accessible to working-class women, who often formulate criticism of the soap opera on these grounds. But criticism is expressed only in terms of realism and escapism, as in the quote above, where a complaint about class norms (having only career women or staying-home wives as characters) is answered by a validation of their function as escapism on these very same grounds (characters whose lives are different from those of the viewers). Any alternative version of the text is impossible for these women to imagine because it is so far beyond the horizon of reasonable expectation.

Postscript: a gendered discourse

Recent audience studies conducted by David Morley and Ann Gray in Great Britain have found women to speak "defensively and self-depreciatingly about their choices and preferences" with regard to television programs.[28] Charlotte Brunsdon argues that these studies confirm the "extremely contradictory position that female viewers seem to occupy in relation to their pleasures."[29] In comparison, our interviews show no such explicitly apologetic overtones. Moreover, they are considerably less informed by what Ien Ang calls "the ideology of mass culture."[30] This non-defensive position about television viewing was held most strongly in interviews conducted in groups where all the participants (informants and interviewers) were women – fifteen of the twenty-six interviews. In part, this suggests significant differences between the United States and Europe in what we might call the social construction of femininity.[31] But it also indicates the importance of situating the decoding of television programs within the context of concrete social exchanges, among subjects whose histories determine the interaction and the kind of discourses which will be used.

To use Benveniste's definition of discourse, the meanings given to soap operas in our interviews depended on the "Is" and "Yous" engaged in a given communicative exchange.[32] Although recent audience studies try to address the discursive "Yous" as historical subjects (rather than as scientific objects), they tend to exclude (as is the academic norm) any systematic account of the researcher's own subjectivity.[33] But discourse analysis focuses on the practices of all participants (including the interviewers) as social and historical beings. This is especially important when dealing with interviews, which unlike "natural" conversations, are, from the beginning, the researcher's creation. Because of the way we initially identified ourselves in the newspaper advertisement ("writing a book"), the discourse of the interviews was to some extent predetermined by our roles and status as: 1) employers, 2) foreigners, 3) academics, and 4) women. The interviewers' initial identification as academics and employers means that a social hierarchy is already at work in the interactions. In order adequately to understand the meanings of soap operas produced in our interviews, we have to recognize the asymmetrical, power-laden nature of the discourse in which they are produced and, more specifically, the significance of the researchers' subjectivities therein.

In retrospect, our communicative strategy was to de-emphasize our role as academics and employers. The position of relatively ignorant but interested "non-initiates" into soap operas and of non-native speakers helped Kreutzner and Warth to counterbalance the initially asymmetrical discursive arrangement.[34] However, in analysing the interview tapes and transcripts, our status as women and our activation of specific patterns of gendered communication emerge as the most decisive factors for the developing interlocutions. These gendered patterns include both what we talked about – fashion, housework, heterosexual relationships, fantasy, sexism – and the way we talked. The interviews evidence what sociolinguists have found to be

> recurring patterns which distinguish talk among women from that in mixed-sex and all-male groups: mutuality of "interaction work" (active listening, building on the utterances of others), collaboration rather than competition, flexible leadership rather than the strong dominance patterns found in all-male groups.[35]

If our identification as academics, foreigners, and employers placed us in the category of "other," gender provided a position of "sameness" in relation to the informants.

In his reflections on ethnographic interviews, James Clifford points to the necessity of an intersubjective ground in any attempt to interact. According to Clifford, such a shared experiental world is "precisely what is missing or problematic for an ethnographer entering an 'alien culture.'"[36] But ethnographic audience studies significantly differ from classic ethnography's attempt to understand "other" cultures. Coming from western, late capitalist, and patriarchal societies, both interviewers and informants spontaneously relied on such a "common sphere," a shared experiential world according to which "sameness" in terms of gender provides specific possibilities to interact. That is, the inter-subjective relations between the discursive "Is" and "Yous" were predominantly constructed according to the historical subjects' gendered identities. In retrospect, our motives for subordinating other social positions to the gendered one can be explained by three factors: 1) the existence of what a German ethnographer has called the researcher's *Angst* created by the transition from the relatively secure and well-known academic (sub)culture to the "unknown" field situation;[37] 2) our own (varying) gender-specific ambivalences concerning our positions as academics;[38] and 3) the fact that such a communicative repertoire is an integral part of female subjectivity practiced since we learned to talk. Indeed, these communicative patterns seem to be so "natural" and "transparent," so much a part of ourselves, that they go unnoticed in everyday activities, and we were scarcely conscious of using them in the interviews.

Our informants, on the other hand, were provided with few other social positions which they could take up discursively. As Susanne Sackstetter points out, ethnographic interviews in which researchers and informants are men can rely on a broad repertoire of possible discursive relations in terms of shared social positions.[39] Except for a gendered one, women have few social positions at their disposal which can be taken up communicatively.

The discursive formation of women talking to women in a domestic setting suggests the construction of a distinctly female space. Such a discursive space corresponds to the one in which most of our female informants reportedly engage with the soap opera text – a private, domestic space which is often characterized by the absence of men. In this social context, the focus is on the women: they are the protagonists, whereas men play supportive, if not subordinate parts. The metaphor of performance illustrates a particular "fit" between women's understanding of their immediate social environment and of the soap opera texts (as both were expressed in the interviews). Here and there, female characters are of absolute priority. The male characters/subjects will add problems, pleasures, and "spice" (e.g. in terms of romance), but they are placed second – the emphasis is on the women who perform and perceive themselves as strong and active subjects. In critical retrospect, the context provided by feminist ethnographic work confirms that such understandings have to be contextualized: interpretations based on this kind of self-perception tend to be expressed only in discursive formations characterized by a collectively shared female identity and by the absence of men. It is significant that the ongoing discourse in the female group interviews was always at some point defined in terms of differing from an "other" one – usually identified as the male perspective on soap operas or in terms of the ideology of mass culture. Some women mentioned their male partner's deprecatory attitude toward the genre, yet such deprecation was not represented as leading to conflict.

This suggests that the opportunity to produce meanings and pleasures by engaging with a discriminated popular text is "paid for" by women's willingness to conceal these pleasures and meanings whenever the dominant discourse is spoken in a social situation. There, women tend to remain silent or describe their own meanings and pleasures from a position which discriminates against itself. If we perceive women's social contexts in terms of a set of interrelating speech practices, the relationship between the gendered and the dominant discourse(s) on soap operas is a monological, unreciprocal one. Within the framework of social relations under patriarchy, women create a gendered, oppositional space to produce their own meanings and pleasures. The closing off of these meanings and pleasures can be seen as a strategy to avoid confrontation and conflict.

By relating differing discourses on soap operas produced in varying social contexts to each other, we can begin to trace the "working" of social power in the cultural production of meaning. Therefore, our future work will address the production of meanings (and pleasures) by historical subjects in at least two interrelating frameworks: 1) one which is constituted by the historical subjects' social practices (in which other discourses on the text are prominent); and 2) one established by the textual determinacy executed by the television program or genre. Both interactions – between a historical subject and a television text and between a historical subject and her social environment – have to be understood as a site of social struggle fought out on the terrain of language and speech practices.

Notes

1 David Morley, *The "Nationwide" Audience: Structure and Decoding* (London: British Film Institute, 1980).
2 David Morley, "'The *Nationwide* Audience' – A Critical Postscript," *Screen Education* 39 (1981): 3-15.
3 Charlotte Brunsdon, *"Crossroads*: Notes on Soap Opera," *Screen* 22, no. 4 (1981): 32-7.
4 Morley, "A Critical Postscript," p. 5.
5 In this context see also Morley's *Family Television: Cultural Power and Domestic Leisure* (London: Comedia, 1986).
6 Janice Radway, *Reading the Romance: Women, Patriarchy, and Popular Literature* (Chapel Hill and London: University of North Carolina Press, 1984), p. 13.
7 Herta Herzog, "On Borrowed Experience. An Analysis of Listening to Daytime Sketches," *Studies in Philosophy and Social Science* 9, no. 1 (1941): 65-95.
8 While German viewers are familiar with US prime-time serials such as *Dallas*, *Dynasty*, and most recently *Flamingo Road*, *Knots Landing* and *Falcon Crest* which are broadcast by West Germany's public broadcast stations ARD and ZDF, it was only with the advent of commercial television that German viewers became acquainted with daytime soap operas like *Guiding Light* and *Santa Barbara* in 1987. US daytime serials had already been adopted by commercial stations in other European countries such as Italy and France, and the expected opening of West German television to these programs was one of the motivations for the Tübingen Soap Opera Project to investigate the genre.
9 James P. Spradley, *The Ethnographic Interview* (New York: Holt, Rinehart & Winston, 1979), p. 2.
10 John L. Caughey, "The Ethnography of Everyday Life: Theories and Methods for American Culture Studies," *American Quarterly* 34, no. 3 (1982): 226.
11 See David Morley, *The "Nationwide" Audience;* Elihu Katz and Tamar Liebes, "Once Upon a Time, in *Dallas*," *Intermedia* 12, no. 3 (1984): 28-32; and James Lull, "How Families Select TV Programs; A Mass-Observational Study," *Journal of Broadcasting* 26, no. 4 (1982): 801-11.
12 James Clifford, "On Ethnographic Authority," *Representations* 1, no. 2 (1983): 128.
13 James Clifford, "On Ethnographic Authority," p. 133.
14 See also James Clifford, "Introduction: Partial Truths," in James Clifford and George E. Marcus (eds) *Writing Culture. The Poetics and Politics of Ethnography* (Berkeley, Calif.: The University of California Press, 1986), pp. 1-26.
15 In-depth analyses will be presented in the forthcoming book : Hans Borchers, Gabriele Kreutzner, and Eva-Maria Warth, *Never-Ending Stories: American Soap Operas and the Cultural Production of Meaning. CROSSROADS: Studies in American Culture* (Trier: Wissenschaftlicher Verlag Trier).
16 E. P. Thompson, "Time, Work-Discipline and Industrial Capitalism," *Past and Present* 38 (1967): 56-97.
17 Gisela Bock and Barbara Duden, "Arbeit aus Liebe – Liebe aus Arbeit. Zur Entstehung der Hausarbeit im Kapitalismus," in their *Frauen und Wissenschaft. Beiträge zur Berliner Sommeruniversität der Frauen* (Berlin, 1977), pp. 118-99.
18 Lesley Johnson, "Radio and Everyday Life. The Early Years of Broadcasting in Australia, 1922-1945," *Media, Culture and Society* 3, no. 2 (1981): 167-78.
19 Nancy Chodorow, *The Reproduction of Mothering: Psychoanalysis and the Sociology of Gender* (Berkeley, Calif.: University of California Press, 1978), p. 36.

20   Ann Gray, "Behind Closed Doors: Video Recorders in the Home," in Helen Baehr and Gillian Dyer (eds) *Boxed In: Women and Television* (London: Pandora Press, 1986), p. 41.

21   Ann Oakley, *The Sociology of Housework* (London: Martin Robertson, 1974).

22   Elihu Katz and Tamar Liebes, "Once upon a Time in *Dallas,*" *Intermedia* 12, no. 3 (May 1984): 28–32.

23   Robert C. Allen, *Speaking of Soap Operas* (Chapel Hill and London: University of North Carolina Press, 1985).

24   Charlotte Brunsdon, "Writing about Soap Opera," in Len Masterman (ed.) *Television Mythologies: Stars, Shows, and Signs* (London: Comedia, 1986), p. 83.

25   Tania Modleski, *Loving With a Vengeance: Mass-Produced Fantasies for Women* (Hamden, Conn.: Archon Books, 1982), p. 92.

26   ibid., p. 94.

27   Allen, *Speaking of Soap Operas*, p. 94.

28   Charlotte Brunsdon's review of Morley and Gray's work in "Women Watching Television," *MedieKultur* 4 (1986): 105.

29   ibid., p. 109.

30   Ang, *Watching "Dallas," Soap Opera and the Melodramataic Imagination* (London and New York: Methuen, 1985), pp. 86–116.

31   The importance of this difference was called to our attention by Charlotte Brunsdon.

32   "Discourse, in Benveniste's classic discussion, is a mode of communication where the presence of the speaking subject and of the immediate situation of communication are intrinsic" (Clifford, "On Ethnographic Authority," p. 131).

33   See also Ien Ang's chapter in this volume, pp. 96–115.

34   Our roles as "students" of soap operas and, for Kreutzner and Warth, as non-native speakers operated on two levels: we could apply them as "strategic devices," e.g. to interrogate particular descriptions and concepts ("What is a 'hunk'?") and to motivate character descriptions or narration of plotlines. However, such a strategic use did not contradict our sincerity as communicative partners (which is essential to intersubjective exchange), since our familiarity with the soap texts was indeed a limited one.

35   Barrie Thorne, Cheris Kramarae, and Nancy Henley, "Language, Gender and Society: A Second Decade of Research," in Barrie Thorne, Cheris Kramarae, and Nancy Henley (eds) *Language, Gender and Society* (Rowley, Mass.: Newbury, 1983), p. 18.

36   Clifford, "On Ethnographic Authority," p. 128.

37   Rolf Lindner, "Die Angst des Forschers vor dem Feld," *Zeitschrift für Volkskunde* 77 (1981): 51–65.

38   In her theoretical reflections on ethnographic interviews on women's lives, Susanne Sackstetter points out that the psychological discomfort caused by the entrance into an "unknown field" must be experienced even more strongly by female scholars whose "space" within academia is much less established than that of men. Moreover, to "go out into the world" may produce conflicts with gendered social norms, both individually and socially. This is especially true in West Germany, where women's public positions are significantly less well established than in the United States. See Susanne Sackstetter, "'Wir sind doch alles Weiber.' Gespräche unter Frauen und weibliche Lebensbedingungen," in Utz Jeggle (ed.) *Feldforschung: Qualitative Methoden in der Kulturanalyse* (Tübingen: Tübinger Vereinigung für Volkskunde, 1984), pp. 159–76.

39   Sackstetter points to Utz Jeggle's account of an ethnographic interview which he calls "Honoratioren unter sich" ("The intimacy of people of rank"). Jeggle argues that in his interview the discursive relationship between ethnographer and informant was constructed via a shared social position as "men of rank" (the interviewer as a university professor and his male informant as a village celebrity); Utz Jeggle, "Geheimnisse der Feldforschung," in *Europäische Ethnologie: Theorie und Methodendiskussion aus ethnologischer und volkskundlicher Sicht* (Berlin: Veröffentlichung des Museums für Völkerkunde Berlin, Staatliche Museen Preussischer Kulturbesitz, 1982).

Select bibliography

Allen, Robert C., *Speaking of Soap Operas*, Chapel Hill and London: University of North Carolina Press, 1985.
—— (ed.) *Channels of Discourse*, Chapel Hill and London: University of North Carolina Press, 1987.
Allor, Martin, "Relocating the Site of the Audience: Reconstructive Theory and the Social Subject," *Critical Studies in Mass Communication* 5 (1988): 217-33.
Althusser, Louis, *Lenin and Philosophy and Other Essays*, trans. Ben Brewster, London: New Left Books, 1971.
—— *For Marx*, trans. Ben Brewster, Harmondsworth: Penguin, 1986.
Ang, Ien, "The Battle Between Television and Its Audiences: The Politics of Watching Television," in Phillip Drummond and Richard Paterson (eds) *Television in Transition*, London: British Film Institute, 1985.
—— *Watching "Dallas" : Soap Opera and the Melodramatic Imagination*, London and New York: Methuen, 1985.
—— "Feminist Desire and Female Pleasure," *Camera Obscura* 16 (1988): 179-90.
Baehr, Helen, and Dyer, Gillian (eds) *Boxed In: Women and Television*, New York and London: Pandora Press, 1987.
Bakhtin, Mikhail M., "The Problem of Speech Genres," in *Speech Genres and Other Late Essays*, trans. Vern McGee, Austin, Texas: University of Texas Press, 1986.
Barthes, Roland, *The Pleasure of the Text*, trans. Richard Miller, New York: Hill & Wang, 1975.
Basso, Keith H., and Selby, Henry A. (eds) *Meaning in Anthropology*, Albuquerque, NM: University of New Mexico Press, 1976.
Bauman, Ricard, and Sherzer, Joel (eds) *Explorations in the Ethnography of Speaking*, Cambridge: Cambridge University Press, 1974.
Bausinger, Hermann, "Media, Technology and Daily Life," *Media, Culture, and Society* 6 (1984): 343-51.
Bennett, Tony, "Text and Social Process: The Case of James Bond," *Screen Education* 41 (1982): 3-14.
Bennett, Tony, Boyd-Bowman, Susan, Mercer, Colin, and Woollacott, Janet (eds) *Popular Television and Film: A Reader*, London: British Film Institute/Open University Press, 1981.
Bernstein, Basil, *Class, Codes, and Control*, 3 vols, London: Routledge & Kegan Paul, 1973.
Bliese, Nancy Wood, "Media in the Rocking Chair: Media Uses and Functions Among the Elderly," in Gary Gumpert and Robert Cathcart (eds) *Inter/ Media: Inter-Personal Communication in a Media World*, New York: Oxford University Press, 1986.

Blumler, Jay G., Gurevitch, Michael, and Katz, Elihu, "Reaching Out: A Future for Gratifications Research," in Karl E. Rosengren, Lawrence A. Wenner, and Philip Palmgreen (eds) *Media Gratifications Research: Current Perspectives*, Beverly Hills: Sage, 1985.

Bobo, Jacqueline, *"The Color Purple: Black Women as Cultural Readers,"* in Deidre Pribram (ed.) *Female Spectators Looking at Film and Television*, London: Verso, 1988.

Bourdieu, Pierre, "The Aristocracy of Culture," *Media, Culture, and Society* 2, 3 (July 1980): 225-54.

—— *Distinction. A Social Critique of the Judgement of Taste*, trans. Richard Nice, Cambridge, Mass.: Harvard University Press, 1984, London: Routledge & Kegan Paul, 1986.

Brody, Gene H., and Stoneman, Zolinda, "The Influence of Television Viewing on Family Interactions," *Journal of Family Issues* 4, 2 (June 1983): 329-48.

Browne, Nick, "The Political Economy of the Television (Super)Text," *Quarterly Review of Film Studies* 9 (summer 1984): 174-82.

Bruck, Peter, "The Social Production of Texts: On the Relation Production/Product in the News Media," *Communication-Information* 4 (1982): 92-124.

Brunsdon, Charlotte, *"Crossroads*: Notes on Soap Opera," *Screen* 22 (1981): 32-7.

—— "Writing About Soap Opera," in Len Masterman (ed.) *Television Mythologies. Stars, Shows, and Signs*, Londo: Comedia, 1984.

—— "Women Watching Television," *MedieKultur* 4 (1986): 100-12.

Brunsdon, Charlotte, and Morley, David, *Everyday Television: "Nationwide"*, London: British Film Institute, 1978.

Butler, Jeremy, "Notes on the Soap Opera Apparatus: Televisual Style and *As The World Turns*," *Cinema Journal* 25 (3) (spring 1986): 53-70.

Bybee, Carl R., "Uses and Gratifications Research and the Study of Social Change," in David L. Paletz (ed.) *Political Communication Research: Approaches, Studies, Assessments*, Norwood, NJ: Ablex, 1987.

Carey, John, "A Primer on Interactive Television," *Journal of the University Film Association* 30 (1978): 35-40.

Cassata, Mary, and Skill, Thomas, *Life on Daytime Television: Tuning-In American Serial Drama*, Norwood, NJ: Ablex, 1983.

Caughey, John L., "The Ethnography of Everyday Life: Theories and Methods for American Culture Studies," *American Quarterly* 34, 3 (Bibliography 1982): 222-43.

Caughie, John, "Television Criticism: 'A Discourse in Search of an Object,'" *Screen* 25, 4-5 (July-October 1984): 109-20.

—— "Popular Culture: Notes and Revisions," in Colin MacCabe (ed.) *High Theory, Low Culture*, Manchester: Manchester University Press, 1986.

Centre for Contemporary Cultural Studies (ed.) *Culture, Media, Language. Working Papers in Cultural Studies, 1972-79*, London: Hutchinson, in association with the Centre for Contemporary Cultural Studies, University of Birmingham, 1980.

Chang, Briankle G., "Deconstructing the Audience: Who Are They and What Do We Know About Them?", *Communication Yearbook* 10, Margaret L. McLaughlin, Beverly Hills: Sage, 1987.

Chodorow, Nancy, *The Reproduction of Mothering: Psychoanalysis and the Sociology of Gender*, Berkeley, Calif.: University of California Press, 1978.

Clifford, James, "Fieldwork, Reciprocity, and the Making of Ethnographic Texts," *Man 15 (1980): 518-32.*

—— "On Ethnographic Authority," *Representations* 1, 2 (spring 1983): 118-46.

Clifford, James, and Marcus, George E. (eds) *Writing Culture. The Poetics and Politics of Ethnography*, Berkeley, Los Angeles, London: University of California Press, 1986.

Collett, Peter, and Lamb, Roger, *Watching Families Watching Television*, Report to the Independent Broadcasting Authority, 1986.

Corcoran, Farrel, "Television as Ideological Apparatus: The Power and the Pleasure," *Critical Studies in Mass Communication* 1 (1984): 131-45.

De Certeau, Michel, "On the Oppositional Practices of Everyday Life," *Social Text* 3 (fall 1980): 3-43.

—— *The Practice of Everyday Life*, Berkeley, Calif.: University of California Press, 1984.

Deming, Robert H., "Discourse/Talk/Television," *Screen* 26 (1985): 88-92.

—— "The Television Spectator-Subject," *Journal of Film and Video* 7 (1985): 49-63.

Derrida, Jacques, *Of Grammatology*, Baltimore, Md.: Johns Hopkins University Press, 1944.

Devereux, Georges, *Angst und Methode in den Verhaltenswissenschaften*, Frankfurt/Main: Suhrkamp, 1984.

Douglas, Jack D., *Understanding Everyday Life*, Chicago, 1970.

Drummond, Phillip, and Paterson, Richard (eds) *Television in Transition*, London: British Film Institute, 1985.

—— *Television and its Audiences: International Research Perspectives*, London: British Film Institute, 1988.

Du Bois, Barbara, "Passionate Scholarship: Notes on Values, Knowing and Method in Feminist Social Science," in Gloria Bowles and Renate Duelli Klein (eds) *Theories of Women's Studies*, London: Routledge & Kegan Paul, 1983.

Duelli Klein, Renate, "How To Do What We Want To Do: Thoughts About Feminist Methodology," in Gloria Bowles and Renate Duelli Klein (eds) *Theories of Women's Studies*, London: Routledge & Kegan Paul, 1983.

Dwyer, Kevin, "On the Dialogic of Field Work," *Dialectical Anthropology* 2, 2 (1977): 143-51.

—— "The Dialogic of Ethnology," *Dialectical Anthropology* 4, 3 (1979): 105-224.

Dyer, Richard, Geraghty, Christine, Jordan, Marion, Lovell, Terry, Paterson, Richard, and Stewart, John (eds) *"Coronation Street"*, London: British Film Institute, 1981.

Easterday, L., Papademas, D., Schorr, L., and Valentine, C., "The Making of a Female Researcher," *Urban Life* 6, 3 (1977): 333-48.

Elliott, Philip, "Uses and Gratifications Research: A Critique and a Sociological Alternative," in Jay Blumler and Elihu Katz (eds) *The Uses of Mass Communication*, Beverly Hills, Calif.: Sage, 1974.

Ellis, John, *Visible Fictions: Cinema Television Video*, London: Routledge & Kegan Paul, 1982.

Emmett, B. P., "The Television and Radio Audience in Britain," in Denis McQuail (ed.) *Sociology of Mass Communications*, Harmondsworth: Penguin, 1972.

Ferment in the Field, Special issue, *Journal of Communication* 33, 3 (1983).

Feuer, Jane, "The Concept of Live Television: Ontology vs Ideology," in E. Ann Kaplan (ed.) *Regarding Television*, Frederick, Md.: University Publications of America, 1983.

—— "Melodrama, Serial Form, and Television Today," *Screen* 25, 1 (1984): 4-16.

—— "Narrative Form in Television," in Colin MacCabe (ed.) *High Theory, Low Culture*, Manchester: Manchester University Press, 1986.

—— "Genre Study and Television," in Robert C. Allen (ed.) *Channels of Discourse. TV and Contemporary Criticism*, Chapel Hill and London: University of North Carolina Press, 1987.

Feyes, Fred, "Critical Communications Research and Media Effects: The Problem of the Disappearing Audience," *Media, Culture, and Society* 6, 3 (July 1984): 219-32.

Fish, Stanley *Is There a Text in This Class? The Authority of Interpretive Communities,* Cambridge, Mass.: Harvard University Press, 1980.

Fiske, John, "Television: Polysemy and Popularity," *Critical Studies in Mass Communication* 3, 4 (December 1986): 392-408.

—— "British Cultural Studies and Television," in Robert C. Allen (ed.) *Channels of Discourse. TV and Contemporary Criticism*, Chapel Hill and London: University of North Carolina Press, 1987.

—— *Television Culture*, London and New York: Methuen, 1987.

Fiske, John, and Hartley, John, *Reading Television*, London and New York: Methuen, 1978.

Flax, Jane, "Postmodernism and Gender Relations in Feminist Theory," *Signs* 12, 4 (1987): 621-41.

Flitterman-Lewis, Sandy, "Psychoanalysis, Film, and Television," in Robert C. Allen (ed.) *Channels of Discourse, TV and Contemporary Criticism*, Chapel Hill and London: University of North Carolina Press, 1987.

Foster, Hal (ed.) *The Anti-Aesthetic*, Port Townsend, Wash.: Bay Press, 1983.

Foucault, Michel, *History of Sexuality*, vol. 1, New York: Random House, 1978.

—— *Power/Knowledge*, New York: Pantheon, 1980.

Fraser, Nancy, and Nicholson, Linda, "Social Criticism Without Philosophy: An Encounter Between Feminism and Postmodernism," *Communication* 10, 3-4 (1988): 345-66.

Garfinkel, A., *Forms of Explanation*, New Haven, Conn.: Yale University Press, 1981.

Garnham, Nicholas, "Concepts of Culture: Public Policy and the Cultural Industries," *Cultural Studies* 1, 1 (1987): 23-37.

Geertz, Clifford, *The Interpretation of Cultures*, New York, 1973.

—— "From the Native's Point of View: On the Nature of Anthropological Understanding," in Keith H. Basso and Henry A. Selby (eds) *Meaning in Anthropology*, Albuquerque, NM, 1976.

Gerbner, George, and Gross, Larry, "Living with Television," *Journal of Communication* 26, 2 (1976):

Gerbner, George, Gross, Larry, Hoover, Stewart, Morgan, Michael, Signorielli, Nancy, Cotugno, Harry, and Wuthnow, Robert, *Religion and Television*, University of Pennsylvania: The Annenberg School of Communications, 1984.

Gerbner, George, Gross, Larry, Morgan, Michael, and Signorielli, Nancy, "Living with Television: The Dynamics of the Cultivation Process," in Jennings Bryant and Dolf Zillmann (eds) *Perspectives on Media Effects*, Hillsdale, NJ: Lawrence Erlbaum Associates, 1986.

Giddens, Anthony. "Positivism and its Critics," in T. Bottomore and R. Nisbet (eds) *A History of Sociological Analysis*, London: Heinemann, 1979.

—— *The Constitution of Society*, Cambridge: Polity Press, 1984.

Giles, Denis, "Television Reception," *Journal of Film and Video* 38 (summer 1985): 12-25.

Glaser, B., *Theoretical Sensitivity*, San Francisco, Calif.: The Sociology Press, 1978.

Gramsci, Antonio, *Prison Notebook: Selections*, trans. Quinton Hoare and Geoffrey Nowell Smith, New York: Internatioanl Publishers Co., 1971.

—— *Selections from Cultural Writings*, ed David Forgacs and Geoffrey Nowell Smith, trans. William Boelhower, Cambridge, Mass.: Harvard University Press, 1985.

Gray, Ann, "Behind Closed Doors: Video Recorders in the Home," in Helen Baehr and Gillian Dyer (eds) *Boxed In: Women and Television*, New York and London: Pandora Press, 1987.

—— "Reading the Audience," *Screen* 28, 3 (1987): 24-35.

Gross, Larry, "The Cultivation of Intolerance," in *Cultural Indicators: An International Symposium*, ed G. Melischek *et al.*, Vienna: Austrian Academy of Sciences, 1984.

Grossberg, Lawrence, "Cultural Studies Revisited and Revised," in Mary S. Mander (ed.) *Communications in Transition*, New York: Praeger, 1983.

—— "Strategies of Marxist Cultural Interpretation," *Critical Studies in Mass Communication* 1, 4 (1984): 392-421.

—— "History, Politics and Postmodernism: Stuart Hall and Cultural Studies," *Journal of Communication Inquiry* 10, 2 (1986): 73-4.

—— "Critical Theory and the Politics of Empirical Research," in Michael Gurevitch and Mark R. Levy (eds) *Mass Communication Review Yearbook, vol. 6*, Newbury Park: Sage, 1987.

—— "The In-Difference of Television," *Screen* 28, 2 (1987): 28-45.

—— "Postmodernity and Affect: All Dressed Up With No Place to Go," *Communication* 10, 3-4 (1988): 271-93.

—— "Wandering Audiences, Nomadic Critics," *Cultural Studies* 2, 3 (1988): 377-91.

Hall, Stuart, "The Hinterland of Science: Ideology and the 'Sociology of Knowledge,'" *Working Papers in Cultural Studies* 10 (1977): 9-31.

—— "Recent Developments in the Theories of Language and Ideology: A Critical Note," in Stuart Hall, Dorothy Hobson, Andrew Lowe, and Paul Willis (eds) *Culture, Media, Language*, London: Hutchinson, 1980.

—— "Encoding/Decoding," in Stuart Hall, Dorothy Hobson, Andrew Lowe, and Paul Willis (eds) *Culture, Media, Language*, London: Hutchinson, 1980.

—— "The Rediscovery of 'Ideology': Return of the Repressed in Media Studies," in Michael Gurevitch, Tony Bennett, James Curran and Janet Woollacott (eds) *Culture, Society and the Media*, London and New York: Methuen, 1982.

Halloran, James, *The Effects of Television*, London: Panther Books, 1970.

—— "The Context of Mass Communications Research," in Emile G. McAnany, Jorge Schnitman, and Noreene James (eds) *Communication and Social Structure: Critical Studies in Mass Media Research*, New York: Praeger, 1981.

Hammersley, Martyn, and Atkinson, Paul, *Ethnography: Principles in Practice*, London and New York: Tavistock, 1983.

Harris, M., *Cultural Materialism: The Struggle for a Science of Culture*, New York: Random House, 1979.

Hartley, John, and O'Regan, Tom, "Quoting not Science but Sideboards: Television in a New Way of Life," in Michael Gurevitch and Michael Levy (eds) *Mass Communication Review Yearbook*, vol. 7, Beverly Hills, Calif.: Sage, in press.

Heath, Stephen, and Skirrow, Gillian, "Television: A World in Action," *Screen* 18, 2 (1977): 7-59.

Hebdige, Dick, *Subculture: The Meaning of Style*, London: Methuen, 1979.

—— "Towards a Cartography of Taste 1935-1962," in B. Waites, Tony Bennett, and G. Martin (eds) *Popular Culture: Past and Present*, London: Croom Helm/Open University Press, 1982.

—— *Hiding in the Light. On Images and Things*, London: Comedia, 1987.

Herzog, Herta, "On Borrowed Experience. An Analysis of Listening to Daytime Sketches," *Studies in Philosophy and Social Science* 9, 1 (1941): 65-95.

—— "What Do We Really Know About Daytime Serial Listeners?", in Paul F. Lazarsfeld and Frank N. Stanton (eds) *Radio Research 1942-1943*, New York: Duell, Sloan & Pearce, 1944.

Hobson, Dorothy, "Housewives and the Mass Media," in Stuart Hall, Dorothy Hobson, Andrew Lowe, and Paul Willis (eds) *Culture, Media, Language*, London: Hutchinson, 1980.

—— "Crossroads": The Drama of a Soap Opera, London: Methuen, 1982.

Hodge, Robert, and Tripp, David, Children and Television, Cambridge: Polity Press, 1986.

Hoggart, Richard, The Uses of Literacy: Aspects of Working-Class Life with Special Reference to Publications and Entertainments, Harmondsworth: Penguin, 1976.

Houston, Beverley, "Viewing Television: The Metapsychology of Endless Consumption," Quarterly Review of Film Studies 9, 3 (summer 1984): 183-95.

Huyssen, Andreas, "Mapping the Postmodern," New German Critique 33 (fall 1984): 5-52.

—— "Mass Culture as Woman: Modernism's Other," in After the Great Divide Bloomington: Indiana University Press, 1986.

Hymes, D. H., "On Communicative Competence," in J. B. Pride and Janet Holmes (eds) Sociolinguistics, Harmondsworth: Penguin, 1972.

Iser, Wolfgang, The Act of Reading: A Theory of Aesthetic Response, London: Routledge & Kegan Paul, 1978.

Jameson, Fredric, "Reification and Utopia in Mass Culture," Social Text 1 (1979) 130-48.

Jeggle, Utz (ed.) Feldforschung: Qualitative Methoden in der Kulturanalyse, Tübingen: Tübinger Vereinigung für Volkskunde, 1984.

Jensen, Klaus Bruhn, Making Sense of the News, Ahrhus: University of Ahrhus Press, 1986.

—— "Qualitative Audience Research: Towards an Integrative Approach to Reception," Critical Studies in Mass Communication 4 (1987): 21-36.

Johnson, Lesley, "Radio and Everyday Life. The Early Years of Broadcasting in Australia, 1922-1945," Media, Culture, and Society 3, 2 (1981): 167-78.

Jules-Rosette, B., "The Veil of Objectivity: Prophecy, Divination, and Social Inquiry," American Anthropologist 80, 3 (1978): 549-70.

—— "Towards a Theory of Ethnography," Sociological Symposium 24 (1978): 81-98.

Kaplan, E. Ann (ed.) Regarding Television. Critical Approaches – An Anthology, Frederick, Md.: University Publications of America, 1983.

Katz, Elihu, "Communications Research Since Lazarsfeld," Public Opinion Quarterly 51, 4 part 2 (winter 1987): S25-S45.

Katz, Elihu, and Liebes, Tamar, "Once Upon a Time in Dallas," Intermedia 12, 3 (May 1984): 28-32.

—— "Mutual Aid in the Decoding of Dallas: Preliminary Notes from a Cross-Cultural Study," in Phillip Drummond and Richard Paterson (eds) Television in Transition, London: British Film Institute, 1985.

Kristeva, Julia, Desire in Language, New York: Columbia University Press, 1980.

Kuhn, Annette. "Women's Genres," Screen 25, 1 (1984): 18-28.

Leavis, F.R., The Great Tradition: George Eliot, Henry James, Joseph Conrad, London: Chatto & Windus, 1950.

Levy, D. J., Realism: An Essay in Interpretation and Social Reality, Manchester: Carcanet New Press, 1981.

Levy, M. R., and Windahl, S., "Audience Activity and Gratifications: A Conceptual Clarification and Exploration," in Karl E. Rosengren, Lawrence A. Wenner, and Philip Palmgreen (eds) Media Gratifications Research: Current Perspectives, Beverly Hills, Calif.: Sage, 1985.

Liebes, Tamar, "Ethnocriticism: Israelis of Moroccan Ethnicity Negotiate the Meaning of Dallas," Studies in Visual Communication 10, 3 (1984): 46-72.

Liebes, Tamar, and Katz, Elihu, "Patterns of Involvement in Television Fictions: A Comparative Analysis," European Journal of Communication 1 (1986): 151-71.

Lindlof, Thomas (ed.) *Natural Audiences: Qualitative Research and Media Uses and Effects*, Norwood, NJ: Ablex Publishing Company, 1987.

Lindner, Rolf, "Die Angst des Forschers vor dem Feld," *Zeitschrift für Volkskunde* 77 (1981): 51-65.

Lovell, Terry, *Pictures of Reality. Aesthetics, Politics and Pleasure*, London: British Film Institute, 1980.

—— *Consuming Fictions*, London: Verso, 1987.

Lull, James, "The Social Uses of Television," *Human Communications Research* 6, 3 (1980): 198-209.

—— "How Families Select Television Programs: A Mass-Observational Study," *Journal of Broadcasting*, 26, 4 (1982): 801-11.

—— "The Naturalistic Study of Media Use and Youth Culture," in Karl E. Rosengren, Lawrence A. Wenner, and Philip Palmgreen (eds) *Media Gratifications Research: Current Perspectives*, Beverly Hills, Calif.: Sage, 1985.

—— (ed.) *World Families Watch Television*, Newbury Park: Sage, 1988.

MacCabe, Colin, *High Theory, Low Culture*, Manchester: Manchester University Press, 1986.

MacCannell, Dean, and Flower Juliet, "Ethnosemiotics: Beyond Structural Anthropology," in Dean MacCannell and Juliet Flower *The Time of the Sign. A Semiotic Interpretation of Modern Culture*, Bloomington: Indiana University Press, 1982.

McQuail, Denis, "With the Benefit of Hindsight: Reflections on Uses and Gratifications Research," *Critical Studies in Mass Communications* 1 (1984): 177-93.

McQuail, Denis, Blumler, Jay G., and Brown, J. R., "The Television Audience: A Revised Perspective," in Denis McQuail (ed.) *Sociology of Mass Communications*, Harmondsworth: Penguin, 1972.

McRobbie, Angela, "The Politics of Feminist Research," *Feminist Review* 12 (October 1982): 46-57.

Mander, Mary, *Communications in Transition,* New York: Praeger, 1983.

Marcus, George E., and Cushman, Dick, "Ethnographies as Texts," *Annual Review of Anthropology*, 11 (1982): 25-69.

Mercer, Colin, "Complicit Pleasures," in Tony Bennett, Colin Mercer, and Janet Woollacott *Popular Culture and Social Relations*, Milton Keynes and Philadelphia: Open University Press, 1986.

—— "That's Entertainment: The Resilience of Popular Forms," in Tony Bennett, Colin Mercer, and Janet Woollacott (eds) *Popular Culture and Social Relations*, Milton Keynes and Philadelphia: Open University Press, 1986.

Modleski, Tania, "The Search for Tomorrow in Today's Soap Operas: Notes on a Feminine Narrative Form," *Film Quarterly* 33 (1979): 12-21.

—— *Loving With A Vengeance. Mass-Produced Fantasies for Women*, Hamden, Conn.: Archon Books, 1982.

—— "The Rhythms of Reception: Daytime Television and Women's Work," in E. Ann Kaplan (ed.) *Regarding Television. Critical Approaches – An Anthology*, Frederick, Md.: University Publications of America, 1983.

—— "Femininity as Masquerade: A Feminist Approach to Mass Culture," in Colin MacCabe (ed.) *High Theory, Low Culture*, Manchester: University of Manchester Press, 1986.

—— "Introduction," in Tania Modleski (ed.) *Studies in Entertainment. Critical Approaches to Mass Culture*, Bloomington, Ind.: Indiana University Press, 1986.

Morley, David, *The "Nationwide" Audience: Structure and Decoding*, London: British Film Institute, 1980.

—— "Texts, Readers, Subjects," in Stuart Hall, Dorothy Hobson, Andrew Lowe, and Paul Willis (eds) *Culture, Media, Language*, London: Hutchinson 1980.

—— "'The Nationwide Audience': A Critical Postscript," *Screen Education* 39 (summer 1981): 3-15.

—— "Cultural Transformations: The Politics of Resistance," in Howard Davis and Paul Walton (eds) *Language, Image, Media*, Oxford: Basil Blackwell, 1983.

—— *Family Television: Cultural Power and Domestic Leisure*, London: Comedia, 1986.

Nelson, Cary, and Grossberg, Lawrence, *Marxism and Cultural Interpretation*, Urbana: University of Illinois Press, 1988.

Newcomb, Horace C., *Television: The Most Popular Art*, New York: Anchor Press, 1974.

—— "American Television Criticism, 1970-1985," *Critical Studies in Mass Communication* 3, 2 (June 1986): 217-28.

—— (ed.) *Television – The Critical View*, 4th edn, New York: Oxford University Press, 1987.

Newcomb, Horace C., and Hirsch, Paul M., "Television as a Cultural Forum: Implications for Research," *Quarterly Review of Film Studies* 8, 3 (summer 1983): 45-55.

Nightingale, Virginia, "What's Happening to Audience Research?" *Media Information Australia* 39 (1986): 18-22.

Oakley, Ann, "Interviewing Women: A Contradiction in Terms," in Helen Roberts (ed.) *Doing Feminist Research*, London: Routledge & Kegan Paul, 1981.

Palmer, Patricia, *The Lively Audience: A Study of Children Around the TV Set*, Sidney: Allen & Unwin, 1986.

Paterson, Richard, "Planning the Family: The Art of the TV Schedule," *Screen Education* 35 (1981): 79-85.

Pecheux, Michel, *Language, Semiotics and Ideology*, London: Macmillan, 1982.

Petro, Patrice, "Mass Culture and the Feminine: The 'Place' of Television in Film Studies," *Cinema Journal* 25, 3 (1986): 5-21.

Poole, Michael, "The Cult of the Generalist: British Television Criticism 1936-1983," *Screen* 25, 2 (1984): 41-62.

Pratt, Mary Louise, "Interpretive Strategies/Strategic Interpretations: On Anglo-American Reader-Response Criticism," in Jonathan Arac (ed.) *Postmodernism and Politics*, Minneapolis: University of Minnesota Press, 1986.

Pribram, Deidre (ed.) *Female Spectators Looking at Film and Television*, London: Verso, 1988.

Probyn, Elspeth, "Memories and Past Politics of Postmodernism," *Communication* 10, 3-4 (1988): 305-10.

Rabinow, Paul, and Sullivan, William M. (eds) *Interpretive Social Science*, Berkeley, Los Angeles, London: University of California Press, 1979.

Radway, Janice, "Women Read the Romance: The Intertextuality of Text and Context," *Feminist Studies* 9, 1 (spring 1983): 53-78.

—— *Reading the Romance: Women, Patriarchy, and Popular Literature*, Chapel Hill: University of North Carolina Press, 1984.

—— "Identifying Ideological Seams: Mass Culture, Analytical Method, and Political Practice," *Communication* 9 (1986): 93-123.

—— "Reading Reading the Romance," in Janice Radway, *Reading the Romance*, London: Verso, 1987.

—— "Reception Study: Ethnography and the Problems of Dispersed Audiences and Nomadic Subjects," *Cultural Studies* 2, 3 (1988): 359-76.

Real, Michael, "The Debate on Critical Theory and the Study of Communications," *Journal of Communication* 34, 4 (1988): 72-80.

Roberts, Helen (ed.) *Doing Feminist Research*, London: Routledge & Kegan Paul, 1981.

Root, Jane, *Open the Box*. London: Comedia, 1986.

Rosengren, Karl Erik, "Communication Research: One Paradigm, or Four?" *Journal of Communication* 33 (1983): 185-207.

Rowland, Willard D., Jr, and Watkins, Bruce (eds) *Interpreting Television: Current Research Perspectives*, Beverly Hills, Calif.: Sage, 1984

Rubin, Alan M., "Media Gratifications Through the Life Cycle," in Karl E. Rosengren; Lawrence A, Wenner, and Philip Palmgreen (eds) *Media Gratifications Research, Current Perspectives*, Beverly Hills, Calif.: Sage, 1985.

Sackstetter, Susanne, "'Wir sind doch alles Weiber': Gespräche unter Frauen und weibliche Lebensbedingungen," in Utz Jeggle (ed.) *Feldforschung: Qualitative Methoden in der Kulturanalyse*, Tübingen: Tübinger Vereinigung für Volkskunde, 1984.

Sahin, Haluk, and Robinson, J.P., "Beyond the Realm of Necessity: Television and the Colonization of Leisure," *Media, Culture, and Society* 3, 1 (1981): 85-95.

Sarris, Andrew, *The American Cinema: Directors and Directions, 1929-1968*, New York: E.P. Dutton, 1968.

Schroder, Kim Christian, "Convergence of Antagonistic Traditions? The Case of Audience Research," *European Journal of Communication* 2 (1987): 7-31.

Seiter, Ellen, "Eco's TV Guide – The Soaps," *Tabloid* 5 (winter 1982): 35-43.

—— "Promise and Contradiction: The Daytime Television Serial," *Film Reader* 5 (winter 1982): 150-63.

—— "Men, Sex and Money in Recent Family Melodramas," *Journal of the University Film and Video Assocation* 35, 1 (winter 1983): 17-27.

Sigman, Stuart J., and Frey, Donald L., "Differential Ideology and Language Use: Readers' Reconstructions and Descriptions of News Events," *Critical Studies in Mass Communication* 2, 4 (1985): 307-22.

Silverstone, Roger, *The Message of Television: Myth and Narrative in Contemporary Culture*, London: Heinemann, 1981.

Simpson, Philip, *Parents Talking Television*, London: Routledge & Kegan Paul, 1987.

Slack, Jennifer Daryl, and Allor, Martin, "The Political and Epistemological Constituents of Critical Communications Research," *Journal of Communication* 33 (1983): 208-18.

Spence, Louise, "Life's Little Problems . . . and Pleasures: An Investigation into the Narrative Structure of *The Young and the Restless*," *Quarterly Review of Film Studies* 9 (1984): 301-8.

Spigel, Lynn, "Installing the Television Set: Popular Discourses on Television and Domestic Space 1948-55," *Camera Obscura* (March 1988): 11-46.

Spradley, James P., *The Ethnographic Interview*, New York: Holt, Rinehart & Winston, 1979.

Streeter, Thomas, "An Alternative Approach to Television Research: Developments in British Cultural Studies in Birmingham," in Willard D. Rowland, Jr, and Watkins, Bruce, (eds) *Interpreting Television: Current Research Perspectives*, Beverly Hills, Calif.: Sage, 1984.

Surlin, Stuart, "Television Criticism in Canada," *Critical Studies in Mass Communication* 2 (1985): 80-83.

Taylor, Laurie, and Mullan, Bob, *Uninvited Guests: The Intimate Secrets of Television and Radio*, London: Chatto and Windus, 1986.

Tulloch, John, *Television Drama: Agency, Audience and Myth*, London: Routledge, forthcoming.

Tulloch, John, and Alvarado, Manuel, *"Doctor Who" : The Unfolding Text*, Basingstoke: Macmillan, 1983.

Tulloch, John, and Moran, Albert, *"A Country Practice" : 'Quality Soap'*, Sidney: Currency Press, 1986.

Turner, Victor, "Process, System, and Symbol: A New Anthropological Synthesis," *Daedalus* 106, 2 (1977): 61-80.

Walkerdine, Valerie, "Video Replay: Families, Films and Fantasy," in Victor Burgin, James Donald, and Cora Kaplan (eds) *Formations of Fantasy*, London and New York: Methuen, 1986.

Webster, Steven, "Dialogue and Fiction in Ethnography," *Dialectical Anthropology* 7, 2 (1982):

Webster, James G., and Wakshlag, Jacob J., "The Impact of Group Viewing on Patterns of Television Program Choice," *Journal of Broadcasting* 26, 1 (1982): 445-55.

Williams, Raymond, *Television: Technology and Cultural Form*, London: Fontana, 1974.

Willis, Paul, "Notes on Method," in Stuart Hall, Dorothy Hobson, Andrew Lowe, and Paul Willis (eds) *Culture, Media, Language*, London: Hutchinson, 1980.

—— *Learning to Labour: How Working Class Kids Get Working Class Jobs*, Farnborough: Saxon House, 1977.

—— *Profane Culture*, London: Routledge & Kegan Paul, 1978.

—— "Cultural Production is Different from Cultural Reproduction is Different from Social Reproduction is Different from Reproduction," *Interchange* 12, 2,3 (1981): 48-67.

Winner, Irene and Thomas, "The Semiotics of Cultural Texts," *Semiotica* 18, 2 (1976): 101-56.

Woal, Michael B., "Defamiliarization in Television Viewing: Aesthetic and Rhetorical Modes of Experiencing Television," *Journal of the University Film and Video Association* 34 (1982): 25-32.

Wollen, Peter, *Signs and Meaning in the Cinema*, London: Secker & Warburg, British Film Institute, 1969.

Woods, P. "Understanding Through Talk," in C. Adelman (ed.) *Uttering, Muttering: Collecting, Using and Reporting Talk for Social and Educational Research*, London: Grant McIntyre, 1981.

Wren-Lewis, Justin, "The Encoding-Decoding Model: Criticisms and Redevelopments for Research on Decoding," *Media, Culture, and Society* 5, 2 (April 1983): 179-97.

—— "Decoding Television News," in Phillip Drummond and Richard Paterson (eds) *Television in Transition*, London: British Film Institute, 1985.

Zimmerman, Patricia R., "Good Girls, Bad Women: The Role of Older Women on *Dynasty*," *Journal of Film and Video* 37 (spring 1985): 66-74.

Index